Irish Republic

WORLD BIBLIOGRAPHICAL SERIES

General Editors:
Robert L. Collison (Editor-in-chief)
Sheila R. Herstein
Louis J. Reith
Hans H. Wellisch

VOLUMES IN THE SERIES

VOLUME 69

Irish Republic

Michael Owen Shannon
Compiler

CLIO PRESS

OXFORD, ENGLAND · SANTA BARBARA, CALIFORNIA
DENVER, COLORADO

© Copyright 1986 by Clio Press Ltd.

British Library Cataloguing in Publication Data

Shannon, Michael Owen
Irish Republic. – (Word bibliographical series; v. 69)
1. Ireland – Bibliography
I. Title   II. Series
016.9417   Z2521

ISBN 1–85109–014–2

Clio Press Ltd.,
55 St. Thomas' Street.
Oxford OX1 1JG, England.

ABC-Clio Information Services.
Riviera Campus, 2040 Alameda Padre Serra.
Santa Barbara, Ca. 93103, USA.

Designed by Bernard Crossland
Typeset by Columns Design and Production Services, Reading, England
Printed and bound in Great Britain by
Billing and Sons Ltd., Worcester

THE WORLD BIBLIOGRAPHICAL SERIES

This series will eventually cover every country in the world, each in a separate volume comprising annotated entries on works dealing with its history, geography, economy and politics: and with its people, their culture, customs, religion and social organization. Attention will also be paid to current living conditions – housing, education, newspapers, clothing, etc. – that are all too often ignored in standard bibliographies; and to those particular aspects relevant to individual countries. Each volume seeks to achieve, by use of careful selectivity and critical assessment of the literature, an expression of the country and an appreciation of its nature and national aspirations, to guide the reader towards an understanding of its importance. The keynote of the series is to provide, in a uniform format, an interpretation of each country that will express its culture, its place in the world, and the qualities and background that make it unique.

SERIES EDITORS

Robert L. Collison (Editor-in-chief) is Professor Emeritus, Library and Information Studies, University of California, Los Angeles, and is currently the President of the Society of Indexers. Following the war, he served as Reference Librarian for the City of Westminster and later became Librarian to the BBC. During his fifty years as a professional librarian in England and the USA, he has written more than twenty works on bibliography, librarianship, indexing and related subjects.

Sheila R. Herstein is Reference Librarian and Library Instruction Co-ordinator at the City College of the City University of New York. She has extensive bibliographic experience and has described her innovations in the field of bibliographic instruction in 'Team teaching and bibliographic instruction'. *The Bookmark*, Autumn 1979. In addition, Doctor Herstein co-authored a basic annotated bibliography in history for Funk & Wagnalls *New encyclopedia*, and for several years reviewed books for *Library Journal*.

Louis J. Reith is librarian with the Franciscan Institute, St. Bonaventure University, New York. He received his PhD from Stanford University, California, and later studied at Eberhard-Karls-Universität, Tübingen. In addition to his activities as a librarian, Dr. Reith is a specialist on 16th-century German history and the Reformation and has published many articles and papers in both German and English. He was also editor of the *American Society for Reformation Research Newsletter*.

Hans H. Wellisch is a Professor at the College of Library and Information Services, University of Maryland, and a member of the American Society of Indexers and the International Federation for Documentation. He is the author of numerous articles and several books on indexing and abstracting, and has also published *Indexing and abstracting: an international bibliography*. He also contributes frequently to *Journal of the American Society for Information Science, Library Quarterly*, and *The Indexer*.

Contents

Contents

Contents

Contents

Contents

Introduction

Ireland, a small nation with a vast history, has contributed an abiding spirit and intellect that have been felt throughout the world. The Irish have nurtured literacy, and artistic and cultural values from ancient times, providing them with protection during the early Dark Ages and then with a burst of missionary activity propagating the best of these values to a mediaeval Europe devastated by conflict. In the modern era Irish dramatists, poets, novelists and artists have commanded international esteem. Yet though a 'literary' people the Irish have, at times, shown a readiness to fight in foreign lands over issues of sovereignty, freedom and independence, rights which have often been denied them in their homeland over the centuries. Personal human values are at the heart of the Irish soul and the Irish have had an enormous impact upon the world through that spirit, outlook and heritage.

Today's Ireland is facing a new phase of industrialization, the modern problems of economic and environmental change, rapid social displacement, the erosion of traditions, and rapid transitions in employment, population, income and living conditions. There is an interplay of a new cosmopolitan outlook in the main cities, urbanization, and the willing acceptance of a growing European role, which may be seen as a mark of nationhood. The casual visitor still may search for ancient roots and the remaining strands of a rural Gaelic culture that has always served to regenerate Ireland after centuries of denial and suffering. These traditional values do still exist in Ireland, shaping public attitudes on questions concerning family life, religion, abortion, marriage, divorce and other contemporary issues.

The present bibliography includes a sampling of some of the better or more popular general works on Ireland. Most of these were published by mid-1985, although a few later works are also included. All periods of Ireland's fascinating and lively history are covered, from prehistoric times to the 1980s. Although some chapters necessarily treat Ireland as a whole entity, for the period after 1922 the bibliography focuses on the twenty-six counties in the South which are now known as the Republic of Ireland. (Northern Ireland will be covered in another volume in this series). For the period before 1922 one must consider the island as a whole.

This bibliography is highly selective. Of the hundreds of thousands of books that have appeared on the country, only a limited number could be included here in order to provide at least some titles on virtually every major topic: history, geography, literature, the arts and all aspects of Irish life and society. Not everyone's favourite book can be listed here: those included are generally an amalgam of prominent, well regarded works, some classic studies, and many that are recent publications, or are readily obtainable, popular rather than esoteric, and from established publishers. A few journal articles are also included where appropriate. This bibliography is designed to assist the general reader, the student, the scholar seeking information in a field other than his own, potential visitors, those with a business interest, or the casual reader needing a brief, annotated guide.

Many who have travelled outside the cities have found Ireland to be a place of magnificent beauty, still retaining large tracts of rugged rural terrain, with a colourful, changing landscape of spectacular cliffs and 2,000 miles of sweeping coastline, gentle beaches in hidden coves, loughs, fjords, glens, valleys, quiet villages, towns, parishes and parks, a relatively mild climate and a friendly population. Accordingly, many pictorial and descriptive works have been published on Ireland, and numerous guide books have also appeared. A small selection of the more attractive volumes have been included here.

There are many dividing points in Ireland's long history that are pivotal to the study of the country. One of the most important of these is 1921, the year of the Anglo-Irish Treaty which divided the country. In its subsequent short history as a modern independent nation the country has been known by several names: Ireland, Éire, the Republic of Ireland. Each form has connotations for those using the term, nationalists, loyalists, defenders and detractors. What then is Ireland? 'Ireland' applies foremost to the whole island of the Irish people. The old English term Irland indicated land of the Irish. The Irish language name for the island is Éire (or in the old Irish, Ériu). To the Romans it

Introduction

was Hibernia. Ireland as a place is easily identified: that entire island to the west of England. However, the name Ireland also applies specifically to the nation, a geographically restricted area of twenty-six of the thirty-two counties of the island, with a boundary set by international agreement following the Anglo-Irish Treaty.

In 1922, following centuries of British rule and a short provisional government, the first independent, modern Irish state was created, the Irish Free State. In 1937 this was changed to simply 'Ireland,' and consequently this term may refer to either the whole island, or just to the free and independent nation with its present jurisdiction over the twenty-six counties in the South. The Irish government under the Constitution lays claim to the whole of the island, though the government admits to its temporary administration over only the Southern portion. The new constitution of 1937 permitted the official use of 'Éire' when the Irish language is used, though 'Ireland' is specified when English is used. In 1948 a legislative act reintroduced the term 'Republic of Ireland', and this is still used in agreements between Great Britain and Ireland. (Ireland had been referred to as a Republic in the Easter proclamation of 1916.) Since 1950 the official, simplified term 'Ireland' has again become the norm, and in international relations all nations are expected to use this term (with the exception of the United Kingdom). To refer to the 'Republic' for some is to emphasize that the Irish government has *de facto* control over most but not all of Ireland. The Irish government avoids referring to twenty-six counties, although when absolutely necessary it will describe its jurisdiction as 'exclusive of the six counties'. The form of government is that of a republic, and it has its own political system and organization developed over the past sixty-five years, quite distinct from Northern Ireland.

Increasingly the economic and social values of the country have also developed along paths which are separate from those of the North. It is largely in the cultural sphere that the present day division between North and South becomes more obscure and tentative, for literature, the theatre, the arts and all the other realms of intellect and imagination can still ignore geographic boundaries and legal barriers. The historic roots and artifacts of both traditional Gaelic communities and later British administration litter the landscape both in Northern Ireland and in the South. Moreover, the Irish people are often recognized by their speech and sometimes by spirit and facial features, regardless of

Introduction

border checkpoints. However, it would be artificial to ignore one of the chief concerns of the Republic: the status of Northern Ireland. Therefore several books are included in this bibliography relating to Northern Ireland in order to guide the reader to some of the larger issues confronting Ireland at present, even though there are those in both Northern Ireland and today's Republic who would rather ignore the existence of the other half. Some of these books are balanced, and a few are controversial.

Knowledge of early Ireland is necessarily dim, befitting its image in the eyes of many, as a place of mystery. This is partly due to the old religions being now poorly understood, and to the long periods of violence which destroyed the knowledge of so much early history. Ireland does appear in the writings of the ancient Greeks and Romans. More important is the oral tradition of Irish history as retold in the early centuries by the shanachies. As is true in many societies throughout the world, especially in some non-Western and 'less developed' regions, oral history may have a particular place in a culture and be held in high regard. The validity of early accounts told through stories, legend and ballad was protected by rules regulating the story tellers. In ancient Ireland such rules were rigorously adhered to (through training, regulation and proscription), and the oral tradition was passed down through generations intact and largely unchanged until the Christian era. From the ancient world we have surviving fragments of legends, history and myths. An important part of early Irish literature and history is to be found in fragmented series of ancient manuscripts, containing annals, genealogies, chronologies, histories, legendary cycles, sagas, voyages and tales. These catagories of mediaeval Irish writings were often based on even earlier tales, and hundreds of these have survived. A few are represented in this bibliography, not for any reason of quaintness but as evidence of an early civilization to be interpreted and reinterpreted by each succession of modern scholars.

Recent research has dated some of the earliest Irish settlements to 9000 BC, among some of the oldest in Europe. Of the pre-Celtic tribes we know little. Celtic Ireland gradually developed its unique culture drawing from each wave of invading groups of the ancient world, from the Continent, the Near East and the East. In time a distinctive Gaelic culture emerged with its own legends, rituals, customs and religion. Later invading forces from a Christianized Western Europe (the English and the Normans especially) encountered an Irish society beyond their compre-

Introduction

hension and experience. To some, Ireland had the image of an uncivilized and mysterious (if not supernatural) place. Ireland was, and is, none of these; its early accounts of invasions, heroic struggles, and its literary conventions were the underpinnings of a society that appears to be in turn fractious, independent, rebellious, sentimental, considerate, poetic, understated, friendly and adventurous. These are the public images but a private lesser known Ireland is also there, determined, hard working, battling the elements, stubborn, generous, open and sharing.

If the surviving literature of ancient Ireland tells us something of the roots of Irish culture, more tangible evidence lies in numerous early artifacts that are remarkable for their beauty and craftsmanship. These treasures, among the finest anywhere in the world, are still, surprisingly, being unearthed today. Some are mentioned in the sections of this book devoted to archaeology; others are noted in the sections covering Irish arts, crafts, manuscripts and metalwork. The early Irish art and manuscripts are significant to world culture, and disprove the 'primitive' nature of the ancient Celts.

Ireland was never conquered by the Romans and much of its way of life survived from ancient times until it gradually succumbed to European influences in the mediaeval period. Much of what was known of early Ireland has either been lost or distorted through the accounts of foreign eyes. During Tudor and later times Ireland was observed by English interpreters, conquerors, ecclesiastics and court officials trained in the written word. Several of their works are listed in this book as historical sources although their accuracy is sometimes called into question.

Special attention is given to some of the major figures in Irish history and several are accorded lengthy notes or separate sections. Although St. Patrick's renowned peaceful conversion of Ireland occured in the 5th century, his venerated memory still exerts a strong influence in the isle. He and the legendary figure Brian Boru, who defeated the Norsemen and their allies at Clontarf in 1014, are both remembered for providing a unity in Ireland, one through the force of religion, and the other through the strengths of arms. Ancient Ireland consisted of five (and later seven) kingdoms or provinces with Tara a central, royal seat, and each province was divided into numerous smaller kingdoms. In the Middle Ages, Viking and Scandinavian forces brought constant destruction, profitable trade and contact with the wider world. Year by year their artifacts are still being uncovered, and many of Ireland's coastal cities such as Dublin were originally

Introduction

Viking settlements. In the 12th century Henry II and Strongbow, his forceful surrogate, extended English rule over Ireland. Ever since, English control and influence have been contested, through a long series of rebellions and resistance, continuing to the present day.

The establishment of the pattern of four provinces and the Irish county system served the convenience of English administration. Irish history, lore, poetry and ballad often allude to the centuries of oppression, domination and cultural loss. Divisions in Irish society were legislated and reinforced by the infamous Statutes of Kilkenny in 1366, which had dire results for centuries. English law was given paramount power in Ireland by Poyning's Law in 1494. Cromwell's cruel suppression and annihilation of the population of whole towns and cities in Ireland occurred in 1649–50. The defeat of Irish forces and those of James II followed by the Treaty of Limerick in 1691, set the stage for further centuries of English rule over Ireland. The 'flight of the Earls' ended many an Irish title and the influence of leading Irish families; the Draconic Penal Laws (1691–1829) brought persecution of religion, language and custom and the severe restriction of basic political rights. A distinguished line of Irish parliamentarians, political gradualists, revolutionaries, and patriots have been the topic of the many biographies listed in this book, including those of Henry Gratton, Edmund Burke, Theobald Wolfe Tone, Robert Emmet, Daniel O'Connell and Charles Stewart Parnell.

'Modern Ireland' is a vague and less than scientific term that has been applied to a period commencing anywhere from the 15th to the 19th centuries. Some Irish textbooks may use the term for the period of the tightening of English control over Ireland, and the consequent emergence of systematic structures of governance. Thus, given Ireland's long history, its emergence as a modern state could be placed as early as the Tudor period. As one of Europe's last underdeveloped nations, a modern Ireland, one could argue, was still emerging in the year 1900. The arrival of a business oriented, industrialized economy in the 19th century was a comparatively late development, and to this day agriculture remains an essential part of the Irish economy.

Many of the books on modern Ireland highlight major themes in the history of the last century: conflict and the constant fight for independence, landlord and tenant issues, the devastation of famine and agricultural reversals, the rise of nationalism, and the reshaping of a national Irish literature to one of world-wide application and respect. The 20th century brought the Easter

Introduction

Rising, which was not the abrupt event which many foreign readers believe it to be, but rather the culmination of a long series of political movements and incidents. Continued agitation and the loss of support for parliamentary representation in London gave way to the guerrilla War for Independence between 1919 and 1921 (sometimes referred to as the Anglo-Irish War). Following cruel hostilities and the use of Black and Tan forces, a treaty was finally negotiated between the two countries, creating an Ireland within the Commonwealth, the Irish Free State, in 1922. There followed a bitter civil war in Ireland, with Britain no longer a direct party to the fighting.

As a result of these events, the state structure and governmental apparatus that we see today was formed. There are many factors distinguishing the present republic from the government of Northern Ireland. The major political parties in the two geographic entities are entirely different. In the Irish Republic political leaders address questions that have been defined by the Irish people South of the border and which are chiefly of interest to them, issues such as the place of abortion and divorce in the Irish constitution for example, or the matter of neutrality and the role of Ireland in a European political framework (involving economic relations within the EEC and the unlikely possibility of NATO military arrangements). Court decisions, tax structure, regional industrial policy, and social services all increase the distance between the Republic and Northern Ireland.

Any bibliography which covers Irish history must include the leading personalities of the time. The limited size of the present bibliography makes it impossible to include a list of books on each major figure. Instead, a few of the more prominent leaders have been selected and given a separate section, including Roger Casement, Michael Collins, James Connolly, Eamon de Valera, Daniel O'Connell, and Patrick Pearse. Many other important or notable figures are mentioned in individual citations. For numerous other Irish figures one should consult the several editions of collective biography that are included here.

Throughout much of Irish history and especially in the last 200 years there has been a search for new opportunities in foreign lands. A significant part of the Irish people has migrated abroad, particularly to the United States, Canada and Australia. In 18th-century North America, long before the famine, the population may have been one-third Irish. A variety of books are listed in this bibliography containing immigration records, histories and ethnic studies of the Irish abroad, genealogical guides, personal reminiscences, notes on the origin of names, and other sources relevant to migration studies.

The population of Ireland has been scrutinized by sociologists and anthropologists. Interesting subjects for study have been found among the tinkers (the Irish 'travelling people' of no fixed address). Minority groups, islanders and the rural population of Western Ireland have been particularly favoured in studies. Certain themes are reported upon regularly and some of the more popular topics have concerned the agrarian Irish striving for survival in a rugged, inhospitable and challenging environment, the waning of rural community traditions, the disappearing family structures of old, and the changing roles of women in Ireland. The present bibliography includes coverage of all these topics.

Ireland faces many of the problems of an industrialized society: environmental pollution, family and minority tensions, drug abuse, wayward youths and the other hazards of contemporary life. However, in Ireland these problems, even now, do not occur so frequently as in many other countries and Ireland may still be seen as a land of beauty, kindness and sentiment. Poverty and unemployment exist, but these have always been problems in the 'Emerald Isle'. The difficulties confronting today's Ireland are discussed in many of the books listed in this bibliography, but these are offset by others, extolling the innumerable benefits of Irish life: a significant culture, literature and art, and a terrain of unsurpassable beauty. A balanced portrayal and listing of works is attempted throughout this bibliography.

Ireland's great gift to the world has been its literature. Its English-language Anglo-Irish writings, including stories, plays and poetry are highlighted here with special attention given to some of the most prominent authors in the international milieu. Sections are devoted to Goldsmith, Swift, Sheridan, Yeats, Joyce, Shaw, O'Casey, Synge and Wilde. The Celtic Renaissance of Irish writing gradually emerged in the 18th century to become a crescendo in the 19th. Unfortunately, all the major Irish writers cannot be mentioned within the scope of this book.

Some emphasis though, has been given to 20th-century essayists, novelists, poets and playwrights, given their wide recognition, fame and influence. A few major Gaelic works are also featured, and some translations from the Irish language are noted in the parts of this bibliography dealing with customs and folklore.

It is not the purpose of this bibliography to list creative works of literature. For many of the writers that are noted here a listing is presented of critical studies and biographies in order to guide the reader. In a few exceptional cases creative works by a major writer will be noted, if the works are about Ireland, or have achieved a particular importance. Thus in some instances the best or preferred edition of collected poems, plays or a significant novel (such as *Ulysses*) will be noted in order to be of service to the reader or the library wishing to improve its Irish collection.

Attention is also paid to Irish art which is an amalgam of the most ancient and the most modern styles. Major works have appeared throughout Ireland's history that have gained world-wide attention and it should be noted that some contemporary Irish art draws upon the ancient literary themes. In architecture Irish castles, towers, townhouses, mansions and cottages have an international following. Examples of Irish Georgian architecture are considered among the most significant in that field, anywhere. Works on various aspects of architecture in Ireland have been included here.

The sampling of Irish newspapers and journals has been assembled by the compiler with an eye on general publications that might also interest an international audience. These are grouped towards the end, except for a few specialized journals which are listed under their appropriate subject categories. Indeed, most books listed throughout this volume have been selected for their general appeal rather than for the specialist working within an established discipline. Some deserving titles have probably escaped notice, and many more will surely have appeared during the preparation of this bibliography. If ancient Ireland largely lacked a written form of literature, this is more than redeemed by the steady outpouring of contemporary Irish writers whose intellectual fervour provides us with a constant renewal and prolific energy for the world of literature today.

As Ireland approaches the last decades of the 20th century the country shows a new political confidence. In every nation there comes a time when novel approaches or a new outlook are required in order to insure continued growth and a peaceful future. In regard to the affairs of Northern Ireland a new *modus vivendi* has been sought by the Republic with the United Kingdom. In November 1985 the Anglo-Irish Agreement, also known as the Hillsborough Agreement, was reached. This offered the prospect of cooperation between the two nations on matters of long concern and potential conflict. The new approach arose, in part, from the unprecedented discussions held among

Introduction

the major political parties of the Republic during the year before, known as the New Ireland Forum. The final proposals are seen by some as forming the basis for a new beginning in international understanding, although the agreement has already faced the concerted opposition of the Ulster Unionists.

This development requires a certain readjustment in the Irish Republic's thinking towards its own borders, and indeed towards some of the fundamental principles of the Irish state. The willingness to face realities (while not abandoning the ideal of a unified Ireland) shows a maturity in the nation's outlook. The Irish proposals of 1984 (a most significant step in Anglo-Irish relations) had received a wide, tacit acceptance in the Republic, even though overt enthusiasm has not been generated. The actual agreement of the following year does not mark a near resolution of the problem of Northern Ireland. Far from it. The provisions of the agreement will undoubtedly be reevaluated and modified over time, with some parts even rejected as eventually unworkable. However, the process of negotiation may become more important than the temporary alleviation of the problem.

The conclusions that have been reached reveal a willingness to face a difficult future with an original, inventive approach, and demonstrate an Ireland of adjustment and change, capable of drawing from its history without being dominated by it. It is the evolutionary aspect of the modern Irish state, the willingness to search for new solutions, that will contribute to the nation's renewal, and enable Ireland to complete its destiny.

Acknowledgements

I wish to express my gratitude to the Research Foundation of the City University of New York which has kindly provided support through its PSC-CUNY Research Awards programme. Lehman College of the City University of New York has also given encouragement, making the commitment to complete this task possible. The Library of Lehman College contains much of the specialized bibliographic records upon which this book is based. The staff of the National Library of Ireland (in Dublin) have provided consistent help whenever needed. Sarah Stubbings of Clio Press has been particularly helpful in seeing this manuscript through to completion, has shown considerable patience and has offered many suggestions. Finally, very special appreciation is due to Mary (Monica) Butler Shannon who has given much understanding, knowledge and advice during the several years of endless, tedious work while this book was in progress.

Glossary

Bord Fáilte Éireann	Irish Tourist Board.
Bord na Gaeilge	The Irish Language Board, the government body supporting the use of the Irish language.
Brehon law	Ancient pre-Norman laws of Ireland extending to the 17th century.
An Chomhairle Leabharlanna	The Library Council.
Coras Tráchtála	The Irish Export Board.
Dáil Eireann	The lower house of the Irish Parliament.
Éire	The proper term for Ireland in the Irish language. The Old Irish form was Ériu. Erin is an improper form of the term.
An Foras Forbartha	National Institute for Physical Planning and Construction Research.
An Foras Talúntais	The Agriculture Institute, the official body devoted to agricultural research.
Gaeltacht	The Irish language speaking area.

Glossary

Irish Free State

Saorstát Éireann (Saor or free, Stát or State). The official term for the Irish nation between 1922–1937.

Oireachtas

The Irish Parliament, located at Leinster House. The Houses of the Oireachtas consist of the Dáil and the Seanad.

Pale

The area surrounding Dublin over which the English exercised effective control after the 14th century.

Seanad Éireann

The Senate, or upper house of the Irish Parliament.

Shanachie

The traditional Irish story teller.

RTE

Radio Telefís Éireann.

Tánaiste

Deputy Prime Minister.

Taoiseach

Prime Minister.

Treaty

The Anglo-Irish Treaty of 1921.

The Country and Its People

General

1   **The importance of being Irish.**
    Alan Bestic.   New York: William Morrow; London: Cassell, 1969.
    199p.
Short essays outline the author's impressions of Ireland's industry, commerce,
farming, tourism, festivals, politics, education, marriage, culture and sports, at
the middle of the 20th century.

2   **The Irish.**
    Donald S. Connery.   New York: Simon & Schuster, 1968. 304p.
Patterns of daily life and living conditions in modern day Ireland are discussed as
Connery attempts to identify the essential character of the Irish. He shows how it
is affected by mass communications, education, marriage, changing politics and
the economy.

3   **Ireland: industrial and agricultural.**
    Edited by William Coyne.   Dublin: Brown & Nolan, 1902. 532p.
    maps.
Although now dated, this account is packed with information on Ireland at the
turn of the 20th century, including coverage of its agriculture, geology,
topography, economy, population, schools and transportation. The volume was
originally prepared by the Irish Department of Agriculture and Technical
Instruction for an international exposition in 1901. It provides an excellent
documentation of the country during a period of change just prior to the rising of
1916.

1

4   **The Irish world: the art and culture of the Irish people.**
Edited by Brian de Breffny.   London: Thames & Hudson; New
York: Abrams, 1977. 296p. bibliog.
Chapters by a number of authors discuss life, culture and the arts of Ireland, from
early times to the 1970s. G. O. Tuathaigh reviews the movement towards
independence between 1801 and 1918 while Kevin Nowlan covers the development of the modern nation of Ireland. A selective, but extensive, bibliography is
included. Overall, this is an attractive, well-illustrated history of Irish life and
society, although there is little information on politics and the economy.

5   **Irish Studies.**
Edited by P. J. Drudy.   Cambridge, England; New York:
Cambridge University Press, 1981- . annual.
Provides a review of current scholarship in many disciplines, including literature,
history, economics, sociology, foreign affairs and government. The papers,
although unrelated and tending towards the miscellaneous, are timely and address
some of the important issues of the day.

6   **Conor Cruise O'Brien introduces Ireland.**
Edited by Owen Dudley Edwards.   New York: McGraw-Hill;
London: Andre Deutsch, 1969. 240p.
Various authors portray aspects of 20th-century Ireland in this account for the
general reader. O'Brien, who is perhaps the best known of the contributors, has
become more controversial since the publication of this book, due to his political
observations and criticisms of Irish society.

7   **Irish heritage: the landscape, the people and their work.**
E. Estyn Evans.   Dundalk, Ireland (Republic): Dundalgan Press,
1967. 178p.
This volume, first published in 1947, portrays the early influences on country life,
crafts, customs and houses. Evans, a prominent geographer, shows the effect of
human activity on the landscape, utilizing many of his own drawings in an
informative study for the general reader.

8   **Facts about Ireland.**
Dublin: Ireland, Department of Foreign Affairs, 1983. 5th ed. 260p.
maps. bibliog.
Regularly issued by the Irish government, this most useful handbook provides an
overall view of the history and politics of both Northern and Southern Ireland,
and also covers the land, geography and resources, industry, arts, society and
social services. Numerous statistics are included. The Department also occasionally
issues free circulars and information sheets on various aspects of Ireland.

9 **Ireland: the challenge of conflict and change.**
Richard B. Finnegan. Boulder, Colorado: Westview, 1983. 166p.
maps.

A good introduction to Ireland by a political scientist who quickly reviews Irish history from Celtic times to the present. Some attention is given to the modernization of Irish society, education and politics during the second half of the 20th century, with critical comments. Two chapters consider the problems of Northern Ireland in a balanced view of Irish affairs. Emphasis is placed on recent transformations in culture, language, religion, the status of women, and the political process, throughout both the North and and the South.

10 **Irish life and traditions.**
Edited by Sharon Bohn Gmelch. Dublin: O'Brien Press, 1986. 256p.

Thirteen writers discuss Irish society and way of life throughout history, covering its traditions, culture and the rural landscape. A well illustrated introductory study, with sections on ancient times, Irish nature, cities, folkways, and music. This volume presents a view of the beauty of Ireland, its society and physical setting. Some chapters cover Irish nature, cities, sports, literature and festivals. Several papers describe life in different rural areas during certain decades between 1890 and 1960. This work will interest those with little prior knowledge of Ireland.

11 **The Crane Bag book of Irish studies.**
Edited by M. P. Hederman, R. Kearney. Dublin: Blackwater, 1983. 937p.

The *Crane Bag* is a literary, political, cultural and social journal published in the Republic of Ireland, each issue of which is generally devoted to one particular theme. This volume is a collection of the best articles published over five years on various aspects of contemporary Ireland. The first ten issues are included. The papers provide a thorough coverage, with an emphasis on literature and culture. The volume is prefaced by author Seamus Heaney.

12 **Irish Free State official handbook.**
Dublin: Talbot Press; London: Benn, 1932. 324p.

Compiled by the Irish government, Saorstát Éireann, this work provides a broad review of many aspects of Irish society, including its history, government, way of life, culture and resources. Each chapter was written for the Ministry of Industry and Commerce by a leading authority and the volume, which is still useful although now dated, is characterized by fine wood block illustrations, prints and design.

13 **Unequal achievement, the Irish experience, 1957-1982.**
Edited by Frank Litton. Dublin: Institute of Public Administration, 1983. 256p.

Seventeen authors contribute to this reassessment of contemporary Irish problems including those of the public sector, the arts, the environment, the economy, local

3

government, politics, culture and the social structure. The volume, which is used as a textbook, also reviews unemployment, emigration, voting and economic decline. This authoritative view from within may seem frank but unduly pessimistic, reflecting the stagnation of the mid-1980s. The volume originally appeared as a special edition of the journal *Administration*, commemorating twenty-five years of the Institute of Public Administration.

14 Ireland and the Irish: Cathleen ni Houlihan is alive and well.

Charles Lucey.   Garden City, New York: Doubleday, 1970. 256p.

Lucey portrays Ireland at mid-century, for the general reader, with observations on numerous topics, including history, society, education, economic growth and population.

15 Wheels within wheels: unraveling an Irish past.

Dervla Murphy.   London: John Murray; New York: Houghton Mifflin, 1980. 248p.

A popular author describes her youth and upbringing in Wexford, and her later travels through Ireland and beyond in this well received book.

16 The Irish.

Sean O'Faolain.   Harmondsworth, England: Penguin Books; Old Greenwich, Connecticut: Devin-Adair, 1979. Rev. ed. 173p.

O'Faoláin, a well-known writer, presents a brief overview of six major types of Irish personality: the Irish peasant, the Anglo-Irish, the rebel, the priest, the politician and the writer. In this study, originally published in 1949, he attempts to identify features of the Irish way of thinking.

17 Ireland, a terrible beauty.

Jill Uris, Leon Uris.   Garden City, New York: Doubleday; London: Deutch, 1976. 288p.

Observations on present-day Irish life in both the Republic and Northern Ireland, are provided in this popular account by a well-known writer. A perspective is presented from the outside by Uris, who, with the aid of more than 400 photographs, portrays the bleakness and problems of Irish society along with the pleasures.

18 The Irish: how they live and work.

Martin Wallace.   Newton Abbot, England: David & Charles; New York: Praeger, 1972. 166p.

Intended for the visitor to Ireland, the volume covers many aspects of Irish life including history, politics, demography, regional characteristics of geography, agriculture and industry, social issues, the quality of family life and the standard of living.

Pictorial

19 **The land of Ireland.**
Brian de Breffny. New York: Abrams; London: Thames & Hudson, 1979. 255p.

A pleasant, if unsystematic history of the four provinces of Ireland. Superior colour illustrations are matched with evocative poems and quotations. The volume includes a chronology, but is basically for recreational reading.

20 **Heritage of Ireland.**
Brian de Breffny. London: Weidenfeld & Nicolson; New York: Bounty Books, 1980. 160p.

An introductory, pictorial history of Ireland covering its people, politics, religion, crafts and particularly its culture. The often dazzling photographs are by George Mott.

21 **Ireland: presences.**
Daniel Kaufman. Dublin: Academy Press; New York: St. Martin's Press, 1980. 112p.

A pictorial record by an internationally recognized professional photographer. The colour photographs of the more pleasing scenes, largely landscapes, have a misty, almost spiritual quality.

22 **Ireland.**
Michael Mac Liammóir, Edwin Smith. London: Thames & Hudson, 1966. 244p.

This introduction to Ireland by an actor and a director, covers history, tradition, the cities and landscape, language, art and the people. Arranged by province with black and white photographs and useful captions, the work conveys a sense of the beauty of the land.

23 **Ireland.**
Terence J. Sheehy. Dublin: Gill & Macmillan; London, New York: Mayflower, 1979. 189p.

A largely pictorial and light-hearted review of twenty-seven aspects of Irish life, with an easy to read narrative on such topics as Ireland's people, geography, arts, literature, humour, culture, games, customs, music and theatre. Sheehy is also the author of another predominantly pictorial work, *Ireland and her people* (New York: Greenwich House, 1983).

24 **Ireland observed.**
May Veber. London: Kaye & Ward, 1980. 131p. map.

A collection of beautiful photographs are used to capture images of the land, its traditions, history and people. Arrangement is by geographic area: the South,

Lakeland, Western lands, and Ulster. Appendixes provide brief comments on the theatre and the arts.

25 Faces of Ireland, 1875-1925, a photographic and literary picture of the period.
Brian M. Walker, Art O'Broin, Sean McMahon.   Belfast: Appletree, 1980. 122p.

This unusually varied collection of over 350 period photographs is presented and arranged by major themes: politics, towns and work. This 'omnibus' edition contains approximately 400 pages of unique photographs grouped by province in addition to the text of contemporary accounts.

26 Ireland.
Gordon Wetmore.   Nashville, Tennessee: Thomas Nelson, 1980. 144p.

Watercolour paintings and drawings portray the Irish people at work and enjoying relaxation. The intent of the book is to convey visual impressions of the inhabitants.

Geography

General

27 **A systematic geography of Ireland.**
Desmond A. Gillmor. Dublin: Gill & Macmillan, 1971. 224p.
In this well illustrated, clearly written and detailed survey, nineteen chapters are presented on physical, economic and political geography, with coverage of the rural landscape, towns and cities, agriculture, transportation and communication. While the book compares regions it also provides a picture of the country as a whole. Intended as a textbook, it may also serve as a reference book.

28 **The geography of Ireland.**
J. P. Haughton, D. A. Gillmor. Dublin: Ireland (Eire)
Department of Foreign Affairs, 1979. 59p. 18 maps. charts.
(Aspects of Ireland, no. 5).
A brief introduction to Ireland's landscape, climate, natural resources, industry, transport, tourism and regional development. The commentary is both clear and succinct.

29 **The Irish landscape.**
George Francis Mitchell. London: Collins, 1976. 240p.
Mitchell describes the evolution of the Irish landscape through history and especially as it has been changed by man. He discusses geological structure, climatic change (especially during the Pleistocene period), botanical features, early farming, and late population changes. The style is simple and lucid, although the study contains considerable technical detail. Many maps, chronological tables, diagrams and illustrations are included.

30 **Ireland.**
A. R. Orme.   London: Longman; Chicago: Aldine, 1970. 276p.
maps. (The World's Landscape).

This is one of a series of volumes that describe environmental change caused by man in various parts of the world. After a general discussion of physical geography, geology, climate and resources the author reviews man-made changes in ecology from ancient times to the present. Lastly, he emphasizes modern trends such as industrialization, regional planning and the growth of towns. Numerous illustrations and maps enhance the text.

31 **Ireland from the air.**
Daphne D. C. Pochin-Mould.   Newton Abbot, England: David & Charles; New York: Arco, 1973. 112p.

A descriptive view of Ireland through captioned aerial photographs. The author identifies earthworks, agricultural patterns, ancient sites, signs of modern development in towns and major types of landforms and features. The work will interest those concerned with geography, history and planning although the detail of coverage lacks consistency.

32 **The climate of Ireland.**
P. K. Rohan.   Dublin: Stationery Office, 1975. 112p.

Major trends and patterns of climate and weather are presented, along with some comments on ancient records, the derivation of averages, extremes and methods of measurement. Extensive tables, maps and a bibliography are included although the main value of the volume lies in its broad perspective and commentary. The Meteorological Service of Ireland's Department of Transportation and Power also publishes a number of monthly to decennial compilations of weather data. See also *Climate of the British Isles* by T. J. Chandler and S. Gregory (New York, London: Longman, 1976. 390p.).

33 **Irish geographical studies in honour of E. Estyn Evans.**
Edited by Nicholas Stephens, Robin E. Glassock.   Belfast: Queen's University, Department of Geography, 1970. 403p. 95 maps.

Twenty-five authors contributed papers in honour of one of Ireland's, and the world's leading geographers. Chapters cover physical, historical, cultural and economic geography from prehistory to the present, in considerable detail, with emphasis on both ancient times and contemporary problems. An important volume.

Place-names

34   **Place-names of Great Britain and Ireland.**
John Field.   Newton Abbot, England: David & Charles; Totowa,
New Jersey: Barnes & Noble, 1980. 208p. maps. bibliog.
Intended for the general reader or the traveller, this dictionary is a selective
listing of some interesting place-names with the derivation of the name, its various
forms and first usage. Both the Irish Republic and Northern Ireland (as well as all
of Great Britain) are included in the 3,000 entries.

35   **A topographical dictionary of Ireland, comprising the several**
counties, cities, boroughs, corporate, market and post towns,
parishes and villages, with historical and statistical information.
Samuel Lewis.   Port Washington, New York: Kennikat Press,
1970. 3 vols. maps.
This gazetteer, originally published in 1837, contains the names and locations of
numerous places, many of which have changed or disappeared in the intervening
century. The last volume contains an atlas.

36   **The meaning of Irish placenames.**
James O'Connell.   Dundonald, Ireland (Republic): Blackstaff
Press, 1979. 96p.
Over 2,300 place-names are described, their origins identified, and Irish roots and
expressions translated. Although a shorter work than *Place-names of Great*
Britain and Ireland (q.v.), this volume deals exclusively with Ireland.

37   **A concise dictionary of modern placenames in Great Britain and**
Ireland.
Adrian Room.   New York: Oxford University Press, 1983. 224p.
The origins of more than 1,000 place-names in Ireland and Great Britain are
given, although the number of places identified in Ireland is not as large as that in
several other available works. However, descriptions are more thorough, and
some districts within cities are identified.

Regional

38   **A regional geography of Ireland.**
George Fahy.   Dublin: Browne & Nolan, 1969. 238p.
This study provides a systematic review of physical and economic geography,
geology and climate, using Ireland as the illustrative example. Not all passages
relate to Ireland in what is intended to be a general textbook, although
comparisons are frequently drawn between different regions of the both the
Republic and Northern Ireland.

39 **Ireland, a general and regional geography.**
Thomas Walter Freeman. London: Methuen, 1972. 4th ed. 559p.
maps. bibliog.
For each region of Ireland Freeman presents background information on its social
life, demography, emigration patterns, housing, agriculture and industry, natural
resources and settlements. The regional analysis oocupies half the volume; the
rest is concerned with a more general discussion of Irish landforms, geology and
historical geography. There is a useful chapter on Northern Ireland, and extensive
bibliographic notes at the end. Numerous statistics are provided although many
are no longer current.

40 **Ireland, a systematic and regional geography.**
Brendan S. MacAodha, E. A. Curry. Dublin: Educational
Company of Ireland, 1968. 297p. maps.
In this basic textbook each region is considered with regard to its resources and
characteristics. An overview is presented of landforms, agriculture, industry and
environment, and the text relates well to the numerous photographs and maps
which are included.

Geology

41 **The geology of Ireland: an introduction.**
John Kaye Charlesworth. Edinburgh: Oliver & Boyd, 1966. 276p.
This is a valuable, coherent introduction to Irish geology, although it is less
detailed than *A geology of Ireland* (q.v.). Charlesworth has also written
Historical geology of Ireland (Edinburgh: Oliver & Boyd, 1963. 565p.).

42 **Handbook of the geology of Ireland.**
Grenville Arthur James Cole, T. Hallisey. London: Thomas
Murby, 1924. 82p.
Cole, a prolific writer and an important contributor to modern geological studies,
did much to popularize the subject. In addition to this short study he also wrote
'Memoir and map of localities of minerals' issued as *Memoir of the geological
survey of Ireland* (Dublin: Stationery Office, 1922. Reprinted, 1956. 155p.).

43 **Ireland.**
Gordon L. Herries Davies, Nicholas Stephens. London: Methuen,
1978. 250p. (Geomorphology of the British Isles).
This work, by two leading authorities, covers the origins of Irish geological
formations and major landforms, the coastline, and geomorphic history.

44 **A geology of Ireland.**
Edited by C. H. Holland.   New York: John Wiley; Edinburgh:
Scottish Academic Press, 1981. 335p. maps.
Various authors provides both great breadth and concise information in this
major publication. Different geological formations are covered in separate
chapters. A paper on the history of Irish geology by Gordon Herries Davies is
included, which reviews the pioneers in the field from 1770. Other contributions
cover economic geology, mapping, the Ordnance Survey and landforms.

45 **Mineral industry of Ireland.**
Tatiana Karpinsky.   Washington, DC: US Bureau of Mines, 1981.
12p.
Frequently the *Minerals Yearbook*, published by the Government Printing Office
in Washington DC, includes this revised chapter on Ireland. This short paper is also
available as an offprint. It contains a useful, up-to-date summary of production,
trade, a commodity review, numerous statistics, and a short commentary. Future
editions will be by different authors.

46 **Geology and Ireland, with physical geography and its geological
background.**
W. E. Nevill.   Dublin: Allen Figgis, 1963. 263p.
This introductory textbook provides a broad view of Irish geology and relates
formations to general geographical features.

47 **Geology and scenery in Ireland.**
John Byron Whittow.   Harmondsworth, England: Penguin Books,
1978. 301p. maps.
Dr. Whittow, an internationally known geographer, considers Ireland by region,
with the first third of the book devoted to Northern Ireland. The study relates
how scenery is created and affected by the underlying geological structure. This
account will interest the general reader as well as the environmentalist,
backpacker and student. It can serve as a field guide and has a glossary, numerous
illustrations, charts and maps.

Special features

48 **The caves of Ireland.**
John Christopher Coleman.   Tralee, Ireland (Republic): Anvil
Books, [n.d.]. 88p.
A brief overview of major cave sites, some of which, such as those at
Mitchelstown and Dunmore, are well known. Further information on caves has
been published in the journal, *The Irish Naturalist*, (vol. 1, 1892), and by the
Speleological Union of Ireland in its annual journal *Irish Speleology*.

49 **Irish rivers.**
Edited by Éamon de Buitléar. Dublin: Country House, 1985.
128p.
Personal observations are offered by several writers on the river systems of
Ireland, life along the banks, fish, birds and wildlife.

50 **Irish peaks.**
Joss Lynam. London: Constable, 1982. 250p. maps. bibliog.
Fifty mountains in Ireland are studied in this volume which includes maps,
photographs and suggestions on routes. Full descriptions are provided of the
surrounding terrain, growth and history, making this a useful reference work.

51 **Management of the River Shannon in the 1980's.**
Administration, vol. 25, no. 2 (Summer 1977), 280p.
This is a special issue devoted to the river and its regional setting. Included are a
wide range of articles on natural resources (fish, power, water), tourism,
navigation, and control. The magazine also reviews some of the major
engineering, governmental and technical studies over the course of a century.

52 **Mountain year: life on the slopes of Slieve Gullion.**
Michael J. Murphy. Dublin: Dolmen; Chester Springs,
Pennsylvania: Dufour, 1964. 63p.
Twelve essays based on experience during a year spent near the mountain Slieve
Gullion. The narrative covers the people and customs of the district and shows
how one mountain can dominate the lives and living patterns of those close by.

53 **The mountains of Ireland.**
Daphne D. C. Pochin-Mould. Dublin: Gill & Macmillan, 1976.
160p.
The major mountain ranges of Ireland are discussed in terms of their geology,
landscape, cultural history and legends. The work is supplemented by aerial
photographs.

Maps and atlases

54 **A paper landscape, the Ordnance Survey in nineteenth century
Ireland.**
J. H. Andrews. Oxford: Clarendon Press, 1975. 350p. maps.
Andrews provides a scholarly though entertaining history of a high point in Irish
mapping, from its uncertain beginnings in the early 19th century through military
improvements, the introduction of unusual scale, technical difficulties, the cultural
outlook of the varied cartographers, and their impressive results.

55 **Irish maps.**
J. H. Andrews. Dublin: Eason, 1978. 25p. maps. (Irish Heritage Series, no. 18).

A basic introduction to the historical mapping of Ireland. Major cartographers, trends and methods are noted from the 16th to the 19th century. Numerous colour reproductions are included of details from estate, large scale and official maps.

56 **An atlas of Irish history.**
Ruth Dudley Edwards. London: Methuen, 1973. 261p. maps.

Maps are used to provide a composite picture of Ireland's physical features, political outlines, commerce, economics, population and social change. The accompanying narrative is useful, although the population figures only go up to 1971. The emphasis of the volume is on the changing geographic face of Ireland through history. Most maps included are on a small scale with limited detail.

57 **Atlas of Ireland.**
Edited by J. P. Haughton, (et al.). Dublin: Royal Irish Academy, 1979. 112p. 250 maps.

In this extensive and reliable atlas, maps of the country are arranged by theme ranging from general to geological, with some relating to water, soils, climate, flora, fauna, population, economics, language and cultural characteristics. The cartography, which is excellent, is a result of the combined efforts of a national team of geographers. This is an important reference volume on Ireland.

58 **Sheets of many colours: the mapping of Ireland's rocks, 1750-1890.**
Gordon L. Herries-Davies. Dublin: Royal Dublin Society, 1983. 242p.

This work outlines the development of the Geological Survey of Ireland from its beginnings to its completion of 205 maps in the one-inch series. Davies covers both political and theoretical battles among geographers and surveyors, British and Irish, military and civilian, in the production of the magnificent, landmark six-inch series.

59 **The Ordnance Survey road atlas of Ireland.**
Dublin: Gill & Macmillan, 1985.

Jointly published by the Ordnance Survey of both the Irish Republic and Northern Ireland, this atlas has thirty-six plates of national maps, supplemented by road maps, maps of urban areas, a gazetteer, and basic touring and driving information.

Travellers' Accounts

60 The south and west of it, Ireland and me.
Oriana Atkinson. New York: Random House, 1956. 303p.

Atkinson describes her personal experiences during a trip through Ireland several decades ago. Although much of the country has since changed, some of the rural areas remain the same, and her recollection of the archaeological excavations at Loch Gur are still interesting. Written for an American audience, the book draws some comparisons between the hills of Ireland, the Catskills in New York and other places with which the author was familiar. Oriana Atkinson was the wife of Brooks Atkinson, a theatre critic who reviewed a number of Irish plays.

61 Irish journal, a traveller's portrait of Ireland.
Heinrich Boll. London: Secker & Warburg, 1983. 127p.

Boll writes of Ireland with a poet's eye, following an extensive stay in 1957. He comments on the social ways, amusements, religion, and habits of the Irish. Boll is critical of the shortcomings that he observed, including inefficiency and the still pervasive poverty of the 1950s. Yet he notes the best qualities of the Irish character, including common thoughtfulness and kindness. This collection of observations, commentary and stories was written just prior to the modernization of Ireland with regard to consumer goods, communications and urban living, aspects of which Boll probably would not have approved. This is a reprint of a 1967 revised edition and translation.

62 A Frenchman's walk through Ireland, 1796–7.
Jacques De Latocnaye, translated by John Stevenson, introduction by John Gamble. Belfast: Blackstaff Press; Dover, New Hampshire: Longwood, 1984. 292p.

The author presents close personal observations of Ireland at the end of the 18th century, based on his experiences during a walking tour of the country. This once popular account provides the distant views of a traveller from the continent. It has been issued in various editions and translations over the last two centuries and was once included in a three volume set by the author, volume one covering the French Revolution, volume two a walk across England, and volume three rambles through Ireland. The present volume is a facsimile of a 1917 edition. As a royalist Chevalier De Latocnaye had fled the French Revolution, and was later to contemplate the perceived benefits of British rule in Ireland, with an unquestioning attitude. Nonetheless, his book does provide a colourful description of 18th-century Ireland, the secret societies, White Boys and other agrarian groups, United Irishmen, Orange Boys, disorder, disputes, migration of refugees, and smuggling. Interspersed is a general look at the countryside, scenic locations, customs, churches, farming methods, markets, courts, and a changing society during a period of declining commerce. There are glances at most regions, including Cork, Donegal, Dublin, Belfast, Armagh, and Dundalk.

63 **Here's Ireland.**
Bryan MacMahon.   Dublin: Butler Sims, 1982. 276p.

The author provides a personal account of his travels throughout Ireland, with discursive, urbane views of the people, places, antiquities and important sites. His observations range from charming to ironic and outspoken. Political issues are avoided.

64 **Ireland beautiful.**
Wallace Nutting.   New York: Bonanza Books, 1975 (reprint).
302p.

For several generations Wallace Nutting has remained a favourite among travel writers, possibly due to his selection of certain locations, according to their romantic, nostalgic or picturesque associations. In this book a happy life in rural Ireland is usually portrayed, even if it is at times unrealistic. Over 300 illustrations reinforce the impressions of natural beauty, although the photographs in this reprinted edition are poorly reproduced. (Superior reproductions appear in a 1925 edition by Plimpton Press, Norwood, Massachusetts). Various Wallace Nutting clubs have been formed among print and book collections.

65 **The gems she wore, a book of Irish places.**
James Plunkett.   New York; Chicago: Holt, Rinehart & Winston,
1972. 208p.

Plunkett, a successful Irish novelist, writer and critic, provides a lyrical guide to Ireland, giving his first hand impressions of some of the varied qualities of Irish places: Dublin, Wicklow, Cork, Kerry, Sligo and Donegal. He includes mention of many of the writers associated with the different locales, and mixed in with Plunkett's own commentary and recollections are some of the stories told by the natives of each area.

66 **The friendly Irish.**
John Scofield.   *National Geographic*, vol. 136, no. 3 (Sept. 1969),
p. 354-91.

Presents a pleasant review of Irish life and character as found by a traveller in various parts of the country. Hardships, changing conditions, work habits and social customs are mentioned.

67 **The grand Irish tour.**

Peter Somerville-Large. London: Hamish Hamilton, 1982. 256p.

Based on a year's journey the author describes the people, towns and land through which he travelled. He draws upon his own recollections of youth and compares the days that he once knew in Ireland to the reports of the 18th- and 19th-century travellers. Many quotations are drawn from the diaries and reports of these earlier visitors. The present book provides a convenient source for some of these earlier observations. As not all the comments are favourable, the book provides an antidote to the often too glowing accounts of the countryside. Diarmaid Ó Muirithe also reviews 19th-century travelling experiences in *A seat behind the coachman: travellers in Ireland, 1800-1900* (Dublin: Gill & Macmillan, 1972. 209p.). Impressions are given of Irish society and economic conditions through contemporary accounts, and some illustrations and music are included.

68 **The Irish sketchbook 1842.**

William Makepeace Thackeray. Belfast: Blackstaff, 1986. Reprint of 1925 edition. 368p.

Thackeray offers many observations on early 19th-century Ireland, based on his sometimes rollicking sojourn through the country, in 1843. His trip was undertaken just before the famine, and he uses a reporter's eye to describe the teeming population, extensive poverty, the poor houses, rural ways, and the cities and towns of Dublin, Cork, Bandon, Killarney, Limerick, Newry, Armagh, and Belfast. He comments on the law courts, all levels of society, the schools of Dundalk and Irish education, and the potato harvests. A number of local stories are interspersed throughout, and there are humorous portraits of his assorted acquaintances in Ireland. Thackeray's observations are those of a Londoner on vacation, picturesque, sometimes astute, often unrealiable and not always sympathetic.

69 **A tour of Ireland, 1776–1779.**

Arthur Young, edited by Constantia Maxwell. Belfast: Blackstaff, 1983. Reprint of 1925 edition. 272p.

Arthur Young's interest in Ireland lay primarily in agriculture, and here he presents his first hand observations on the 18th-century farming methods, produce and livestock which he encountered during his travels through the countryside. He offers numerous comments on rural life, the economy, and suggests methods for their improvement during that period.

Tourism and Travel Guides

70 **Touring Ireland.**
Edited by T. J. Barrington.   Dublin: Touring Ireland. 8 tapes.

A series of cassette tapes (purchasable individually), each of which covers a section of itinerary largely in the southwest of Ireland (Dingle, Kerry and Killarney). The tapes, which run for an hour or more, discuss ancient history and sites, natural history, traditions and the people of each locale. Most of the journeys outlined cover a hundred miles or so by car.

71 **AA touring guide to Ireland.**
Edited by Russell Beach.   London: British Tourist Authority; Bridgeport, Connecticut: Merrimack, 1979. 336p. maps.

This detailed guidebook (first post-war edition 1956) covers towns, cities, geography and history, and is arranged by place-name. The volume is useful as a reference sources, although unwieldy for the traveller. It is enhanced by excellent maps. The Automobile Association has also produced a shorter guide: *AA Ireland, where to go, what to do* (1981, 208p.), with the same publishers.

72 **Rambles in Ireland, a county-by-county guide for discriminating travelers.**
Monie Begley.   Old Greenwich, Connecticut: Devin-Adair, 1977. 382p. maps.

A short introduction to Ireland's history, genealogy, people, culture and countryside is followed by a guide to particular areas, hotels and guesthouses, food and entertainment. An attempt is made to depart from the terseness of standard travel handbooks, and observations are included based on conversations with various Irish writers and prominent figures.

73 **Arthur Frommer's guide to Dublin and Ireland.**
Beth Bryant, Susan Poole. New York: Simon & Schuster, 1984.
232p.

A standard, current guide, this volume highlights the major sights although in less
detail than *Fodor's Ireland, 1984* (q.v.). Emphasis is given to hotels and stores,
and a short section on Northern Ireland is included. This volume will be most
useful for a first time visitor to Ireland on a short stay, who may not need a
detailed volume. Paper quality is poor.

74 **Let's halt awhile in Ireland, 1982-1983.**
Ashley Courtenay. New York: Hastings, 1982. 128p.

Reissued regularly with updated versions, this volume of standard travel
information provides current tips for the visitor to Ireland.

75 **Ireland observed, a guide to the buildings and antiquities of Ireland.**
Maurice Craig, the Knight of Glin. Dublin; Cork: Mercier Press,
1981. 120p.

A very useful guide to buildings, historic locations, sites, and antiquities. The
volume is thoroughly illustrated and is arranged alphabetically by location for
quick reference. Appendixes contain a glossary, bibliography, and references to
map grids.

76 **Around Ireland.**
Catharina Day. Chicago: Regnery, 1982. 321p.

A useful general travel guide, with numerous travel tips, remarks on Irish history
and legends, and some out of the way locations. Includes references to guest
houses and employment opportunities.

77 **Planning for amenity and tourism.**
Michael Dower. Dublin: An Foras Forbartha (National Institute
for Physical Planning and Construction Research), vol. 1 1966; vol.
2. 1976.

This United Nations financed manual is designed to assist planning authorities in
selecting and improving local resources and amenities that will be attractive to
tourists in Ireland. The study discusses financial methods of analysis and
managerial considerations in evaluating resources. A study of County Donegal's
potential for tourism is presented in *Ekistics*, vol. 23, no. 137 (1967), p. 238-45.

78 **The magic of the Shannon.**
John M. Feehan. Cork: Mercier Press, 1980. 128p.

Feehan covers the passage and the lands bordering 200 miles of the River
Shannon and provides a commentary on the towns, the people and the important
sites as if they were being observed from a boat. For similar, general impressions
of the region see *The Shannon guide* by Ruth Heard and Terence Mallagh
(Dublin: Inland Waterways Association, 1978. 51p.); and 'Where the Shannon
River flows' by Allan C. Fisher in the *National Geographic Magazine*, vol. 154,
no. 5 (Nov. 1978), p. 652-79.

79   **Fodor's Ireland, 1984.**
New York: David McKay, 1984. 308p. maps. (Fodor's Travel
Guides).
One of the better travel guides, Fodor's has permanent reference value.
Following a useful introduction to the country and numerous facts at the fingertip
the major part of the book in divided by region. The narrative includes many
references to history. Contains adequate maps, good local town plans, and
suggestions for trips. Twenty or so pages cover Northern Ireland. The volume is
convenient to carry, and usful to retain afterwards.

80   **Ireland: convention planners' guide.**
Dublin: Convention Bureau of Ireland, [n.d.]. 104p.
This useful handbook for travel and booking agents and tour planners, provides
diagrams, floor plans and photographs for a number of hotels, with data on the
facilities available in each. General travel requirements are also listed, though
frequency of publication is uncertain. The Convention Bureau of Ireland was
established by Bord Fáilte as a coordinating body for the promotion and
marketing of travel, conventions, sales meetings and related forms of business.

81   **The Ireland guide.**
Dublin: Irish Tourist Board (Bord Fáilte Eireann), 1977. 260p.
maps. bibliog.
An excellent guide, arranged by province and county, this volume provides a wide
range of information on ancient locations, ruins, history, geography, terrain,
natural history and interesting sights. A biographical section covers Irish
literature. The volume maintains a good balance between travel tips and
background information.

82   **The essential Dublin.**
Terry Kelleher.   Dublin: Gill & Macmillan, 1979. 224p.
A general guidebook for the traveller to the city, this volume also attempts to
identify some of the less usual sites and locales.

83   **Shell guide to Ireland.**
Lord Killanim, M. V. Duignan.   London: Ebury, 1969. 512p.
An extensive guide to the antiquities and early monuments of the country, its
architecture and museum collections. The section on Dublin is useful though
somewhat dated. The focus of the book is on history and art rather than on
geography or scenery. Descriptive information on places is arranged alphabetically.

84   **Irish walk guides.**
Edited by Joss Lynam.   Dublin: Gill & Macmillan, 1979-
A series of pamphlet guides, each about forty pages and covering a different part
of the country. Each suggests possible routes for the walker with notes on
distances, inclines, climate, flora, natural habitat, geology and parking. Guides
for the following regions have appeared: east, southeast, west, southwest, and
northwest.

85   **Michelin red guide to Great Britain and Ireland.**
Geneva: Michelin, 1983. 600p. (Red Guide Series).

A standard travel guide for the motorist, though with the larger part of the volume devoted to England. Useful directions, distances and destinations are plotted with suggestions on sightseeing and accommodation.

86   **Outings in Ireland.**
Hugh Oram.   Belfast: Appletree; Bridgeport, Connecticut: Merrimack, 1983. 216p. maps.

This compact guide provides a brief history and summary of major towns and cities with their important sites. More than sixty maps are augmented by photographs and drawings.

87   **Goodly Barrow, a voyage on an Irish river.**
T. F. O'Sullivan.   Dublin: Ward River, 1983. 288p. maps. bibliog.

Inland Ireland is viewed from the sweep of a major Irish river. More than just a navigational guide, this well written volume, illustrated with maps, photographs, engravings and drawings, provides observations on the history, land and people along the river's banks. The author served as Ireland's ambassador to the United States. A more general work on Irish rivers is *Holiday cruising in Ireland, a guide to inland waterways* by P. J. Ransom (Newton Abbot, England: David & Charles, 1971).

88   **Ireland.**
Ian Robertson.   London: Benn; Chicago; New York: Rand McNally, 1979. Reprinted, New York: Norton, 1984. 359p. maps. (Blue Guide Series).

This useful guidebook, which includes a good index, suggests detailed, planned trips and provides considerable information on buildings and sites. Excellent coloured maps are provided and there is a good historical introduction. This serves as a helpful reference for the traveller.

89   **Tourism plan, 1975-1978.**
Dublin: Irish Tourist Board (Bord Fáilte), 1975. 131p.

The potential and future of Irish tourism is considered, with a recommended four year plan of action.

90   **The west: Clare, Galway, Mayo.**
Tony Whilde.   Dublin: Gill & Macmillan, 1978. 93p.

Intended as a guide for walkers, this volume includes information on trails, provides hints for the walker and suggests excursions through rural and scenic areas, many of which are of interest to the naturalist.

91 **Dumont guide: Ireland.**
Wolfgang Ziegler, Russell Stockman. New York: Stewart, Tabori
& Chang, 1984. 302p. maps.

This is one of the more attractive tour guides on Ireland. Much historical background is included, with the first eighty pages devoted to a general introduction to Irish history. The remainder of the volume is divided by province and county with appendixes containing helpful hints, a chronology and a bibliography. The volume will be most useful to those preparing for an extended trip. Many 19th-century engraved illustrations are reproduced along with recent photographs of historic sites. The book has been faulted for a few inaccuracies in the text.

City and Regional Studies

General

92 **The Irish countryman: an anthropological study.**
Conrad Maynadier Arensburg. New York: Natural History Press, 1968. 216p.

In this classic study, first published in 1937, the author describes rural life in County Clare, covering family life, living conditions in the early 20th century and the role of the individual within an agricultural community.

93 **Discovering Kerry, its history, heritage and topography.**
Thomas J. Barrington. Tallaght, County Dublin: Blackwater Press, 1976. 336p. maps. bibliog.

An interesting review of Kerry's archaeological and architectural heritage, natural history, important locations, folklore and other topics. This detailed account is supplemented with maps, prints, photographs and drawings. (Barrington, a former director of the Institute of Public Administration, has also prepared an hour-long Ring of Kerry cassette for the traveller). *Discovering Kerry* is a major study of the region, which includes extensive research material.

94 **The story of Cork.**
Seán Beecher. Cork: Mercier Press, 1971. 127p.

In this rather summary account the author provides a general description of the city, its history, society and inhabitants.

95 **Inishkillane: change and decline in the West of Ireland.**
Hugh R. Brody.   Harmondsworth, England: Penguin, 1973.
Reprinted, New York: Schocken, 1974; London: Jill Norman &
Hobhouse, 1982.226p. bibliog.

West coast economics and social conditions are discussed in this study of a parish
in County Clare. Rural patterns, family life, intercommunity relations, the place
of the pub, shop and church, marriage, local business and demography are all
interwoven in this study of difficult living conditions.

96 **The history and antiquities of the Diocese of Ossory.**
William Canon Carrigan.   Kilkenny, Ireland (Republic): Roberts
& Wellbrook, 1981. 4 vols.

This enormous history is considered a model of local historical research,, and it is
one of the finest produced in Ireland on the limited area of Leinster.
Archaeology, and ecclesiastical, family, architectural and linguistic history are
interwoven in this discourse covering mediaeval times to the beginning of the 20th
century. First published in 1903, with 300 illustrations, this reprint has a new
introduction by John Bradley of the University College Dublin Department of
Archaeology.

97 **The Midlands.**
Leo Daly.   Dublin: Albertine Kennedy, 1979. 79p.

A short, popular survey of the counties of Longford, Cavan, Laois, Westmeath,
Roscommon, Monaghan and Offaly. Literature, ancient locations, history and
geology are among the topics considered.

98 **The land and people of nineteenth century Cork; the rural economy
and the land question.**
James Donnelly.   London: Routledge & Kegan Paul, 1975. 440p.

Against the backdrop of rural Cork in the 19th century, the author analyses social
and economic conditions in a period of drastic change. Famine, disorder, living
conditions, changing land use and ownership are all aspects of an important
period in Irish agricultural history. The author draws upon a huge range of
historical documentation in this thorough study.

99 **Sweet Cork of thee.**
Robert Gibbings, in association with John Treacey.   Leicester,
England: Remploy, 1983. 235p.

In this charming work, Gibbings provides a rambling account of both city and
country life in the South of Ireland, the folk-ways and friendships. This reprint of
a 1951 edition incorporates a number of illustrations that convey a sense of the
beauty of the area. A companion volume by Gibbings is *Lovely is the Lee*,
published by Dent.

100 **The west of Ireland.**
Seán Jennett. London: Batsford; New York: Norton, 1980. 150p.
bibliog.
Intended for leisurely reading this volume contains general comments on such topics as history, geography, local lore and important sites. Although not in the format of a guidebook it covers the counties of Clare, Galway, Mayo and Sligo and includes an appendix on Irish place-names. Jennett has written several other popular books on different regions of Ireland, including *Munster* (London: Darton, Longman & Todd, 1966) and *Connacht: the counties of Galway, Mayo, Sligo, Leitrim and Roscommon in Ireland* (London: Faber, 1970).

101 **The history of the county of Mayo to the close of the sixteenth century.**
H. T. Knox. Dublin: Hodges Figgis, 1908. Reprinted, Castlebar, County Mayo, Ireland (Republic): De Burca, 1982. 451p.
An extensive history of early County Mayo from prehistory to the first monastic settlements, and into the Tudor and later periods. The author's love for the county is evident in this fact filled summary. The De Burca reprint is in a finely printed, limited edition.

102 **Steps and steeples: Cork at the turn of the century.**
Colm Lincoln. Rathgar, County Dublin: O'Brien Press, 1981. 146p. maps. bibliog. (Urban Heritage, no. 1).
Based on early photographs by Robert French and supplemented with street-maps, the book looks at the ancient city as it was a century ago, including its buildings, bridges, water, railways and people. Lincoln provides a good introduction to the photographs.

103 **Our like will not be there again: notes from the west of Ireland.**
Lawrence Millman. Boston, Massachusetts: Little, Brown, 1977. 209p.
A nostalgic appreciation of the people in the west of Ireland and the changing conditions that confront them. Millman weaves together tales, first-hand observations, humour and monologues to describe the work, craft, and rural ways of a society which is now disappearing.

104 **Irish Midland studies.**
Edited by Harmon Murtagh. Athlone, Ireland (Republic): Old Athlone Society, 1980. 270p. maps.
Includes a wide range of topics on the interior counties of the Irish Republic, with particular attention to archaeology, history, ancient sculpture, artifacts and folklore. Twenty-three authors contribute papers ranging from studies of mediaeval times to observations on the customs and folk-ways of the present century. The volume is illustrated with numerous plates, drawings, and maps. The book is a memorial to historian N. W. (Billy) English.

105 **Tipperary: history and society.**
Edited by William Nolan.   Dublin: Geography Publcications,
1985. 493p.
A scholarly, detailed, and major study of the county of Tipperary, with nineteen
interdisciplinary essays that review a wide range of topics. Those on archaeology,
geography, mediaeval history, literature, and the presence of the Catholic Church
in the county from 1700-1900, are excellent. Other papers on history and
economics are narrowly focused and specific. A final chapter on planning provides
a general overview of modern day problems. The work is augmented by maps,
charts and forty-three pages of references. No attempt is made to present a
complete view of the county, past and present.

106 **Galway: town and gown, 1484-1984.**
Edited by Díarmuid Ó Cearbhaill.   Dublin: Gill & Macmillan,
1985. 310p.
A series of lectures on the history of the city, tracing its evolution from an ancient
centre of commerce, to more recent times, with a place for higher education,
scholarship and science.

107 **The history, topography, and antiquities of the county and city of
Waterford, with an account of the present state of the peasantry of
that part of the South of Ireland.**
R. H. Ryland.   Kilkenny, Ireland (Republic): Wellbrook, 1982.
419p.
This account, first published in 1824 provides an historical sketch of the city from
the time of Henry II to the end of the 17th century. The Reverend Ryland
comments on topography, scenery, antiquities and historical sites, trade,
commerce and government. Though he attempted to correct the inaccuracies of
the past, his opinions are now dated.

108 **The ancient and present state of the county of Kerry.**
Charles Smith.   Cork; Dublin: Mercier, 1980. 320p.
An updated version of a history written in 1756 covering religious, political and
military events in Kerry. This should be read in conjunction with John
O'Donovan's *Antiquities of the county of Kerry* (Cork, Ireland (Republic): Royal
Carberry Books, 1983), which criticises and correct much of Smith's account.

109 **In Wicklow, West Kerry and Connemara.**
John Millington Synge, with essays by George Gmelch, Ann
Saddlemyer.   Totowa, New Jersey: Rowman & Littlefield, 1980.
166p. maps.
These three essays by the famous dramatist, first published in 1911 (Dublin:
Maunsel) present sensitive portraits of the rural landscape, its inhabitants and the
daily life of the farmers, fishermen and tinkers of the day. The work was first
published with drawings by Jack B. Yeats, an uncle of poet W. B. Yeats. In this
new edition, essays are included by Gmelch and Saddlemyer, which place Synge

in the perspective of literature and anthropology, and show how the work provided the material for his later plays. The addition of maps and sixty photographs by Gmelch serve to document the scenes and their changes since Synge's day.

110 **Another life.**
Michael Viney, Ethna Viney.   Dublin: Irish Times, 1979. 159p.

The Vineys give a highly personal view of modern life in rural Ireland following their relocation after some years in the cosmopolitan surroundings of the cities. Their rather individualistic observations cover a range of subjects, including social life in rural towns and attitudes toward employment and housing. A sequel, *Another life again* (Dublin: Irish Times, 1982) concentrates more on rural living conditions and patterns, and the sea. The book is illustrated with line-drawings by Michael Viney.

Dublin

111 **Dublin made me.**
C.S. Andrews.   Cork: Mercier, 1979. 312p.

A vivid view of the city in the early 20th century is presented in this first hand account of history, politics and daily life.

112 **A history of the county of Dublin, the people, parishes and antiquities from the earliest times to the close of the eighteenth century.**
Francis Elrington Ball.   Dublin: Thom, 1902-1920. Reprinted, Dublin: Gill & Macmillan, 1980. 6 vols.

A modern reprint of a standard, thorough account of the city and county. The last two volumes cover the outlying areas of Howth and Southern Fingal. The set does not include later archaeological findings or modern social analysis, yet the volumes include much of the traditions, locations and historical evidence still observable at the turn of the century in Dublin and surrounding areas.

113 **Dublin.**
Robert Ballagh.   Dublin: Ward River Press, 1982. 128p.

A collection of photographs by one of Ireland's leading artists, who has also had architectural training. The volume concentrates on street scenes, details and buildings, many of which have since disappeared. An introductory essay discusses the artist's life and work, and his emphasis on colour, contrast and the beauty which may be found in unexpected places.

114   **Tom Corkery's Dublin.**
Tom Corkery.   Dublin: Anvil Books, 1981. 128p.
With nostalgia and humour the author observes Dublin during the 1940s and 50s. The book draws on thirty or so of Corkery's weekly columns for the *Irish Times*, with a number of photographs added to document a past style of life in the city, its markets, characters, rogues, streets and leisurely pace.

115   **Where they lived in Dublin.**
John Cowell.   Dublin: O'Brien Press, 1980. 128p.
Cowell identifies the locations of and describes the lives of 160 better-known members of Dublin society, including literary, artistic and political figures such as Handel, Joyce, Synge, Yeats, Shaw, George Moore, Robert Emmett, Pearse, Churchill, de Valera and others. The biographies are both pithy and poignant and the book, with photographs of many of the homes, serves as both a reference work and a guidebook.

116   **Dublin, 1660-1860, a social and architectural history.**
Maurice James Craig.   Dublin: Allen Figgis, 1950. rev ed. 1980. 362p. maps.
A solid historical portrait is given of the city in different periods, reflecting the times of the Ormonds, Swift and Henry Grattan. An appendix contains eighty plates of photographs relating the city's architecture to cultural forces. Also included are lists of streets, buildings and building suppliers. Craig has also prepared an introduction to a reprinted map of Dublin in 1728 showing the principal buildings and topography of the city with twenty-two vignettes. This is a separate publication.

117   **A history of the city of Dublin.**
John Thomas Gilbert.   Dublin: Gill & Macmillan, 1978. 3 vols.
Gilbert, a 19th-century historian, provides a detailed history of the city. This is a reprint of the set first published between 1854 and 1859. A new index is provided.

118   **The Liberties of Dublin: its history, people and future.**
Edited by Elgy Gillespie.   Dublin: O'Brien Press, 1973. 120p.
Papers by sixteen specialists discuss the Viking and mediaeval part of the city that was originally outside the jurisdiction of the high sheriff. In this both serious and entertaining work particular attention is focused on conditions of poverty, 19th-century working conditions, Viking finds, daily conditions and life in the 20th century and the old town walls.

119   **Dublin 1913, a divided city.**
Gary Granville, (et al.).   Dublin: O'Brien Press, 1973. Reprinted, 1982. 111p. maps.
Prepared by the Curriculum Development Unit as an introductory text, this brief volume provides an excellent picture of Dublin at a crucial point in its history just prior to the Easter Rising of 1916. Vivid photographs and narrative document the contrast between poverty and high society during this turbulent period. Numerous

quotations from leading figures and authors of the day are included, and particular attention is given to labour disputes and the city-wide lockout of that year.

120 **Dublin, the people's city.**
Nevill Johnson. Dublin: Academy Press, 1981. 192p.
This work, which includes a selection of 140 photographs of Dublin, records the variety of buildings, street scenes, games, life and customs prevalent in the 1950s. Winner of the International Book Award in Leipzig, the volume, through its black and white illustrations, provides a scene of contrasts in shabbiness and texture of everyday existence.

121 **Dublin.**
Edited by Benedict Kiely. London, New York: Oxford University Press, 1983. 120p.
This anthology combining the author's narrative with passages on the city drawn from the works of a number of writers, including Joyce, Swift, Shaw, Moore, Behan, and Yeats, presents a series of literary impressions for the vistor.

122 **Dublin, ninety drawings.**
Brian Lalor. London; Boston, Massachusetts: Routledge & Kegan Paul, 1981. 136p.
Ninety very sensitive pen drawings illustrate Dublin street scenes, architectural forms and patterns. Mediaeval and Georgian locations are shown with a fresh perspective. The narrative covers politics, social classes, history and religion, but the particular value of the book lies in its everyday views of the streets, riveting attention on environmental details.

123 **Dublin.**
Brendan Lehane. Amsterdam: Time-Life Books, 1978. 200p. (Great Cities Series).
In this often elegant and sensitive account, impressions are given of the city's literary, architectural and social heritage. This highly illustrated volume provides a valuable introduction to the city for the prospective visitor, although it is not, however, a guidebook.

124 **A history and topography of Dublin City and County.**
Samuel Lewis. Cork: Mercier, 1979. 242p.
First published in 1837, this volume provides an account of 19th-century institutions, commerce, economic, political and social conditions in the city, and is often referred to as a standard source for the period.

125 **Guide to historic Dublin.**
Adrian MacLoughlin. Dublin: Gill & Macmillan, 1980. 222p.
The physical growth of the city is shown over a period of centuries through comments, photographs, drawings and maps, in this comprehensive guide.

126 **Me jewel and darlin' Dublin.**
Eamonn MacThomais. Dublin: O'Brien Press, 1983. 144p.
A lively and entertaining social history of the city, with particular attention paid
to amusements, customs, daily life, living conditions, commerce, neighborhoods
and newspapers. Some emphasis is given to markets, Trinity College and the
city's mediaeval core. Companion volumes by the same author and publisher
include *Janey Mack, me shirt is black* (1983), which covers childhood and street
lore; *Gur cakes and coal blocks* (1976), a social journal of Dublin in the war
years, and *The Labour and the Royal* (1982), continuing a picture of Dublin into
the postwar years. All the volumes are well illustrated and entertaining.

127 **A picturesque and descriptive view of the city of Dublin . . . 1799.**
James Malton, introduction by Maurice Craig. Mountrath,
County Laois, Ireland (Republic): Dolmen Press; Atlantic
Highlands, New Jersey: Humanities Press, 1981. 144p. maps.
A reprint of a well-known collection of 18th-century views of fine buildings,
parks, streets and locations. Drawn in 1791 and published in 1799, Malton's
acquatint views were considered the finest to have ever appeared of the city. A
new introduction is provided by the Knight of Glin, a leading authority on
Georgian architecture.

128 **Dublin under the Georges, 1714-1830.**
Constantia Maxwell. Dublin: Gill & Macmillan, 1979. 350p.
Originally published in 1936 and revised in 1956 (Faber & Faber) this is an
account of the development and growth of the city during its most architecturally
and socially significant period. Attention is given to the life styles of both the
successful and the poor, and to the city's commerce, culture and society.

129 **Bloomsday images: an evocation of Joyce's Dublin in words and
pictures.**
David Norris, Kieran Hickey. Dublin: Academy Press, 1979.
180p.
The Dublin of Joyce's day is described in quotations from his works. Norris has
also written a pamphlet, *Joyce's Dublin* (Dublin: Eason, 1982. Irish Heritage
Series, no. 36). Both are well-illustrated. Another guide to the city for followers
of Joyce is *Dublin in Bloomtime: the city James Joyce knew* by Cyril Pearl (New
York: Viking, 1969).

130 **Mister: a Dublin childhood.**
Michael O'Beirne. Dublin: Blackstaff Press, 1979. 144p.
A warm view is given of a Dublin childhood in the early 20th century, with a
child's view of family life and social history up to 1924.

131 **Dublin, a portrait.**
V. S. Pritchett. New York: Harper & Row, 1967. 99p.

The dark and bright sides of Dublin are described in its various moods and temperaments. There are some comments on political and literary Dublin but the book's chief asset lies in the many photographs by Evelyn Hofer.

132 **Dublin.**
Peter Somerville-Large. North Pomfret, Vermont: Hamish
Hamilton, 1979. 319p. maps. bibliog.

This well written volume covers the history of the city from ancient times to shortly after 1916. Particular attention is paid to Dublin's society, politics, architecture and to the preservation of the city. Numerous illustrations are included and there is a considerable amount of historical detail, although the book is intended as a general introduction. Among recent histories of the city this is one of the most highly recommended for the casual reader. A very different view of Dublin is presented by Mary E. Daly in *Dublin: the disposed capital; a social and economic history, 1860-1914* (Cork: Cork University Press, 1984). Daly provides an unsentimental view of the problems confronting the city between the famine and the First World War, which was a time of concern in the realms of commerce, business, industry, unemployment, health and housing.

133 **An historical guide to the city of Dublin.**
George Newenham Wright. Dublin: Irish Academic Press &
Four Courts Press, 1979. 442p.

A reprint of a major guide to Georgian Dublin, published originally in 1825. Detailed descriptions are given of principal buildings, institutions and societies with facsimiles of engravings (after the drawings of George Petrie). This volume provides a thorough review of the city at a particular point in time.

Islands

134 **Gola, the life and last days of an island community.**
F. H. A. Aalen, H. R. Brody. Cork: Mercier Press, 1969. 127p.

The community of Gola exemplifies the harsh realities of island life along the northwest coast of Ireland. Using the results of first hand observations the authors trace the reasons for economic and demographic decline over a long period of the island's history.

135 **The Western island: or the Great Blasket.**
Robin Flower. Oxford: Clarendon Press, 1944. Reprinted,
London: Oxford University Press, 1978. 141p.

Flower, an important translator of other accounts of Blasket, has, in this work, compiled an elegant set of impressions of island life in prose and verse. He shows both the savage rigours, and yet at times beautiful existence there, as reflected in its literature, customs and superstition. Flower's observations are based on the years 1910 to 1930.

136   **The Tory islanders: a people of the Celtic fringe.**
Robin Fox.   London, New York: Cambridge University Press, 1978. 215p.

In this anthropological account Fox provides a thorough survey of the people, life and social structure on Tory Island. He describes the islanders' work, their sharing of limited resources and the measures taken over the centuries to meet the needs of the community.

137   **Inishmurray, ancient monastic island.**
Patrick Heraughty.   Dublin: O'Brien, 1982. 128p.

A history of society on the island, from the 6th century early monastic times (the sites are still intact) to the present, which includes interesting comments on smuggling, folk customs, medicine and other traditional activities.

138   **North Bull Island, Dublin Bay, a modern coastal natural history.**
Edited by D. W. Jeffrey.   Dublin: Royal Dublin Society, 1977. 158p. maps. bibliog.

There are a number of good books on the islands of Ireland, but this one is different. It does not concern the population in the west, but rather an uninhabited area that serves as a natural preserve and wildlife habitat. Seventeen authors and scientists have contributed to this survey of fauna, flora, ecology and conservation, which contains numerous maps and colour plates.

139   **Skellig, island outpost of Europe.**
Des Lavelle.   Dublin: O'Brien Press, 1976. 112p.

A short history of the island's rugged life and inhabitation, including early settlement, religious traditions, legends and bird lore.

140   **Islands of Ireland.**
Donald McCormick.   London: Osprey, 1974. 160p.

This guidebook to the more than 100 islands off Ireland will be useful to the naturalist with its discussion of often unique flora and fauna. Numerous maps and illustrations are included.

141   **Achill.**
Kenneth McNally.   Newton Abbot, England: David & Charles, 1973. 239p.

McNally portrays the natural history and the disappearing life, customs, settlements and living conditions on Achill in this well-rounded view of the island.

142   **The islands of Ireland.**
Kenneth McNally.   New York: Norton; London: Batsford, 1978.
168p.

This is a convenient guide for the identification of each island off the coast of Ireland. A detailed account is given of each in terms of its location, terrain, history and customs and life. Photographs of each are included.

143   **The islands of Ireland; their scenery, people, life, and antiquity.**
Thomas H. Mason.   New York: Scribners; London: Batsford,
1938. Reprinted, Cork: Mercier Press, 1967. 135p.

This short work, which has been reprinted several times, concentrates on the sights, attractions and the often unique culture that has developed on the major islands off the coast of Ireland.

144   **Inis Beag, isle of Ireland.**
John C. Messenger.   New York: Holt, Rinehart & Winston, 1969.
131p.

A view of Irish rural life, customs and culture on the brink of change.

145   **Letters from the Great Blasket.**
Éibhlís Ní Shúilleabháin.   Dublin; Cork: Mercier Press,
1977. 87p.

Ní Shúilleabháin views the decline of island life in the West of Ireland over a twenty year period, from the rare and poignant perspective of a woman resident. The author, who was the wife of the writer Tomás Ó Crohan, studies rural Irish life during a critical period of change with an insider's knowledge.

146   **The island man.**
Tomás Ó Crohan, translated from the Irish by Robert
Flower.   London: Oxford University Press, 1978. 245p.

Ó Crohan (Criomhtháin) provides a valuable impression of a unique and dying culture of subsistence living on Great Blasket, an island off the Western coast of Ireland. This unsentimental and direct account portrays the daily life and language of a people largely cut off and little adapted to the modernization of Irish society. The work was written in 1929.

147   **Cliffmen of the West.**
Thomas O'Flaherty.   Dublin: At the Sign of the Three Candles;
London: Sands, 1936. 285p.

O'Flaherty describes his childhood and rough life on the Aran Islands. Aran, celebrated in folklore, literature and cinema, is also covered in Pat Mullen's *Man of Aran* (London, Faber & Faber, 1934. Reprinted, Cambridge, Massachusetts: MIT Press, 1970. 286p.).

148 **The man from Cape Clear.**
Conchúr O Síocháin. Dublin; Cork, Irish Republic: Mercier
Press, 1975. 171p. bibliog.
The author recalls an entire life spent on Cape Clear, off County Cork, including
his years as a farmer and a fisherman. He relates seafaring traditions, techniques,
stories, and the island topography. His account provides an interesting balance to
the more scientific work of John Sharrock, *The natural history of Cape Clear
Island* (Berkhamsted, England: Poyser, 1973. 207p.).

149 **Aran: island of legend.**
P. A. O'Siochain. Old Greenwich, Connecticut: Devin-Adair,
1963. 192p.
The Aran Islands are placed in both their geographic and historical setting in this
discussion of old settlements and sites, the land and the customs of the people.

150 **Twenty years a-growing.**
Maurice O'Sullivan. London: Oxford University Press, 1983.
312p.
In this venerable account first published in 1933, the author recounts his
childhood years spent on Blasket Island and the Irish coast at the beginning of the
20th century. He writes of the local customs and way of life from vivid memories
and with humour. In the last part of the narrative the author confronts radically
different surroundings as a member of the Civic Guard in Dublin.

151 **The Aran Islands.**
Daphne D. C. Pochin-Mould. Newton Abbot, England: David &
Charles, 1972. 171p.
The author, a photographer, provides a detailed look at the historical remains on
the Arans, and through her numerous photographs gives an account of life there.

152 **Peig: the autobiography of Peig Sayers of the Great Blasket Island.**
Peig Sayers, translated by Bryan MacMahon. London: Oxford
University Press, 1978. 131p.
In this classic of modern Gaelic literature Sayers retells the bleak, harsh life of the
islanders on Great Blasket. She traces rural childhood, youth, marriage,
traditions, holidays, daily life, aging and finally tragedy in this story of poverty,
hardship and survival. Unromantic, the book yet has an optimistic spirit. See also
the translation by Seamus Ennis of Peig Sayers' *An old woman's reflections*
(London: Oxford University Press, 1978).

153 **Aran Islands, a personal journey.**
Dennis Smith. Garden City, New York: Doubleday, 1980. 143p.
From his personal observations Smith provides an impressionistic account of the
recent history and ongoing life of the Arans. The work, which includes many
photographs, is an excellent review of the physical surroundings, land settlement
patterns, and social conditions. A good, vivid picture of contemporary island life.

154 **Day visitor's guide to the Great Blasket Island.**
Ray Stagles. Dublin: O'Brien Press, 1982. 48p. maps.

This short guidebook contains useful information on traveling to Great Blasket Island, its history, wildlife and nature, ruins and locations. An earlier work on the people of Great Blasket before its abandonment is *Next parish America: Blasket Islands*, by Joan Stagles and Ray Stagles (Dublin: O'Brien Press, 1979. 144p.). The study traces the island community from its earliest recorded presence, through the difficult years of the famine and on to the last inhabitants in 1953, with comments on the important writers there, the environment and living conditions.

155 **The Aran Islands.**
John Millington Synge. London: Oxford University Press, 1979. 173p.

This classic work by the prominent writer was first published as early as 1906 and has gone through many editions. Its popularity is due to the way Synge retells the sparse, heroic and rugged existence of the islanders. A modern guidebook by Ruth Shaw, *J. M. Synge's guide to the Aran Islands* (Old Greenwich, Connecticut: Devin-Adair, 1975. 123p.), rearranges the stories of Synge, and with the inclusion of recent photographs it serves as a literary visitor's guide. Another study by Lilo Stephens, *My wallet of photographs: the collected photographs of J. M. Synge* (Dublin: Dolmen Press, 1971), includes some Aran photographs.

156 **A world of stone; life, folklore and legends of the Aran Islands.**
Dublin: O'Brien Educational Press, 1977. 248p.

A popular history and description of Aran, this volume provides a thorough review of the natural setting, geology, climate, history, crafts, trades, folklore and stories of the islands. The book was sponsored by the Curriculum Development Unit (Dublin), and has also been divided into and separately published as three paperbacks: *World of stone*, *Field and shore*, and *Island stories*. Excellent historic and recent photographs enhance the text.

Flora and Fauna

General

157 **The landscape of Slieve Bloom: natural and human heritage.**
John Feehan.   Tallaght, County Dublin: Blackwater Press, 1979.
304p. maps.
A geologist studies the natural and human history of this mountain area of central Ireland. He shows in some detail the effects on rockforms, plant life, history (from ancient times to modern communities) and topography of development, farming, famine and neglect. The work contains numerous illustrations.

158 **Irish nature.**
Norman Hickin.   Dublin: O'Brien Press, 1980. 240p. maps.
A good, reliable account is given of the entire natural habitat of Ireland including its birds, fish, mammals, insects, plants, ferns, fungi, mosses, and seaweed, with information on status, distribution and size. Nearly 340 black and white illustrations help identification. However, this is not a field guide. The text is entertaining, with tales of the author's experiences. Species are covered with evolutionary order reversed, starting with the more advanced forms. Includes a useful index to species and Latin names.

159 **The Burren.**
Maryangela Keane.   Dublin: Eason & Son, [n.d.]. 26p.
The Burren, a ragged and largely deserted area in the west of Ireland, is noted as a naturalist's paradise, with its particular and often minute flora and peculiar formations. This short collection of colour photographs and narrative provides a valuable introduction to the area.

160   **A natural history of Ireland.**
      Christopher Moriarty.   Cork; Dublin: Mercier Press, 1972. 192p.
A general natural history of Ireland, arranged by county in an entertaining
manner suitable for both school children or adults. An outline is provided of the
Irish environment, flora and fauna.

161   **The way that I went, an Irishman in Ireland.**
      Robert Lloyd Praeger.   Dublin: Figgis, 1969. 394p.
Based on a lifetime of observation of the Irish countryside, geography and
geologic structure, Praeger presents a personalized history of the land, discussing
his finds in archaeology, flora and fauna. Praeger has also compiled a collection
on the lives of his colleagues entitled *Some Irish naturalists; a biographical
notebook* (Dundalk, Irish Republic: Tempest, 1949).

162   **The natural history of Ireland, a sketch of its flora and fauna.**
      Robert Lloyd Praeger.   London: E. P. Group, 1972. 350p.
A sensitive, comprehensive history of Ireland's natural habitat. Much detail is
given on fauna and flora, which Praeger takes great care to relate to the larger
environment. The author was a distinguished botanist, naturalist, and former
president of the Royal Irish Academy. The work was first published in 1950
(Dublin: Collins).

163   **A natural history of Britain and Ireland.**
      Eric Simms.   London: Dent, 1979. 258p.
A general, illustrated natural history of the British Isles, which places Ireland's
flora and fauna within the larger context.

Flora

164   **A student's illustrated Irish flora.**
      John Adams.   Ashford, Kent, England: L. Reeve, 1931. 343p.
An adequate, standard handbook to the indigenous seed plants of Ireland, which
is still useful.

165   **Trees and shrubs hardy in the British Isles.**
      W. J. Bean.   London: J. Murray; New York: St. Martin's Press,
      1970-1980. 8th ed. 4 vols.
This thorough guide covers all major species, which are listed alphabetically
throughout the four volmes. Each volume of over 800 pages contains instructions
on tree care, cultivation, characteristics and use in the garden. Extensive
illustrations make this set useful to both the amateur and specialist gardener,
botanist or nurseryman.

166 **Flora of the British Isles.**
Arthur Roy Clapham, T. G. Tutin, E. F. Warburg. Cambridge, England: Cambridge University Press, 1957-1965. 4 vols.
For the specialist, this extensive guide includes much of the Irish flora with detailed description and references. A basic volume of 1,270 pages was issued in 1962, followed by several volumes of illustrations.

167 **The botanist in Ireland.**
Robert Lloyd Praeger. Dublin: Hodges Figgis, 1934. Reprinted, London: E. P. Group, 1976. 460p.
Ireland's leading botanist and natural scientist writes of his research and discoveries in the early 1900s. He presents a sensitive and readable account of Irish flora and environmental factors in changing Ireland. His many other works include *Tourist's flora of the west of Ireland* (Dublin: Hodges Figgis, 1909. 243p.), and a revision of S. A. Stewart and T. Corry's, *Flora of the north east of Ireland* (Belfast: Belfast Naturalists Field Club, 1938. 472p. looseleaf). Both these volumes are useful but *Botanist in Ireland*, while not a guidebook, provides particularly pleasant reading.

168 **Irish wildflowers.**
Ruth Isabel Ross. Dublin: Easons, 1978. 24p. (Irish Heritage Series).
An attractive, general essay highly illustrated with colour photographs, which provides a good introduction, although with little depth or detail.

169 **Irish trees.**
Ruth Isabel Ross. Dublin: Easons, 1979. 24p. (Irish Heritage Series).
Ross briefly describes the trees which are most prevalent in Ireland, such as the yew, elm, beech, arbutus, hawthorn and eucalyptus, and comments on the state of Irish forests, some protected and many endangered. The booklet is well illustrated.

170 **An Irish florilegium; wild and garden plants of Ireland.**
Wendy Walsh, Ruth Isabel Ross, Charles Nelson. London: Thames & Hudson, 1983. 224p.
Chiefly a collection of forty-eight beautiful, hand-tipped coloured plates by Walsh, with descriptive botanical notes added by Nelson of the National Botanical Gardens. Ross covers the history of Irish horticulture and plant collecting from earliest times. Gardens, ferns and trees are also well covered, in this largely pictorial work, with accurate paintings often showing the stages from bud to bloom.

171 **An Irish flora.**
David A. Webb.   Dundalk, Ireland (Republic): Dundalgan Press,
1977. 277p. bibliog.
This useful guide to Irish flora has had numerous editions. Identification and a full
description of the wild flowers and other native plants of Ireland, a glossary and
name index are included, but the illustrations are inadequate.

Fauna

172 **An angler's paradise; recollections of twenty years with rod and line
in Ireland.**
Fred Drummond Barker.   London: Faber, 1929. 296p.
Personal reminiscences not only retell the experiences of the sportsman but also
give an account of the prevalence of many species of fish at the turn of the
century, before much of the modern ecological change had taken place.

173 **Sea birds of Britain and Ireland.**
Stanley Cramp.   London: Collins, 1975. 288p. maps.
Cramp, a leading authority on the birds of the world, outlines the major species,
location and distribution of sea birds, although the book does not concentrate
particularly on Ireland. This second, revised edition contains thirty-two maps.

174 **The guide to the birds of Ireland.**
Gordon D'Arcy.   Dublin: Eason, 1981. 192p. 150 maps.
This delightful volume has been described as a complete colour guide to Irish
birds. Nearly 400 birds are described, 219 are illustrated, mostly in colour.
Practical information is provided for the identification of species, and 150 maps
show both winter and summer distribution. Some species are nearly extinct.
Suggestions are made for bird watching, and comments are given on the history
and future of Irish brids. The author writes from a lifetime of personal
observation and study in Ireland's Forest and Wildlife Service.

175 **Irish wild mammals, a guide to the literature.**
James S. Fairley.   Galway, Ireland (Republic): University
College, Galway, Department of Zoology, 1971. 128p.
This bibliography lists almost one thousand references to Irish mammals. While
providing a useful starting point for in-depth research, the list now needs
extensive updating. The author has also compiled a more popular guide, *The Irish
beast book, a natural history of Ireland's wild mammals* (Belfast: Blackstaff, 1984.
352p.). This volume presents numerous interesting accounts of all of Ireland's
furred wildlife: foxes, otters, badgers, shrews and others. Another interesting
study by Fairley is *Irish whales and whaling* (Belfast: Blackstaff, 1981. 244p.).
This provides a vivid review of the industry, the hunt, its history and folklore.

176   **The Shell guide to the birds of Britain and Ireland.**
James Ferguson-Lees, Ian Willis, J. T. R. Sharrock.   London:
Michael Joseph, 1983. 329p.

This excellent field guide, for the advanced reader, is divided into sections on
common and on rare species. Some 488 species are covered in terms of eating
habits, nesting and breeding. New maps show both the distribution and size of the
bird population. Willis' fine paintings illustrate the full range of plumage, through
changing age and season, and the volume contains numerous colour plates.
Although the number of Irish birds included is substantial, a large part of the
book does not relate to Ireland.

177   **The seals.**
Monk Gibbon.   Dublin: Figgis, 1970. 247p.

A very personal appreciation of the seals of Ireland, describing the challenge of
survival through long years of hunting. Gibbon presents first hand impressions
and also discusses the wider significance of man and environment.

178   **Fisheries in Ireland, 1849.**
Great Britain. Parliament.   Dublin: Irish Academic Press.
Reprint. 832p. (British Parliamentary Papers Series).

These official reports present a detailed analysis of Ireland's freshwater fish,
inland fisheries and economic potential in the mid 19th century. With its many
illustrations this is a prime source for the history of fish in Ireland.

179   **Irish birds.**
Paul Hillis.   Dublin: Eason, 1979. 24p. (Irish Heritage Series).

A short introduction to the occurrence and major species of birds in Ireland.
Numerous photographs are included.

180   **Birds of Ireland, an account of the distribution, migrations, and
habits.**
P. G. Kennedy, R. Ruttledge, G. Humphreys.   Dublin:
Stationery Office, 1954. 437p.

An extensive list for the advanced observer or researcher.

181   **A guide to Irish birds.**
Christopher Moriarty.   Cork: Mercier Press, 1967. 176p.

For the new observer, this introduction to Irish birds covers the behaviour,
features, and location of more than 350 species. Moriarty's concise but useful
summaries provide a basic and entertaining foundation to the topic.

182   **The future of Irish wildlife, a blueprint for development.**
Fergus O'Gorman, Edna Wynnes.   Dublin: An Foras Taluntais,
1973. 218p.

This study prepared for the Irish Agricultural Institute outlines the problems of
survival faced by many Irish species in a time of rapid development.

183 **Extinct terrestrial mammals of Ireland in the National Museum.**
C. E. O'Riordan. Dublin: Stationery Office, 1980. 37p.

A guide intended for popular use, on the mammals in Ireland immediately after the Ice Age (with some surviving to later periods). A pen drawing and short narrative is provided for each species.

184 **The fauna of Ireland, an introduction to the land vertebrates.**
Fergus O'Rourke. Cork: Mercier Press, 1970. 176p. maps. bibliog.

The author, a professor of zoology, provides a thorough review of Irish fauna for the amateur or the less knowledgable student, which describes the more important birds, mammals, fish and reptiles.

185 **Birds of Ireland.**
Richard Dunscombe Parker. Dundonald, County Down, Northern Ireland: Blackstaff Press, 1983. 120p.

Outstanding bird paintings of the 19th century are reproduced for the first time in this finely published, limited edition. Parker (1805-1881) was known as 'Ireland's Audubon'. Forty paintings are in colour. Notes and introduction have been added by Martyn Anglesea.

186 **Wildlife in Britain and Ireland.**
Richard Perry. London: Croom Helm, 1978. 256p.

Studies the survival of various forms of wildlife throughout history, changes in climate and the challenge of man. The volume, which was commissioned by the World Wildlife Fund, provides a broad perspective and contains sixty illustrations.

187 **Saltees: islands of birds and legends.**
Richard Roche, Oscar Merne. Dublin: O'Brien Press; Toronto: Macmillan, 1978. 152p. bibliog.

The Saltee Islands contain a major bird sanctuary off the east coast of Ireland, and this work, with the aid of numerous photographs, discusses their natural habitat, birdlife, and the folklore and history of human settlement, including centuries of occupation by hermits and smugglers.

Prehistory

188   **The Boyne Valley vision.**
   Martin Brennan.   Portlaoise, Ireland (Republic): Dolmen Press,
   1980. 120p. maps.

The author speculates on the meanings and significance of ancient rock carvings
and prehistoric remains in Ireland. Using clear drawings and maps he provides a
highly personal interpretation of archaeological remains, relating early Irish
culture and art to those of other societies. His interpretation is debatable at times,
but the volume is elegant and well designed.

189   **The stars and stones, ancient art and astronomy in Ireland.**
   Martin Brennan.   London: Thames & Hudson, 1983. 208p.

Brennan, from the viewpoint of an artist, observes the placement, orientation and
direction of ancient Irish megalithic mounds and carvings in the Boyne Valley and
Loughcrew Mountains, and he searches for a wider possible significance. The
work includes over 300 illustrations, most of which are drawings, that support his
conclusion that there is some astronomical reasoning in the design of the ancient
mounds and art.

190   **Rings of stone; the prehistoric stone circles of Britain and Ireland.**
   Aubrey Burl.   London: Weidenfeld & Nicholson, 1979. 280p.
   maps.

A balanced view of the many stone circles throughout Great Britain and Ireland,
with a discussion of major types, materials, possible uses, and traditions
associated with selected examples. A gazetteer helps locate some of these
prehistoric remains, and over 200 excellent photographs supplement the text.
Intended for the non-specialist.

Prehistory

191 **The Celtic world.**
Barry Cunliffe. New York: McGraw-Hill, 1979. 224p. maps.
bibliog.
The ancient Celtic world in all its aspects is evoked in this story of a race faced
with the challenge of survival. Celtic influence and creativity are shown as
extending throughout Europe, during all periods, from early times to the present.
Many illustrations and examples are drawn from the Irish experience in this
sumptuously illustrated volume.

192 **Ireland in pre-history.**
Michael Herity, George Eogan. London; Boston, Massachusetts:
Routledge & Kegan Paul, 1977. 302p. maps. bibliog.
A thorough summary of Irish archaeology, spanning the Stone Age to Celtic
times. This college level text provides a revised chronological framework of early
Irish history. Attention is focused on tombs, cairns, art, utensils and other
artifacts, and their manufacturing. Numerous illustrations and maps are included.

193 **The Celts, the people who came out of the darkness.**
Gerhard Herm. London: Weidenfeld & Nicolson, 1976.
Reprinted, New York: St. Martin's, 1977. 312p.
Celtic history throughout Europe is traced from pre-Roman times to the days of
King Arthur in this history for the general reader. Ireland is covered on p. 233-74.
A similar history, better illustrated but with less information, is *The Celts* by
George Dotlin (Geneva: Minerva, 1977. 142p.).

194 **A social history of ancient Ireland.**
P. W. Joyce. London, New York: Longmans, Green; Dublin:
Gill, 1908. Reprinted, New York: Arno, 1980. 2 vols.
This pioneering and now classic study of ancient Irish society includes information
on the evidence of early population, literature, kingship, territory, government,
warfare, social classes and rank, law and punishment, religion, learning,
mythology, the Druids, Christianity, education (academic programmes and
degrees), language, the Ogham alphabet, libraries and books, ancient annals,
historical tales and cycles, art, music, medicine, marriage and family, homes,
food, dress, agriculture, building, crafts and trades, sports, customs, death and
burial. Exceptionally detailed and engrossing, this volume must, nevertheless, be
read with caution in the light of later research findings.

195 **The history of Ireland from the earliest period to the English
invasion.**
Geoffrey Keating, translated by John O'Mahony. Kansas City,
Missouri: Irish Genealogical Foundation, 1983. 3 vols.
A most important early source on Irish history, this account was written during
the 17th century. The present set is a reprint of an 1866 edition with the addition
of notes and references to the equally important Annals of the Four Masters. In a
preface Keating provides a memoir of his life from approximately 1570 to 1644,
and describes his years of persecution. In the text itself he weaves legends, myths

and traditions of oral history, as heard on the European continent. While much is not entirely factual, the work is an essential source on traditional prehistory as it was once believed to be. The volume includes a description of early invasions, the arrival of separate groups in pre-Christian times, pagan writers and later history to the arrival of the Normans. Volume three contains various appendixes, indexes, and a geographical guide. The information recorded by Keating provides the foundation for many of the later Irish histories.

196 Celtic Ireland.
Eoin MacNeill.   Dublin: University Press of Ireland, 1983. 224p.

First published in 1921 this has remained an important work on Gaelic culture and early Irish civilization. MacNeill, a founder of the scientific method in Irish history, provides a dependable summary based on primary sources. Emphasis is given to pre-Norman periods and a new introduction comments on other sources.

197 Celtic civilization.
Jean Markale.   London, New York: Gordon & Cremonesi, 1976. 320p. maps.

Markale discusses the origin of Celtic myths and history, the Gaels and Celtic peoples in Ireland, ancient Irish poetry, the early Christian Church, Druidism, superstition and mythology. The study attempts to identify remaining Celtic influences in thought and literature. Some passages relate to the Continent. For the advanced reader.

198 The Celts.
T. G. E. Powell.   London, New York: Thames & Hudson, 1980. 232p.

An illustrated introduction to Celtic life, chronology, belief in the supernatural, archaeology and literature. Includes a general treatment of European antiquities, including the Irish.

199 The Celts.
Edited by Joseph Raftery.   Cork; Dublin: Mercier, 1964. 83p.

Six authorities contribute short papers on Celtic language, religion, archaeology and society. The editor also compiled *Pre-historic Ireland* (London: Batsford, 1951).

200 Celtic Leinster, towards an historical geography of early Irish civilization AD 500-1600.
Alfred Smyth.   Dublin: Irish Academic Press, 1983. 197p. maps.

Heralded as an important contribution to mediaeval scholarship, this study searches for the geographic conditions that made the Irish midlands into a heartland of Gaelic civilization. The landscape of dense forest and bog is seen shaping settlement patterns of small independent units of Celtic culture. This elaborate, illustrated volume, with frequent source material included, also has an historical atlas appended, showing early tribes and the routes and boundaries of the ancient kingdoms.

Archaeology

201 **Viking Dublin exposed: the Wood Quay saga.**
Edited by John Bradley. Dublin: O'Brien Press, 1985. 184p.
Papers from a symposium of the Friends of Medieval Dublin outline attempts to save a major archaeological site in the city. Exploration of the site and its background from 1900 to 1976 is discussed with comments on the controversial decision to close the location, the politics of the dispute, and the public outcry against it. Several authors review the important artifacts gathered from the site. A more popular account is provided by Jonathan Bardon and Stephen Conlin in *1000 years of Wood Quay* (Belfast: Blackstaff, 1984. 36p.). Bardon and Conlin utilize illustrations and drawings to present a reconstruction of the site, showing its development from Viking times to the present day.

202 **New Grange and other incised tumuli in Ireland.**
George Coffey. Poole, Dorset, England: Dolphin, 1977. 127p.
This classic account, first published in 1912, looks at Ireland's examples of some of the finest megalithic art in Europe, finding Mediterranean parallels in the circles, spirals and other motifs. This pioneer study of Irish archaeology provides a good introduction to the great monument of New Grange, although it was written long before the latest findings or conclusions.

203 **Survey of the megalithic tombs of Ireland.**
Ruaidhrí de Valera, Seán Ó Nualláin. Dublin: Stationery Office, 1983- . 4 vols.
This major series provides an extensive survey of the tombs in various Irish counties. Volume four covers Cork, Kerry, Limerick and Tipperary. The series has been produced by the Ordnance Survey and includes their maps.

204 **Excavations at Knowth. Volume one.**
George Eogan. Dublin: Royal Irish Academy, 1985.
An authoritative, detailed study of the great Neolithic passage tomb of Knowth (including the complexes of New Grange and Dowth). The author discusses the passage graves in general, artifacts, designs, the surrounding areas, and the possible living patterns and food of the original inhabitants. This is the first of a three volume set intended for advanced research. Volume two will cover the occupation of Knowth from the Iron Age to Norman times; volume three will study the largest of the tombs. Hundreds of photographs and drawings are included, supporting the evidence of a developed Boyne Valley civilization.

205 **Prehistoric and early Christian Ireland.**
Emyr Estyn Evans. London: Batsford, 1966. 241p. bibliog.
A useful guidebook for those wishing to visit early sites, with a convenient gazetteer included.

206 **Guide to the national monuments in the Republic of Ireland.**
Peter Harbison. Dublin: Gill & Macmillan, 1970. 284p. maps. bibliog.
A very useful guidebook alphabetically arranged by county, then locality, with map references and access directions. An historical summary is given for each site. Nearly 800 monuments are described with some 300 illustrations and maps.

207 **The archaeology of Ireland.**
Peter Harbison. Dublin: Gill & Macmillan; New York: Scribners, 1976. 120p.
A basic introduction to archaeology in Ireland from the earliest inhabitants, later periods of the first Christians, Viking, mediaeval, and Norman times. Comments are included on search, discovery, excavation and preservation techniques. For the novice.

208 **Irish passage graves, Neolithic tomb-builders in Ireland and Britain 2500 B. C.**
Michael Herity. New York: Barnes & Noble, 1975. 308p. maps. bibliog.
The author provides a very detailed review of significant prehistoric tombs, their types, location, ornament and symbolism, various finds of artifacts, and the scope of the Boyne Valley culture. A major part of the volume consists of an inventory of finds, arranged by county. Fully illustrated, this is a good reference work for the specialist.

209 **The archaeology of late Celtic Britain and Ireland, c. 400-1200 A. D.**
Lloyd Laing. London: Methuen, 1975. 450p.
A comprehensive, illustrated review of the archaeology of the Celtic speaking areas in Wales, Scotland, Ireland and southwest England. Ireland is discussed in

its larger, regional aspects, and the Irish settlements in Britain and the impact of the Vikings are mentioned. The early Christian Celts are covered, including their ornament, art, dress, crafts, industry, and architectural remains. Photographs, diagrams, and drawings are included in this very handy introduction.

210 **The archaeology of Ireland.**
R. A. S. Macalister.   New York: Arno, 1972. 363p.

A thorough work on early Ireland, describing prehistoric society and that of Iron Age, early Christian, Scandinavian and mediaeval Ireland, based on historical evidence and artifacts. Written evidence, art and architecture are included. The study, which is still useful, was written in 1927 and has gone through many editions. Also by Macalister is *Ancient Ireland, a study in the lessons of archaeology and history* (New York: Arno Press, 1978. 307p.). This is a reprint of a 1935 edition.

211 **Digging up Dublin: a future for our past.**
Edited by Nick Maxwell.   Dublin: O'Brien Press, 1980. 64p. 25 maps.

Based on a symposium of the Dublin Archaeological Research Team, this volume presents a series of proposals to safeguard ancient sites and findings in the future, following the destruction of the early Wood Quay site. Maps and illustrations pinpoint and document the remaining historical deposits.

212 **The early development of Irish society.**
E. R. Norman, J. K. S. St. Joseph.   Cambridge, England: Cambridge University Press, 1969. 126p.

The remains of early Irish society are discussed in this work based on seventy aerial photographs (this being the third volume of the Cambridge Air Surveys). A useful and vivid perspective is provided of the outlines of the ancient sites, although the text is sparse.

213 **Newgrange: archaeology, art and legend.**
Michael J. O'Kelly.   London: Thames & Hudson, 1982. 240p.
(New Aspects Of Antiquity Series).

This excellent, detailed study, based on excavations from 1962 to 1975, is intended to be the definitive account of one of Europe's greatest prehistoric sites, an elaborately carved and constructed 5,000 year old tomb. The author comments upon recent discoveries, the ancient farming communities encompassing much technical skill and studies some literary allusions and traditions, the excavations and the finds. Attention is focused on pre-Christian art and ornamentation from the site. Methods of construction, precise orientation and measurements are also covered in this review of the intact structures older than Stonehenge, Mycenae or the Pyramids. While written for the serious reader, the superior photographs and drawings make this volume also suitable for quick perusal. Claire O'Kelly in one chapter writes of New Grange's significance in early Irish art and literature. She previously compiled a shorter *Illustrated guide to Newgrange and other Boyne monuments* (Cork, Irish Republic: the author, 3rd ed. 1978. 139p.). New Grange was considered the burial place of the pagan kings of Tara, Dagda, the good god, and the Tuatha De Danann, one of the original tribes of Ireland. Another short account of New Grange is provided by George Coffey in *New Grange and other incised tumuli in Ireland* (q.v.). More detail is included in a British Archaeological Report *Newgrange, Co. Meath* edited by Claire O'Kelly (Oxford: BAR, 1984. International Series S190). Descriptive information and drawings are provided by the contributors, who include Michael O'Kelly.

214 **New Grange and the bend of the Boyne.**
Seán P. Ó Ríordáin, Glyn Daniel. London: Thames & Hudson, 1964. 218p.

New Grange and the accompanying Dowth and Knowth passage graves are described in terms of their history, present condition, motifs and structure. Seventy black and white photographs and twenty-three line drawings supplement a readable text which provides a useful introduction, but the volume predates latest scientific findings.

215 **Antiquities of the Irish countryside.**
Seán P. Ó Ríordáin. London, New York: Methuen, 1979. 5th ed. 182p.

A standard work on the topic, this short account, revised by Ruaidhri de Valera conveniently divides ancient sites into forts, earthworks, homes, tombs and other categories. This is sufficient for a general understanding without technical details. No conclusions are drawn, but as a field guide to visible, largely pre-Norman remains this is a good introduction. A convenient and inexpensive volume, this is recommended for upper level students. Another volume which is useful for interpreting ancient remains in their physical setting is the more popular work by Richard Muir, *Reading the Celtic landscape* (London: Michael Joseph, 1985. 288p.). Muir describes the evidence from agricultural methods, and the walls, towers and other structures, remaining after thousands of years in Ireland, Scotland, Cornwall and Wales.

216 **Early Ireland: a field guide.**
Anthony Weir. Dundonald, County Down, Northern Ireland: Blackstaff Press, 1980. 245p. bibliog.

A clear and detailed field guide with directions, map locations and short historical descriptions of hundreds of sites, both ancient and later. The guide is arranged by county and its many illustrations (of only fair quality) are of remote places not easily found in other reference guides.

History

General

217 **Confrontations: studies in Irish history.**
James Camlin Beckett. Totowa, New Jersey: Rowman &
Littlefield, 1972. 175p.

Concentrating on the Anglo-Irish experience and on the confrontation between
various segments of Irish society, the author provides an in-depth analysis of some
aspects of Irish history, from the 17th century onwards.

218 **A short history of Ireland.**
James Camlin Beckett. London: Hutchinson, 1979. 191p. bibliog.

A valuable introduction to Irish history up to the mid-20th century is presented,
with emphasis placed on the modern period. (Chapter 1 covers all of Irish history
up to the 15th century). First published in 1952.

219 **Ireland and the Irish: a short history.**
Karl S. Bottigheimer. New York: Columbia University Press,
1982. 301p. maps. bibliog.

This sweeping, condensed history concentrates on main themes and historic forces
beginning with early habitation and environmental conditions, followed by the
heroic age of the Celt and Viking and the mediaeval period. The author outlines
the development of Irish nationalism from the 17th century to the 1970s,
emphasizing the Protestant ascendancy, religious influences, and English policy
towards Ireland since the Union. The study has an independent, detached stance
and avoids apportioning blame. This will provide a useful introduction for the
general reader.

220 **Ireland, a documentary record.**
James Carty. Dublin: Fallon, 1949-1958. 3 vols.

Carty provides the text of numerous documents of Irish history from Stuart times onwards, and relates each with a continuous commentary. The first volume covers 1607 to 1782, from the flight of the earls to Grattan's parliament; volume two studies the period 1783 to 1850, from Grattan to the great famine; and volume three covers 1857-1921, from the famine to the treaty granting Dominion status to Catholic Ireland.

221 **A short history of Ireland.**
Roger Chauviré. New York: Devin-Adair, 1961. 145p.

An intelligent distillation of Irish history up to the end of the 19th century. Gaelic society and traditional Irish ways are stressed. For the general reader.

222 **Ireland, three: union to the present day.**
Mary Elizabeth Collins. Dublin: Educational Company of Ireland, 1972. 264p.

One of a three volume series of competent, illustrated textbooks designed to hold the interest of secondary level students. Interesting detail is given in each. The other volumes are *Ireland, one: earliest times to 1485* by M. de Paor and P. Holohan's *Ireland, two: 1485-1800*. Mary Collins has also compiled *Outline of modern Irish history, 1850-1951* (1974, 424p.) for the Educational Company, a leading publisher of Irish school books below the college level.

223 **Studies in Irish history presented to R. Dudley Edwards.**
Art Cosgrove, Donald McCartney. Dublin: University College; Gerrards Cross, England: Colin Smythe, 1980. 354p.

Miscellaneous papers by leading academics include those on Gaelic society and the English in Ireland during the 16th and 17th centuries, rural conditions, social change, modernization in more recent times, and the Irish policies of successive British governments during the 19th century.

224 **Helicon history of Ireland.**
Edited by Art Cosgrove, Elma Collins. Dublin: Educational Company of Ireland, 1981- . maps.

A projected ten volume history intended for school students in Ireland. Each volume is about 150 pages with both hard cover and paperback editions, and each focuses on a major theme and period of Irish history from mediaeval times to the present.

225 **Life in Ireland.**
Lewis Michael Cullen. London: Batsford; New York: Putnam's Sons, 1979. 178p.

An illustrated history of Irish society, settlements and living conditions, from 800 AD to modern times. Emphasis is placed on rural life and change, especially during the 18th and 19th centuries. Cullen explores the rural crisis in post-famine

Ireland and studies matters of employment, prices, living conditions and pastimes in recent years.

226 **Irish historical documents, 1172-1922.**
Edited by Edmund Curtis, R. B. McDowell. London: Methuen; New York: Barnes & Noble, 1943. Reprinted, 1968. 331p.
This useful collection consists of a wide variety of original sources and documents on Ireland from mediaeval times to independence. Emphasis is given to political history and the editors provide references and descriptive comments.

227 **A history of Ireland.**
Edmund Curtis. London: Methuen; New York: Barnes & Noble, 1969. 6th ed. 434p.
A general, thorough history up to the attainment of independence, this has served for years as a leading textbook, although it no longer reflects the most current scholarship.

228 **A dictionary of Irish history since 1800.**
James E. Doherty, Denis J. Hickey. Dublin: Gill & Macmillan; New York: Barnes & Noble, 1980. 617p.
A most useful reference work with more than 1,000 entries devoted solely to events in Ireland. Brief commentary is given on the many aspects of Irish life since 1800, including cultural and social affairs, religious developments, literature and the arts, folk customs, economics, population, politics, military events, government and biography. This handy, basic guide is arranged alphabetically.

229 **A new history of Ireland.**
Ruth Dudley Edwards. Dublin: Gill & Macmillan; Toronto: University of Toronto Press, 1972. 272p.
A competent history suitable for college use, with a current viewpoint.

230 **The Irish in Ireland.**
Constantine Fitzgibbon. New York: Norton; Newton Abbot, England: David & Charles, 1983. 328p.
An illustrated portrayal of the Irish through history from pre-Celtic times up to the early 20th century, with the author's own observations on what has contributed to an Irish sense of identity. For the general reader.

231 **Gill history of Ireland.**
Edited by James Lydon, Margaret MacCurtain. Dublin: Gill & Macmillan, 1972-1975. 11 vols.
A highly regarded series of eleven short, scholarly paperback volumes covering the whole history of Ireland. Each include maps, illustrations, and bibliographies, and are suitable as introductory works at college level. The volumes are: *Ireland before the Vikings*; *Ireland before the Normans*; *Anglo Norman Ireland*; *Gaelic*

Ireland in the Middle Ages; *Church in Medieval Ireland*; *Later Middle Ages*; *Tudor and Stuart Ireland*; *Ireland in the 18th century*; *Ireland before the famine*; *Modernization of Irish society*; and *Ireland in the 20th century*.

232   **The making of Ireland and its undoing, 1200-1600.**
Alice Stopford Green.   Freeport, New York: Books for Libraries Press, 1972. 511p.

An impassioned and outspoken account, first published in 1908, of the centuries of political suppression of Irish trade, education and enterprise, covering many aspects of a hidden culture sruggling for survival. Most of the incidents described relate to the 15th and 16th centuries.

233   **Ireland, 6000 BC-1972: a chronology and fact book.**
William D. Griffin.   Dobbs Ferry, New York: Oceana, 1973. 154p. bibliog.

This reference sourcebook is divided into two parts, a thirty page chronology of Ireland from ancient to modern times (which for prehistoric and early periods may now need minor revisions), and the text of collected documents which are important to Irish history, for the most part selected from the modern era. The volume includes documents from 1494 to 1972, although emphasis is given to political events such as the Easter Rebellion, the independence struggle, and events in Ulster. This is not a factbook of current statistical or directory-type data.

234   **The antiquities of Ireland.**
Francis Grose.   Kilkenny, Ireland (Republic): Wellbrook Press, 1982. 2 vols.

First published in 1791 this work includes numerous engravings as a testimony to the chief monuments in Ireland at the end of the 18th century. Many of these have now changed and some have disappeared. Much of the book was compiled by Edward Ledwich, carrying out the ideas of Grose. Arranged by county, descriptive information is provided on ancient ruins. Reproduction of plates in this reprint is unfortunately weak. In the introduction, Ledwich concentrates on Irish military history, unrelated to the rest of the volume.

235   **A history of Irish flags from earliest times.**
G. A. Hayes-McCoy.   Dublin: Academy Press; Boston, Massachusetts: G. K. Hall, 1979. 240p.

The history of Ireland is traced through an evocative and rich collection of emblems and banners. Political slogans and flags document past aspirations and include St. Patrick's cross, the green harp, shamrocks and the plough and the stars. Ancient accounts mention banners among the Celts. Numerous coloured illustrations show examples of regimental flags of Irish units and banners marking political divisions, orange versus green, 1601, the later rise of romantic nationalism, and insurrection. There are also illustrations of coins, medals, maps, and battle scenes.

236 **Irish battles.**
> G. A. Hayes-McCoy.   London: Longman, 1969. Reprinted,
> Dublin: Gill & Macmillan, 1980. 320p.

A history of military forces, units, leaders and battles in Ireland extending from Clontarf in 1014 to the Battle of Arklow in 1798.

237 **The story of Ireland.**
> Brian Inglis.   London: Faber & Faber, 1966. 2nd ed. 274p.

A widely used and popular general history of Ireland, now somewhat dated.

238 **Ireland's sea fisheries: a history.**
> John de Courcy Ireland.   Dublin: Glendale Press, 1982. 184p.

A leading historian of the sea traces Ireland's destiny as a maritime state, covering the vital trade in the Middle Ages, Tudor control and restrictions, and later cycles of decline, neglect, encouragement and prosperity.

239 **Ireland and the Irish in maritime history.**
> John de Courcy Ireland.   Dun Laoghaire, Ireland (Republic):
> Glendale Press, 1985. 416p.

A major review of the relationship between the Irish and the sea from ancient times to the present. That experience has encompassed invasion and warfare, social, economic and commercial history, and the lives of a significant part of the Irish population.

240 **Ireland: a concise history from the twelfth century to the present.**
> Paul Johnson.   St. Albans, Hertfordshire, England: Granada;
> Chicago: Academy Chicago, 1982. 272p.

This paperback edition by an English journalist outlines the major elements of Ireland's political, social and economic history over 700 years, from the Norman invasion to the present disorders in the North. A fair and objective review. The earlier hardcover edition was entitled *Ireland: land of troubles.*

241 **A history of Ireland.**
> Edited by Margaret MacCurtain.   Dublin: Gill & Macmillan,
> 1969. 3 vols.

This set of three titles, each by a different author, provides an attractive, interesting and illustrated introductory history for those beginning secondary level education. Included are *Celts and Normans* by Mary Collins, and *The birth of modern Ireland*, by Mark Tierney and Margaret MacCurtain.

242 **The story of the Irish race.**
> Seumas MacManus.   Old Greenwich, Connecticut: Devin-Adair,
> 1981. 737p.

A perennial favourite, first published in 1921 with at least thirty-five reprintings, this volume of eighty-two short, concise essays (some written by different authors) provides a detailed and emotional survey of the major events and themes of Irish history. Intended for an American audience, the book looks at Irelands's ideals, accomplishments and culture within the framework of its political history from ancient times to the aftermath of the treaty of 1921. Stress is placed on the independent culture of Ireland until mediaeval times, and on the conflict with Britain since then Suitable for adult or secondary school level readership.

243 **A new history of Ireland.**
Edited by Theodore William Moody, F. X. Martin. Oxford: Clarendon Press, 1976- . 10 vols.

This authoritative set, compiled under the direction of the Royal Irish Academy, provides a most thorough, continuous narrative of the whole of Irish history, and a distillation of contemporary scholarship relating to political, economic, social and cultural themes. Volume one is on prehistoric and early mediaeval Ireland; volume two covers mediaeval Ireland 1169 to 1534; volume three studies early modern Ireland from 1534 to 1691; volume four the 18th century, 1691-1800; volume five Ireland under the union, part one, 1807-70; volume six Ireland under the union, part two, 1870-1921; volume seven Ireland since 1921; volume eight consists of companion to Irish history part one, a chronology, maps and reference material and volume nine contains part two of companion, a digest of parliamentary elections since 1801, genealogical tables, and a historical atlas. Given its definitive character, this set should be in all historical collections where research will be undertaken.

244 **The course of Irish history.**
Edited by Theodore William Moody, F. X. Martin. Cork: Mercier, 1984. 484p. bibliog.

An excellent introduction, based on a television script, of Irish history from ancient times to the mid-1960s. Twenty-one leading scholars have contributed chapters in their area of speciality. The work includes a good bibliography and chronology and is suitable for recreational reading.

245 **The Irish sea province in archaeology and history.**
Donald Moore. Aberystwyth, Wales: National Library of Wales for the Cambrian Archaeology Association, 1970. 125p.

The sea has always been an integral part of Irish life and this work shows how it has affected Irish culture, economy and history throughout the centuries.

246 **The Irish people, an illustrated history.**
Kenneth Neill. Dublin: Gill & Macmillan; New York: Mayflower, 1979. 238p.

A general history of the Irish from prehistory, through the Celtic and mediaeval periods, conquest, colonization, nationalism, famine, rebellion and civil war. Weight is given to the mid-19th and early 20th century. The text is superficial but well coordinated with over 400 illustrations, the best feature of the book. The author also pays attention to social history and to aspects of ordinary life.

247 **A concise history of Ireland.**
Máire O'Brien, Conor Cruise O'Brien.   London: Thames &
Hudson; New York: Beekman, 1972. 192p.
A well illustrated but very abbreviated general history of Ireland, concentrating
on the years of conflict and progress towards nationhood. For quick perusal.

248 **The Ireland reader.**
Compiled by Helen O'Clery.   New York: Franklin Watts, 1963.
339p.
This attractively arranged collection of writings covers Ireland from ancient times
to the 1960s, through excerpts from the work of leading, modern Irish authors.
While lacking the continuity of a single theme, the many short excerpts provide
an entertaining scan of the main themes of Irish history, in poems, narrative and
drama. For popular reading.

249 **The Celtic consciousness.**
Edited by Robert O'Driscoll.   New York: Braziller; Mountrath,
Ireland (Republic): Dolmen; Edinburgh: Canongate; Toronto:
McClelland & Stewart, 1982. 642p.
Based on lectures given during a 1981 symposium in Toronto, a variety of
scholarly papers subject to scrutiny elements that have dominated Celtic society
through history, including literature, language, music, myths, arts and
archaeology. The fifty-five essays emphasize but are not confined to Ireland, and
go as far afield as Central Europe and the East. The modern remnants of Celtic
customs in Ireland are seen from a world perspective. Some papers have great
depth of perception, others are silly. The varied perspectives are confusing but
those who are interested in identifying the 'Celtic' spirit or tradition in all periods
of time including the present will find this volume of great interest. For the
serious and discerning reader.

250 **Story of the Irish people.**
Sean O'Faolain.   New York: Avenal, 1982. 180p.
The distinguished novelist, writing in 1942, describes Irish traits and character. He
interweaves history, politics, life, culture, mythology, literature and social
analysis. Drawing heavily on ancient accounts and on the invaders, O'Faolain sees
their influence in the rebels, writers and clergy of the 20th century. This short
work provides only the briefest outline of Irish history, society and culture, with
examples drawn from literature.

251 **Irish history and culture: aspect of a people's heritage.**
Edited by Harold Orel.   Lawrence, Kansas: University Press of
Kansas; Dublin: Wolfhound, 1976. 398p.
A comprehensive history of Ireland with particular emphasis given to culture,
society and population. An introductory reader that balances the arts with
history.

252 **Ireland: an illustrated history.**
John Ranelagh.   Oxford: Oxford University Press, 1981. 252p.
A brief but well written narrative of Ireland and the fortunes of Gaelic culture.
Ranelagh describes the integrity and accomplishments of the Celtic world and its
decline and destruction under successive invasions. A large format book, with 150
photographs, illustrations and maps.

253 **A short history of Ireland.**
John Ranelagh.   Cambridge, England: Cambridge University
Press, 1983. 280p.
Presents a broad history, partly based on hundreds of interviews, of Ireland from
the earliest times to the present.The author includes political and cultural events,
literature, the role of religion, recent developments in British-Irish relations, and
in Northern Ireland.

Early and mediaeval history

254 **The round towers of Ireland: a study and gazetteer.**
George Lennox Barrow.   Dublin: Academy, 1979. 228p.
A comprehensive study of 128 of the towers that figure in Irish history, landscape
and monastic settlements. Using hundreds of photographs and drawings, the
author presents their history, measurement and confused origins. The work will
also interest those concerned with archaeology, architecture or travel.

255 **Statutes, ordinances and acts of the Parliament of Ireland, John to
Edward IV.**
Edited by H. F. Berry, J. F. Morrissey.   Dublin: Stationery
Office, 1907-1939. 4 vols.
An important collection of source documents, this set provides translations of the
original acts and laws, many of which were destroyed during the Civil War in
1922. The first three volumes by Berry document the beginning of English control
from John to Henry IV in volume one; Henry VI in volume two; and Edward IV
in volume three. Morrisey continues from the thirteenth year of Edward's rule.

256 **Ireland: harbinger of the Middle Ages.**
Ludwig Bieler.   Oxford: Oxford University Press, 1963. 160p.
Bieler, a prolific scholar on the Middle Ages, traces the extension of Irish culture
to continental Europe and shows the influence of missionary work both to and
from Ireland. Some primary sources are included. This illustrated account was
first published in German in 1961.

257 **Corpus iuris Hibernici, a diplomatic edition of all the extant vellum manuscripts of early Irish law.**
D. A. Binchy. Dublin: Institute for Advanced Studies, 1978.
6 vols.

A most important source of documentation on the history of law in Ireland, which centuries after the conquest retained a specifically Irish identity, philosophy and procedure. This edition includes new introductory material.

258 **The history and topography of Ireland (topographia Hiberniae).**
Giraldus Cambrensis. Mountrath, Ireland (Republic): Dolmen; Atlantic Highlands, New Jersey: Humanities; Harmondsworth, England: Penguin, 1982. 128p.

Giraldus, from Wales was one of the Norman invaders of Ireland. Here, he provides a view of 12th-century Ireland in a conversational tone. This is an indispensable source of first hand observations, although considered distorted and biased. He captures a picture of Irish civilization and native customs in the year 1185, a time of encroachment by influences from the continent. This edition is well printed and includes contemporary illustrations and a map from a manuscript copy at the National Library in Dublin. Other editions of Giraldus include *Expungnatio Hibernica, the conquest of Ireland* edited by A. Scott and F. X. Martin (Dublin: Royal Irish Academy, 1978. New History of Ireland Series) with a new translation; an earlier translation by M. Kelly in a fine edition (Dublin: Celtic Society, 1848); and a reprint of an 1896 edition with paralleled texts (New York: Haskell House, 1969. 172p.).

259 **History of medieval Ireland from 1086-1513.**
Edmund Curtis. London: Methuen; New York: Gordan, 1961.
Reprinted, New York: Barnes & Noble, 1968. 433p.

Once the standard work for the mediaeval period, this may still be useful for the study of Irish towns, laws and families of the Gaelic period, but is now largely supplanted by later works. An Irish language edition was published by the Stationery Office, Dublin.

260 **Early Christian Ireland**
Máire de Paor, Liam de Paor. London: Thames & Hudson; New York: Praeger, 1960. 2nd rev. ed. 264p. bibliog. (Ancient Peoples and Places, no. 8).

Using the evidence of archaeology and ancient literature, the beginnings of Christianity in Ireland are traced showing the gradual development of the golden age of Irish art, culture and scholarship. Chapters are on Ireland and Rome, monasteries, daily life, the Vikings, the Renaissance and the Reformation. Ireland's early Christian culture (legend, literature, arts and scholarship) is treated as a whole. Excellent photographs are included.

261   **Anglo-Norman Ireland.**
Michael Dolley.   Dublin: Gill & Macmillan, 1973. 213p.
A short work detailing the development of Irish political institutions, English
influence and continental events of the 12th and 13th centuries.

262   **Ireland and the making of Britain.**
Benedict Fitzpatrick.   London, New York: Funk & Wagnalls,
1922. 363p.
This volume covers the early missionary and mediaeval periods, the Irish
contribution to Carolingian Europe, Iona, Scotland and England, and the state of
scholarship at the time. Irish educational proficiency is seen as a bridge between
the ancient world of learning and the new.

263   **Saint Patrick: his writings and Muirchu's life.**
Edited and translated by A. B. E. Hood.   Totowa, New Jersey:
Rowman & Littlefield, 1978. 101p. (History From the Source
Series).
Various original sources are presented from both Latin and English works on the
life of Saint Patrick, including a fragment of his *Confessio* written after 540.
Among the other early texts included is the 7th century life of Patrick by
Muirchu. A more popular but less academically satisfying work is Alice-Boyd
Proudfoot's *Patrick, sixteen centuries with Ireland's patron saint* (New York:
Macmillan, 1983. 212p.). Proudfoot combines personal observations and
experiences with numerous writings from both primary and secondary sources to
give a kaleidoscopic view of Patrick's life, the legend and folklore surrounding
him, and his impact on the modern world. A major sourcebook remains the
Tripartite life of Patrick, which contains mediaeval texts translated by Whitley
Stokes in the British 'Rolls Series' (London: Public Record Office, 1888.
Reprinted, New York: Kraus Reprints). For the student, the present volume by
Hood is particularly reliable and convenient. Ludwig Bieler has edited *Four Latin
lives of Saint Patrick*, by mediaeval authors with English translations, for the
Dublin Institute of Advanced Study. A speculative but realistic and reasonable
biography is provided by E. A. Thompson in *Who was St. Patrick?* (Woodbridge,
Suffolk, England: Boydell; New York: St. Martin's, 1986). Thompson dispenses
with the quaint and unlikely stories surrounding Patrick, while presenting a
popularized but more likely portrayal, based on verifiable or existing early
records and sources.

264   **Celtic monasticism: the modern traveller to the early Irish church.**
Kathleen Hughes, Ann Hamlin.   New York: Seabury, 1981. 131p.
A description is given of the functioning of the monastic community and the
ancient inhabitants who faced the onslaught of the Norsemen. The volume can be
used as a guide to present day ruins. Hughes has also published *The Church in
early Irish society* (1966), a useful text on the Church in pre-Norman times.

265 **The Irish Text Society.**
Dublin: The Society, 1899-.
The series issued over several decades includes several score volumes of texts in early Irish, usually with translations, copious notes and extensive introductions. Volumes are numbered and are occasionally reprinted, though often with vague imprints. Early and mediaeval texts are included and this edition can be considered definitive. The set is essential for the detailed study of folklore, tradition, literature, and the historical usage of the Irish language. Included are volumes on literature, medicine, law and a dictionary. Volume seven, *Duanaire Finn*, the book of the lays of Fionn, was edited by Eoin MacNeill.

266 **England and Ireland in the later Middle Ages.**
Edited by James Lydon. Dublin: Irish Academic Press, 1981.
286p. maps.
Various authors contribute chapters on the relationship between the two countries, the settlement of Limerick, King John and Edward I in Ireland, English expeditions, O'Neill and Ulster, and the reign of Richard II. Many examples are given of the political consequences for Ireland of problems which were local to England. The work is provocative but narrowly focused and requires some previous knowledge of Irish history.

267 **Phases of Irish history.**
Eoin MacNeill. Dublin: Gill & Macmillan, 1968. 364p.
This series of essays by Ireland's famous historian, scholar and political figure, became a landmark in Irish history after it first appeared in 1919. Now considered more a curiosity, these twelve lectures cover pre-Celtic times to the Middle Ages, with the author's defence and preference for the old Gaelic structures of society.

268 **Ireland before the Vikings.**
Gearóid MacNiocaill. Dublin: Gill & Macmillan, 1972. 184p.
(Gill History of Ireland, no. 1).
A short introduction to the period of the consolidation of tribal power into kingships, and the emergence of a unifying culture and economy prior to the 9th century.

269 **Brian Boru, king of Ireland.**
Roger Chatterton Newman. Dublin: Anvil, 1982. 224p.
A readable, full biography of Ireland's great king (941-1014). His character and achievement as a unifying force are discussed. Boru is seen as both a military leader and a skilled administrator, confronting Danes and Norsemen while establishing a rule of law, liberty, and sporadic peace. Illustrations document historical evidence and excavations. The study provides a scholarly foundation. A very popular account, also well-researched but fictional, is *Lion of Ireland: the legend of Brian Boru* by Morgan Llywelyn (Boston, Massachusetts: Houghton Mifflin; London: Bodley Head, 1980. 528p.).

270 **Gaelic and gaelicised Ireland in the Middle Ages.**
Kenneth Nicholls. Dublin: Gill & Macmillan, 1972. 197p. (Gill
History of Ireland, no. 4).
An overview is given of Ireland in the Middle Ages with emphasis on rural,
Gaelic society beyond the boundaries of English control.

271 **Ireland before the Normans.**
Donncha Ó Corráin. Dublin: Gill & Macmillan, 1972. 210p.
A good introduction to Irish society prior to the Norman invasions, covering the
conflict between local chiefs and kings, battles with the Norsemen, ecclesiastical
change, and Irish institutions up to the 12th century.

272 **Lectures in the manuscript materials of ancient Irish history.**
Eugene O'Curry. New York: Burt Franklin, 1965. 722p.
This reprint of the 1861 edition provides a most detailed and comprehensive
account of the major Irish mediaeval manuscripts, including the important Irish
annals, chronicles, devotionals, missals, tales, romances, poems and genealogies.
O'Curry identifies the principal sources of recorded Irish history, evaluates and
comments upon them and the existing collections, libraries, ancient education and
writers, and upon the vicissitudes faced over centuries of plunder, ruin and
neglect. Another interesting collection of lectures by O'Curry is *On the manners
and customs of the ancient Irish* (Dublin: W. B. Kelly; London: Williams &
Norgate; New York: Scribners, 1873. Reprinted, New York: 1971. 3 vols).

273 **Annals of the kingdom of Ireland, by the Four Masters, from the
earliest period to the year 1616.**
Edited by John O'Donovan. London: Cass; New York: AMS,
1966. 7 vols.
A prime source of collected Irish history, the Four Masters were among the last to
record the traditional ancient history of Ireland largely from oral accounts and the
then extant manuscripts. Chronologically arranged, the work is useful for
determining the sequence of events and in many instances remains the only
confirming source of names and events. Much of the renewal of Irish
historiography of the 19th century incorporates details from the annals.
O'Donovan, a founder of the Irish Archaeological Society, completed this
translation in 1854, and it has become the standard edition. Another edition
translated from the original Irish by Owen Connellan, was published in 1846. *The
Annals* are useful primarily for the advanced student.

274 **Early Irish history and mythology.**
Thomas O'Rahilly. Dublin: Institute for Advanced Studies, 1976.
568p.
This scholarly study details Irish history prior to the introduction of Christianity in
AD 432. Using recorded tradition, linguistic evidence, and the work of classical
authors it traces the course of early occupations, invasions and eventual
settlement. Includes chapters on the dating of the early Irish annals and the
separation of history and fable. For the advanced student this analysis carefully

weighs evidence and is an important and careful contribution to Irish historiography of the early periods.

275   **Ireland under the Normans, 1169-1333.**
      Goddard Henry Orpen.   Oxford: Clarendon Press, 1968. 4 vols.
      maps.
This valuable account, first published 1911-1920, is especially rich in detail and is generally accurate. It covers changing Irish conditions under foreign dominance and influence just prior to the statutes of Kilkenny. Some later historians have suggested minor revisions but this work remains a good, in-depth study.

276   **History of medieval Ireland.**
      A. J. Otway-Ruthven.   London: Benn; New York: St. Martin's,
      1980. 2nd ed. 472p. maps. bibliog.
A thorough, accurate study of Ireland and its political, ecclesiastical and economic establishment from the 12th to the end of the 15th centuries. The work is considered an authoritative standard history of the mediaeval period.

277   **Sex and marriage in ancient Ireland.**
      Patrick Power.   Cork: Mercier Press, 1967. 96p.
Social customs and marriage under Gaelic law and in ancient times were far different, and in some ways more liberal than those of the modern day. Some positive implications can be drawn from the status of women in early times as outlined in this book.

278   **The administration of Ireland, 1172-1377.**
      H. G. Richardson, G. O. Sales.   Dublin: Irish Manuscript
      Commission, 1963. 300p.
A selection of documents and treasury accounts are reprinted up to the year 1416, providing a picture of centralized government as described in original sources. A useful introduction is included.

279   **The Norman invasion of Ireland.**
      Richard Roche.   Dublin: Anvil, 1979. 134p.
A concise account of the political intrigue and involvements surrounding the 12th-century invasion. The study comments on the cultural heritage at the time of conquest, warring parties, military engagements, and the eventual subjugation of Ireland. For the new student of Irish history, and the general reader.

280   **The flowering of Ireland: saints, scholars and kings.**
      Katharine Scherman.   Boston, Massachusetts: Little, Brown;
      London: Victor Gollancz, 1981. 368p.
Recounts the story of Ireland from the 5th to the 12th centuries, when the remaining pagan Celts who had made so important a contribution to the Irish arts were confronted by missionaries from a classical tradition. The study covers the prehistory of Ireland, the saints, the breakdown of the old society and subsequent

invasions. Attention, however, is focused on the cultural flowering in education, poetry, scholarship, art, metalwork and writing. The missionaries are seen not as individuals but as a social force (such as Patrick), or as innovators (such as Enda, Finian and Brigid), and travellers (Brendan, Columba and Columbanus). This review of the amalgamation of cultures contains enough detail, colour, and interest to make it enjoyable reading.

281 **Scandinavian York and Dublin; the history and archaeology of two related Viking kingdoms.**
Alfred P. Smyth.   Dublin: Templekieran Press; Atlantic Highlands, New Jersey: Humanities, 1979. 361p.

This study demonstrates the interrelationships and commercial ties that existed between the two mediaeval cities and kingdoms, by inspecting literature, sagas, monastic traditions and archaeological evidence. Chapters explore the urban economy, material culture, and topography and comparisons are made with Eastern Europe. Genealogical charts of the Irish kings are included. The later results of modern excavations from 1974 to 1980 in the ancient Viking areas of Dublin are discussed by Patrick Wallace in *Viking and medieval Dublin, 900-1315, the archaeological evidence at Wood Quay* (Dublin: University Press of Ireland, 1980. 224p.).

282 **Britain and Ireland in early Christian times, A. D. 400-800.**
Charles Thomas.   New York: McGraw-Hill; London: Thames & Hudson, 1971. 144p.

A well illustrated, introductory account of the period following the end of Roman Britain. The volume studies the rise of the various invading groups, the colonizers, monastic life, the home and agricultural life. Numerous pictures of Irish art are included.

283 **Ireland in early medieval Europe.**
Edited by Dorothy Whitelock, Rosamond McKitterick, David Dumville.   Cambridge, England; New York: Cambridge University Press, 1982. 406p.

This collection includes essays on martyrs, ancient art (the crosses of Kells), the Vikings in Ireland and political expansion. The chapters of this Festschrift are varied but an overview of the mediaeval Irish world is not provided. For the advanced reader.

284 **The northern world: history and heritage of northern Europe, A. D. 400-1100.**
Edited by David Wilson.   New York: Harry Abrams; London: Thames & Hudson, 1980. 248p. maps. bibliog.

An attractive, handsomely produced survey by an international group of professors who comment on Germanic myths and tribes, the Celtic contribution in Ireland and elsewhere, and the Scandinavians, both Viking and other. For general readership, this places Irish culture within the larger European context. Various examples of Celtic art are included.

Tudor and Stuart period

285 **The Elizabethan conquest of Ireland: a pattern established 1565-1576.**
Nicholas P. Canny. Brighton, England: Harvester; New York: Barnes & Noble, 1976. 205p.

The author traces the problems of British relations with Ireland to the 16th century. The social, political and cultural customs and mores of the Irish race which the English failed to understand, resulted in centuries of clashes and resistance.

286 **The upstart earl: a study of the social and mental world of Richard Boyle, first Earl of Cork, 1566-1643.**
Nicholas P. Canny. Cambridge, England: Cambridge University Press, 1982. 211p.

A picture of court politics, social and family history is given in this study of a 16th-century Anglo-Irish Elizabethan adventurer. Included is a view of his accumulated estates through expropriations in Munster. The volume provides a most readable account of the successful life of Boyle who rose from a penniless status to a position on the Privy Council during years of intrigue.

287 **Owen Roe O'Neill.**
Jerrold I. Casway. Philadelphia: University of Pennsylvania; London: Academic and University Publishers Group, 1985. 353p.

A portrait of 17th-century Ireland is presented in this biography of the nephew of the Earl of Tyrone (the great Hugh O'Neill.) Owen Roe O'Neill received military training in Spain and later led forces in Ireland in an effort to reclaim lost lands. Casway discusses the changing alliances and politics of the day, local feuds and rivalries, and the organization and control of armies. Primary historical sources have been used and maps are included.

288 **Granuaile: the life and times of Grace O'Malley, 1530-1603.**
Anne Chambers. Dublin: Wolfhound, 1980. 212p.

This biography of Ireland's famous 'sea queen' provides insights into diplomacy, rebellion and commerce during the 16th century. Granuaile, who exercised authority over the O'Mally clan, was responsible for many of the fortresses and sea rovers of the period. The study comments on social history, local Gaelic conditions and on the Elizabethan court.

289 **The image of Irelande, with a discoverie of Woodkarne.**
John Derricke. Belfast: Blackstaff; Dover, New Hampshire: Longwood, 1984. 224p.

An eyewitness report on Elizabethan Ireland, in verse, considered as a primary source for the period. This is an illustrated, fine press, limited edition.

290 **Ireland in the age of the Tudors: the destruction of Hiberno-Norman civilization.**
R. Dudley Edwards. London: Croom Helm; New York: Barnes & Noble, 1977. 222p.

The author discusses English expansion and the Irish reaction during the Reformation in this largely political account of British inroads and cultural ruin of Ireland. Much emphasis is placed on a detailed analysis of Irish parliamentary legislation and its effect on society. An appendix covers Irish historiography of the 16th century. Edwards has also written *Church and state in Tudor Ireland*, (q.v.) which is the standard work on the history of the penal laws up to James 1st.

291 **The letters of Saint Oliver Plunkett.**
Edited by John Hanly. Portlaoise, County Kildare, Ireland (Republic): Dolmen, 1979. 624p.

This beautifully produced collection of letters provides insights into the social and political state of Ireland during the 17th century. A commentary relates the papers to the ecclesiastical situation at a time of persecution. A valuable source of contemporary comment.

292 **Holinshed's Irish chronicle: the historie of Irelande from the first inhabitation thereof, unto the yeare 1509.**
Raphael Holinshed, edited by Liam Miller, Eileen Power. Mountrath, County Laois, Ireland (Republic): Dolmen; Atlantic Highlands, New Jersey: Humanities, 1979. 363p.

The chronicle, continued to the year 1547 by Richard Stanyhurst, was first published in 1577. While faulted for its accuracy, Holinshed affords an important view of English Tudor knowledge and interpretation of Irish history. Sections of the text suppressed by the Privy Council are now restored, original woodcuts are included and the text now includes a critical introduction and six appendixes. This is a limited edition, fine presentation of a major historical source. A comparison can be made with an equally biased Elizabethan account, namely, Edmund Spenser's *View of the present state of Ireland*, (revised edition by W. Renwick, Oxford: Oxford University Press, 1979). D. B. Quinn elsewhere provides an overview of the problem of interpreting contemporaneous accounts by Englishmen of Gaelic Ireland in *The Elizabethans and the Irish* (Ithaca, New York: Cornell, 1966).

293 **Richard Stanihurst the Dubliner, 1547-1618: a biography.**
Colm Lennon. Blackrock, County Dublin, Ireland (Republic): Irish Academic Press, 1981. 186p.

Stanyhurst was an important Elizabethan historian of Ireland, and an accomplished scholar, scientist, physician and diplomat. He has been blamed for the creation of erroneous impressions of Ireland but in time his views changed, he was forced into exile and eventually became a priest. This biography of the Dublin humanist is also a history of the society of the time. Excerpts from Stanyhurst's writings on Ireland are included.

294 **The English in medieval Ireland.**
Edited by James Lydon. Dublin: Royal Irish Academy, 1984.
160p.

Many facets of the English experience in Ireland are covered in these papers of a 1982 conference sponsored by the Royal Irish Academy and the British Academy.

295 **Tudor and Stuart Ireland.**
Margaret MacCurtain. Dublin: Gill & Macmillan, 1972. 211p.
(Gill History of Ireland, no. 7).

MacCurtain provides a useful, condensed overview of the interrelationship between England and Ireland and the effects of warfare and conquest on Ireland's political, social and economic life. Intended for general readership.

296 **Irish life in the seventeenth century.**
Edward MacLysaght. Dublin: Irish Academic Press, 1979. 320p.

An important and also entertaining work on the social history of Ireland between 1660 and 1700, with information on the traits, behaviour, home life and recreation of both the gentry and peasantry, including commentary on political forces and living conditions.

297 **Elizabethan Ireland: a selection of writings on Ireland by Elizabethans.**
James Myers. London: Archon; Hamden, Connecticut: Shoe
String Press, 1983. 261p.

The English outlook on Ireland is traced through the writings of an aide to Mountjoy, Edmund Spenser, John Davies and others. The author identifies a pervasive bias and animosity towards the Irish during the 16th and early 17th centuries in the writings of the period.

298 **The great O'Neill.**
Sean O'Faolain. Cork; Dublin: Mercier, 1981. 284p.

The classic study of one of the most powerful forces in Ireland in the Elizabethan period, Hugh O'Neill, Earl of Tyrone. First published in 1942, the volume traces the political and military turmoil of the time, the armed resistance in Ulster during the Renaissance and the eventual fall of the Gaelic order.

299 **Sir John Davies and the conquest of Ireland.**
Hans S. Pawlisch. Cambridge, England: Cambridge University
Press, 1985. 246p.

A thorough study of the growth of Jacobean control over Ireland, largely through judicial interpretations fostered by Davies (1569-1619), the English Attorney General of Ireland. The study traces the growing manipulation of the law against old Gaelic society, privilege and ownership. (Davies was also a noted humanist, poet and antiquarian.)

300   **The political anatomy of Ireland.**
Sir William Petty, introduction by John O'Donovan.   Dublin:
Irish Academic; Totowa, New Jersey: Rowman & Littlefield, 1961.
Reprinted, 1970. 230p.

A contemporary account of Ireland written in 1672. Petty, a well educated and
experienced English administrator accompanied Cromwell to Ireland. After his
arrival there he gave considerable thought to reordering the country's economic
life. His observations, though somewhat prejudiced, were considered important at
the time and are still referred to by scholars.

18th-19th centuries

301   **The making of Ireland.**
James Camlin Beckett.   New York, London: Faber & Faber,
1981. 2nd rev. ed. 496p. bibliog.

An excellent survey of three centuries of Irish history, first published in 1966.
Beckett considers the divisions of Irish society, rebellion and the beginnings of the
modern state. A good bibliography is included, which is especially informative on
local history. Some emphasis is given to 19th-century political struggles,
confiscation and economics. Useful as a school textbook or for the general reader.

302   **Land and the national question in Ireland, 1858-1882.**
Paul Bew.   Dublin: Gill & Macmillan; New York: Humanities,
1979. 250p.

A detailed study of the rural, local conditions of 19th-century Ireland, the
economic plight of tenant farmers, and the organization of the Land League.
Dr. Bew focuses on the league as an experiment that drew support across class
lines, and he attempts to relate that experience to wider social movements. For
university level research.

303   **The passing of the Irish Act of Union; a study of parliamentary
politics.**
Geoffry Bolton.   London: Oxford University Press, 1966. 239p.

A history of interparty manoeuvering in Dublin and London. Partisan politics and
the fear of Irish rebellion are seen as leading to direct rule under a United
Kingdom, with the abolition of the Irish parliament at the beginning of the 19th
century.

304   **Crown and castle, British rule in Ireland, 1800-1830.**
Edward Brynn.   Dublin: O'Brien, 1978. 172p.

The author explores the office of viceroy through an examination of both the
private and public papers of the incumbents, in this study of government
administration.

305 **Views of the Irish peasantry, 1800-1916.**
Daniel Casey, Robert Rhodes. Hamden, Connecticut: Archon Books, 1977. 225p.

Describes 19th-century agricultural life and society, literature, tradition and migration. A somewhat narrower view is given by Kenneth Connell in *Irish peasant society, four historical essays* (London: Oxford University Press, 1968. 161p.). Connell concentrates on specific social issues, such as marriage and alcoholism, while Casey and Rhodes present a more rounded view of Irish life as a whole. For a different view of social and economic history see *Irish peasants, violence and political unrest, 1780-1914*, edited by Samuel Clark and James S. Donnelly Jr. (Madison, Wisconsin: University of Wisconsin Press, 1985).

306 **Social origins of the Irish land war.**
Samuel Clark. Princeton, New Jersey: Princeton University Press, 1979. 418p.

Land disputes, the peasants' economic plight and social unrest characterized the conflicts over the control and ownership of agricultural lands. Concentrating on the period 1879 to 1882 Clark analyses post-famine politics, the struggles for power and the ultimate collective movement towards reforms. Well researched and written, this study will be of interest chiefly to those involved in advanced research. Clark, with James Doherty, has edited *Irish peasants: violence and political unrest 1780-1914* (Madison, Wisconsin: University of Wisconsin, 1983. 416p.), in which many of today's problems are traced back to the organization of the farming sector in the late 19th century.

307 **Charles J. Kickham 1828-82: a study in Irish nationalism and literature.**
R. V. Comerford. Dublin: Wolfhound, 1979. 255p.

Kickham (1828-1882) was a popular author, and president of the Irish Republican Brotherhood. This study illuminates the movements of nationalism, Fenianism and revolutionary politics, and provides a valuable and detailed view of the time.

308 **The Fenians in context: Irish politics and society, 1848-82.**
R. V. Comerford. Dublin: Wolfhound Press; Atlantic Highlands, New Jersey: Humanities, 1985. 272p.

A dispassionate study of the motivations of those drawn to the Fenian movement, which aimed for Irish independence, and the rise of nationalism in the Victorian era between the famine of 1845-1849, and the land wars. Comerford sifts considerable evidence in order to evaluate some of the political factors of the time: election results, relative economic prosperity, and corruption.

309 **Priests and people in pre-famine Ireland, 1780-1845.**
Sean Connolly. New York: St. Martin's Press, 1982. 340p. maps. bibliog.

By contrasting pre- with post-famine periods this study points to changing conditions and the impact of the clergy in shaping 19th-century Ireland. Suppressed popular and often superstitious beliefs, enforced political and moral stability, and social change, eventually moulded Ireland into a very different form of society.

310 **The emergence of modern Ireland, 1600-1900.**
Louis M. Cullen. New York: Holmes & Meier; Dublin: Gill & Macmillan, 1981. 292p. bibliog.

This detailed history analyses the various groups that make up Irish society from the time of their arrival until 1900. Cullen presents a great amount of detail on colonists, habits, diet and the famine, housing, agrarian society, culture and sectarian changes. For the more advanced reader.

311 **Dispatches from United States consuls.**
Washington, DC: U.S. National Archives and Records Service. Microfilm.

Records of 19th-century American consular reports and dispatches provide a contemporary view of conditions in Ireland, covering such topics as the economy and emigration. These are arranged by city of origin and date on various reels.

312 **Ireland: land, politics and people.**
Edited by P. J. Drudy. London; Cambridge, England; New York: Cambridge University Press, 1982. 331p. (Irish Studies, no. 2).

Twelve essays weave together the major land issues of the last century: agrarian class conflict, rural unrest in the period 1885 to 1900, politics and change in small communities, economic growth, regional problems, the Land League, and family structure. More recent policies, especially those from 1922 to 1960 are included, as is the influence of the European Economic Community (EEC), and current national politics. Maps and statistics are incorporated. For advanced research. Two other studies of the land question are *Landlord or tenant? A view of Irish history* by Magnus Magnusson (London: Bodley Head, 1978. 155p.), and *The Irish Land League crisis* by Norman Palmer (New York: Farrar, Straus & Giroux, 1978. 340p.).

313 **Young Ireland: a fragment of Irish history, 1840-1850.**
Charles Gavan Duffy. New York: Da Capo, 1973. 778p.

The Irish national leader, Daniel O'Connell is a leading figure in this narrative, and there is a full account of his trial and conviction and its aftermath, as well as accounts of other 19th-century controversies. The correspondence of Smith O'Brien and Thomas Davis is included in this reprint of an 1881 edition. Duffy was an important publisher and nationalist figure of the period.

314 **Pre-famine Ireland: a study in historical geography.**
Thomas Walter Freeman. Manchester, England: Manchester University Press, 1957. 352p.

Using the census returns of 1841 and many other sources Freeman is able to provide a useful overview of Ireland in the early 19th century, before the devastating effects of the famine.

315 **Documents relating to Ireland, 1795-1804.**
John T. Gilbert. Shannon, Ireland (Republic): Irish University Press, 1970. 250p.

The selected documents cover a period of political disturbances, imminent invasion by France, demands for Catholic emancipation, and parliamentary reform. Among the papers reproduced are some relating to the United Irish movement, the Orange Order, the rising of 1798, and secret service payments to highly placed informers. This is a facsimile of an 1893 edition compiled by the Secretary of the Public Record Office of Ireland. For research collections.

316 **Paddy's lament, Ireland, 1846-47.**
Thomas Gallagher. New York: Harcourt Brace Jovanovich, 1982. Reprinted, Dublin: Wolfhound, 1985. 352p.

A popular, vivid account of the harsh famine years, including the difficulty of survival, and emigration to America. The account is made compelling through its tragic stories of many individuals.

317 **Elections, politics and society in Ireland, 1832-1885.**
K. T. Hoppen. Oxford: Clarendon Press, 1984. 596p.

Hoppen provides extensive statistics and an interesting commentary in this examination of Irish political developments from the times of O'Connell to Parnell. He notes the degree of change in society and in political organizations, especially at the local level, with effects persisting to today.

318 **The green flag.**
Robert Kee. London: Weidenfeld & Nicholson; New York: Delacorte Press, 1972. 870p.

An intensive and detailed account of Irish history and nationalism since the 12th century, concentrating particularly on the 19th and 20th centuries. Kee inspects the many disputes which have characterized Anglo-Irish relations and studies the rise of mass popular movements in Ireland. The paperbound edition has been divided into three volumes: *The most distressful country*, covering the period up to the famine years; *The bold Fenian men* (to 1916); and *Ourselves alone*, which studies the Easter Rising through the civil war period. An engrossing history for general or college readership.

319 **Ireland: a history.**
Robert Kee. London: Weidenfeld & Nicholson; Boston, Massachusetts: Little, Brown, 1982. 256p.

Following a brief outline of early Irish history, the volume focuses on the troubles and political conflict of the 19th and 20th centuries, up to early 1970. Based on a controversial BBC/RTE television series the study highlights particular incidents of confrontation, especially regarding Northern Ireland, but attempts to understand each side without apportioning blame. (Advocates of either side in the present difficulties are dissatisfied with this account). Kee vaguely urges a future confederation and the forgetting of past anguish as a way out of the Irish dilemma. This balanced portrayal provides a useful and well written, albeit simplified history, for the general reader. Many illustrations are included.

320   **The Roman Catholic Church and the creation of the modern Irish state, 1878-1886.**
Emmet J. Larkin.   Philadelphia: American Philosophical Society;
Dublin: Gill & Macmillan, 1975. 436p. (Memoirs of the American
Philosophical Society, no. 108).

The interrelationship between the Church, government and politics is graphically portrayed through excerpts from contemporary papers and correspondence of the 19th century. Larkin emphasises the influence of the hierarchy in interpreting and manipulating events in this and three later volumes: *The Roman Catholic Church and the Plan of Campaign in Ireland, 1886-1888* (Cork, Irish Republic: Cork University Press, 1978. 334p.); *The Roman Catholic Church in Ireland and the fall of Parnell* (Chapel Hill, North Carolina: University of North Carolina Press, 1979. 316p.); *The making of the Roman Catholic Church in Ireland, 1850-1860* (Chapel Hill, North Carolina: University of North Carolina Press, 1980). For advanced readers.

321   **The history of Ireland in the eighteenth century.**
William Edward Lecky.   London: Longmans, Green; New York:
Appleton, 1893. 5 vols.

A detailed look at social, economic and political Ireland before the Act of Union, in 1800. A now dated account that does not reflect current scholarship, it is still important to the researcher. Volume one covers 1700-1760; volume two 1760-90; and volumes three to five cover the period 1790-1800.

322   **The modernization of Irish society, 1848-1918.**
Joseph J. Lee.   Dublin: Gill & Macmillan, 1973. 192p. bibliog.
(Gill History of Ireland Series).

The second half of the 19th century is seen as a time of great social change, with the development of a new political awareness in the populace, a conflict in land ownership, and economic transition.

323   **Ireland since the famine.**
Francis S. L. Lyons.   London: Fontana; New York: Scribner,
1973. 880p.

A valuable survey of society in post-famine Ireland, with the concurrent economic, political and cultural changes. The modern history of Ireland is traced through the legacy of the Young Ireland movement, the home rule campaign, the revolution and Sinn Fein. The emergence of the Irish Republic is studied and social policies, and Northern Ireland politics to 1972 are also included.

324   **Ireland under the Union: varieties of tension.**
Edited by Francis Stewart L. Lyons, R. A. Hawkins.   Oxford;
New York: Oxford University Press, 1979. 290p.

Focusing on the 19th century, the authors outline the many cultural and political issues between England and Ireland, including the suppression of Gaelic culture and language, economic constraints and the repression of tenant farmers. The various papers included evaluate British policies from the separate viewpoints of the Irish, English and Anglo-Irish. A provocative study for college-level reading.

325 The Republic of Ireland.
D. R. O'Connor Lysaght.   Cork: Mercier Press, 1970. 255p.

A revisionist interpretation of Irish history and society for the period 1800 to the mid-20th century.

326 Tone and his times.
Frank MacDermont.   Dublin: Anvil, 1981. 306p.

First published in 1939 this is one of the better biographies of Theobald Wolfe Tone, leader of the 1798 rebellion, and founder of the Society of United Irishmen. A shorter biography by Henry Boylan, *Theobald Wolfe Tone* is in the Gill Irish Lives series (Dublin: Gill & Macmillan, 1981). Tone's autobiography was published in 1826 with added notes by his son. Sean Cronin and Richard Roche provide a short biography of Tone *Freedom the Wolfe Tone way* (Dublin: Anvil), which relates excerpts from Tone's writings to revolutionary politics today.

327 Social life in Ireland, 1800-1845.
Robert Brendan McDowell.   Dublin: Cultural Relations
Committee of Ireland, 1950. Reprinted, Dublin: Mercier, 1973.
120p.

Based on a series of radio talks on the cultural, social and living conditions of the period.

328 The Irish administration, 1801-1914.
Robert Brendan McDowell.   London: Greenwood, 1977. 328p.
bibliog.

An excellent, detailed study of politics and the machinery of government in Ireland during the 19th century. A valuable bibliography of original sources makes this a particularly useful reference guide.

329 Ireland in the age of imperialism and revolution, 1760-1801.
Robert Brendan McDowell.   London, New York: Oxford
University Press 1979. 740p. bibliog.

A review of 18th-century Ireland ending with the union and including an analysis of governmental administration and politics, intellectual and religious life, parliamentary reform, English constitutional conflicts (the American War of Independence, Anglo-Irish settlements), the French Revolution, agitation and insurrection. A careful, well-written study, with many quotations from contemporary sources, that concentrates on the economic, political and social relationship between England and Ireland.

330 **Public opinion and government policy in Ireland, 1801-1846.**
Robert Brendan McDowell.   London, New York: Oxford
University Press, 1979. 74p.

McDowell outlines support of and elements of opposition to governmental
policies at a time of critical change. It is one of the few books to cover the history
of public opinion. The volume is a sequel to *Irish public opinion, 1750-1800*
(London: Faber & Faber, 1944. 306p.).

331 **The Irish question, 1840-1921: a commentary on Anglo-Irish
relations.**
Nicholas Mansergh.   London: Allen & Unwin, 1975. 3rd ed.
344p.

This substantial analysis of 19th-century government and politics explores the
many ways in which Anglo-Irish relations have been affected by the social and
political forces that led up to the Easter Rising and its aftermath.

332 **Why Ireland starved: a quantitative and analytical history of the
Irish economy, 1800-1850.**
Joel Mokyr.   London: Allen & Unwin, 1983. 330p. bibliog.

Studies some of the causes of Ireland's slow economic development, low
productivity and problems of capital formation that led to the famine which
claimed more than a million victims between 1846 and 1851. Putting aside some of
the traditional explanations, Mokyr concentrates on a statistical analysis of
mortality and demographic patterns, agricultural methods and income levels. The
value of the account is in its evaluation of agricultural patterns of little planning
and low productivity. The volume has a somewhat controversial, left-wing
orientation. For advanced research.

333 **The Fenian movement.**
Edited by T. W. Moody.   Cork: Mercier Press, 1978. 128p.

A popular review of the revolutionary Fenian movement from the mid-19th
century, covering its American connection, and its organization, aims and
leadership. For general readers.

334 **Davitt and Irish revolution, 1846-82.**
Theodore William Moody.   Oxford; New York: Oxford
University Press, 1982. 712p. maps. bibliog.

This is the most detailed account of Michael Davitt's life, including his activities
as founder of the Land League in 1879, and as a defender of tenant farmers with
his own approach to nationalism and human justice. The volume also covers
home rule, Fenianism in America, penal servitude, evictions and other agrarian
outrages. An exhaustive account, which draws upon numerous primary sources.

335 **The shaping of modern Ireland, 1880-90.**
Edited by Conor Cruise O'Brien. Toronto: University of Toronto Press, 1960. 201p.

Biographical portraits of various leading figures of the day are presented, and these provide an introduction to late 19th-century Ireland.

336 **Devoy's post bag, 1871-1928.**
Edited by William O'Brien, Desmond Ryan. Dublin: Academy Press, 1979. 2 vols.

This is an important, first-hand source on the Fenians, based on the extensive correspondence of its leader, John Devoy, from his exile in America. The papers shed light on the political experiences of the 19th-century Irish-American, intertwined with that of the people remaining in Ireland during times of agitation and revolutionary activity.

337 **Revolutionary underground: the story of the Irish Republican Brotherhood, 1858-1924.**
Leon O'Broin. Totowa, New Jersey: Rowman & Littlefield, 1976. 245p.

A full account is given of the history of the Irish Republican Brotherhood (IRB), its tactics, organization and policies in the years before the formation of the Irish Republican Army (IRA). O'Broin has also written *Protestant nationalists in revolutionary Ireland; the Stopford connection* (Dublin: Gill & Macmillan, 1985. 234p.).

338 **Recollections of Fenians and Fenianism.**
John O'Leary. Dublin: Irish University Press, 1969. 554p.

O'Leary recalls his days in the Fenian movement in this account published in 1896. As editor of the *Irish People* he suffered arrest and nine years banishment. He comments on nationalist sentiments, Young Irelanders, Parnelites, and rural conditions.

339 **Family and farm in pre-famine Ireland: the parish of Killashandra.**
Kevin O'Neill. Madison, Wisconsin: University of Wisconsin, 1985. 233p.

A study of population and economic forces in County Cavan, as an example of a rural society undergoing great change. Farm holdings, prices and exports are closely examined. For the advanced reader.

340 **The three lives of Gavan Duffy.**
Cyril Pearl. Dublin: O'Brien, 1980. 200p.

A biography of the founder of the newspaper the *Nation* and the Young Ireland movement, and a political figure who achieved fame a second time, in Australia by becoming a prime minister. Duffy died in 1903.

341 **The struggle for land in Ireland, 1800-1923.**
John Edwin Pomfret. New York: Russell & Russell, 1969. 334p.
A major cause of contention and conflict during ·the 19th century was the ownership of land following colonization, the forced acquisition and the later removal of tenants and the destruction of rural homes. Pomfret provides a vivid account of a most turbulent period. A shorter, more concentrated and scholarly work by Barbara Solow is *The land question and the Irish economy, 1870-1903* (Cambridge, Massachusetts: Harvard University Press, 1971. 247p.).

342 **Bishop Stock's 'narrative' of the year of the French: 1798.**
Bishop Joseph Stock, foreword by Michael Garvey, introduction by Grattan Freyer. Ballina, Ireland (Republic): Irish Humanities Centre, 1982. 144p.
Stock, an accomplished cleric, gives a vivid eye-witness account of the French landing at Killala in 1798, in support of the Irish rebels, at the urging of Napper Tandy and Wolfe Tone. The bishop's home served as headquarters for the insurgents. This is a reprint of the 2nd edition of 1809.

343 **The birth of modern Ireland.**
Mark Tierney. Dublin: Gill & Macmillan, 1969. 256p.
Tierney provides a competent review of the political and cultural forces of the 19th century that have contributed to the formation of the modern state. This illustrated volume has served as a textbook.

344 **Modern Ireland since 1850.**
Mark Tierney. Dublin: Gill & Macmillan, 1978. rev. ed. 241p.
A general introductory history, for use in the secondary school or at lower college level, covering post-famine Ireland of 1850 to 1870, the land question, home rule, the Ulster situation to 1969, nationalism, the Easter Rising, the Civil War, and Free State politics.

345 **Political violence in Ireland: government and resistance since 1848.**
Charles Townshend. London; Oxford: Oxford University Press, 1984. 400p.
Townshend examines the historical circumstances that have generated violence in Ireland from the famine days to the present and discusses the British response to it. He sees a relationship between the imposition of government authority through coercive legislation and armed force and the use of terror and intimidation by resistance groups, which he suggests has become a pattern from the 19th century onwards. Based on archival sources, this is suitable for advanced level or college readership.

346   **The penal laws, 1691-1760: church and state from the Treaty of
      Limerick to the accession of George III.**
      Maureen Wall.   Dundalk, Ireland (Republic): Dublin Historical
      Association, 1961. 72p.

A good review is given of the repressive legislation against Ireland's traditional
culture, religion and education that did so much to further divide society. Similar
coverage is given by R. Dudley Edwards in *Church and state in Tudor Ireland*
(q.v.), and by Thomas Bartlett and D. Hayton in *Penal era and golden age, essays
in Irish history, 1690-1800* (Belfast: Ulster Historical Foundation). Wall's account
is especially suited for class use.

347   **The great hunger: Ireland 1845-1849.**
      Cecil Woodham-Smith.   London: New English Library, 1977.
      429p. bibliog. Revised, New York: Dutton, 1980. 519p.

This classic account of the famine of the 1840s is a detailed, accurate and well-
researched study which covers all the contributory causes of the starvation and
disease, including governmental mismanagement. Different editions have
appeared from various publishers since 1962; the shorter paperback edition by the
New English Library does not include an extensive bibliography. Other standard
works on the famine are T. D. Williams' *The great famine* (New York: Russell &
Russell, 1976); and Robert Dudley Edwards and T. Desmond Williams' *The
great famine, studies in Irish history, 1845-52* (Dublin: Browne & Nowlan; New
York: New York University Press, 1976. 517p.). An excellent source for detailed
research are the eight volumes of British Parliamentary papers on the great
famine reprinted by the Irish Academic Press (Dublin) which provide unrivaled
source material. A catalogue of contents for these volumes is available.
Woodham-Smith's study is suitable for general adult reading; Edwards' is the
more scholarly. For popular reading a fine work is *Paddy's lament, Ireland 1846-
1847: prelude to hatred* (New York: Harcourt Brace, Jovanovich, 1982. 345p.).
This meticulously researched account (based on the oral history archives of the
Irish Folklore Department) gives an emotional, compelling and vivid story of
several fictional characters and the effects of famine, emigration and slum life in
New York. An extensive bibliography by Gallagher, is included.

George Berkeley

348   **Berkeley.**
      Harry M. Bracken.   New York: St. Martins Press, 1974. 173p.

A good and concise description of Berkeley's life, with a short biographical
survey, a chronological listing of his major works, and a review of his major
philosophical ideas.

349   **Berkeley.**
      A. Campbell Fraser.   London: Blackwood, 1884. 243p.

An older, venerable account reviewing Berkeley's philosophical thought, and
including some biographical material. Fraser provides information on Berkeley's

early years in Ireland, his boyhood, student days, and the later discovery of Berkeley's manuscripts. Other biographical works include J. Wild's *George Berkeley: a study of his life and philosophy* (1962. Reprint of 1936 ed.), and *Bishop Berkeley* by J. M. Hone and M. M. Rossi, with notes by William B. Yeats (1931).

350 **The development of Berkeley's philosophy.**
G. A. Johnston.   New York: Russell & Russell, 1965. Reprint of 1923 edition. 400p.

Reviews Berkeley's thought and philosophy concerning metaphysics, knowledge, ethics, religion and mathematics. The influences of Locke and Cartesianism are shown. An edition of *Berkeley's philosophical writings* has been compiled by D. M. Armstrong (1965), and Armstrong has also completed a commentary, *Berkeley's theory of vision* (1960).

351 **Bishop Berkeley's *Querist* in historical perspective.**
Joseph Johnston.   Dundalk, Irish Republic: Dundalgan Press, 1970. 220p.

An important discussion of Berkeley's response to rural Irish life as the newly created Bishop of Cloyne, in 1735. Berkeley wrote the *Querist* to help reconcile his observations on rural poverty and social problems with a more enlightened philosophical view of life. The work advocates a national currency and credit system based on an equitable distribution of income in a just society. A variety of editions of the *Querist* were published in Berkeley's lifetime up to 1752, each containing a long series of leading questions on banking, money, wealth, consumption, waste, labour, social justice and wise administration. The present edition is prefixed with essays supplied by Johnston on Ireland in the colonial system, the banking experience in Ireland during the 18th century, agricultural policies and rents, commercial expansion and Berkeley's idealistic philosophy. Most books on Berkeley's philosophy ignore this phase of his life.

352 **The life of George Berkeley.**
A. A. Luce. Westport, Connecticut; London: Greenwood Press, 1968. Reprint of 1949 edition. 260p.

Luce provides a definitive biography of Berkeley, who was born in Kilkenny in 1685, became Dean of Derry, and left a lasting impression on the major philosophical thinking of the next two centuries. A. A. Luce with T. E. Jessup has edited the standard edition of Berkeley's own works in 9 volumes (1948-1957). Other works by Luce include *Berkeley's immaterialism* (1945. Reprinted 1968), and the *Dialectic of immaterialism* (1963), both with competent accounts of Berkeley's philosophy.

353 **George Berkeley, a reappraisal.**
A. D. Ritchie.   Manchester, England: Manchester University Press; New York: Barnes & Noble, 1967. 189p.

A good review of Berkeley's *New theory of vision*, and his arguments for faith in God, clear reasoning, and morality in life and politics.

354 **Berkeley, the philosophy of immaterialism.**
I. C. Tipton. London: Methuen, 1974. 392p. bibliog.
Tipton reviews Berkeley's philosophical approach to knowledge and his psychological and innovative exploration of perception and its relationship to being. The role of common sense in Berkeley's thought is underscored.

355 **Berkeley.**
G. J. Warnock. Harmondsworth, England: Penguin, 1969. 250p.
Warnock reviews Berkeley's major essays and his theories on language, the material world, perception, existence, science and mathematics.

Edmund Burke

356 **The philosophy of Edmund Burke.**
Edited by Louis Bredvold, Ralph Ross. Ann Arbor, Michigan: University of Michigan Press, 1960. 276p.
A good analysis of Burke's philosophy on law, legislation, the state and society, human nature, colonial policies, politics, gradual reform and the importance of tradition. The standard edition of Burke's best known work, *Reflections on the revolution in France* has been edited by Conor Cruise O'Brien (Harmondsworth, England: Penguin, 1960. 400p.).

357 **Edmund Burke, the practical imagination.**
Gerald Chapman. Cambridge, Massachusetts: Harvard University Press, 1967. 350p. bibliog.
Chapman provides a general review of Burke's positions on constitutional reform, the French Revolution, and Britain's colonial policies in India, America, and Ireland. Burke's cautionary and prudent approach is shown in issues confronting trade policies, taxation and economics. Special mention is made of Burke's involvement with Ireland (p. 68-115), and a list of major events in Burke's life is included.

358 **Edmund Burke.**
George Fasel. Boston, Massachusetts: Twayne, 1983. 151p.
(Twayne's English Authors Series).
Fasel describes Burke through his writings, first as the political outsider, and then as the conscience of constitutional ways, and supporter of humanism, consistency and conservatism. Burke's moral voice is shown in his role as leader of a crusade against revolution. For a review of Burke's writing style see Christopher Reid's *Edmund Burke and the practice of political writing* (Dublin: Gill & Macmillan; New York: St. Matin's Press, 1985. 238p.).

359   **Edmund Burke.**
Edited by Isaac Kramnick.   Englewood Cliffs, New Jersey:
Prentice-Hall, 1974. 180p. (Great Lives Observed Series).
A short but useful study of Burke's parliamentary career and the main strands of
his political philosophy, his response to radicalism and his view of the world.
Kramnick also discusses how Burke was viewed by his contemporaries, his
position in history, and his standing as evaluated by modern writers, ranging from
conservative to Marxist. Many excerpts from Burke's writings are included.
Kramnick has also written a useful biography, *The rage of Edmund Burke:
portrait of an ambivalent conservative* (New York: Basic Books, 1977. 225p.). This
includes a psychological interpretation of Burke as the prophet of conservation. A
brief review is given of Burke's Irish youth, from 1729 to 1749.

360   **The political philosophy of Edmund Burke.**
John MacCunn.   London: Edward Arnold, 1913. 272p.
A valuable review of Burke's principles, his conservatism, opposition to radical
reform, and his general toleration and preference for the tested wisdom of the
past. Contrasting views of Burke can be found in the left-wing interpretation by
C. B. Macpherson, *Burke* (New York: Hill & Wang, 1980. 83p.). Macpherson
gives a revisionist view of Burke as an adventurer, politician, and bourgeois
political economist. A more even evaluation is given by Francis Canavan in *The
political reason of Edmund Burke* (Durham, North Carolina: University of North
Carolina Press, 1960. 222p.). Canavan, like MacCunn, stresses some of the key
elements of Burke's thought: political and social order, legitimacy and sound
reasoning as basic foundations of society.

361   **Edmund Burke, a life.**
Philip Magnus.   New York: Russell & Russell, 1939. 367p.
Magnus provides a thorough, detailed look at Burke, the 'Irish patriot'. Attention
is focused on Burke's youth, public and private life, the cause of American
independence, his views on India, the impeachment of Hastings, the French
Revolution, and the major issues confronting Ireland (p. 260-85). An appendix
provides further information on Burke's family and personal life.

362   **Edmund Burke and Ireland.**
Thomas H. Mahoney.   Cambridge, Massachusetts: Harvard
University Press, 1960. 413p. bibliog.
Mahoney gives some emphasis to Burke's early days and activities in Ireland, a
part of his life which is often overlooked. He also covers Burke's parliamentary
career, his opposition to Pitt on Irish free trade, and Burke's position on Catholic
emancipation. This book provides a good retrospective evaluation of Burke's
political career, rather than his private life. An appendix contains a useful
summary of the penal laws, and Catholic relief legislation.

363 **Edmund Burke, a historical study.**
John Morley.   New York: AMS, 1968. Reprint of 1867 edition.
216p.

This short biography provides a somewhat dated view of Burke's years in
Parliament, and his positions on economic reform and British politics. The book
ends with comments on Burke's visits to Ireland, his last years and his literary
character. Morley's earlier view of Burke can be balanced by the more recent
work by Alice P. Miller, *Edmund Burke and his world* (Greenwich, Connecticut:
Devin-Adair, 1979. 232p.). Miller gives a popular account of the great range of
Burke's activity and philosophical thought, and his contributions to the cause of
freedom.

364 **Edmund Burke, his political philosophy.**
Frank O'Gorman.   Bloomington, Indiana; London: Indiana
University Press, 1973. 153p.

A broad, convenient review of Burke's outlook on the British constitution,
Parliament, political parties, and imperialism (in Ireland, India, and America).
Underscored are Burke's preferences for conciliation, moderation, property
rights, and electoral change.

365 **Memoir of the life and character of the Right Honorable Edmund
Burke.**
James Prior.   New York: Burt Franklin, 1968. Reprint of 1854
edition. 2 vols.

Prior presents a biography of Burke's personal life and Parliamentary office. This
detailed account was written in 1837 and the language is somewhat cumbersome.
Prior does, however, provide numerous excerpts from Burke's writings and
letters, and he discusses Burke's visits to Ireland.

Nationalism

366 **Nationalism in Ireland.**
David George Boyce.   Dublin: Gill & Macmillan; London:
Croom Helm; Baltimore, Maryland: Johns Hopkins, 1982. 441p.
bibliog.

Using a wide range of sources Boyce traces the roots of Irish nationalism from
Tudor and even earlier times, although concentrating particularly on the last two
centuries. He explains that a nationalist ideology has so far failed to achieve its
goal of unifying all creeds and classes into a single state because of an ingrained
sectarian outlook. The volume suggests that nationalism draws upon certain
unstable elements, such as regionalism and religious antagonism, and is
reaffirmed by popular culture and literature. An extensive bibliography covers
nationalism into the 20th century. Suitable for college level reading and
recommended for all collections of Irish history.

367   **Irish nationalism: a history of its roots and ideology.**
Sean Cronin.   New York: Continuum; Dublin: Academy Press,
1981. 391p.
An important study of political theory and partisan politics in modern Ireland.
Cronin traces the roots of a nationalist movement through the centuries but
especially from Wolfe Tone in 1791 to the Easter Rising. He observes the chief
facets of the nationalist ideology: traditionalism (Gaelic and Catholic): consti-
tutionalism; culture; force; radicalism; and republicanism. The account explores
the problems of Northern Ireland which the author expects will continue as long
as the nationalist movement stimulates conflict by excluding major segments of
society, especially the Protestants of the North. A stimulating review, based on
numerous interviews and reports and containing an extensive bibliography. Many
will not subscribe to Cronin's solution to the Irish problem, namely that of a
united, socialist republic, but his background analysis is thorough and should be
made available to any upper level college student with an interest in modern
Ireland.

368   **Faith of our fathers, the formation of Irish nationalist ideology,
1890-1920.**
Maurice Goldring.   Dublin: Repsol, 1982. [not paginated].
A passionate look at the formation and effects of Irish nationalism is made by the
Frenchman. Goldring uses as examples (and stereotypes) rural priests and urban
intellectuals. He criticizes rural traditions and the pattern of political violence
from a Marxist perspective.

369   **Conflict of nationality in modern Ireland.**
A. C. Hepburn.   London: Edward Arnold; New York:
St. Martin's, 1980. 221p. (Documents of Modern History).
The text of collected documents is presented to illustrate the course of nationalist
sentiment. Sources include official papers of both the Irish and British
governments, newspapers, ephemera and speeches. The documents date from the
19th century to 1979, and cover the Home Rule Bill, United Irishmen and Young
Ireland movements, the Easter Rising, and the Civil War. This is a useful
supplement to readings on the conflict between Northern Ireland and the Irish
Republic.

370   **Irish culture and nationalism, 1750-1950.**
Oliver MacDonagh, W. F. Mandle, P. Travers.   New York:
St. Martin's, 1983. 289p.
Collected essays on narrow topics provide supplementary material on the growth
of Irish nationalism. Topics include Burke, the 18th-century church, 19th-century
recreation, myths in literature, the Anglo-Irish and historians during the period
1830 to 1980. The typescript is poor.

20th century

371 **Guerilla days in Ireland.**
Tom Barry.   Dublin: Anvil, 1981. 254p. maps.
The famous leader of one of Ireland's guerilla units provides a first-hand account of the independence struggle, the Black and Tans, and the attacks on regular military units. Published in various editions, this is an expanded version with maps and appendixes. An exciting and a one-sided approach by an active participant, this account gives a picture of a 'liberation struggle' from the inside. A companion story from the same side and period is that of Dan Breen, who in *My fight for Irish freedom* gives a more exuberant and personal account of the Irish Republican Army (IRA), and its struggle during the 1917-1921 war. (Dublin: Anvil Books, 1981. 192p.). Barry's *Guerilla days*, has become a classic in military academies with its description of tactics and innovations. His life as a prominent insurgent is told by Meda Ryan in *The Tom Barry story* (Cork: Mercier, 1982).

372 **The secret army, the IRA, 1916-1979.**
J. Bowyer Bell.   London: Sphere, 1962. Reprinted, Cambridge, Massachusetts: MIT Press, 1980. 478p. bibliog.
One of the most thorough histories of the Irish Republican Army, this study looks back to its early roots in the republicanism of Wolfe Tone in the 18th century. The work goes on to trace the development of an ideology in the revolution and Civil War of 1916-1921, and studies the later campaigns, factions and new tactics into the 1970s. Through hundreds of interviews Bell provides a detailed review of modern Irish politics and the long guerilla conflict.

373 **The Black and Tans.**
Richard Bennet.   London: Hulton; Boston, Massachusetts: Houghton Mifflin, 1960. 228p.
A popular account of the violent and ultimately disastrous fighting and the sufferings of the Irish at the hands of the British troops, the Black and Tans, prior to the treaty of 1921, granting Dominion status to Catholic Ireland.

374 **Sean Lemass and the making of modern Ireland 1945-66.**
Paul Bew, Henry Patterson.   Dublin: Gill & Macmillan, 1980. 224p.
A study of government policy in Ireland. Lemass was a government minister who succeeded Eamon de Valera as *taoiseach* (prime minister) in 1959, continuing his programmes and adjusting them to changing conditions. The study details national economic planning and industrial change up to 1966. A contrasting view of Lemass as the 'architect of modern Ireland' rather than the implementer of de Valera's policies is given in Brian Farrell's biography *Sean Lemass* (Dublin: Gill & Macmillan, 1983. 164p.), in the Irish Lives Series.

375 **The war in Clare, 1911-1921.**
Michael Brennan. Dublin: Irish Academic Press, 1980. 112p.
This memoir by a one-time leader of the Irish Volunteers provides a vivid, personal account of the war of independence. Brennan describes joining the Irish Republican Brotherhood at age fifteen, the military training and tactics of the IRB, the Easter Rising, and his imprisonment. He later became chief of staff of the Irish Army, from 1931 to 1939.

376 **Ireland: a social and cultural history, 1922 to 1979.**
Terence Brown. London: Fontana; Ithaca, New York: Cornell University Press, 1985. Rev. ed. 368p.
A discussion of Irish society, literature, art and culture since the founding of the Irish Republic, up to 1979.

377 **Lucky eyes and a high heart: the life of Maud Gonne.**
Nancy Cardozo. Indianapolis, Indiana: Bobbs-Merrill; London: Gollancz, 1979. 489p.
An admiring, skillfully written and detailed life of the revolutionary leader, patriot and nationalist, Maud Gonne McBride. This is the best biography of her available, although a useful shorter account is provided by Eibhlin Ni Eireamhon in *Two great Irish women: Maud Gonne McBride and Constance Markievicz* (Dublin: Fallon, 1972).

378 **American opinion and the Irish question, 1910-1923: a study in opinion and policy.**
Francis M. Carroll. Dublin: Gill & Macmillan; New York: St. Martin's, 1978. 319p.
A thorough study of the relationship between Irish-American opinion and the nationalist movement in Ireland. It outlines the range of interest, support and hostility shown towards Ireland by different segments of the American population. Drawing on a wide range of sources, the author documents the importance of particular leaders, their competing influence, and their following in both countries. He also considers public attitudes towards home rule and independence. A useful analysis is provided of President Wilson's avoidance of Irish issues.

379 **The Easter rebellion.**
Malachy Francis Caulfield. London: Muller; New York: Holt, Rinehart & Winston, 1963. Reprinted, Westport, Connecticut: Greenwood, 1975. 375p.
In a journalistic style, the author outlines the progress of the rebellion and its shifting fortunes, step by step.

380 **Agony at Easter; the 1916 Irish uprising.**
Thomas Coffey. New York: Macmillan, 1969. 271p. maps.
A vivid portrait of Dublin during the uprising with much detail and local information.

381 **The I.R.A.**
Timothy Patrick Coogan. London: Pall Mall Press; New York: Praeger, 1970. Reprinted, London: Fontana, 1971. 2nd rev. ed. 446p.
This edition brings the history of the IRA up to 1970, and provides a fairly detached assessment of Irish motivation. The study is valuable for its understanding of the origin of one of the major influences in Irish politics, but needs updating for the post-1970 period of organizational splinter groups and continued violence. For general readership.

382 **Ireland since the rising.**
Timothy Patrick Coogan. London: Pall Mall; New York: Praeger; Westport, Connecticut: Greenwood, 1976. 355p.
Coogan, a journalist and newspaper editor provides a sound review of Irish political solutions from the formation of the Irish Republic to the 1960s. The emphasis is on the domestic politics of Éire, the Northern Ireland issue, de Valera, and the continued development of Irish society and culture.

383 **Damned Englishman; a study of Erskine Childers (1870-1922).**
Thomas Cox. Hicksville, New York: Exposition Press, 1975. 374p.
A penetrating study of this complex figure, who was a soldier, author, clerk of the House of Commons, secretary in the 1921 treaty negotiations, and revolutionary. Includes discussion of the 1921 treaty and the resultant civil war, which led to Childers' execution. Two other biographies are by Andrew Boyle, *The riddle of Erskine Childers* (London: Hutchinson, 1978. 351p.) and Burke Wilkinson, *The zeal of the convert* (Gerrards Cross, England: Colin Smythe, 1978. 317p.).

384 **The birth of the Irish Free State, 1921-1923.**
Joseph M. Curran. University, Alabama: University of Alabama Press, 1980. 356p.
A solid, nonpartisan account of the origin of the Irish Free State, formed in January 1922. Immediately after its foundation, civil war broke out between its supporters and those who refused to accept the partition of Ireland and the retention of any ties with Britain. Curran presents a balanced discussion of political roles and partisan activity in the 1920s, a period which did much to shape the future government of Ireland. This work partially replaces another valuable study by N. Mansergh, *The Irish Free State, its government and politics* (1934). Also on the Free State, Donald O'Sullivan focuses on the period 1922 to 1939 and more particularly on the senate of which he was the clerk, in *The Irish Free State and its senate, a study of contemporary politics* (London: Faber & Faber, 1940. Reprinted, New York: Arno, 1972. 666p.).

385 **The damnable question: a study in Anglo-Irish relations.**
George Dangerfield.   Boston, Massachusetts: Little, Brown, 1976.
400p. bibliog.
A thorough review of British policy and Irish affairs in the early 1900s, leading to
rebellion, cooperation in the First World War, and protracted, difficult
negotiations afterwards.

386 **Arthur Griffith and non-violent Sinn Fein.**
Richard Davis.   Dublin; Tralee, Ireland (Republic): Anvil Books,
1974. 232p.
A biography of Griffith, political leader, advocate of passive resistance and self-
reliance, and first president of the Irish Free State. The study charts the debates
within Sinn Fein between violent and non-violent philosophies and shows
Griffith's influence throughout. A shorter study of Griffith by Calton Younger is
Arthur Griffith (Dublin: Gill & Macmillan, 1981. 160p.), in the Irish Lives Series.

387 **Irish neutrality and the U.S.A., 1939-47.**
T. Ryle Dwyer.   Dublin: Gill & Macmillan, 1977. 254p.
Heavily documented with a wide range of archival sources, this work examines
Irish-US interrelationships and frictions during the Second World War, Éire's
position of neutrality, American clashes with de Valera, and the correspondence
between Ambassador Grey and Roosevelt.

388 **Independent Ireland.**
Ronan Fanning.   Dublin: Educational Company of Ireland;
Dover, New Hampshire: Longwood, 1984. 23p. (Helicon History
of Ireland, no. 9).
This clearly written account traces the forces shaping the emergence of
contemporary Ireland, from the formation of the Irish Free State in 1922 to the
present time. Attention is focused on successive governments, political change,
and the relations between the two Irelands. Appropriate as a college text.

389 **Politics and Irish life, 1913-1921, provincial experience of war and
revolution.**
David Fitzpatrick.   Dublin: Gill & Macmillan; Atlantic
Highlands, New Jersey: Humanities, 1979. 394p.
An excellent study of rural conditions prior to and during the revolution, and the
warfare leading to independence. Considerable use is made of a wide range of
contemporary documents.

390 **The life of John Redmond.**
Denis Rolleston Gwynn.   New York: Arno Press, 1977. 610p.
A full biography of this political leader who advocated the cautious road of
constitutional reform in gaining independence for Ireland. Many excerpts from
the Redmond papers are provided.

391   **The evolution of Sinn Fein.**
Robert Mitchell Henry.   New York: Arno, 1977. 284p.

A number of accounts of Sinn Fein have appeared, most of them issued during or immediately after the war of independence. Henry's study, originally published in 1920, provides a first-hand look at the organization by a scholar. Other works on Sinn Fein include Patrick Sarsfield O'Hegarty's *The victory of Sinn Fein* (Dublin: Talbot, 1925); Aodh De Blácam's *What the Sinh Fein stands for* (Dublin: Melifont Press, 1921); and Francis Jones' *History of the Sinn Fein movement and the Irish rebellion of 1916* (New York: Kenedy & Sons, 1920. 447p.).

392   **Protest in arms; the Irish troubles, 1916-1923.**
Edgar Holt.   London: Putnam; New York: Coward-McCann, 1961. 328p.

A detached account of the struggle for independence up to the end of the Civil War. The author provides much detail in this unemotional, balanced approach to the subject.

393   **The Irish Civil War.**
Michael Hopkinson.   Dublin: Gill & Macmillan, 1985. 220p.

The Irish Civil War of 1919-1921 is analysed with regard to its many causes and factions, and its repercussions in recent Irish history.

394   **The partition of Ireland, 1911-1925.**
Michael Laffan.   Dublin Historical Association, 1983. 138p.

A useful textbook intended for upper-secondary or college level, providing a concise view of the political conflicts surrounding the origin of the Irish Free State.

395   **James Larkin, Irish labour leader, 1876-1947.**
Emmet Larkin.   London: Routledge & Kegan Paul, 1965. 334p.

An excellent study of organized labour activity in Ireland is provided in this biography. James Larkin was a leader of the Belfast disputes of 1907 and the Dublin lock-out of 1913, and subsequently organized trade union activity in America and Ireland in the following decades.

396   **Britain and Ireland, 1914-23.**
Sheila Lawlor.   Dublin: Gill & Macmillan; Totowa, New Jersey: Barnes & Noble, 1983. 291p.

An examination of British internal politics and their effect on events in Ireland, especially the rise of Lloyd George, the exercise of authority in Ireland prior to independence, and the Treaty negotiations. Extensive use is made of private diaries, papers, official documents and other contemporary accounts. For advanced students. For the following two decades Professor Paul Canning provides a scholarly review in *British policy towards Ireland: 1921 to 1941* (Oxford: Clarendon Press, 1985), a crucial period covering the beginning of the Second World War, Éire's emerging position of neutrality, and a foreign policy strongly divergent from that of the United Kingdom.

397 **Ireland 1945-1970.**
Edited by J. J. Lee. Dublin: Gill & Macmillan; New York:
Barnes & Noble, 1979. 184p. (Thomas Davis Lectures).
Essays by various authorities describe a changing Ireland, with particular regard
to its way of life, and to politics, economics, education, culture, religion, media,
environment, social conditions and history. A wide-ranging and important study,
it shows Ireland as a dynamic society.

398 **The Irish uprising, 1916-1922.**
Goddard Lieberson. New York: Macmillan, 1966. 164p. (CBS
Legacy Collection Series).
For popular reading, this photographic essay on the Easter Rising includes
antique views of Dublin, passages from the works of Padraic Pearse, James
Connolly, and Benedict Kiely, and an introduction by Eamon de Valera. A vivid
portrayal is given of the violence and revolt.

399 **Culture and anarchy in Ireland, 1890-1939.**
Francis Stewart L. Lyons. Oxford; New York: Oxford University
Press, 1979. 184p.
Four conflicting cultures are seen in modern Ireland, both in the North and in the
Republic: the English, Irish, Scots-Irish, and Anglo-Irish. Within a narrow time
frame, Lyons scrutinizes the interplay between these groups and the divisions that
occurred at the end of the First World War, with lasting effects on the culture of
each.

400 **The Irish Republic: a documented chronicle of the Anglo-Irish
conflict and the partitioning of Ireland.**
Dorothy MacCardle. New York: Farrar, Straus & Giroux, 1965.
Reprinted, London: Corgi Books, 1968. 4th ed. 989p. bibliog.
An exceptionally detailed account of the steps leading to revolution, the
independence struggle and the civil war that followed. Based on extensive source
material.

401 **British policy and the Irish administration, 1920-22.**
John McColgan. London: Allen & Unwin, 1983. 178p.
In discussing the transfer of power to Ireland following independence, the author
examines the features that were carried over from the past: government
organization, public employees and civil servants and the policies towards
Northern Ireland that proved so divisive.

402 **Ireland: the union and its aftermath.**
Oliver MacDonagh. London: Allen & Unwin, 1977. 176p.
For more advanced students of Irish history, this volume reviews the development
of the Irish government, the economy and political movements. There is some
emphasis on Anglo-Irish relations since the turn of the century and on Northern
Ireland.

403 **Changing times: Ireland since 1898.**
Edward MacLysaght.   Gerrards Cross, England: Colin Smythe;
Atlantic Highlands, New Jersey: Humanities, 1978. 248p.

An Irish historian views the changing politics and culture of the country during and since the struggle for independence.

404 **The years of the great test, 1926-1939.**
Edited by Francis MacManus.   Cork: Mercier, 1967. 184p.
(Thomas Davies Lectures).

Twelve authors contributed papers for a radio series, which cover the period immediately following the creation of the Irish Free State and study the issues that faced it in government, education, foreign policy and domestic politics. A competent review is given of Ireland in the inter-war period, during which the governmental structures and political parties developed and matured. The Second World War period is covered by Joseph Carroll in *Ireland in the war years* (New York: Crane, Russak; Newton Abbot, England: David & Charles, 1975. 190p.).

405 **The Irish question, 1840-1921.**
Nicholas Mansergh.   London: Allen & Unwin; Toronto:
University of Toronto Press, 1965. 316p.

Provides a commentary on Anglo-Irish relations from the years of the famine, covering the gradual social reform, eventual revolution and independence. A competent and balanced history.

406 **The Irish Volunteers, 1913-1915.**
Edited by Francis X. Martin.   Dublin: James Duffy, 1963. 228p.

A collection of reminiscences about the founding members of the Irish Volunteers just prior to the Easter rebellion.

407 **Leaders and men of the Easter Rising: Dublin 1916.**
Francis X. Martin.   London: Methuen; Ithaca, New York:
Cornell University Press, 1967. 276p.

This balanced account explores the motivations and attitudes held by both Unionists and Nationalists during the rebellion.

408 **The scholar revolutionary: Eoin MacNeill, 1867-1945, and the making of a new Ireland.**
Edited by Francis X. Martin, F. J. Byrne.   Shannon, Ireland
(Republic): Irish University Press, 1973. 429p.

Fifteen papers are presented, including three which have been reprinted from the writings of MacNeill, on Gaelic language, culture, and the political movement to reestablish an Irish identity. These were encouraged by MacNeill, who also helped reform Irish historiography. He was one of the organizers of the Gaelic League and the Irish Volunteers.

409   **Irish political documents, 1916-1949.**
      Edited by Arthur Mitchell, P. Ó Snodaigh.   Dublin: Irish
      Academic Press, 1985. 254p.

A collection of 146 documents, which are either significant *per se*, or which shed light on political developments. Both Republican and Unionist views are represented.

410   **The Irish Civil War, an illustrated history.**
      George Morrison.   Dublin: Gill & Macmillan, 1981. 142p.

The Civil War commencing in 1922 used to be spoken of very seldom. Through an extensive photographic record and vivid period illustrations this volume dramatically records that tragic era.

411   **Ireland in the twentieth century.**
      John A. Murphy.   Dublin: Gill & Macmillan, 1975. 160p. (Gill
      History of Ireland Series).

A brief review of Ireland since 1918, covering the struggle for independence, the creation of the modern state and later political development up to 1974. This college textbook provides a valuable, balanced, historical account.

412   **The making of 1916; studies in the history of the rising.**
      Edited by Kevin B. Nowlan.   Dublin: Stationery Office, 1969.
      338p.

Various authors explore the causes of unrest and dissatisfaction that led to the Easter Rising and also comment on the Gaelic movement, nationalism, Sinn Fein, Unionism, and other aspects. The volume is good on the background to the rebellion. Nowlan has also completed a study on Ireland in the 1840s in the *Politics of repeal* (Toronto: University of Toronto Press, 1975. 248p.). For a vivid account of the 1916 rising see *The insurrection in Dublin* (q.v.).

413   **Ireland in the war years and after, 1939-51.**
      Edited by Keven B. Nowlan, T. Desmond Williams.   Dublin: Gill
      & Macmillan; Notre Dame, Indiana: University of Notre Dame
      Press, 1970. 219p.

This collection of essays reviews various aspects of Irish society during and after the Second World War, including industry and labour, church and state, foreign policy, economic conditions, government, politics, education and Northern Ireland. The volume extends into an analysis of the postwar readjustment until 1951, and includes a chapter on the 'changing pattern of Irish society' by General Quinn.

414   **The chief secretary: Augustine Burrell in Ireland.**
      Leon O Broin.   London: Chatto & Windus; Hamden,
      Connecticut: Archon; Toronto: Clarke, Irwin, 1969. 232p.

Covering the period 1907 to 1916, this biography of the chief secretary is useful for providing an understanding of government policy at the time. See also Leon

O'Broin's *Dublin Castle and the 1916 rising* (New York: New York University Press, 1971).

415 **The times I've seen: Oliver St. John Gogarty, a biography.**
Ulick O'Connor. New York: Obolensky, 1963. 365p.

A picture of life in Dublin during the early 20th century is presented in this biography of Gogarty, a literary figure, surgeon and one-time activist. An entertaining account for general readership.

416 **A terrible beauty is born: Irish troubles 1912-1922.**
Ulick O'Connor. London: Granada, 1981. 192p.

A popular history of 1916, the war of independence and its aftermath, for general readership.

417 **Insurrection fires at Eastertide.**
Compiled by M. O'Dubhghaill. Cork: Mercier, 1966. 337p.

This anthology combines a variety of first hand reports and memoirs to create a vivid picture of the Easter Rising drawn from contemporary sources.

418 **The Sean Mac Eoin story.**
Padraic O'Farrell. Cork: Mercier, 1981. 182p.

This short, clearly written biography studies the contrasts of a man who in the guerilla days was the figure most wanted by the police. Mac Eoin rose to be chief of staff of the Irish Army at its foundation, eventually becoming an active politician noted for his gentleness and humanity.

419 **On another man's wound.**
Ernie O'Malley. Dublin: Anvil, 1979. 343p.

An exceptionally well-written account of the guerilla struggles after 1916, as seen by a participant. O'Malley provides a sensitive narrative of the struggle, daily life in rural areas and wartime events. The account ends in 1921, and is resumed in *The singing flame* (q.v.). O'Malley has also written about his personal experiences in offensive actions during 1920 and 1921, in *Raids and rallies* (Dublin: Anvil, 1983. 209p.).

420 **The singing flame.**
Ernie O'Malley. Dublin: Anvil Books, 1978. 312p.

An exciting account of military activity in the republican cause covering the civil war period of 1921-1924, during which O'Malley served as a leader of the Republican forces.

421 **The origins of Irish neutrality in World War II, 1932-1938.**
Paul Francis O'Malley. Ann Arbor, Michigan: University Microfilms, 1980. 659p. (Dissertation no. 8024209).

This dissertation, completed for Boston University, provides a detailed review of the foreign policy of de Valera, the Irish government at the beginning of the

Second World War, earlier, unpromising results under the League of Nations, Britain's relinquishing of its control over Irish ports in 1938, concessions to Northern Ireland, and Éire's gradual shift into a neutral position.

422   **Where mountainy men have sown.**
Michael O'Sulleabhain.   Dublin: Anvil, 1965. 186p.
Vivid recollections of the warfare during 1916 to 1921 in rural areas of Cork, and in the open countryside of mountains and passes by one who fought there as a youth. For popular reading.

423   **Peace by ordeal.**
Frank Pakenham (Earl of Longford).   London: Sidgwick & Jackson, 1972. Rev. ed. 318p.
An account is given of the complex negotiations, the difficult circumstances of the Irish participants, and the signing of the Anglo-Irish Treaty of 1921. First-hand sources are included.

424   **The insurrection in Dublin.**
James Stephens.   Gerrards Cross, England: Colin Smythe; Atlantic Highlands, New Jersey: Humanities, 1978. 116p.
A lively, eye-witness account of the Easter Rising, by a prominent writer.

425   **The imagination of an insurrection: Dublin, Easter 1916, a study of an ideological movement.**
William I. Thompson.   London: Oxford University Press; New York: Harper & Row, 1967. Reprinted, Dublin: O'Brien Press, 1982. 262p.
A useful study of the underlying causes of the rebellion, and especially of the contributions that Irish culture and nationalist sentiment made to the political movement. For the serious reader.

426   **Eoin MacNeill, scholar and man of action, 1867-1945.**
Michael Tierney, edited by F. X. Martin.   Oxford: Clarendon Press, 1980. 409p. bibliog.
This substantial biography paints a favourable picture of MacNeill, pioneer scholar, academic, political leader, founder of the Gaelic League and leader of the Irish Volunteers. The study covers the IRB, MacNeill's role in the Easter Rising, the birth pangs of the Irish Free State, the Boundary Commission and the Northern Ireland problem. This is a useful, thorough account of the period and one of its leading figures. The author was the son-in-law of MacNeill. The volume was completed after Tierney's death by Martin. Much of the work is based on MacNeill's own memoir which is as yet unpublished. Unfortunately Tierney's presentation has been criticised for its one-sidedness. For another account of MacNeill see *The scholar revolutionary: Eoin MacNeill, 1867-1945, and the making of a new Ireland* (q.v.).

427 **The best of decades, Ireland in the 1960's.**
Fergal Tobin. Dublin: Gill & Macmillan, 1984. 246p.

A portrait of a nation reaching maturity, during a decade of optimism, relative
political quiet, prosperity, advances in mass communication, and new international roles. In the following decades some of these positive aspects were
unfortunately to be moderated.

428 **The British campaign in Ireland, 1919-1921; the development of
political and military policies.**
Charles Townshend. Oxford; New York: Oxford University
Press, 1975. 256p.

An important, serious and scholarly study of the political background and military
actions taken by the British government during the war of independence.

429 **Constance de Markievicz: in the cause of Ireland.**
Jacquelin Van Voris. Amherst, Massachusetts: University of
Massachusetts, 1967. 384p.

Several biographies of the countess, an influential figure in the 1916 Rising, have
been written: see Sean O'Faolain's *Constance Markievicz, or the average
revolutionary* (London: Cape, 1934. 321p.); Anne Marreco's *The rebel countess*
(London: Corgi, 1969. 320p.); and Eibhlin Ni Eireamhon's *Two great Irishwomen:
Maud Gonne MacBride and Constance Markievicz* (Dublin: Fallon, 1972). The
best of these is by Voris who emphasises the important years of 1904 to 1927,
including political events throughout the Civil War period.

430 **Ireland's Civil War.**
Carlton Younger. London: Fontana, 1979. 542p.

A solid study of the Civil War, drawing upon first hand sources, the official papers
of the British cabinet, and recollections of participants.

The Northern Ireland question

431 **De Valera and the Ulster question, 1917-1973.**
John Bowman. London, New York: Oxford University Press,
1983. 369p.

Bowman provides a new perspective on the policies of de Valera towards
Northern Ireland. He suggests that de Valera's primary aim of a neutral and Gaelic
Ireland thwarted his secondary objective of a unified Ireland. According to the
author any future solution for a divided Ireland will have to consider positions
originally established by de Valera. The book contains an excellent analysis of the
evolution of the Republic's policies toward the North during a crucial period. De
Valera is portrayed as more conciliatory and moderate than is usually
acknowledged. Any hope for a thorough and rational compromise on the North
was upset by the war years, and de Valera's approach to Ulster is now held by
Bowman to be contradictory and eventually a failure. Bowman faults de Valera

for having a too restricted view of a unified Ireland that excluded the Northerners he hoped to induce to join. New archival sources are included.

432 **Ireland: a positive proposal.**
Kevin Boyle, Tom Hadden. Harmondsworth, Middlesex, England: Penguin, 1985. 127p.

The authors accept as their premise the legitimacy of Northern Ireland as a separate state, due to the existence of a divided population at the time of its origin. The book strongly endorses the new Anglo-Irish accords of 1985, and advocates changes in the Irish constitution to facilitate future unity. The authors scrutinize all the proposals that have been made to date for peace in Northern Ireland, and they fault the wide variety of arrangements and compromises made in the past. They also offer their own suggestions for a change in the legal status of Northern Ireland, for new economic cooperation between the two states, and for constitutional changes in the Republic. There is a good discussion of the relative merits of all proposed solutions, but the author's own solutions to strife may not have any more likelihood of success. Boyd and Hadden aim towards objectivity. This book can be contrasted with *Ireland after Britain*, edited by Martin Collins (London: Pluto; Dover, New Hampshire: Longwood, 1985. 173p.). In the Collins volume sixteen essays evaluate the prospects and fears associated with British withdrawal from Ireland. Collins urges immediate withdrawal and an unlikely rapprochement between the republicanism of Sinn Fein, and the Labour Party in Britain. A similar stance is taken by Geoffrey Bell in his book *The British in Ireland, a suitable case for withdrawal* (London: Pluto Press, 1983. 120p.). Bell argues for an immediate withdrawal and a socialist future in a unified country, while Boyle and Hadden avoid insisting on a philosophical reorientation of the majority of the population.

433 **The Forum issue.**
Edited by Mark Patrick Hederman, Richard Kearney. *Crane Bag*, vol. 7, no. 2 (1983). Special issue.

Some thirty essays review elements of Irish culture in the context of a future unified society. Both divisive and unifying aspects are noted in Irish education, religion, the arts and psychology. The authors speculate on how the ancient beliefs and preoccupations of the majority can be adapted and modified for the creation of a new Irish society. An earlier issue of *Crane Bag* (vol. 4, no. 2 1980) was devoted to Northern Ireland, and contained articles on casualties between 1960 and 1980, the structure of Unionism, and special warfare in the province.

434 **Northern Ireland: the background to the conflict.**
Edited by John Darby. Belfast: Appletree; New York: Syracuse University Press, 1983. 272p. bibliog.

This collection examines community relations in Northern Ireland and the effects of strife. Chapters by nine authors urge attitudinal adaptation on both sides, in order to ease conflict. Each paper considers a different aspect of the Northern Ireland problem, and attention is given to economic and social inequality, police procedures, an oppressive judicial system, social organization and psychology, the demography of violence, and the reemergence of the IRA. A more detailed look is given at those areas where accommodation has occurred. The authors deplore Catholic intransigence that favours a separate identity. The book concentrates on experiences since 1970 and provides a good review of some of the major concerns of a divided society. A twenty-four page bibliography is included. For more historical background see George Dangerfield's *The damnable question, a study of Anglo-Irish relations* (q.v.). Dangerfield provides excellent coverage for the century and a half following 1800, with much on British-Irish relations. Although the Easter Rising is central, the author continues the account to more recent turbulence. The Darby volume provides a deeper analysis of the varied outlooks within the communities of Northern Ireland however. These ten essays give the general impression that the Republic should not be involved in the search for a solution to the question of Northern Ireland. They stress the need to find any permanent answers within Northern Ireland itself, rather than in Dublin or London.

435   **Them and us, Britain, Ireland and the Northern question, 1969-1982.**
James Downey.   Dublin: Ward River Press, 1983. 258p.

Downey, a columnist for the *Irish Times*, offers a personal perspective on Northern Ireland in which he urges both Britain and Ireland to reevaluate their positions. A very brief historical survey is given of the Ulster question from the 18th century. For the current situation Downey provides short biographical portraits of the leading participants. Considerable attention is given to the period after 1960 and the relations between England and Ireland. The Sunningdale Agreement is explored as is the collapse of power sharing in the North which brought to an abrupt end a brief hope of compromise. Downey utilizes the trained eye of a reporter, providing details and anecdotes. He offers no clear conclusions for the future, however.

436   **Conflict in Northern Ireland.**
D. P. Doumitt.   New York, Bern: P. Lang, 1985. 247p.
(American University Studies, series 9. History, no. 5).

Doumitt traces the history of Northern Ireland from Tudor times, through centuries of injustice, repression and domination. The author strives to understand the origin of prejudices and he urges reforms in the economy, employment policies, housing, and public attitudes. He notes some successful cases of cooperation between contending groups, but he also faults the impact of demagogues.

437   **Northern Ireland, the Orange State.**
Michael Farrell.   London: Pluto Press, 1980. 406p. bibliog.

An extensive history is given of Northern Ireland during the 20th century. The author covers the major conflicts that have occured there since 1922, and emphasizes the Catholic drive for minority rights. Farrell was an organizer of the 1969 marches, and was once imprisoned, becoming a hunger striker. He now advocates a socialized Ireland brought about after the ending of partition. The book calls for a class struggle in both the Republic and Northern Ireland following British withdrawal, and the creation of a unified socialist Ireland. It is well-researched however, and provides a convenient history of the period, with an enumeration of violent acts. In discussing a united Ireland the book is on less sure ground.

438 **The history of partition (1912-1925).**
Denis Rolleston Gwynn.   Dublin: Browne & Nolan, 1950. 244p.
A history of the steps leading to the Anglo-Irish Treaty (1921), and the division of Ireland. The author, an academic historian, argues against the partition, using the papers of the treaty participants.

439 **Report of the Irish Boundary Commission.**
Introduction by Geoffrey J. Hand.   Shannon, Ireland (Republic): Irish University Press, 1969. 264p.
This document, which was so far reaching in the destiny of Ireland, relates to the establishment of the border between the Republic of Ireland and Northern Ireland. Compiled in 1925 to implement the Anglo-Irish Treaty of 1921 this report was highly contested and supressed for some years. Dr. Hand provides a useful introduction to what remains a technical study of economic and geographic considerations of the border area of the 1920s.

440 **The Irish border as a cultural divide: contributions to the study of regionalism in the British Isles.**
M. W. Heslinga.   Assen, The Netherlands: Van Gorcum, 1979. 225p.
An important study is presented of the effects of partition upon the major regions of Ireland. Considered are the social and economic effects of the border separation, and the humanistic and intellectual results. The author reviews the existing literature on partition and he describes the arguments both for and against dual states. In reference to Ulster he provides a condensed history from ancient times, through periods of colonization. Heslinga discusses more fully the uneasy status of the dual communities in Northern Ireland, and he notes the special terminology that has arisen to describe the situation.

441 **Too long a sacrifice life and death in Northern Ireland since 1969.**
Jack Holland.   New York: Dodd, Mead, 1981. 226p.
Holland presents a laudable account of the Northern Ireland conflict and turmoil, but he also looks to underlying causes with an evenhandedness, searching into the Nationalist and Unionist camps for the roots of violence and the reasons for its continuance. Holland has the perspective of a Belfast-born journalist of mixed Catholic-Protestant heritage. He offers personal observations from his experiences in Northern Ireland, and his accounts are both vivid and fair when describing the seemingly ever-worsening sectarian violence. Holland supports the unification of Northern Ireland with the Republic, and is strongly critical of some Protestant groups. The book makes passing references to Dublin, but the Republic seems far from any significant involvement in the daily problems of the North.

442 **The Ulster question.**
T. W. Moody. Cork; Dublin: Mercier Press, 1978. 3rd ed. 134p.
A good introduction is given to the conflict in Northern Ireland. Moody, a prominent historian from Dublin, reviews events in Ulster between 1603 and 1973, although the book emphasizes recent history. He demonstrates that the history of Northern Ireland is intertwined with that of the whole of Ireland. This short textbook, which has been noted for its impartiality, seeks to discover the underlying causes of violence.

443 **New Ireland Forum.**
Dublin: Stationery Office, 1983-1984. (various reports).
The New Ireland Forum began in March 1983 as a means of discussion between three major political parties of the Republic, and the one Catholic oriented party in Northern Ireland. An attempt was made to develop some form of a concensus platform on a new form of acceptable government structure for a united Ireland. Several reports and special studies were issued over the course of the year, with a final report appearing in May 1984. The final report offered several alternative solutions: a unitary state, a federal/confederal state, or a measure of joint authority between Northern Ireland and the Republic. Other papers issues in the series and published as parliamentary publications included 'A comparative description of the economic structure, North and South;' 'The cost of violence arising from the Northern Ireland crisis since 1969;' 'The economic consequences of the division of Ireland since 1920;' 'Macroeconomic consequences of integrated economic policy, planning and coordination in Ireland;' and 'The legal system, North and South.' Several useful papers have appeared on the results of the Forum. An excellent article is by William V. Shannon on 'The Anglo-Irish Agreement' in *Foreign Affairs*, vol. 64, no. 4 (Spring 1986) p. 849-70. Shannon reviews the recent history that contributed to the accords of 1985, tracing the rise of political disorders in Northern Ireland since 1969, the religious dimension of the problem, the unprecedented approach and agreement of the New Ireland Forum, and the evolution of the British position from intrasigence to compromise. The Forum is seen as a major step in the progress toward a final agreement. A paper by Paul Arthur appeared on 'Anglo-Irish relations and the Northern Ireland problem', in *Irish Studies in International Affairs*, vol. 2, no. 1 (1985) p. 37-50. Arthur discusses changing Anglo-Irish relations from 1922, through shifts in party platforms and government pronouncements. He shows the difficulties faced by both Dublin and Belfast in framing issues politically and legally which are devoid of rhetoric. The paper by Arthur ends as the Forum strategy was still evolving; William Shannon's paper written a year after its conclusion, covers its aftermath.

444 **The uncivil wars, Ireland today.**
Padraig O'Malley. Boston, Massachusetts: Houghton Mifflin; Belfast: Blackstaff, 1983. 481p.
An excellent survey of the troubles in Northern Ireland. The volume provides a thorough analysis of the problems based on extended interviews with a number of key leaders among various factions in Northern Ireland, Britain, the Republic, and the United States. Intended for advanced readers this book utilizes a wide range of evidence, including public opinion polls. There is fair treatment (and often condemnation) of all groups in the Northern Ireland conflict. The author

offers no quick solutions, but in examining the attitudes of each group he urges that they accept limitations to their expectantions.

445 **Political cooperation in divided societies.**
Edited by Desmond Rea. Dublin: Gill & Macmillan, 1982. 250p.
In this collection twelve papers offer different options for a solution to the conflict in Northern Ireland, and the prospects of each of these is evaluated according to past attempts to solve similar problems elsewhere in the world. Various models of political cooperation are examined. In this study, financed by the European Economic Community, it is maintained that discriminating measures in Northern Ireland could have been abandoned a generation ago, before the deaths of thousands.

Collected biography

446 **A dictionary of Irish biography.**
Henry Boylan. Dublin: Gill & Macmillan, 1978. 385p.
A particularly useful volume that provides in alphabetical order more than 1,000 entries. Includes famous Irish individuals deceased by 1977. All the entries are concise but include the essential information. This volume belongs in all reference collections or any collection on Ireland.

447 **Who's who in Ireland.**
Compiled by Maureen Cairnduff. Dublin: Vesey, 1984. 231p.
Biographical sketches have been included for 'the influential 1,000.' All individuals are living, and some photographs are included. All the major professions are represented, although some significant names are not.

448 **Portraits in leadership.**
Barry O'Brien. Fermoy, Ireland (Republic): Eigse na Mainistreach Publications, 1980-1982. 2 vols.
Two, short paperback volumes provide very brief biographical sketches of military leaders in Ireland from ancient times to the present, including soldiers at home and in foreign forces, and revolutionary figures.

449 **Who's who in the Irish war of independence, 1916-1921.**
Padraic O'Farrell. Cork; Dublin: Mercier, 1980. 188p.
A useful reference source listing over 1,000 participants in the struggle, including both Irish and British, and those in supporting roles as well as the activists. The brief biographical statements are drawn from information in numerous archives. A chronology of events and a list of casualties are included.

450   **Irish lives: biographies of fifty famous Irish men and women.**
Bernard Share.   Dublin: Allen Figgis, 1974. 420p.

An interesting, illustrated collection of biographies of leading Irish figures
arranged in five groups: patriots and politicians; scholars and teachers; writers,
artists and musicians; scientists and businessmen; and the Irish abroad. Although
highly selective in its choice of fifty people, all periods are covered from the
Middle Ages to the 1940s. Suitable for young adults or for recreational reading.

451   **100 Irish lives.**
Martin Wallace.   Newton Abbot, England: David & Charles;
New York: Barnes & Noble, 1983. 184p.

Brief and selective biographies arranged chronologically by birth. Includes
references for further reading and for places to visit, under each entry. A
convenient volume for cursory reading, this is not intended to be definitive.

452   **Irish chiefs and leaders.**
Paul Walsh, edited by Colm O'Lochlainn.   Dublin: Sign of Three
Candles, 1960. 334p.

Biographies of Irish leaders throughout history, including military figures.

453   **A compendium of Irish biography: sketches of distinguished
Irishmen and of eminent persons connected with Ireland by office or
by their writings.**
Alfred John Webb.   New York: Lemma, 1970. 598p.

A reprint of the 1878 Dublin edition by Gill, this volume contains very brief
biographies of thousands of notable figures who were no longer alive in that year.
Thorough, but antiquated.

Prominent figures of the 19th and 20th centuries

Roger Casement

454   **The life and death of Roger Casement.**
Denis Rolleston Gwynn.   London: Jonathan Cape, 1930. 444p.

This useful, solid biography is tactful and compassionate, but lacks the later
evidence about Casement's diaries. Casement (1864-1916), was a British consular
agent and Irish rebel. He joined the Irish Nationalists, was opposed to Irish
participation in the First World War, and was hanged by the British as a traitor.

455 **Roger Casement.**
Brian Inglis. London: Hodder: New York: Harcourt, Brace
Jovanovich, 1974. 448p.

Inglis provides one of the best standard biographies, using both official and other
important sources. This is a balanced, compassionate study, relatively free of
rancour and blame.

456 **Roger Casement: a new judgement.**
Rene MacColl. New York: Norton, 1956. 328p.

A reassessment of Casement in the light of the then available evidence, leading to
a generally unfavourable view of him, one that accepts Casement's diaries as real
but also views him as an unfortunate victim of administrative and legal
persecution.

457 **The lives of Roger Casement.**
B. L. Reid. New Haven, Connecticut: Yale University Press,
1976. 532p.

A lively and understanding account of the adventurous British consul who
exposed inhuman colonial servitude, was knighted and finally hanged after
supporting the Easter Rising and German intervention. This is a vivid, well-
documented, and enthusiastic story of the romantic, but fallen hero.

458 **Casement: the flawed hero.**
Roger Sawyer. London: Routledge & Kegan Paul, 1984. 199p.
bibliog.

Sawyer presents the life of Casement as one filled with extreme contradictions and
emphasizes the roles of philanthropist and revolutionary, as well as Casement's
quirky sexual mores. The study provides some depth of biographical information,
with data from diplomatic papers, but stresses Casement's faults and naiveté.

459 **Black diaries; an account of Roger Casement's life and times with a
collection of his diaries and writings.**
Peter Singleton-Gates, Maurice Girodias. New York: Grove;
London: Sidgwick, 1959. 536p.

The diaries have long played a key and controversial part in the assessment of
Casement, due to their random reference to his sexual peculiarities. Some
editions have had offending pages deleted. The authenticity of the diaries has
been questioned by some defenders of Casement. This collection includes a
judicious weaving together of diaries and other background information,
including some of the offensive pages. Another collection of the diaries was
published in 1922, *Sir Roger Casement's diaries* (Munich: Arche, 1922. 226p.).
The allegations of forgery are looked at by Herbert Mackey in *Roger Casement:
the truth about the forged diaries* (Dublin: Fallon, 1966. 183p.); and William
Moloney: *The forged Casement diaries* (Dublin: Talbot, 1936. 275p.).

460   **The mystery of the Casement ship.**
Karl Spindler.   New York: Westerman, 1931. Reprinted, Dublin: Anvil, 1965. 218p.

A spirited narrative by the former captain of Casement's ship during the secret voyage. Spindler gives an exciting summary of events leading up to the Easter Rising. The author blames Irish sources for having warned the English of Casement's arrival.

Michael Collins

461   **Michael Collins and the making of a new Ireland.**
Piaras Béaslaí.   London: Harrap; Dublin: Phoenix, 1926. 2 vols.

A standard biography written a few years after the ambush and death of Collins in 1922. Using original sources and documents the volume traces the revolutionary leader and organizer through participation in the Easter Rising, service as government minister, head of the provisional government and commander in chief of the military forces of the Irish Free State. A valuable history of the times.

462   **Michael Collins.**
Leon O Broin.   Dublin: Gill & Macmillan, 1980. 160p.

A brief biography that evaluates the personality and roles of Collins as a successful administrator, organizer and pragmatist. O Broin has edited the first volume to appear of Collins' correspondence, *In great haste* (Dublin: Gill & Macmillan, 1983. 233p.); with letters addressed to his fiancée, in which Collins provides much detail on the turbulent period after 1917.

463   **The big fellow: Michael Collins and the Irish revolution.**
Frank O'Connor.   Dublin: Poolbeg; London: Corgi, 1969. 222p.

A riveting, well written and objective study of Collins' life and charismatic personality, focusing on the time of the revolution. For another assessment of Collins see a thorough biography by Margery Forester, *Michael Collins, the lost leader* (London: Sphere, 1972. 370p.).

James Connolly

464   **Young Connolly.**
Sean Cronin.   Dublin: Repsol Publications, 1978. 110p.

Using the papers of Connolly and those of his associates, Cronin presents a vivid view of the harsh times faced by Connolly, financial stress, family life and the often thankless years of organizing in Ireland and the United States. Connolly was a member of Sinn Fein and was commander in chief in the Easter Rising.

465 **James Connolly.**
Ruth Dudley Edwards. Dublin: Gill & Macmillan, 1981. 160p.
(Gill's Irish Lives Series).
A straightforward, detached biography of the trade unionist, socialist and
revolutionary, who was executed during the 1916 rising.

466 **James Connolly: selected writings.**
P. Berresford Ellis. Harmondsworth, England: Penguin; New
York: Monthly Review Press, 1974. 317p.
This selection, largely on Irish and socialist themes, includes representative
writings on nationalism, trade unionism, women's rights, religion, Marxism and
guerilla warfare. Connolly's major work was *Labour in Irish history* (1910).
Further writings have been edited by Owen Dudley Edwards and Bernard
Ransom in *Selected political writings* (London: Cape; New York: Grove, 1973.
382p.).

467 **The life and times of James Connolly.**
C. Desmond Greaves. London, New York: Lawrence & Wishart,
1972. 448p.
One of the most extensive biographies on Connolly to have appeared, viewing
him against the turmoil and background of labour disputes, poverty and the tragic
aftermath of the Easter Rising.

468 **James Connolly, a biography.**
Samuel Levenson. London: Quartet, 1977. 352p.
A useful biography covering the full life of Connolly.

469 **James Connolly and the United States: the road to the 1916 Irish
rebellion.**
Carl Reeve, Ann Barton Reeve. Dublin: Academy; Atlantic
Highlands, New Jersey: Humanities, 1979. 307p.
An account of Connolly's years as a labour organizer and agitator in the United
States (to 1910), and his part in the wider continuing struggle culminating in the
Easter Rising. A left-wing political orientation is used in evaluating Connolly's
achievements.

Eamon de Valera

470 **De Valera's darkest hour, 1919-32.**
T. Ryle Dwyer. Cork; Dublin: Mercier Press, 1982. 190p.
The first of a two volume political biography, this provides a concise, readable
introduction to de Valera's earlier, controversial career. Descriptions are given of
the Easter Rising, de Valera's assumption of a leadership position, sentence of
death, sojourn in the USA, the Civil War days and treaty disputes, and his

triumphant return to politics. Dwyer has the detached view of a non-Irish author and is able to raise a few questions of de Valera's judgement. The second volume, *De Valera's finest hour, 1932-59* (Cork; Dublin: Mercier, 1982. 210p.), concentrates more on the international role of Ireland, the League of Nations, neutrality, and Northern Ireland policies.

471   **Eamon de Valera, 1882-1975; the controversial giant of modern Ireland.**
Dublin: Irish Times, 1976. 144p.

A popular biography designed for general readership, with numerous period illustrations, covering both de Valera's personal and political life, from his childhood to his death in 1975. This collection of essays forms a memorial tribute and includes some interviews with de Valera.

472   **Speeches and statements by Eamon de Valera, 1917-1973.**
Edited by Maurice Moynihan.   New York: St. Martin's, 1980. 634p.

A comprehensive selection of the speeches and statements of de Valera, and chosen in part by him for inclusion here. The documents trace his long public career of fifty-six years from his days as leader of the Republican movement to his eventual presidency. The work contains a chronology of his life and includes descriptive comments on the papers. This is a useful, standard collection of documentary sources for the period. A shorter volume, *Quotations from Eamon de Valera* compiled by Proinsias Mac Aonghusa is available (Cork: Mercier, 1983).

473   **De Valera and his times.**
Edited by John P. O'Carroll, John A. Murphy.   Cork: Cork University Press, 1983. 208p.

A varied collection of thirteen conference papers describe elements of de Valera's times: his personality, charisma, achievements, economic policy, views of sovereignty, cabinet politics and governmental administration. A chronology and glossary are included. The volume lacks the flow of a single narrative and is suited for the more advanced reader.

474   **Eamon de Valera.**
Frank Pakenham (Earl of Longford), Thomas P. O'Neill.   London: Hutchinson; Boston, Massachusetts: Houghton Mifflin, 1971. 499p.

An authorized, highly favourable and uncritical biography. A shorter account of de Valera is Constantine FitzGibbon's *The life and times of Eamon de Valera* (Dublin: Gill & Macmillan. 1973. 150p.).

Daniel O'Connell

475   **Daniel O'Connell and his works.**
R. Dudley Edwards.   London: Thames & Hudson, 1975. 112p.
Professor Edwards, head of the Archives Department at University College,
Dublin, provides a vivid, clear account of O'Connell's career as political leader,
reformer, statesman, lawyer and advocate of change. This straightforward
account gives an adequate appraisal of O'Connell but does not probe his
character.

476   **The world of Daniel O'Connell.**
Edited by Donald McCartney.   Dublin; Cork: Mercier, 1980.
240p.
Fourteen essays evaluate the impact of O'Connell on both the Irish political scene
and the world-wide arena, as a folk hero with a moral force. This is a stimulating
collection of scholarly studies.

477   **The correspondence of Daniel O'Connell.**
Edited by Maurice R. O'Connell.   Dublin: Blackwater, 1972-
1980. 8 vols.
This large collection represents a major undertaking in modern Irish scholarship.
The monumental gathering of papers of O'Connell, known as 'the Liberator'
reflects his brilliance, sharp wit and dynamic force as a barrister, leader and
member of the House of Commons, and also shows him as a family man and
defender of the poor. Volume eight contains extensive indexes. The editor, a
professor at Fordham University and a descendent of O'Connell, prepared the
papers for the Irish Manuscripts Commission.

478   **King of the beggars, a life of Daniel O'Connell.**
Sean O'Faolain.   London: Greenwood, 1976. Reprinted, Dublin:
Poolbeg, 1980. 338p.
O'Faolain, a distinguished Irish writer provides a literate history of the period and
an evaluation of O'Connell's personality and accomplishments in the light of a
growing nationalist movement. A thorough, forceful portrait is presented.

479   **Daniel O'Connell.**
Fergus O'Ferrall.   Dublin: Gill & Macmillan, 1981. 150p. (Gill
Irish Lives).
A short, lively biography of O'Connell, (1775-1847), emphasizing the major
events of the times.

480 **The great Dan, a biography of Daniel O'Connell.**
Charles Chenevix Trench. London: Cape, 1984. 345p.

This sympathetic portrait presents 'the Liberator' as both a loyal subject and as a reformer who abjured violence. A balanced judgement is provided in this rehabilitation of the leader, although his limitations of personality are noted. Good use is made of O'Connell's collected letters.

Charles Stewart Parnell

481 **Charles Stewart Parnell.**
Paul Bew. Dublin: Gill & Macmillan, 1980. 160p. (Gill's Irish Lives).

This short study concentrates on Parnell's political career as a driving force in the land reform and home rule movements, in the period following the tragic famine years. The land question is shown to have had a lasting effect up to the present. Bew also explores the eventual dissipation of Parnell's leadership. An account which is lacking detachment but is important for its first hand observations is Katherine Parnell O'Shea's *Charles Stewart Parnell, his love story and political life* (Reprinted, London: Cassell, 1973. 2 vols.).

482 **Charles Stewart Parnell, the man and his family.**
Robert Foster. Brighton, England: Harvester, 1979. 403p.

The story of the intertwined private and public life that led to Parnell's downfall. His career was ruined in 1890 by a divorce suit which proved his adultery with the wife of William Henry O'Shea. Other studies of Parnell are *The Fall of Parnell* by Francis S. L. Lyons (Toronto: University of Toronto Press, 1960. 364p.) and Jules Abels' *The Parnell tragedy* (London: Bodley Head, 1966. 408p.), both exploring a life ending with political and personal trauma resulting from charges made in the famous divorce action.

483 **Charles Stewart Parnell.**
Francis S. L. Lyons. London, New York: Oxford University Press, 1977. 704p.

An excellent, thorough and extensive account of Parnell and his times, suitable for college level readership. This revises and brings up to date the leading earlier assessment by Richard O'Brian, *The life of Stewart Parnell, 1846-1891* (Westport, Connecticut: Greenwood, 1969. 2 vols.), which was first published in 1898.

484 **Parnell and his party, 1880-90.**
Conor Cruise O'Brien. Oxford: Clarendon Press, 1964. 373p.

A valuable portrayal of Parnell's role and personality during his important political years, and the party politics of the late 19th century.

Patrick Pearse

485 **Patrick Pearse: the triumph of failure.**
Ruth Dudley Edwards. London: Faber & Faber; New York:
Taplinger, 1977. 384p.

A careful, sensitive and well written biography tracing Pearse's life as an educator, playwright and leader of the Easter Rising, and describing a time of great political and cultural change.

486 **The letters of P. H. Pearse, 1879-1916.**
Edited by Séamas O'Buachalla. Gerrards Cross, England: Colin
Smythe, 1979. Reprinted, Atlantic Highlands, New Jersey:
Humanities, 1980. 528p.

This is a definitive edition of 500 of Pearse's letters. An edition of his *Collected works* appeared in 1917 (Dublin: Maunsel); and a selection of *Political writings and speeches* in 1962 (Dublin: Talbot Press). In O'Buachalla's edition of Pearse's letters, several appendixes provide short biographies of his major correspondents.

Population

487 Has Ireland a population problem?
R. E. Blackith. Dublin: Irish Conservation Society, 1973. 57p.

A short study which predicted the difficulties ahead for Ireland in the event of over-population. A decline in economic benefits, employment and standards of living were forecast and in part these did happen, but were more likely the result of world economic conditions. Brendan Walsh also observes some of the negative characteristics of Irish population growth (migration, unemployment and mental illness) in *Some Irish population problems reconsidered* (Dublin: Economic and Social Research Institute, 1968. 41p.).

488 Census of Population.
Central Statistics Office. Dublin: Stationery Office.

Now issued at five yearly intervals with both general and topical reports on population, family conditions, employment, housing, and education. Information is updated by the annual *Report on Vital Statistics* and a quarterly report on births, deaths and marriages. A microfiche edition of the census for the period 1813-1911 is available from Irish Microforms of Dublin, and Clearwater Publishing of New York. In the 19th century, volumes of the Irish census have been issued at least since 1813. During subsequent decades, volumes have appeared usually as command papers in the British Parliamentary Records Series (1821-1911. every ten years). After independence, the census of population was issued by the Irish Free State Department of Industry and Commerce (Dublin: 1928-34), and the Ireland Department of Industry and Commerce in 1936. The Central Statistics Office has issued the census since 1946 at five yearly intervals.

489 **The population of Ireland, 1750-1845.**
Kenneth H. Connell. Oxford: Clarendon Press, 1950. Reprinted,
New York: Greenwood, 1976. 293p.

Connell explores the great population increase in Ireland prior to the famine years, and includes much data on births, mortality, disease, marriage and family size.

490 **Irish population, economy and society: essays in honour of the late K. H. Connell.**
Edited by J. M. Goldstrom, L. A. Clarkson. Oxford; New York:
Oxford University Press, 1981. 322p. bibliog.

The contributors explore the characteristics of the Irish population from 1600 to later periods, and the related factors of diet and disease, rural economy and society, emigration, famine, railway construction and agricultural reform. An important chapter covers the accuracy of available statistics. The papers are narrow in focus and are for the specialist.

491 **The Irish: emigration, marriage, and fertility.**
Robert Emmet Kennedy. Berkeley, California: University of
California Press, 1973. 236p. bibliog.

Broad social and economic developments are shown to affect family structure, population, Irish culture and standard of living. Concentrating on the period 1841 to 1961 and including the famine years, the author presents an array of statistics and analysis showing the interrelationship of family size, emigration, celibacy and high fertility in marriage, farm size, the transition of cultivated land to pasture, and rural to urban living.

492 **Population and employment projections, 1971-86.**
National Economic and Social Council. Dublin: Stationery
Office, 1976. 84p. (NESC Publication, no. 14).

Conclusions are drawn of future needs for social planning and housing, based on statistical projections. Another paper, by Brendan Walsh, (number 5 in the series) is *The structure of unemployment in Ireland* (Dublin: Economic and Social Research Institute, 1974. 80p.).

493 **The vanishing Irish: the enigma of the modern world.**
Edited by John Anthony O'Brien. New York: McGraw-Hill;
London: Allen, 1954. 258p.

Several writers discuss the changing social conditions in Ireland and the sharp decline in population which took place from the mid-19th to the mid-20th centuries. The transition and growth in the Irish population and the changed social mores of later decades are not projected.

494   **Irish historical statistics: population 1821-1971.**
Edited by W. E. Vaughan, A. J. Fitzpatrick.   Dublin: Royal Irish
Academy, 1978. 372p.

In spite of its limited focus, this is a very interesting and useful collection of data
on health, economic and social conditions and the wide fluctuations in the
population figures for the period, providing indices of Ireland's changing
conditions. Vaughan and Fitzpatrick provide statistics by county, province and
town, with some figures on religious denominations, age groups, conjugal status,
and vital statistics. Data for an earlier period is provided by Joseph Lee in *The
population of Ireland before the nineteenth century* (Farnborough, Hampshire,
England: Gregg International, 1973. 464p.).

Minorities

495 **The Anglo-Irish tradition.**
James Camlin Beckett. London: Faber & Faber, 1976. 158p.
Beckett reviews the influence of the Anglo-Irish (usually those with established lands and English heritage), from the 12th to the 20th centuries. He notes their roles, contributions and gradual decline as a controlling force in Éire after the Treaty of 1921. The study is sympathetic to the Anglo-Irish.

496 **Protestants in a Catholic state: Ireland's privileged minority.**
Kurt Bowen. Dublin: Gill & Macmillan, 1983. 237p.
A thorough sociological study is made of the Protestant minority in the Republic of Ireland. Concentrating particularly on the postwar years, the author notes that the Protestants have peacefully integrated into community, social and business patterns, while maintaining a separate and unassimilated cultural heritage. Bowen discusses the declining influence of religion in the South and the social and economic behaviour of both segments of the population since the 1920s.

497 **The Irish tinkers, the urbanization of an itinerant people.**
George Gmelch. Menlo Park, California: Cummings Publishing, 1977. 178p. bibliog.
An anthropological and sociological study of the effects of change upon the Irish tinkers, (gypsies). Gmelch, an authority on the topic, includes data on the modern urban environment, poverty, welfare services, and the unusual lifestyle of the closed society of the tinkers.

498 **Tinkers and travellers.**
Sharon Bohn Gmelch. Dublin: O'Brien Press, 1975. 144p.
A valuable, illustrated general introduction to the 'travelling people' in Ireland, covering their origins, traditions, mores, language, and their often abrasive

relationship with more established society. A scholarly history of the group is presented by Artelia Court in *Puck of the Droms: the lives and literature of the Irish tinkers* (Berkeley, California: University of California Press, 1985). Court describes the lives and experiences of several 'average' tinkers, showing how their aspirations and lifestyle diverge from Irish society. Both Gmelch and Court provide useful studies of this separate culture.

499   **Prejudice and tolerance in Ireland.**
Mícheál Mac Gréil.   Dublin: College of Industrial Relations; New York: Praeger Scientific, 1977. 634p.

An important study of intergroup attitudes with more than 700 tables and charts. This monumental work, based on detailed interviews with 3,000 Dublin adults, discusses a wide range of issues and attitudes on topics including ethnicity, religion, social class, mobility, education, and employment. The author considers the psychological origins of attitudes, prejudice, minority group responses, and the social-cultural environment.

500   **The Jews of Ireland.**
Louis Hyman.   Shannon, Ireland (Republic): Irish University Press; London: Jewish Historical Society, 1972. 403p. bibliog.

A history of the small, dwindling, yet once more prominent Irish Jewish community, concentrating on the period from mediaeval times to 1900. Family, geographic, demographic and business patterns are discussed. Nearly half of the book consists of notes, a bibliography and supporting documentation. This updates Bernard Shillman's *Short history of the Jews of Ireland* (Dublin: 1945).

501   **Minorities in Ireland.**
Edited by Timothy Kearney.   *Crane Bag*, vol. 5, no. 1 (1981).

This is a special issue devoted to the status of different minorities in Ireland, with contributions by historians and academic and political figures. Among the groups discussed are the poor, the insane, tinkers, artists, homosexuals, Protestants in the Republic, and Catholics in the North. An analysis is provided of governmental and religious influences towards tolerance.

502   **Being Protestant in Ireland.**
Edited by James McLoone.   Belfast, Dublin: Cooperation North, 1985. 97p.

The Protestant experience in present day Ireland, both North and South, is reflected in seven papers from a conference held in Kilkenny in 1984.

503   **Irish tinkers.**
Janine Wiedel.   London: Latimer New Directions; New York: St. Martin's 1979. 121p.

A short, photographic essay on the tinkers and their nomadic life, based on close observation and numerous interviews.

Overseas Population

504 **The Irish in Ontario, a study in rural history.**
Donald Harmon Akenson.   Toronto: McGill-Queen's University
Press, 1984. 404p.

An important study of the cultural adaptation and survival of both Irish Catholics
and Protestants in rural Canada. The two groups are compared, statistics
presented on the experiences of each, and immigrant folklife discussed on the
basis of the remaining evidence.

505 **Real lace: America's Irish rich.**
Stephen Birmingham.   New York: Harper & Row, 1973. 322p.

A social history written in a popular style of Irish-American high society. The
climb towards the upper class is traced through the lives of successful individuals
and families. Suitable for general readership, the volume does not always present
a complimentary picture.

506 **The Molly Maguires.**
Wayne G. Broehl.   Cambridge, Massachusetts: Harvard
University Press, 1965. 409p.

The life of the Irish immigrant among the labouring classes is presented in this
vivid picture of the 19th-century coalfields of Pennsylvania. Turbulence, poverty,
revolutionary organization and violent politics are some of the conditions of the
time.

507 **Irish-American nationalism, 1870-1890.**
Thomas N. Brown.   Westport, Connecticut: Greenwood;
Philadelphia: Lippincott, 1966. 206p.

This work comments on the origins of nationalism in Ireland, 19th-century rural
life there, political life in the United States and the ties of the American Irish to

the major issues in Ireland. The Clan na Gael movement and the lives of Davitt, Devoy and Carroll are discussed. The study, although it is not thorough, contains interesting comments on violence, frontier life in America, the frustration of the immigrants and political accommodation in the 19th century.

508   **The American Irish revival.**
Edited by Kevin Cahill.   New York: Associated Faculty Press, 1984. 806p.

This compilation draws together numerous works previously published in the *Recorder*, a journal of the American Irish Historical Society. Essays, personal experiences and scholarly and creative writing are included. There are contributions by such writers as Garret FitzGerald, Padraic Colum, Seamus Heaney, Thomas Kinsella, James Farrell, Benedict Kiely, and Ronald Reagan. An American view of Irish affairs is presented.

509   **The Irish in Philadelphia: ten generations of urban experience.**
Dennis Clark.   Philadelphia: Temple University Press, 1982. 263p.

A social history covering the rise of the Irish after ten generations to positions of relative affluence and influence in an American city after the initial fight for survival.

510   **Irish relations: trials of an immigrant tradition.**
Dennis Clark.   Rutherford, New Jersey: Fairleigh Dickinson University Press; London; Toronto: Associated University Presses, 1982. 255p.

Clark concentrates on the difficult industrial and labour conditions faced by the immigrants as factory workers, or later as servants. Social progress is weighed against a century of victimization, from the 1830s to the 1930s. Clearly written and engrossing, the book's locale is Philadelphia, from the days of indenture to recent times. The relationship of the Irish to other groups in similar circumstances is shown to be often poor. Includes numerous notes and references.

511   **The Irish directory.**
John Joseph Concannon.   Pearl River, New York: the author, 1983. [not paginated].

Thousands of Irish-American organizations are listed with their names, addresses and phone numbers. Histories of major groups are included, as are lists of parades, media, gift shops, and Irish government agencies in America.

512   **The Irish-American who's who.**
John Joseph Concannon, Francis Eugene Cull.   N.P.: Port City Press, 1984. 971p.

Two thousand biographies are included from a wide range of living Irish-Americans of varying degrees of importance. Little selectivity is shown although a cross section of all types and status is provided. An appended, more useful section has biographies of 250 Irish-Americans prominent in history.

513 **The Irish race in America.**
Edward Condon. New York: Ogham House, 1976. 325p.
This reprint of an 1887 edition provides an interesting history of the Irish by geographic region in the United States, from the American revolution to the post-Civil War period.

514 **The McGarrity papers: revelations of the Irish revolutionary movement in Ireland and America, 1900-1940.**
Sean Cronin. Dublin: Anvil, 1972. 224p.
The extensive personal papers of Joseph McGarrity illuminate Irish-American politics and relationships. McGarrity was one of the leading figures of the Irish revolutionary movement in the United States.

515 **The Fenian movement in the United States: 1858-1880.**
William D'Arcy. New York: Russell & Russell, 1947. 453p. bibliog.
A history of the Fenian movement in America from its origins through to the Civil War period, and the subsequent often violent, political action which it has taken in the United States. A very extensive bibliography is included.

516 **Erin's daughters in America, Irish immigrant women in the nineteenth century.**
Hasia R. Diner. Baltimore, Maryland; London: Johns Hopkins University Press, 1983. 192p.
The hardships and patterns of immigrant life in America are discussed with views on the changing status of women, work and wages, social problems and stress, various support services, and 19th-century relations between men and women in the working world. Extensive notes are included. For advanced readership.

517 **America and Ireland, 1776-1976: the American identity and the Irish connection.**
Edited by David Noel Doyle, Owen Dudley Edwards. Westport, Connecticut: Greenwood Press, 1980. 348p. bibliog.
Based on the papers of a conference held in Ireland, this volume contains twenty-three essays on the 'American identity', the Irish presence in the USA and interrelationships between the two countries. Topics include politics, religion, labour, literature, the American revolution and the American West.

518 **Ireland, Irishmen and revolutionary America, 1760-1820.**
David Noel Doyle. Dublin; Cork: Mercier for the Cultural Relations Committee of Ireland, 1981. 257p.
During the 18th century the Irish influence in America was probably larger than that of later times, due to emigration and extensive economic and political contacts. The population of Ireland then significantly outnumbered that of the American colonies. This study examines the part played by the Irish in the American revolution and the later effects of that event on Ireland itself. Many misconceptions are challenged and numerous references to sources are provided.

519 **The Irish in the United States.**
John B. Duff.   Belmont, Califoria: Wadsworth, 1971. 87p.
A general overview of the Irish experience in the United States.

520 **Irish-Americans: identity and assimilation.**
Marjorie Fallows.   Englewood Cliffs, New Jersey: Prentice Hall,
1979. 158p.
A concise review of immigrant life, expectations, assimilation, the decisive famine
experience, reception in the USA, social adaptation, poverty and the dynamics of
the Irish neighbourhood and the upper classes. The study identifies the main
currents and trends which flowed between the two countries, family patterns in
the United States and the style of American politics. Interesting use is made of
Connecticut oral histories.

521 **Passenger and immigration lists bibliography, 1538-1900.**
Edited by P. William Filby.   Detroit, Michigan: Gale, 1981. 195p.
Some 1,200 citations guide the researcher to immigration records and lists in the
United States and Canada for the period 1538-1900. A useful subject index is
included. The bibliography lists major immigration records, histories and journal
articles.

522 **Passenger and immigration lists index.**
Edited by P. William Filby, Mary Meyer.   Detroit, Michigan:
Gale, 1981. 3 vols. supplements.
Nearly half a million immigrants are identified by name with details on their date
of arrival, port of entry and accompanying relatives. Supplementary volumes
provide additional names. Many nationalities are included for both the United
States and Canada.

523 **Irish American voluntary organizations.**
Edited by Michael F. Funchion.   Westport, Connecticut:
Greenwood Press, 1983. 323p. (Ethnic American Voluntary
Organizations Series).
Some seventy major organizations are listed and fully described with information
on their historical background, organizational structure, purpose, leaders, major
activities, achievements and failures. Most organizations are national in scope,
range from the 18th century to the present, and nearly all have exerted some
important influence on the American scene. Included are charitable, fraternal,
social, cultural, political and educational groups. This is a major reference work
on the Irish-American experience.

524 **The famine immigrants, lists of Irish immigrants arriving at the port of New York, 1846-1951.**
Edited by Ira Glazier, Michael Tepper.   Baltimore, Maryland: Genealogical Publishing, 1983- . 6 vols.

An exhaustive tabulation of the tremendous Irish migration following the agricultural disaster and evictions of 1845-46. Arrival lists enumerate all Irish passengers arriving in New York and give their personal name, date of arrival, ship, occupation, and family relationship. The volumes are chronologially arranged, and were compiled under the supervision of Temple University which holds the original records in its National Immigration Archives.

525 **Colonisation from Ireland, 1847.**
Great Britain. Parliament.   Shannon, Ireland (Republic): Irish Academic, 1971. (reprint of 1847 edition). 864p.

This volume includes a reprint of an 1847 report of a House of Lords Committee on the results of the great famine of 1845-1849. Irish poverty, starvation, opportunities abroad and emigration are discussed in detail. A companion volume *Colonisation from Ireland 1947-49* (Shannon, Ireland (Republic), 1971. 612p.) continues the review of emigration from Ireland, and discusses trade opportunities around the world.

526 **That most distressful nation: the taming of the American Irish.**
Andrew M. Greeley.   Chicago: Quadrangle, 1972. 281p.

Greeley discusses the history of the Irish-American community, church and family, the life of the immigrant and the gradual diminishing of a separate Irish identity.

527 **The Irish Americans: the rise to money and power.**
Andrew M. Greeley.   New York: Harper & Row, 1981. 215p.

Reviews the Celtic inheritance of the Irish, the history of English invasions, migration, the nationalist cause, the Irish personality, achievements, family life, religion, politics and Irish-American creative literature. The development of an Irish-American identity is traced through changing social trends, patterns and attitudes and is shown to have survived although with some unpleasant characteristics.

528 **The Irish in America, 550-1972, a chronology and fact book.**
Compiled and edited by William D. Griffin.   Dobbs Ferry, New York: Oceana, 1973. 154p.

The first part of the volume consists of a chronology of major events in Irish exploration, immigration and achievement in America. The second part contains the text of a varied selection of documents, letters, speeches, newspapers and other contemporary sources. A selective bibliography and statistical information are also included.

529   **A portrait of the Irish in America.**
William D. Griffin.   New York: Charles Scribner, 1981. 260p.

A pictorial history of the origins of the Irish, their life in exile, hardship, struggle in America, elements of success, various leaders, the role of politics, the nationalist cause, cultural heritage and social patterns. This is an excellent review for the general reader of Irish life from the 6th century to the early 1980s.

530   **The great migration; the Atlantic crossing by sailing ship since 1770.**
Edwin C. Guillet.   New York: J. S. Ozer, 1971. 284p.

Emphasizing the experiences of the Irish, the author describes British migration and ocean voyages during the 19th century. Originally published in 1937, the volume covers travel to both the United States and Canada.

531   **Boston's immigrants (1790-1880); a study of acculturation.**
Oscar Handlin.   Cambridge, Massachusetts: Harvard University Press, 1959. Enlarged ed. 382p. (Harvard Historical Studies no. 1).

The contributions of various immigrants to the development and changing society of Boston is traced, with a particularly close look at the Irish, their families, employment and politics. Originally published in 1914.

532   **The Australian colonists: an explanation of social history, 1788-1870.**
K. S. Inglis.   Melbourne, Australia: Melbourne University Press, 1974. 319p.

Inglis traces the contributions of various groups towards the development of Australia, and includes several sections on the Irish.

533   **The Irish in Britain.**
John Archer Jackson.   London: Routledge; Cleveland, Ohio: Western Reserve University Press, 1963. 208p.

A useful review of the Irish in Britain, their major concentrations, history, way of life, and social and economic status. This study can be supplemented by the journal, *Irish Studies in Britain*, which includes timely articles on the current status of the culture of the Irish in Britain. Jackson has also written *Migration* (Cambridge, England: Cambridge University Press, 1970. 304p.).

534   **The Scots and Scots-Irish in America.**
James E. Johnson.   Minneapolis, Minnesota: Lerner, 1966. 86p.

Provides a short general history of the Scots-Irish presence in America, covering the characteristics and identity of the group.

535 Ireland and Australia.

Edited by Colm Kiernan. Dublin; Cork: Mercier Press, 1984. 85p.

A collection of six Dublin radio broadcasts on the intertwined destiny of the two countries, and the history of the Irish in Australia. The essays discuss convict transportation to Australia, the growth of Irish education there, the period of the Gold Rush, and the eventual acceptance of the Irish into Australian society. The Ulster Historical Foundation in Belfast has sponsored a source book, *Letters from Irish Australia, 1825-1829*, edited by Patrick O'Farrell (Belfast: Ulster Historical Foundation, 1985. 244p.). The correspondence graphically demonstrates the hard life of the immigrant during the early 19th century.

536 Exiles of Erin: Irish migrants in Victorian London.

Lynn Hollen Lees. Ithaca, New York: Cornell University Press, 1979. 264p. bibliog.

Drawing upon primary records, the volume charts the gradual adaptation of the Irish to London's urban life, and their successful development as a minority with an individual culture.

537 The Irish and Irish politicians, a study of cultural and social alienation.

Edward M. Levine. Notre Dame, Indiana: University of Notre Dame Press, 1966. 241p.

A detailed account of Irish-American political 'bosses', patronage, political machines, social values, patterns and identity. This solid, sociological study is also critical at times of the Irish political experience.

538 The Scotch-Irish: a social history.

James G. Leyburn. Chapel Hill, North Carolina: University of North Carolina Press, 1962. 377p. bibliog.

A valuable, well-rounded and highly informative study of the long history of the Scots-Irish in America. Includes an extensive bibliography.

539 Irish nationalism and the American contribution.

Edited by Lawrence J. McCaffrey. New York: Arno, 1976. 90p.

Includes five previously published essays on Irish nationalism, religion, peasant life, and the American involvement in the Irish problem during the period 1899 to 1921.

540 The Irish in America.

John Francis Maguire. London: Longmans, Green, 1868. Reprinted, New York: Arno, 1969. 653p. (American Immigrant Collection Series).

A thorough study of the Irish in the United States and Canada at the middle of the 19th century. Although now dated, the volume presents an early view of opportunities and hazards for the immigrant, Western areas, the status of women and minorities, the established church, anti-Irish movements, the American Civil War, and the feelings of the Irish towards England.

541 **Irish settlements in Eastern Canada: a study of cultural transfer and adaptation.**
John Mannion.   Toronto: University of Toronto Press, 1974.
219p. bibliog.

This analysis of immigrant farming methods in rural Canada between 1810 and 1835 shows the initial persistence of Irish customs in settlement patterns, architecture, tools and land use. Cultural traits were quickly lost however. An 1877 view is provided by Nicholas Flood Davin in *The Irishman in Canada* (Reprinted, Shannon, Ireland (Republic): Irish University Press, 1969. 718p.).

542 **Emigrants and exiles: Ireland and the Irish exodus to North America.**
Kerby A. Miller.   London, New York: Oxford University Press, 1985. 640p.

An excellent history is presented of Irish immigration to the United States and Canada, over a three hundred year period. Miller provides a careful and sensitive look at the effects of migration on more than five million Irish. He is particularly adept at describing some of the traditions and images that arose surrounding this mass movement of population, and the songs, dances and oral stories about the plight of the Irish exile. He reviews the dismal economic conditions of past centuries in Ireland, and gives a broad portrait of a new life in America. Miller is careful to note where this popular image departs from reality. He also considers the context of emotional longing for a return to Ireland felt by so many, as part of an ethos of forced leaving (exile) that had been a pattern in Irish history for hundreds of years. Miller shows how certain aspects of Irish culture and language differentiated the Irish from other immigrant groups in the manner of their assimilation. This scholarly but readable and engrossing study also includes numerous excerpts from the letters of immigrants.

543 **Irish settlers in America.**
Michael H. O'Brien.   Baltimore, Maryland: Genealogical Publishing, 1979. 2 vols.

A collection of articles reprinted from the *Journal of the American Irish Historical Society*. These range from the general to the very specific, with articles on particular locations, families, states or communities, and some which provide a broader perspective on the Irish in America. Genealogical extracts are included.

544 **Dreamers of dreams: portraits of the Irish in America.**
Donal O'Donovan.   Bray, County Wicklow, Ireland (Republic): Kilbride Press, 1984. 187p.

Biographies of twenty-five successful Irish-Americans, including leaders in the corporate, academic, and cultural worlds, although most are not popularly known.

545 **The Irish emigrant's guide for the United States.**
Reverend John O'Hanlon. New York: Arno, 1976. 274p.
A reprint of an 1851 edition with a new introduction and commentary by Edward J. Maguire. The added notes place the study in the context of 19th-century emigration, with further comments on other works and O'Hanlon's life. The original volume contained sage advice on church groups, relief agencies, and aid available to the immigrant, government policies, and the difficulties of travel and adjustment. This is a most useful source on immigration of the period.

546 **The Catalpa rescue.**
Sean O Luing. Dublin: Anvil Books, 1984. 182p.
The story of the daring rescue of six Fenians from penal service in Australia provides an exciting account that takes in the difficult times in 19th century Ireland, and eventual freedom in America. The volume was formerly published as the *Freemantle Mission* (1962), and the new title takes its name from the rescue ship.

547 **To the golden door, the story of the Irish in Ireland and America.**
George Potter. Boston, Massachusetts; Toronto: Little, Brown, 1960. 631p.
This excellent history of Irish migration to the United States covers political and economic conditions, the voyage, American life in the 19th and 20th centuries, Fenianism and American politics. The work comments upon the reasons for limitations in the success of the Irish in American society and their preference for civil service occupations. Suitable for both general and college level readership.

548 **The Fenians in England, 1865-1872.**
Patrick Quinlivan, Paul Rose. London: Calder, 1982. 197p.
(Historical Perspectives Series, no. 11).
A retelling of the violent exploits of the Fenians in 19th-century England with details on specific raids, their organizational planning, subsequent trials and the beginnings of an amnesty movement. Supported by the Arts Council of Great Britain, the volume provides a history rather than an analysis. Bombing attempts in the following decade, the 1880s, are covered by Kenneth Short in *The dynamite war: Irish American bombers in Victorian Britain* (Dublin: Gill & Macmillan, 1979. 278p.).

549 **The Brendan voyage.**
Timothy Severin. New York: McGraw-Hill, 1978. 292p.
The author has duplicated the supposed voyage of Brendan from Ireland to America in the 6th century. The dangers and techniques of primitive travel are clearly shown in this sometimes exciting account.

550 **The American Irish.**

William Shannon. New York: Macmillan; London:
Collier-Macmillan, 1963. 458p.

In this study, Shannon, who was later a US ambassador to Ireland reviews the
Irish inheritance throughout history and Irish attitudes in the United States, civil
war politics, struggles to gain control of the cities, the Irish political style,
Tammany machine, changing images, education, and the Boston style. Al Smith
and Jim Curley are discussed as archetypes of the Irish-American politician. The
volume also covers literary movements, drama, and the main currents of Irish
conservatism. A substantial political history, with extensive notes, which is well
written and accurate.

551 **Harvard encyclopedia of American ethnic groups.**

Edited by Stephan Thernstrom. Cambridge, Massachusetts;
London: Harvard University Press, 1980, p. 524-45.

A short essay on the Irish provides a concise summary of their American
experience with regard to immigration, their history from the days of American
revolution, social change, settlement patterns, occupations, quality of life,
families, community and church, nationalism, the labour movement, cultural
divisions, achievements and politics.

552 **Wearing of the green; the lore, literature, legend and balladry of
the Irish in Australia.**

Edited by Bill Wannon. Melbourne, Australia: Lansdowne, 1965.
328p.

A selection of passages on the history of the Irish in Australia, drawing upon a
variety of documentary sources.

553 **The Irish in America.**

Carl Frederick Wittke. Baton Rouge, Louisiana: Louisiana State
University Press; New York: Russell & Russell, 1956. 319p.

In this history of the Irish-Americans, the author covers their previous life in
Ireland, migration, urban and rural experiences, religion, politics, prejudice, the
Fenians, nationalism, society, attitudes of the Irish towards others, the arts, sports
and business. An honest, straightforward appraisal, but one that does not go
beyond the beginning of the 20th century.

Genealogy

554 In search of your British and Irish roots.
Angus Baxter.   New York: William Morrow, 1982. 304p.

An outline guide to the basics of genealogical research. Major record collections and types of data are succinctly noted in chapters on the Republic and Northern Ireland.

555 Irish genealogy: a record finder.
D. F. Begley.   Dublin: Heraldic Artists, 1983. 256p.

A useful guide to tracing one's Irish ancestors through census returns, wills and deeds, directories, newspapers, legal records, papers of the Irish Manuscripts Commission, and recorded gravestone inscriptions. References are made to 2,000 sources, and a list of record repositories is provided. Another volume by Begley is *Handbook on Irish genealogy* (Dublin: Heraldic Artists, 1985. 160p.).

556 Irish family names: arms, origins, and locations.
Brian de Breffny.   New York, London: Norton, 1982. 192p.

A brief outline of the principal families of each county in Ireland is followed by a fuller discussion of family history, arranged by name.

557 Irish and Scotch-Irish ancestral research.
Margaret Dickson Falley.   Baltimore, Maryland: Genealogical Publishing, 1984. 2 vols.

A full review of the sources of genealogical information throughout Ireland, both North and South. Volume one lists sources in Ireland and the United States of birth, marriage and burial records, wills, census, land, tax and other data. Volume two is a guide to available family histories in a variety of institutions.

558 **Handbook on Irish genealogy: how to trace your ancestors and relatives in Ireland.**
Dublin: Heraldic Artists, 1984. 6th ed. 160p.
A useful basic guide for the beginner, this identifies important record collections and includes illustrative pages selected from major indexes, inventories, estate records, censuses, tax and account books, parish registers and passenger lists. Access to major repositories is discussed.

559 **Irish families: their names, arms, and origins.**
Edward MacLysaght. Dublin: Hodges Figgis, 1972. 368p. 3rd rev. ed.
A copious compendium of Irish family names, and short histories of each. This is updated by *More Irish families* (Dublin: Irish Academic Press, 1982. rev. ed. 400p.), by the same author. It also includes an essay on Irish chieftainries. Together, the two volumes form a most useful reference set with much entertaining and incidental information. The Irish Academic Press has announced a revised edition for 1985, with new appendixes, glossaries and illustrations.

560 **The surnames of Ireland.**
Edward MacLysaght. Dublin: Irish Academic Press, 1978. 404p. bibliog.
First published in 1969, this volume identifies major Irish surnames and their origins. It also contains an extensive bibliography, that has later been revised and separately published as *Bibliography of Irish family history* (Dublin: Irish Academic Press, 1982. 64p.).

561 **Burke's Irish family records.**
Edited by H. M. Massingberd. London: Burke's Peerage, 1976. 1,350p.
A good source for delineating history and lineage of the more established families.

562 **The complete book for tracing your Irish ancestors.**
Michael C. O'Laughlin. Kansas City, Missouri: Irish Genealogical Foundation, 1982. 224p. bibliog.
A general outline is provided for carrying out genealogical research, with a discussion of types of records, terms used in Ireland, repositories in church, government and public institutions, censuses and surveys, and parish registers. Helpful societies in Ireland, England, America and Canada are listed, old county maps are reproduced and a bibliography of other genealogical sourcebooks is also included.

Language and Dialects

General

563 **The fortunes of the Irish language.**
Daniel Corkery.   Cork; Dublin: Mercier Press, 1968. 128p.
The fluctuations in the popularity of the Irish language are traced through very different periods of usage, from ancient times to 1919.

564 **The great silence: a study of the relationship between language and nationality.**
Seán de Fréine.   Cork: Mercier Press, 1978. 121p.
In discussing reasons for the decline of the native Irish language, the author identifies the importance of the ancient language and literature for cultural identity. Both are seen as a means of expression suited to Irish ways but endangered by changing society.

565 **The decline of the Celtic languages.**
Victor Edward Durkacz.   Edinburgh: John Donald; Atlantic Highlands, New Jersey: Humanities, 1983. 272p.
A study of the interrelationship between linguistic, cultural and religious conflicts in Ireland, Scotland and Wales from the Reformation to the 20th century. The reduction in usage of the Gaelic languages is partly attributed to English administrative and political history, forced cultural assimilation to reduce individual Celtic identity, and official educational policies. Only a portion of the book deals with Ireland. The use of hedge schools in Ireland is criticized and the author is at times unclear on the use and decline of the Irish language.

566 **Celtic: a comparative study.**
D. B. Gregor.   Cambridge, England; New York: Oleander Press,
1980. 398p. bibliog.

A comparative study of the six Celtic languages: Irish, Gaelic, Manx, Scottish,
Welsh and Breton. Each is separately examined against a background of history,
literature and cultural destiny. Decline is attributed to disunity, loss of status, lack
of instruction and schools, limited reading matter, religious influence, migration,
and the impact of the mass media. The development/of word-forms is traced,
though the history of early usage is sketchy.

567 **English as we speak it in Ireland.**
P. W. Joyce, introduction by Terence Dolan.   Dublin: Wolfhound, 1980. 384p.

A scholarly but readable introduction to the use of the English language in
Ireland and its peculiar idioms, patterns and phrases. Some terms are traced back
to their Irish roots and there are chapters on topics such as pronunciation and
swearing. An extensive glossary of Anglo-Irish words is included.

568 **Synge and the Irish language.**
Declan Kiberd.   London: Macmillan; Totowa, New Jersey:
Rowman & Littlefield, 1979. 294p.

Synge's investigations of the Irish language are traced through his unpublished
letters, which are related to his major plays.

569 **The Irish language and culture.**
Edited by Declan Kiberd.   *Crane Bag*, vol. 5, no. 2 (1981).

This entire issue is devoted to a range of contemporary views by writers, critics,
scholars and artists of the present state of the Irish language, which is strong in
current literature, but weak in both schools and everyday society. A balanced
assessment.

570 **Catalogue of Gaelic manuscripts in selected libraries in Great
Britain and Ireland.**
Compiled by John Mackechnie.   Boston, Massachusetts: G. K.
Hall, 1973. 2 vols.

Some 73,000 entries catalogue and describe the historic corpus of Gaelic
manuscripts, a large number of which are Irish.

571 **Bilingualism and primary education: a study of the Irish experience.**
John MacNamara.   Edinburgh: Edinburgh University Press, 1966.
173p.

Lessons are drawn on the abilities of children and the effectiveness of teaching
both English and Irish in Irish schools.

572 **Irish dialects and Irish-speaking districts: three lectures.**
Brian Ó Cuiv.   Dublin: Dublin Institute for Advanced Studies,
1951. 95p.

Three lectures describe the decline of spoken Irish, the changing form of the language, and its use in Cork. The author has also edited *A view of the Irish language*, published by the Irish Government (Dublin: Stationery Office, 1969. 159p.).

573 **How the Irish speak English.**
Padraic O'Farrell.   Cork; Dublin: Mercier Press, 1980. 111p.

The use of Irish sayings expressed in the English language is shown through a series of folk stories, some of which are amusing.

574 **The English language in Ireland.**
Edited by Diarmuid Ó Muirithe.   Cork; Dublin: Mercier Press,
1977. 152p.

Nine essays cover the unique elements of English as spoken in Ireland, including the way it is influenced by the Irish language, patterns which are peculiar to individual writers, and local dialects. Contributors include well known literary figures.

575 **Irish dialects past and present, with chapters on Scottish and Manx.**
Thomas O'Rahilly.   Dublin: Dublin Institute for Advanced Studies, 1972. 303p.

A comparison is drawn between modern and earlier forms of the language in varied locales, showing the evolutionary process. First published in 1932.

576 **Linguistic atlas and survey of Irish dialects.**
Heinrich Wagner, Colm O'Baoill.   Dublin: Dublin Institute for
Advanced Studies, 1958-1969. 4 vols.

A comprehensive survey of the Irish language. Volume one covers phonetics and vocabulary, volume two studies the language in Munster, volume three Connaught, and volume four Ulster and the Isle of Man.

577 **Studia Celtica.**
Edited by J. E. Caerwyn Williams.   Aberystwyth, Wales: University College of Wales, 1966-1978. 13 vols.

Papers on various aspects of Celtic language and philology, for advanced readership. Each volume also contains a list of recently published books, articles and theses, a necrology and reviews of new works. Only some of the papers relate to the Irish language.

Dictionaries

578 **English/Irish dictionary.**
Tomás de Bhaldraithe. Dublin: Stationery Office, 1959. 894p.
An excellent dictionary that gives the current, multiple usages of words, with occasional reference to older literature for further explanation where necessary. The companion Irish to English Dictionary is *Foclóir Gaeilge-Bearla* (q.v.).

579 **An Irish-English dictionary.**
Patrick S. Dineen. Dublin: Educational Company of Ireland, 1970. 1,374p.
Published originally in 1927 for the Irish Text Society, and covering 'the words, phrases and idioms of the modern language', this is a useful, reliable volume for everyday use.

580 **Foclóir Gaeilge-Bearla. (Irish to English dictionary.)**
Edited by Nial O. Donaill, Tomás de Bhaldraithe. Dublin: Stationery Office, 1977. 1,308p.
This exhaustive Irish to English dictionary provides full definitions, and covers pronunciation and the current context of words in phrases.

581 **The pocket Irish phrase book.**
Paul Dorris. Belfast: Appletree; Newton Abbot, England: David & Charles, 1982. 70p.
A small, convenient guide to 1,000 words and phrases in everyday use, with grammar and pronunciation for the beginner. Different dialects are noted and terms are translated into English.

582 **The illustrated Gaelic-English dictionary to which is prefixed a concise Gaelic grammar.**
Edward Dwelly. Glasgow: Gairm Publishing, 1971. 1,034p.
This was first published in 1901. Gairm have also issued *Gaelic self-taught* by James Maclaren (1971. 224p.), *Everyday Gaelic* by Morag Macneill (1984. 110p.) and the *Etymological dictionary of the Gaelic language* (1982. 472p.).

583 **Combined Irish-English, English-Irish dictionary.**
Michael O Siocfhradha. Dublin: Talbot Press, 1972. 321p.
A good, general dictionary intended for the beginner.

584 **Dictionary of the Irish language based mainly on Old and Middle Irish materials.**
Royal Irish Academy.   Dublin: The Academy, 1913-1976.
25 parts.
A definitive dictionary covering the older forms of the language in more than 2,500 pages. A compact edition of this dictionary, edited by E. G. Quin, was published by the Academy in 1984 with 638p. For the specialist in mediaeval Irish. Originally published in twenty-four parts, with an introduction appearing in 1976.

Grammars

585 **New Irish grammar.**
Christian Brothers.   Dublin: Fallons, 1980. 152p.
This compact grammar for the beginner is basic but clearly written. For those beyond this level there is another and larger Christian Brothers grammar written in Irish, *Graiméar Gaeilge na mBráithre Chriostai* (Dublin: McGill & Son, 1960. 432p.). Another useful grammar is by Brian Mac Giolla Phadraig *Réchúrsa Gramadaí* (Dublin: Longman, Brown & Nolan, [n.d.]. 387p.).

586 **Teach yourself Irish.**
Myles Dillon, Donncha Ó Cróinín.   London: English Universities Press, McKay, 1961. 243p.
A basic-level guide, which is part of an introductory series to various different languages.

587 **An introduction to Old Irish.**
R. P. M. Lehman, W. P. Lehman.   New York: Modern Language Association, 1975. 196p.
This handbook for the serious student includes selections from Old Irish texts, with glosses and annotations. After each passage of text there is an analysis, phonetic transcription, translation, and grammatical points, which vary according to the selections.

588 **Buntús Cainte, a first step in spoken Irish.**
Tomás Ó Domhnalláin.   Dublin: Stationery Ofice, 1983. Set.
A series of pamphlet textbooks and tape cassettes guide the student through a progression of some 200 lessons in the language, grammar and vocabulary of Irish as currently spoken. The pamphlets and eight tapes may be purchased individually or as a set. Produced with the support of the Minister for Education, and RTE, this series is intended for students who may not have access to a teacher. It is well designed, illustrated with cartoons, and forms the basis of a television series.

589 **Learning Irish, an introductory self-tutor.**
Mícheál Ó Siadhail. Dublin: Institute for Advanced Studies,
1980. 331p.

Thirty-six lessons are included with appendixes on spelling, pronunciation, Irish-English and English-Irish vocabularies, and a table of sounds. The volume is intended for those with no previous knowledge of Irish. It teaches the language as it is spoken in one locale of Connemara. Three tape cassettes accompany the book with passages read by several speakers.

590 **A concise Old Irish grammar and reader.**
Julius Pokorny. New York: AMS Press, 1982. 2 vols. bibliog.

Volume one contains a grammar and volume two the reader in this reprint of a 1914-1923 edition. For the advanced reader interested in the historical usage of Irish.

591 **A grammar of Old Irish.**
Rudolf Thurneysen, translated by D. A. Binchy, Osborn
Bergin. Dublin: Dublin Institute of Advanced Studies, 1946.
668p.

This enlarged and corrected English language edition of a work originally published in Germany in 1909 is useful for providing a detailed study of the language. The Institute has also published two grammars edited by Parthalan Mac Aogain, written by 17th century Franciscans and reflecting the style of the old Irish bardic schools. See also *Graomeir Ghaeilge na mBrathar Mionur* by Giolla Brighde O hEodhasa (Dublin: Dublin Institute of Advanced Studies, [n.d.]. 2 vols.). Most of the first volume is in Latin; the second is in Irish.

Religion

History

592 **Churches and abbeys of Ireland.**
Brian de Breffny, George Mott.   London: Thames & Hudson,
1976. 208p.
More than 250 illustrations are included in this comprehensive history of the
churches, cathedrals and monastic sites of Ireland. The account begins with the
Celtic Church, covers the Romanesque period, later gothic buildings, abbeys and
their architecture, the ecclesiastical disestablishment, and finally, the modern
structures of the 20th century.

593 **The Irish priests in the penal times (1660-1760).**
William Burke, introduction by Patrick Corish.   Shannon, Ireland
(Republic): Irish University Press, 1969. 491p.
A reprint of a 1914 edition with a new introduction that evaluates the original
work. The study makes considerable use of source material and excerpts from
documents in the public records offices of London and Dublin, the Bodleian
Library, Oxford and the British Museum. It illustrates the official English view of
the clergy from the reigns of Charles II to Anne, and comments upon
persecutions in different provinces, the case of Oliver Plunkett and various plots
and their penalties.

594 **A history of Irish Catholicism.**
Edited by Patrick J. Corish.   Dublin: Gill & Macmillan, 1967-
1969. 6 vols.
This extensive history provides a comprehensive account of the Catholic Church
in Ireland. Each volume is written by a different expert, and the set provides

coverage from the early mediaeval period of St. Patrick up to the 20th century, including the expansion of the Irish Church abroad. This will be a standard source on the Irish Catholic Church. Corish also provides a one-volume history of the Church (ancient, mediaeval and modern, up to 1960) in *The Irish Catholic experience* (Dublin: Gill & Macmillan, 1985).

595   **The Catholic community in the seventeenth and eighteenth centuries.**
Patrick J. Corish.   Dublin: Educational Company of Ireland, 1981. 156p. (Helicon History of Ireland Series no. 5).
Irish social, religious and cultural life is shown to have been affected by the severe post-Reformation restrictions, a pattern that explains the deep conservation which was still found in the Church long after the disuse of the penal laws.

596   **The saints of Ireland, a chronological account of the lives and works of Ireland's saints and missionaries at home and abroad.**
Mary Ryan D'Arcy.   St. Paul, Minnesota: Irish American Cultural Institute, 1974. 241p.
This account summarizes the lives of some 200 saints, both famous and little known. Biography, historical place and interwoven legend are included in chapters on the early Christian periods, Irish saints in Scotland, England and on the Continent, the post-Viking period, later martyrs and modern missions.

597   **Church and state in Tudor Ireland: a history of penal laws against the Irish Catholics, 1534-1603.**
Robert Dudley Edwards.   London: Longman, 1935. Reprinted, 1972. 352p. bibliog.
A balanced, scholarly and fully documented account from the reign of Henry VIII to Elizabeth I, which makes extensive use of original sources and manuscripts, and includes a thorough bibliography. For advanced students.

598   **Ecclesiastical history of Ireland.**
W. D. Killen.   London: Macmillan, 1875. 2 vols.
A useful work, though now dated, and with a somewhat Presbyterian approach. Many references are made to historical sources. Killen also wrote several other books on the ancient church, and on the Old Catholic, Presbyterian, and Unitarian churches.

599   **The holy wells of Ireland.**
Patrick Logan.   Gerrards Cross, England: Colin Smythe; Atlantic Highlands, New Jersey: Humanities, 1980. 170p.
Some of the 3,000 wells in Ireland are described according to their type, seashore or mountain, healing powers, folk practices and religious beliefs, pilgrimages, ancient remains and lore of wildlife and tree. Written by a physician this account includes some observations on folk medicine. An engrossing account for popular reading.

600 **The Celtic churches: a history, A.D. 200 to 1200.**
John T. McNeill. Chicago; London: University of Chicago Press,
1974. 289p. bibliog.
Beginning with the pagan Celts, the author reviews the beginnings of Christianity
in Ireland, the Irish in Europe, including Brittany, Scotland and England, the
monastic tradition, the growth of the Church, and its learning, art, and missionary
activity. Extensive notes cover both documentary sources and archaeological
discoveries.

601 **The saints and martyrs of Ireland.**
H. Patrick Montague. Gerrards Cross, England: Colin Smythe,
1981. 138p.
This brief work presents short biographies of the major Irish saints, causes and
martyrs. A chronological description is given of important feast days.

602 **Celi De, spiritual reform in Ireland, 750-900.**
Peter O'Dwyer. Dublin: Editions Tailliúra, 1982. 2nd rev. ed.
213p.
Drawing upon recent archaeological discoveries and a considerable amount of
manuscript references this study focuses on the ecclesiastical reforms from the 8th
century to the end of the 10th century and on a significant mediaeval literature.

603 **The monasteries of Ireland, an introduction.**
Daphne D. C. Pochin-Mould. London: Hippocrene Books, 1976.
188p. bibliog.
An outline of the life and goals of monks from the 6th to 10th centuries is
provided in this photographic essay. Included are the Celtic period, various
religious orders through the centuries, local traditions, art, architecture, politics
and theology. The book has a gazetteer, chronology, and good building plans.

604 **The crosses and culture of Ireland.**
Arthur Kingsley Porter. New York: Arno, 1979. 141p.
Through an analysis of the iconography of surviving crosses and sculpture a
review is provided of Irish religious history from early centuries to the Viking
times. This is a reprint of five lectures at the Metropolitan Museum of Art in
1930.

605 **Irish saints.**
Robert T. Reilly. New York: Avenel Books, 1981. 169p.
A brief review of the twelve major Irish saints, each given a short chapter. For
popular reading only.

606   **The Church and the two nations in medieval Ireland.**
      John Watt.   Cambridge, England: Cambridge University Press;
      Dublin: Gill & Macmillan, 1972. 225p. bibliog. (Cambridge Studies
      in Medieval Life and Thought, 3rd series, no. 3, Gill History of
      Ireland Series).
A concentrated study of the interplay between the forces of colonization and the
native Irish from the Anglo-Norman invasion in the 12th century, until the 14th
century. The view is of an often bleak period for the Irish Church. This careful
study discusses both local affairs and developments on the continent.

Roman Catholicism

19th century

607   **Paul Cardinal Cullen and the shaping of modern Irish Catholicism.**
      Desmond Bowen.   Dublin: Gill & Macmillan; New York: Orbis,
      1983. 311p.
An important look at Cullen, who was a major influence on the 19th-century
Church during a transition between the rule of the traditionalists and those who
advocated a new, stronger administration and discipline. A discussion is provided
of Cullen's educational reforms, his fights with the Fenians and British policies
toward the universities. While strengthening the position of the Roman Catholic
Church, Cullen is seen to have made a negative contribution in widening the
chasm between the Protestant and Catholic religions.

608   **The struggle for Catholic emancipation.**
      D. Gwynn.   London, New York: Longmans, 1928. 290p.
The struggle of the native Catholic Irish against religious persecution from the
mid-18th century to their emancipation under O'Connell in 1829 is recounted.
This short survey outlines the major religious, political and economic forces of the
period.

609   **The Catholic Church in nineteenth century Ireland.**
      Desmond Keenan.   Dublin: Gill & Macmillan, 1983. 308p.
Keenan describes the revival of religious influence and its place in the world of
politics following the lapse of the penal laws. This scholarly account studies the
rapid growth during the 19th century of the institutions and administrative
structure of the church, its strong system of education and its charities. At times,
the author strongly criticises the domination of Irish society by an episcopacy of
narrow views.

610   **Peel, priests and politics: Sir Robert Peel's administration and the Roman Catholic Church in Ireland, 1841-1846.**
Donal A. Kerr.   Oxford: Clarendon Press, 1983. 399p.

A detached and heavily documented look at the relationship between Ireland, England and the Catholic Church and some of the leading figures of the period: O'Connell, Cullen, Archbishop Murray and others. The interplay of politics in both countries is shown in response to Peel's programme of support for charities, Maynooth and the Queen's Colleges.

611   **The Roman Catholic Church in Ireland and the fall of Parnell 1888-91.**
Emmet Larkin.   Liverpool, England: Liverpool University Press; Chapel Hill, North Carolina: University of North Carolina Press, 1979. 368p.

An important work on the position of the Church hierarchy in Irish politics at the end of the 19th century, its position of 'consensus' with the established political leadership, and its opposition to the more extreme agrarian reformers. The abandonment of Parnell is seen as a reassertion of the Church's role in Irish politics that would continue long into the next century. Larkin's *The historical dimensions of Irish Catholicism* (Washington, DC: Catholic University, 1984. 139p.) is also concerned with the changing dynamics of the Church and religious practice in 19th-century Ireland.

612   **The Catholic Church and Ireland in the age of rebellion, 1859-73.**
E.R. Norman.   Ithaca, New York; London: Cornell University Press, 1965. 485p.

A very detailed and well-researched account of church politics, the position of the bishops and such issues as land tenure, the disestablishment of the official church, and Cardinal Newman's proposals for a university in Ireland.

613   **Priests, politics and society in post famine Ireland.**
James O'Shea.   Dublin: Wolfhound, 1983. 300p.

This study focuses on County Tipperary during the period 1850 to 1891, and on the influential role held by the clergy in an Irish society facing drastic social and political change.

614   **Edmund Ignatius Rice: the man and his times.**
Desmond Rushe.   Dublin: Gill & Macmillan, 1981. 156p.

Rice (1762-1844) was founder of the influential Brothers of the Christian Schools. This study traces his extraordinary change of career and subsequent dedication to charity and the improvement of education, which had an impact in many countries.

20th century

615   **Church and state, essays in political philosophy.**
Desmond Clarke.   Cork: Cork University Press, 1984. 250p.
A somewhat controversial view of the individual in a society dominated by
established churches acting with great influence in the politics of the state.

616   **The Church now.**
Edited by John Cumming, Paul Burns.   Dublin: Gill & Macmillan, 1980. [not paginated].
Collected essays describe and provide a critique of the contemporary Roman
Catholic Church and some of its problems. Critical note is made of administrative
bureaucracy, centralization, and a perceived lack of freedom. Popular complaints,
declining support, and a few useful educational programmes are alluded to by
several religious and sociological commentators.

617   **The changing face of Catholic Ireland.**
Desmond Fennell.   London: Geoffrey Chapman, 1968. 223p.
The modern Roman Catholic Church is shown to be beset by changing public
norms and by a shift in religious interpretations following the second Vatican
Council.

618   **Is Irish Catholicism dying?**
Peadar Kirby.   Dublin; Cork: Mercier, 1984. 93p.
An analysis of the contemporary role of the Catholic Church in Ireland, its lack of
a critical stance on issues needing reform in Ireland, and its waning influence in
public opinion. The author makes several recommendations.

619   **Irish spirituality.**
Edited by Michael Maher.   Dublin: Veritas, 1982. 160p.
These collected essays range in time from early Irish monasticism and idealism to
the modern period which questions established rules while reaffirming spirituality.
Suggestions are made for a renewed theology that retains the distinctiveness of
Ireland's cultural heritage.

620   **Irish Catholics, tradition and transition.**
John J. Ó Riordáin.   Dublin: Veritas, 1980. 98p.
A short description of the traditional values and outlooks held by Irish Catholics
today, and some of the roots that have shaped a modern spirituality, including
elements from both the highly centralized Roman Church and English puritanism.

621   **Church and state in modern Ireland, 1923-79.**
J. H. Whyte.   Dublin: Gill & Macmillan, 1980. 2nd rev. ed. 480p.
A review of the Church's role in government policy since independence and the
positions that it has taken on many social and political issues. First published in
1971, this second edition provides much updated information.

Protestant churches

622 **A Protestant in purgatory: Richard Whately, Archbishop of Dublin.**
Donald Harman Akenson.   Hamden, Connecticut: Archon, 1981.
225p.
The eclipse of the Church of Ireland as a central force is traced through this
biography of the sometimes eccentric, 19th-century archbishop. Whately, a liberal
and a reformist, fostered a programme of changing church roles, programmes for
the poor, and public education. Many of his positions were not accepted and the
influence of the Church declined in the period of economic and political change.
Akenson has also written: *The Church of Ireland: ecclesiastical reform and
revolution, 1800-1885* (New Haven, Connecticut: Yale University Press, 1971).

623 **Protestant dissent in Ireland, 1687-1780.**
J. C. Beckett.   London: Faber, 1948. 161p. bibliog. (Studies in
Irish History, no. 2).
Beckett, a leading historian, presents a somewhat Presbyterian view of Church
history during a period of political turbulence.

624 **The Protestant crusade in Ireland, 1800-70.**
Desmond Bowen.   Dublin: Gill & Macmillan; Montreal: McGill-
Queens University Press, 1978. 412p.
A study of Protestant-Catholic relations between the Act of Union and the final
disestablishment of the Church of Ireland by Gladstone in 1869. Among the
elements of tension which are discussed are the French Revolution and its
influences, the Protestant mind in Ireland, Church evangelicals and leading figures
in controversies, famine and changing economic conditions, crusades, missions,
and the roots of religious conflict leading towards the 20th century.

625 **The Church of Ireland in the age of Catholic emancipation.**
Edward Brynn, edited by Peter Stansky, Leslie Hume.   New
York: Garland, 1982. 306p. (Modern British History Series).
The 19th-century Church of Ireland is depicted as besieged in an era of change,
and challenged by political movements (such as that of O'Connell), by the rising
Catholic voice, and by charges of privilege and of aloofness. Under parliamentary
reform church prerogatives were curtailed, especially in the area of national
education.

626 **Historical sketches of congregations in the Presbyterian Church in
Ireland.**
Belfast: Presbyterian Church House Historical Society, 1982. [not
paginated].
Short reviews of the different Presbyterian congregations throughout Ireland are
provided. For an historical overview see also J. S. Reid's *History of the*

Religion. Protestant churches

Presbyterian Church in Ireland, edited by W. D. Killen (Belfast: W. Mullan: 1867. 3 vols.) which is the standard work.

627 **Irish Anglicanism, 1869-1969.**
Michael Hurley. Dublin: Figgis, 1970. 236p.
A century of evolution is shown in the Anglican Church, with a shift of focus from a position of established order to one of involvement in social issues and reform.

628 **The Church of Ireland, 1869-1969.**
R. B. McDowell. London; Boston, Massachusetts: Routledge, 1975. 157p. bibliog. (Studies in Irish History, 2nd Series, no. 10).
The Church of Ireland's position in Irish society is studied since its disestablishment in 1869. In a period of waning influence a picture is presented of church organization and the clergy, including their work, opinions and background. The Church is seen as a pocket of peace during the changing economic and political circumstances of the 20th century.

629 **History of the Church of Ireland from the earliest times to the present day.**
Edited by Walter Alison Phillips. London: Oxford University Press, 1933-1934. 3 vols. bibliog.
A reliable, thorough study of the Church and its antecedents with some emphasis on the mediaeval and Renaissance periods. Chapters by various historians trace the progress of the Christian Church following the invasions of the Danes, and end with the disestablishment of the Church of Ireland in the 19th century, and a new direction in the 20th. Written from an Anglican point of view.

Social Conditions

General

630 **Family and community in Ireland.**
Conrad Maynadier Arensburg, Solon T. Kimball.   Cambridge,
Massachusetts: Harvard University Press; London: Oxford University Press, 1968. 2nd ed. 417p.

An important, pathfinding work in Irish sociology that scrutinizes the patterns and habits found in a small town. Comparisons are drawn between town and farm environments, and the lives of farmers, workers, shopkeepers and those in business, their families, marriages and circles of acquaintances.

631 **Rural industrialization and social change in Western Ireland.**
Mary E. Cawley.   *Sociologia Ruralis*, vol. 19, no. 1 (1979),
p. 43-59.

The incursion of town and commuter life into rural areas and the consequent changes in social life and values are having a major effect on the stability of Irish society in agricultural communities. Further evidence of this is seen in a government study of the National Economic and Social Council by P. Commins, et al., on *Rural areas: change and development* (Dublin: Stationery Office, 1978. 183p.).

632 **Ireland, a sociological profile.**
Edited by Patrick Clancy, Sheelagh Drudy, Kathleen Lynch, Liam O'Dowd.   Dublin: Institute of Public Administration, 1986. 434p.

This far ranging study reviews many aspects of changing Irish society in the 1980s. Scholarly papers from twenty-two academic writers identify a number of factors and influences on society and suggest future directions concerning demographic change, the effects of industrialization and employment, religion and growing secularization, social stratification, social class, marriage and the family, and rural society. The papers are separated into those dealing with the Republic and those on Northern Ireland. A final section contains several papers dealing with the whole of Ireland with regard to sex roles, crime, the mass media and communications. As the volume is a collection of papers by varied authors on specific topics, it is somewhat uneven and does not achieve a unified conclusion or summary of the totality of Irish society. However, it does identify many of the major issues of the 1980s. The book was published in conjunction with the Sociological Association of Ireland. An important issue in contemporary Irish society is that of marriage and divorce. The traditional concepts surrounding marriage have recently been under stress. Nonetheless, Irish religious values have been reaffirmed by a popular vote against the legalization of divorce in 1986. Several books shed light on the strong legal adherence to marriages in the Republic. In *Marriage in Ireland*, edited by Art Cosgrove (Dublin?: College Press, 1985) a series of papers are included from those delivered before the Dublin Historical Association in 1983-84. These cover marriage traditions and practices from the 5th century to the present, and some of the papers mention various forms of family unions other than marriage during past centuries, as well as the availability of divorce and remarriage. After the 12th century, gradual change brought about a uniform marriage custom protected by church law. Additional complexity occurred in times of religious supression during the Tudor and later periods. A book advocating the loosening of marriage law has been edited by John O'Conner, *Social reform of marriage in Ireland* (Dublin?: Divorce Action Group, 1984). O'Connor suggests 'pratical steps for legal change', and while advocating support for marriage in distress, he also calls for the humane acceptance of failed marriages. The 1986 defeat of the divorce referendum however has rendered this position moot in Ireland. Three publications which support the existing marriage law in Ireland, while attacking divorce are: *Marriage or divorce: the real issue* by Joseph McCarroll (Dublin: Four Courts Press, 1986); *Ireland must choose* by the Bishop of Limerick, Jeremiah Newman (Dublin: Four Courts Press, 1984. 96p.); and *Is divorce the answer?* by William Binchy (Dublin: Irish Academic Press, 1984).

633 New Dubliners: urbanization and the Irish family.
Alexander J. Humphreys. London: Routledge & Kegan Paul; New York: Fordham University Press, 1966. 295p.

The transition to a growing urban lifestyle is shown from the viewpoint of twenty-nine families in Dublin. Changing patterns are shown in social behaviour and daily life.

634 Power, conflict and inequality.
Mary Kelly, Liam O'Dowd, James Wickham. Dublin: Turoe, 1983. 222p. bibliog.

This collection of eleven essays, sponsored by the Sociological Association of Ireland, looks at political and social structures which the authors feel reinforce inequality and poverty. Numerous statistics are included. Suitable for advanced readership.

635   **Contemporary Irish society: an introduction.**
      Michel Peillon.   Dublin: Gill & Macmillan; Atlantic Highlands,
      New Jersey: Humanities, 1982. 231p.
A sociological perspective on contemporary Ireland and its traditional ways.
Major groups are identified (farmers, the bourgeoisie, white-collar workers, small
businessmen, professional and working class), and each is discussed with regard to
its demographic, social and political characteristics, and contribution to Ireland.
Also covered are the Church, the Gaelic movement, government and social forces
and ideologies. The state is seen as a consolidating social mechanism, unifying
Ireland's diverse elements. A valuable, theoretical work, although it comes to
some debatable conclusions.

Women

636   **Cumann na mBan and the women in Ireland, 1913-25.**
      Lil Conlin.   Kilkenny, Ireland (Republic): People, 1969. 312p.
Cumann na mBan, the leading women's political organization of volunteers at the
time of the Easter Rising is described, along with the activist role of the Countess
Markievicz and others in the following years.

637   **Daughters of Erin: five women of the Irish renaissance.**
      Elizabeth Coxhead.   London: Secker & Warburg; Gerrards Cross,
      England: Colin Smythe, 1979. 236p.
The biographies of five famous Irish women: Maude Gonne, Constance de
Markievicz, Sarah Purser, Sara Allgood and Maire O'Neill.

638   **Woman in Irish legend, life and literature.**
      Edited by S. F. Gallagher.   Gerrards Cross, England: Colin
      Smythe; Totowa, New Jersey: Barnes & Noble, 1983. 156p. (Irish
      Literary Studies, no. 14).
Nine essays describe how the life of Irish women has been portrayed through the
writings of Irish authors, poets, playwrights and historians. Imagery ranges from
ancient, heroic proportions, to the more transient qualities of the modern age.
These papers were presented at a 1981 seminar of the Canadian Association of
Irish Studies.

639   **Handbook for single women in Ireland.**
      Lorna Hogg.   Dublin; Cork: Mercier, 1982. 128p.
A practical guide to the everyday requirements of living in Ireland, with legal and
financial information and social hints which are relevant mainly to Dublin.

640   **Hanna Sheehy-Skeffington, Irish feminist.**
Leah Levenson, Jerry H. Natterstad.   Syracuse, New York:
Syracuse University Press, 1986. 240p.

A biography of an unusual woman born in County Cork in 1877. Hanna Sheehy combined a career as writer and lecturer with the dedicated outlook of a pacifist, ardent feminist, Irish nationalist and socialist. A popular speaker in Ireland and the United States, she long advocated the causes of women's rights, human rights, and an independent Ireland. This book recounts her life (which ended in 1946) and places it in the context of the more traditional society which surrounded her: her Irish Catholic family, friends and the church. Her pacifist role, however, often did not appeal to those favouring more revolutionary means. The programme that she espoused are still timely decades later.

641   **Women in Irish society, the historical dimension: a study of socialization and role conflict.**
Edited by Margaret MacCurtain, Donncha Ó Corráin.   Dublin:
Arlen House; Westport, Connecticut: Greenwood Press, 1979.
133p. (Contributions to Women's Studies, no. 11).

This pathfinding volume began as a series of radio broadcasts to commemorate Women's International Year. It reviews both the present status of women in Ireland and their changing roles at different stages in history, from ancient times to the mid-1970s. Chapters by various authors discuss women's domestic roles, employment, place in society, political roles, voting, and religious influence. Suitable for the college level, this book will also be useful for programmes of comparative women's studies.

642   **Irish women: image and achievement.**
Edited by Eilean Ní Chuilleanáin.   Dublin: Arlen House, 1984.
240p.

Ten essays trace the contributions of women to Irish culture, principally in the arts, throughout history. Experts discuss women, their achievements, and their image in art, folklore, religion and the law.

643   **Images of the Irish women.**
Edited by Christina Nulty.   *Crane Bag*, vol. 4, no. 1 (1980).

This special issue is devoted to tracing the important role of Irish women through history, literature, the arts and tradition from ancient to modern times. Special attention is focused on the Irish woman today as affected by legislation, economics and religion.

644   **Smashing times, a history of the Irish women's suffrage movement,
1889-1922.**
Rosemary Cullen Owens.   Dublin: Attic, 1984. 159p.

The active roles undertaken by a number of women's organizations in labour and politics are outlined for the turbulent years leading to revolution and independence. The women's platforms, manoeuvering and active participation is described along with comments on opposing forces.

645 **The female experience, the story of the woman's movement in Ireland.**
Catherine Rose. Dublin: Arlen House, 1976. 110p.
The modern-day Irish woman is seen to be in an unequal position due to religious influences and limited legal rights. The prognosis is given for improvement and reform. A major issue concerning women's rights and obligations in Irish society is that of abortion. Although this issue has been hotly debated in the Irish press (with some liberal views represented in the leading Dublin papers) most Irish publications have opposed the legalization of abortion. A typical Irish perspective is given by Andrew Rynne in *Abortion, the Irish question* (Dublin: Ward River Press, 1982). Rynne, a medical doctor and chairman of the Family Planning Association of Ireland, reviews all sides of the debate and discusses the results of a questionnaire to leading advocates and opponents. Although some 10,000 abortions are said to be performed on Irish women per year, this book opposed legalization in Ireland as unnecessary. A constitutional amendment in favour of limited access to abortion is seen as both divisive and contrary to Irish family traditions. Also opposing abortions on religious and ethical grounds are two books: *Abortion and the law*, edited by Austin Flannery (Dublin: Dominican Publications, 1983. 130p.), and a collection of documents on the issue, *Abortion no: constitutional amendment?* (Dublin: Dominican Publications, 1985. 74p.).

646 **Women's rights in Ireland, with a checklist of children's rights.**
Ailbhe Smyth, (et al.). Dublin: Ward River Press, 1982. 221p.
Produced for the Irish Council for Civil Liberties, this practical handbook serves as a guide to information, readings and organizations relating to employment, equal rights legislation, health, child care, family law, welfare and educational opportunities. Shortcomings and restrictions for women in each of these fields are noted.

647 **Unmanageable revolutionaries: women and Irish nationalism.**
Margaret Ward. Dingle, County Kerry, Ireland (Republic): Brandon; London: Pluto, 1984. 289p.
The women's movement in Ireland at the turn of the century is seen in its twin roles as a feminist cause and as a force supporting revolutionary activity. Organizations such as the Ladies' Land League and the Cumann na mBan are reviewed, although their influence is found to have been limited by society.

Social issues

648 **Rural exodus.**
Damian Hannon. London: Geoffrey Chapman, 1970. 348p.
The extensive transition of rural to urban Ireland is described, based on the mobility of Irish youth from County Cavan in the late 1960s.

649 **One million poor?**
Edited by Sister Stanislaus Kennedy. Dublin: Turoe Press, 1982. 272p.

Written by social workers, academics and lawyers, this volume describes persistent poverty in contemporary Ireland, the poor living standards of one quarter of the population, economic causes of poverty, and insufficient public policy and governmental response. Statistics on poverty are also provided by John Roche in *Poverty and income maintenance policies in Ireland, 1973-80* (Dublin: Institute of Public Administration, 1984. 293p.).

650 **The distasteful challenge.**
Charles McCarthy. Dublin: Institute of Public Administration, 1968. 116p.

Irish society is challenged to adopt a more pluralistic, democratic and receptive approach to shared responsibility in both social and economic planning issues. The author outlines what he sees as some of the ills of Irish society, namely that it is submissive, accepting and alienated.

651 **One thousand years of Irish whiskey.**
Malachy Magee. Rathgar, Ireland (Republic): O'Brien Press, 1981. 144p.

The production, use and misuse of alcohol is traced through parliamentary debates, illegal production, war and fraudulent means. Magee reviews economic changes in the industry, social patterns, the temperance movement in Ireland and political disputes. This, and John McGuffin's *In praise of poteen* (q.v.) are entertaining accounts of a social problem. Balance can be found in a volume of British parliamentary papers on *Drunkenness, 1878-79* (Reprinted, Dublin: Irish Academic Press, 824p.), which provides official source documentation. The Irish temperance movement has also had a long and lasting effect, often overlooked in the popular image of the country. An interesting history of the Irish abstinence movement is provided by Elizabeth Malcolm in *Ireland sober, Ireland free* (Dublin: Gill & MacMillan, 1986). Malcolm provides a detailed look at aspects of Ireland's culture, politics and society during the 19th and early 20th centuries.

652 **The dynamics of Irish housing.**
Paul Alfred Pfretzchner. Dublin: Institute of Public Administration, 1965. 137p.

A general review is made of community needs for increased public and private housing, and the available resources. Statistics and a different assessment is provided by T. J. Baker and L. O'Brien in *The Irish housing system: a critical overview* (Dublin: Economic and Social Research Institute, 1979. 272p.). Patrick Meghen describes housing programmes between 1921 and 1964 in *Housing in Ireland* (Dublin: Institute of Public Administration, 1965. 85p.).

653   **The lost children: a study of charity children in Ireland, 1700-1900.**
Joseph Robins.   Dublin: Institute of Public Administration, 1980.
366p.

A sad and poignant social history outlining the fate of numerous children in
workhouses, charity schools, prisons, and foundling hospitals, in which thousands
perished. An important work on social reform.

654   **Saints, scholars, and schizophrenics: mental illness in rural Ireland.**
Nancy Scheper-Hughes.   Berkeley, California: University of California Press, 1979. 260p.

This well received and authoritative volume studies the high incidence of mental
illness in isolated, rural areas of Ireland. A readable account based on
questionnaires covering childhood, marriage and inter-group relationships, this
book provides a detailed look at living and family conditions, personal roles and
social activities.

Social Services

655 **The Irish social services.**
John Curry. Dublin: Institute of Public Administration, 1979.
224p.
A brief history of the sometimes uncoordinated development of social services in Ireland is followed by a discussion of policies, available resources and organization. This is a convenient, outspoken survey of public services in the fields of housing, health, welfare and education.

656 **Directory and guide to social welfare, health, housing, legal services and other social services in Dublin.**
Dublin: Turoe Press, 1985. 160p.
Published for the social action group, Focus-Point, this provides an extensive listing of services in the Dublin area.

657 **Directory of national voluntary organizations, social service agencies and other useful public bodies.**
Dublin: National Social Service Board, 1985. 104p.
A short listing of social service organizations and addresses, intended for referrals.

658 **Community and social services directory.**
Edited by Raphael Gallagher. Dublin: Gill & Macmillan, 1970.
200p.
This guide to the services available in the greater Dublin area, although useful, is now somewhat dated. AnCo, the Dublin based industrial training body, has issued a later, revised community services directory.

Start. ..

659 Social policy in the Irish Republic.
Peter Robert Kaim-Caudle. London: Routledge & Kegan Paul;
New York: Humanities, 1967. 120p.
Provides a background review of some of the Irish services in the fields of health,
welfare, economic and family assistance, social insurance and housing. This study
is somewhat updated by J. D. Roche's *Social planning in Ireland, its purposes and
organizational requirements* (Dublin: National Economic and Social Council).

660 Who should care? The development of Kilkenny social services.
Sister Stanislaus Kennedy. Dublin: Turoe Press, 1981. 228p.
This study traces the development of the social services in Kilkenny over a period
of nearly two decades, showing the changing needs of the population, the quality
of services and the changes in their administration.

661 Who's minding the children.
Ronit Lentin, Geraldine Niland. Dublin: Arlen House, 1981.
137p.
A comprehensive guide to preschool and daycare facilities, with suggestions on
staff training and organizing techniques. Some questionable and superficial
comparisons are made with the experiences of other countries.

662 Guide for the disabled.
Richard Mooney. Dublin: Ward River, 1982. 250p.
A guide to locating and obtaining services in Ireland for the physically disabled. A
discussion of 'major issues in planning services for mentally and physically
handicapped persons' can also be found in report no. 50 of the National
Economic and Social Council in Dublin.

**663 Whose children? An analysis of some aspects of child care policy in
Ireland.**
Valerie Richardson. Dublin: University College Dublin, Family
Studies Unit, 1985. [not paginated].
Based on research undertaken in 1977 involving 151 Dublin children needing
residential care, Richardson examines the family background that leads to
children having special needs. She makes recommendations for new social
policies, family and adoption services.

664 Fifty years young, the story of An Oige.
Terry Trench. Dublin: An Oige, 1981. 136p.
A description of the development of Ireland's leading youth hostels organization,
covering its formative years, the war period, and its present service for young
people, as well as the cause of environmental conservation.

Health and Medicine

665 **The history of medicine in Ireland.**
John F. Fleetwood. Dublin: Skellig Press, 1984. 2nd rev. ed.
360p.

The history of Irish medicine is traced from pre-Christian times to the present, with numerous biographical portraits of leading professionals. Comments are given on the growth of hospitals, medical schools and societies, journals and governmental health services.

666 **The health services of Ireland.**
Brendan Hensey. Dublin: Institute of Public Administration, 1979. 3rd ed. 276p.

This standard work has been updated to describe the health services of the late 1970s, their origin, legislation, organization and financing. Further information can be found in the conference proceedings edited by Pauline Berwick and Margaret Burns, *Future directions in health policy* (Dublin: Council for Social Welfare, 1984. 328p.), and *Some major issues in health policy* by A. J. Culyer, A. K. Maynard, et. al. (Dublin: National Economic and Social Council, 1977. 94p.).

667 **Irish country cures.**
Patrick Logan. Belfast: Appletree, 1981. 192p.

This guide to traditional folk medicine describes the methods, supplies and skills of the healer. A reliable work, written by a physician and authority on the topic.

668 **Brief lives of Irish doctors, 1600-1965.**
J. B. Lyons. Dublin: Blackwater, 1979. 182p.

The lives of fifty leading Irish doctors and authors are briefly given, and an introduction reviews Irish medicine from 9,000 BC to the modern era.

669 **A portrait of Irish medicine.**
Eoin O'Brien, Anne Crookshank.   Dublin: Ward River Press,
1984. 256p.

Seven essays provide an illustrated social history of Irish medical practice,
architecture, and physicians through former centuries.

670 **Royal College of Surgeons in Ireland.**
Eoin O'Brien.   Dublin: Eason, 1984. 24p. (Irish Heritage Series,
no. 40).

A brief history of the College founded in 1784, and its growth into a leading
medical institution.

Politics

General

671 **What kind of country: modern Irish politics, 1968-1983.**
Bruce Arnold. London: Jonathan Cape, 1984. 241p.
An episodic account of election issues and parliamentary fights over partisan issues of the day. Written by a newspaper columnist, the book provides a summary of political disputes and power politics local to Ireland, but offers little in the way of a theory or a vision of the future. For popular reading.

672 **The Republic of Ireland, its government and politics.**
Morley Ayearst. London: London University Press, 1970. 241p.
A useful introduction on Irish politics and battles from the 17th century to the present is followed by short chapters on political developments since the Treaty of 1921, and recent Irish society (up to the 1960s), government, the constitution, political parties, elections and pressure groups.

673 **Harpstrings and confessions: an anthropological study of politics in rural Ireland.**
Mart Bax. Amsterdam: University of Amsterdam; Assen, Netherlands: Van Gorcum; Atlantic Highlands, New Jersey: Humanities, 1977. 224p.
An interesting look at political control in rural Irish areas, the local political élite, and the tension between government at the national level and the voting public in agricultural areas of the west.

674 **Magill book of Irish politics.**
Edited by Vincent Browne, Brian Trench, (et al.). Dublin:
Magill, 1983. 112p.

Information is provided on 600 political leaders and Members of Parliament, 20 political parties, and the election results for a 60 year period since 1923. This volume includes charts and illustrations. More than a directory, the work includes a number of pithy observations, and sometimes controversial assessments of selected political leaders.

675 **The government and politics of Ireland.**
Basil Chubb. London: Longman; Stanford, California: Stanford
University Press, 1982. 2nd ed. 396p. bibliog.

A major work covering the fundamentals of Ireland's government, civil service, politics and performance, foreign policy and social issues. This second edition contains much updated factual and statistical information.

676 **Source book of Irish government.**
Edited by Basil Chubb. Dublin: Institute of Public
Administration, 1983. 2nd rev. ed. 255p.

An anthology on Irish politics and government, with excerpts drawn from government documents, debates, constitutions, treaties, and party platforms. The second edition has been greatly expanded beyond the 1964 volume but it has been the cause of dispute, the author charging censorship. Nonetheless this remains a basic volume for political research.

677 **The Irish political elite.**
A. S. Cohen. Dublin: Gill & Macmillan, 1972. 88p.

A brief look at the changing background of political leadership, from the revolutionary figures of former days to the modern bureaucrat and technician.

678 **Towards a new Ireland.**
Garret FitzGerald. Dublin: Gill & Macmillan, 1973. 2nd ed.
190p.

In this volume written a decade before his election as Taoiseach (Prime Minister) FitzGerald evaluates the divisions of Irish society and the paths that might lead to unification. He discusses economic, social and political differences and social welfare provisions in both the Republic and Northern Ireland and views the future for a united Ireland. The son of a Northern Presbyterian mother and a Southern Catholic father, FitzGerald became a leading, if controversial, spokesman for political and economic unification.

679 **The boss, Charles J. Haughey in government.**
Joe Joyce, Peter Murtagh. Dublin: Poolbeg, 1984. 400p.

A journalistic account of Charles Haughey as prime minister during 1982, his role as leader of the Fianna Fail, Ireland's largest political party, and political infighting, which the authors view with some disdain as a cynical example of expediency.

680 **Nealon's Guide.**
Ted Nealon, Seamus Brennan. Dublin: Platform Press, 1978.
176p.
A directory to the Irish parliament with biographies of members of the
government, election results, bibliographies, and a limited political analysis. First
published by the Institute of Public Administration as *Ireland: a parliamentary
directory* (1974. 240p.).

681 **Political culture in Ireland: the views of two generations.**
John Raven, (et al.). Dublin: Institute of Public Administration,
1976. 206p.
Theoretical papers are included on public attitudes towards social questions and
political institutions. The conclusions are drawn from a survey of 1,200
individuals. For advanced readership.

682 **The Donegal mafia: an Irish political machine.**
Paul Sacks. New Haven, Connecticut: Yale University Press,
1976. 241p.
A valuable discussion of politics in the west of Ireland, where the milieu of
Donegal has seen the decline of agricultural influences and the consequent rapid
change in farm life and society. The author examines party leadership and
struggles, local and national issues, the use of patronage, family ties, attitudes
towards government, corruption, and the system of proportional representation.

683 **The houses of the Oireachtas.**
John McGowan Smyth. Dublin: Institute of Public
Administration, 1979. 4th ed. 62p.
A description of the lower house Dáil Éireann and the upper house Seanad of the
Irish Parliament, covering their procedures, political roles and responsibilities.
The history of the Dáil from 1919 to 1948 is provided by J. L. McCracken in
Representative government in Ireland (Oxford: Oxford University Press, 1958.
229p.). Thomas Garvin's *The Irish Senate* (Dublin: Institute of Public Administra-
tion, 1969. 100p.) reviews the history of the Seanad from 1922 to 1968.

Political parties and elections

684 **Party and parish pump: electoral politics in Ireland.**
Riki Carty. Dingle, County Kerry, Ireland (Republic): Brandon
Press; Gerrards Cross, England: Colin Smythe; Waterloo, Ontario,
Canada: Wilfrid Laurier University Press; Atlantic Highlands, New
Jersey: Humanities, 1981. 160p.
A critical analysis of the Irish electoral system which raises questions about the
system of proportional representation and the possibilities for corruption. Carty, a

148

Canadian, discusses slow political development in a rural society, party symbols, long term loyalties and the shift of attention to urban, economic, industrial and social issues.

685 **Political parties in the Republic of Ireland.**
Michael Gallagher. Manchester, England: Manchester University Press, 1985. 174p.

The origin, development, aims, organization, financing and membership of both major and minor political parties are described. Survey findings are used to analyse the composition of each party. This scholarly account discusses the background of Fine Gael, Fianna Fail, Sinn Fein and its factions, the Labour, and Farmers parties. Gallagher has also written *The Irish Labour Party in transition, 1957-81* (Manchester, England: Manchester University Press, 1983. 240p.). The present volume on political parties provides an excellent introduction to the topic, and the author also speculates on the future of the Irish party system.

686 **Guide to political parties in Ireland.**
Edited by Gerry Kennedy, Maeve Good. Killala, County Mayo, Ireland (Republic): Morrigan, 1984. 64p.

A short review of the development of Irish political parties since 1914 with brief comments on their objectives.

687 **Irish political parties.**
Maurice Manning. Dublin: Gill & Macmillan, 1972. 128p.

A general review of the major Irish political parties and issues during the years 1922 to 1970.

688 **Communism in modern Ireland: the pursuit of the workers' republic since 1916.**
Mike Milotte. Dublin: Gill & Macmillan, 1985. 326p.

From within the Communist movement, Milotte provides a criticism of party tactics and close adherence to foreign policy platforms, and notes the party's failures to achieve wide public support.

689 **Irish elections, 1918-77; parties, voters, and proportional representation.**
Cornelius O'Leary. Dublin: Gill & Macmillan; New York: St. Martin's, 1979. 134p.

A convenient review of the Irish political parties, elections and system of voting from 1918, with a substantial amount of statistical information.

690 **Results of presidential elections and referenda, 1937-1979.**
Dublin: Stationery Office, 1979. 39 leaves.

Statistical data on election results with some additional information on voting procedures.

691   **The party, inside Fianna Fail.**
       Dick Walsh.   Dublin: Gill & Macmillan, 1986. 158p.

A case-study and history of one of Ireland's major political parties, tracing its advance through sixty years under the leadership of de Valera, Lemass, Lynch and Haughey. Some mention is made of the party's original objective of national unity.

Constitution, Constitutional Law and Civil Rights

692 **The constitution and constitutional change in Ireland.**
Basil Chubb.   Dublin: Institute of Public Administration, 1978.
122p.

The development of the Irish constitution from its early stages in the first Dáil and the Free State is traced, and compared with the form and structure of government in later decades. Chubb reviews the role of judicial interpretations, European Economic Community (EEC) membership, the growth of political parties, individual rights and the powers of the president.

693 **Constitutional law and constitutional rights in Ireland.**
Brian Doolan.   Dublin: Gill & Macmillan, 1984. 194p.

A comprehensive introduction to Irish law and rights, with comments on equality, liberty, family law, and property rights. One hundred leading cases decided by the Irish courts are summarized with the author's comments as to their significance. He stresses the growing importance of judicial review in Ireland.

694 **Your rights as an Irish citizen.**
Irish Association of Civil Liberties.   Dublin: Ward River Press, 1982. 80p.

A short summary of basic rights pertaining to freedom of assembly, expression, arrest, home ownership, and union membership.

695 **Fundamental rights in the Irish law and constitution.**
John Maurice Kelly.   Dublin: Allen Figgis; New York: Oceana, 1968. 355p.

The leading analysis of the rights and liberties guaranteed under the constitution and the Irish system of government. Described as a 'Magisterial survey' by the *Sunday Press* (Dublin).

696 **Constitutional law of Ireland.**
David Gwynn Morgan.   Blackrock, Ireland (Republic): Round
Hall Press (Irish Academic), 1984. 270p.

A discussion of the major elements of government (the President, administration, Oireachtas, courts and judiciary), with a commentary on some modern, major political cases and crises.

697 **Cases and materials on the Irish Constitution.**
James O'Reilly, Mary Redmond.   Dublin: Incorporated Law
Society of Ireland, 1980. 712p.

A textbook for law students covering the provisions and basic rights under the Irish Constitution, with excerpts from numerous court cases and other public documents.

Law

Legal history

**698   Liberty, order and law under native Irish rule, a study in the book
of the ancient laws of Ireland.**
Sophie Bryant.   London: Harding & More, 1923. 398p.
This introduction to the ancient laws of Gaelic society is well presented in a fine
press edition. Included are laws and practice relating to landlords and tenants,
ecclesiastical policy, the secular law, a synopsis of early commentators on the
structure of Irish society, public duties and privileges, maintenance of the sick,
inheritance, the rights of women and the family in ancient times.

699   Irish at law.
James Comyn.   London: Secker & Warburg, 1981. 262p.
A selection of famous and unusual cases from 1671 to 1976 with comments on
personalities involved, the historical context and their significance. Included are
the cases of Oliver Plunkett, Wolfe Tone, Robert Emmet, Roger Casement,
Oscar Wilde, and Robert Erskine Childers.

700   George Gavan Duffy, 1882-1951.
G. M. Golding.   Dublin: Irish Academic Press, 1981. 240p.
One of the few studies of an Irish judicial leader. The philosophy, approach, life
and decisions of Duffy are covered. He had served as Ireland's first Minister of
Foreign Affairs, was a defender of Roger Casement, and eventually became a
distinguished President of the High Court.

701 **The old Munster circuit, a book of memories and traditions.**
Maurice Healy.   Dublin; Cork: Mercier, 1979. 272p.

A collection of monologues and reminiscences from 1891, by a barrister and local official in Munster. Amusing anecdotes help describe a period of 19th-century legal practice under British rule.

702 **Ancient laws and institutes of Ireland.**
Edited by Richard Oakes.   Buffalo, New York: William S. Hein, 1983. 378p.

First published in 1885, this volume reviews the Senchus Mor, the body of ancient Gaelic law extending back to pre-Christian and Brehon society. The text of the Brehon law is given in Irish, with English translation, and it provides a window into the structure of indigenous Irish society and its government for a period of twelve centuries, up the early 1600s.

703 **Lives of the Lord Chancellors and Keepers of the Great Seal of Ireland.**
J. Roderick O'Flanagan.   New York: Augustus Kelly, 1971. 2 vols.

A history of Irish law through biographies of leading legal officials from ancient to Victorian times. First published in 1870.

Law, legal practice and the administration of justice

704 **The Irish judiciary.**
Paul C. Bartholomew.   Dublin: Institute of Public Administration, 1971. 86p.

A review of the Irish court system, judges, the legal process and civil liberties.

705 **The administration of justice in Ireland.**
V. T. Delany.   Dublin: Institute of Public Administration, 1978. 5th ed. 90p.

A short, popular and convenient survey of the development of the Irish legal system, its courts and profession.

706 **Principles of Irish law.**
Brian Doolan.   Dublin: Gill & Macmillan, 1981. 300p.

An introductory textbook on Irish legal practice. Covered are statute law, court cases, the Constitution, legal history, government, fundamental rights, contracts, criminal law, torts, equity, land law, family, inheritance and labour law. A wide and very useful overview of the Irish flavour of the law. Tables list 120 statutes and 260 cases cited.

707 **Introduction to law in the Republic of Ireland.**
Richard Grimes, Patrick Horgan. Dublin: Wolfhound Press, 1981. 384p.

Intended for law students as well as for the general reader, this volume describe the origin, history from Brehon times, and modern development of Irish law, covering the courts, legal procedure, jurisprudence, evidence and the influence of the European Economic Community (EEC).

708 **Irish Law Reports Monthly. Volume one.**
Dublin: Round Hall Press in association with Irish Academic Press, 1981.

Complete coverage is given to the judgements of the High Court which are reported in full. Those of superior courts in the Republic are listed, and in some instances printed. The same publisher has also reinstated the *Irish Law Times*, first published between 1867 and 1981, and beginning in a new series (vol. 1, 1983-.) An abridgement of the *Irish law reports monthly* has been compiled as the *Handbook of Irish case law*. The 1985 volume contains 120p.

709 **Crime and punishment.**
Edited by Sean MacBride. Dublin: Ward River Press, 1982. 188p.

Several studies and papers are included on the Irish penal system, prisoners' rights, capital punishment, prostitution, and the need for systematic, university level research. More than sixty recommendations are made. MacBride was a Nobel Prize winner.

710 **In the eyes of the law.**
Neill McCafferty. Dublin: Ward River Press, 1981. 185p.

A reprint of columns from the *Irish Times* describing individual legal cases and the daily functioning of Dublin's District Courts in the 1970s. The author criticizes the system of criminal justice, probation and social welfare, all of which are viewed as insufficient.

711 **Irish law of torts.**
Bryan M. McMahon, William Binchy. Abingdon, Oxfordshire, England: Professional Books, 1981. 620p.

This textbook shows how Irish statutes and case law has affected the common law with respect to civil disputes and personal disputes between individuals. Included is material on negligence, trespass, breach of duty, product liability, privacy, nuisance, and trade and business relationships.

Law. Law, legal practice and the administration of justice

712 **Business law.**
Liam O'Malley.   London: Sweet & Maxwell, 1982. 222p. (Irish Law Texts Series).
A detailed review of Irish business law through cases and statutes, with chapters covering incorporation and organization, property and premises, transactions and contracts, sales, marketing and labour relations. Also published by Sweet & Maxwell in the same series are *Contract*, by R. Clark (1982), *Tax law* by K. Corrigan (1983), and *Company law* by P. Ussher (1983). Of related interest is *Cases and comment on Irish commercial law and legal technique* (Blackrock, Irish Republic: Round Hall Press, 1985), which covers contracts, sales, credits, insurance, banking, competition and remedies.

713 **Irish company law, 1973-1983; a guide and handbook.**
B. J. Power.   Dublin: Gill & Macmillan, 1984. 208p.
A guide to legal regulations governing the organization of companies, their assets and share-holding. Both Irish law and European Community regulations are included.

714 **The Irish criminal process.**
Edward F. Ryan, Philip Magee.   Dublin; Cork: Mercier, 1983. 600p.
A thorough study of criminal procedure relating to serious offences, and Irish courts, arrests, prosecution, search and seizure, bail, trials, sentencing, and the appeals process. A table conveniently lists offences and penalties. Mercier Press has also published *Irish cases on criminal law* by J. S. Cole (240p.).

715 **Family law in the Republic of Ireland.**
Alan J. Shatter.   Dublin: Wolfhound, 1981. 2nd rev. ed. 448p.
The standard work on family law, revised to February 1, 1981.

716 **Irish conveyancing law.**
J. C. Wylie.   Abingdon, Oxfordshire, England: Professional Books, 1979. 921p.
A scholarly and comprehensive survey of the law, arranged chronologically. This is intended to complement Wylie's *Irish land law* with the same publisher (1975, 1026p. + supplements).

Administration and Local Government

717 **Administration Yearbook and Diary.**
Dublin: Institute of Public Administration, 1968-. annual.
A major, comprehensive directory, listing thousands of organizations; including private bodies, all the main departments of the national government, county councils, local government, the defence forces, major religious groups, larger companies, the media, press, higher education and women's interest groups. Good coverage is provided for trade organizations and social, cultural and political groups. The address of each is given, and for government agencies a brief description is added. Details of the latest census and other statistical information on agriculture, industry, population and other factors are particularly useful. Brief information is also included on postal charges and social insurance. Some bibliographic references are provided and there is a good listing of periodicals. A US edition entitled *Ireland: a Directory* (Detroit, Michigan: Gale Research) is also available.

718 **Man of no property.**
C. S. Andrews.   Dublin; Cork: Mercier, 1982. 328p.
The second part of a two-volume autobiography by a former official who served in a number of major government posts, including those dealing with peat, electric power, transportation, radio and television. Covering the years 1924 to 1980, Andrews also comments on life in Dublin and Connemara early in the century, and on other public officials encountered in over fifty years of service. The tone of the account ranges from sensitive to outspoken.

719 **From big government to local government.**
T. J. Barrington.   Dublin: Institute of Public Administration, 1976. 238p.
The author stresses the need for reforming government administration in Ireland, especially the transfer to local and regional levels of some of the present centralized functions of the national government.

Administration and Local Government

720 **The Irish administrative system.**
T. J. Barrington. Dublin: Institute of Public Administration, 1980. 256p.
A former director of the Institute and an expert on the civil service describes government administration, its problems, promises and public employees.

721 **The Irish police.**
Seamus Breathnach. Dublin: Anvil Books, 1974. 219p.
A review of the origin and development of the Garda Síochána, Ireland's police force, its historical antecedents and place in modern society. Breathnach provides a popular approach. For more detailed information on the contemporary police force in the Irish Republic see Conor Brady's *Guardians of the peace* (Dublin: Gill & Macmillan, 1974. 254p.).

722 **The office of Attorney General in Ireland.**
J. P. Casey. Dublin: Institute of Public Administration, 1980. 256p.
A description is provided of the office of Attorney General, its functioning in an advisory role to the government, and its participation in the courts and legal profession.

723 **The Irish civil service.**
Sean Dooney. Dublin: Institute of Public Administration, 1966. 56p.
A short but useful review of public employees and the civil service system, government performance and organization. Now somewhat dated.

724 **The Irish Department of Finance, 1922-1958.**
Ronan Fanning. Dublin: Institute of Public Administration, 1978. 707p.
An excellent, highly detailed review of the history and organization of the department and of public finance, showing the changes which have taken place during several crucial periods as the government emerged and matured.

725 **Chairman or chief, the role of Taoiseach in Irish government.**
Brian Farrell. Dublin: Gill & Macmillan, 1971. 110p.
The position and authority of the Irish Prime Minister, as both head of government and as party leader, is analysed. The role of individual office holders is described through recent history.

726 **No man's man: a biography of Joseph Brennan.**
Leon O Broin. Dublin: Institute of Public Administration, 1983. 192p.
With wide experience as a public administrator, and as an expert in government finance, Brennan's career traces the development of the civil service from British

rule into the emerging Irish state. Brennan served as governor of the Central
Bank for many years.

727 **How Ireland is governed.**
James D. O'Donnell.   Dublin: Institute of Public Administration,
1979. 160p.
A basic introduction to the functioning of the Irish government, including the civil
service, various departments and agencies and local government.

728 **Local government in Ireland.**
Desmond Roche.   Dublin: Institute of Public Administration,
1982. rev. ed. 391p. bibliog.
The major publication on Irish local government originally written by P. J.
Meghen and revised through various editions. The book includes the historical
origin of local government, its growth and its present responsibilities for roads,
traffic, education, welfare, recreation, housing, planning and certain environmental matters.

729 **The parish pump.**
Myles Tierney.   Dublin: Able Press, 1982. 126p.
A study of local government in Ireland, covering the advantages of devolution of
power, and the complexities of public finance, by a member of the Dublin County
Council.

Foreign Relations

730 **Inside the EEC, an Irish guide.**
Ruth Barrington, John Cooney.   Dublin: O'Brien Press, 1984.
200p.
This simplified guide and commentary provides an Irish perspective on the
European Economic Community (EEC), its history, organization, politics, people
and contact points, and its policies on business, finance, agriculture and law.

731 **Ireland and the European communities; ten years of membership.**
Edited by David Coombes.   Dublin: Gill & Macmillan, 1983.
220p.
Nine papers prepared for the National Institute of Higher Education (Limerick)
provide a valuable survey of the effects that EEC membership has had on the
constitutional and legal system of the Republic of Ireland, on public opinion,
government and foreign policy, agriculture, and the economy.

732 **The foreign policy of Eamon de Valera, 1919-59.**
T. Ryle Dwyer.   Dublin: Gill & Macmillan, 1981. 220p.
An examination of Irish foreign policy under the leadershp of de Valera, covering
his attitudes on independence, international participation, and the role of small
states in the wider world.

733 **Irish unification and N.A.T.O.**
William FitzGerald.   Dublin: Dublin University Press, 1982. 85p.
The author argues for Ireland's acceptance of a role in the North Atlantic Treaty
Organization (NATO), (and perhaps the abandonment of neutrality), in exchange
for unification with Northern Ireland, an unlikely scenario. An opposing position
is taken by Patrick Comerford in *Do you want to die for NATO?* (Dublin; Cork:

Mercier, 1984. 104p.), and by Bill McSweeny in *Ireland and the threat of nuclear war* (Dublin: Dominican Publications, 1984. 212p.).

734 **The road to Europe, Irish attitudes 1948-61.**
Miriam Hederman.   Dublin: Institute of Public Administration,
1984. 304p.

The author explores the slow evolution of an Irish foreign policy endorsing EEC membership in 1961, and the first steps toward political integration with Europe. Also described are the influences of pressure groups, the media and public attitudes toward Europe, Ireland's rejection of NATO membership, and its maintenance of an independent stance.

735 **A place among the nations: issues of Irish foreign policy.**
Patrick Keatinge.   Dublin: Institute of Public Administration,
1978. 287p.

A wide ranging review of both domestic and international issues affecting Irish foreign policy in the late 1970s. The author focuses on the process of policy-making, the principle of neutrality (especially as it has emerged in Anglo-Irish relations), and Ireland's support of independence, order and justice abroad. Keatinge has also written *The formulation of Irish foreign policy* (Dublin: Institute of Public Administration, 1973. 323p.).

736 **A singular stance, Irish neutrality in the 1980s.**
Patrick Keatinge.   Dublin: Institute of Public Administration,
1984. 162p. bibliog.

A critical analysis of Irish foreign policy and its doctrine of neutrality. The author, a political scientist, covers both the historical roots and current applications of the principle. He notes comparisons with other European states, local Irish politics, the EEC, and NATO. Several additional papers on current Irish neutrality can be found in the *Irish Studies in International Affairs* vol. I, no. 3 (1982), and in the *Journal of Common Market Studies* (March 1982).

737 **Republicans and imperialists: Anglo-Irish relations in the 1930s.**
Deirdre McMahon.   New Haven, Connecticut: Yale University
Press, 1984. 340p.

A well-documented review of relations between Britain and Ireland in the angry aftermath of the Treaty negotiations, showing the various shifts, and the development of an Irish foreign policy in the 1930s.

738 **Irish Studies in International Affairs.**
National Committee for the Study of International Affairs.   Dublin: Royal Irish Academy, 1977-. annual.

An academic journal covering Irish participation in international affairs. Articles include the history of Irish foreign policy, Ireland's position on current questions, and world events in general from an Irish perspective.

739 **Dublin from Downing Street.**
John Peck. Dublin: Gill & Macmillan, 1980. 241p.

An inside view with an English perspective of important events in the Irish Republic from 1970 to 1973, during which time the author served as British ambassador to Dublin. Irish political manoeuvering is described from first hand knowledge, and comments are given on Northern Ireland, the burning of the British embassy, 'Bloody Sunday,' and the beginnings of internment. After retirement, Peck chose to live in Dublin.

740 **Up in the park.**
Elizabeth Shannon. Dublin: Gill & Macmillan; New York: Atheneum, 1983. 358p.

The diary of the wife of the American ambassador to the Republic of Ireland, during her four years of residence in Dublin, from 1977 to 1981. The author presents a witty, 'safe' and colourful account of diplomatic life in the city. This chronological review describes public reactions to events, various interviews and inspection tours, and Irish government officials. Also included are anecdotes on country folk ways and remarks on the women's movement. Chiefly of interest to an American audience.

741 **Under the blue flag.**
Raymond Smith. Dublin: Aherlow Publications, 1980. 242p.

A review of the experiences of Irish military units operating with UN peacekeeping forces, in the Middle East, the Congo and Cyprus. A closer look at Irish military organization is provided in P. D. Kavanagh's *Irish defense forces handbook* (Dublin: An Casantoir, 1974. 56p.). See also 'The changing nature of Irish defense policy,' by Trevor Salmon, *World Today*, vol. 35, no. 11 (Nov. 1979), p. 462-70.

Economy, Finance and Banking

742 **The emergence of the Irish banking system.**
G. L. Barrow.   Dublin: Gill & Macmillan; Toronto: Macmillan, 1975. 284p.

The history of the Irish banking system is reviewed during a twenty-five year period of expansion (1820-1845) of both provincial and centralized services.

743 **Economic policy in Ireland.**
Edited by John Bristow, A. A. Tait.   Dublin: Institute of Public Administration, 1968. 320p.

Various experts discuss different industries, the business and economic sectors of the Irish economy, the potential growth of each and the ways in which they might be encouraged by government policy.

744 **Economic development and planning.**
Basil Chubb, Patrick Lynch.   Dublin: Institute of Public Administration, 1969. 362p.

Irish economic theory, growth, government policy, and planning are discussed by the two specialists and academics, for the period 1950 to 1968. Some statistics are included.

745 **An economic history of Ireland since 1660.**
Louis M. Cullen.   London: Batsford, 1972. 208p.

Growth and fluctuations in the Irish economy are covered from the 17th century to 1921, and the author weaves together trends in Irish population and industrial development. Cullen has edited a shorter study of Ireland's economy from the 18th century to the 1970s, entitled *Formation of the Irish economy* (Cork: Mercier, 1978. 128p.).

746 **Doing business in the Republic of Ireland.**
Dublin: Price Waterhouse, 1977. 150p.

Designed for the business investor, this report presents data on economic and labour conditions, new business opportunities, and the requirements of banking, trade, taxation and accounting. A more theoretical work with a geographical outlook on business and industry is provided by Desmond A. Gillmor in *Economic activities in the Republic of Ireland* (Dublin: Gill & Macmillan, 1985. 394p.).

747 **Irish economic policy: a review of major issues.**
Edited by Brendan R. Dowling, J. Durkin. Dublin: Economic and Social Research Institute, 1978. 410p.

A useful overview of Ireland's economic standing, covering its agriculture, industry, labour force and employment, health and environmental policies, the problems affecting government budgets, planning, and European developments.

748 **Planning in Ireland.**
Garrett FitzGerald. Dublin: Institute of Public Administration, 1968. 246p.

FitzGerald, who is currently Ireland's Prime Minister (or Taoiseach), reviews the state of the Irish economy at mid-century, and offers several alternatives for economic planning and direction.

749 **Economic activity in Ireland: a study of two open economies.**
Edited by Norman Gibson, John Spencer. Dublin: Gill & Macmillan, 1977. 272p.

Various papers compare the Republic and Northern Ireland in an analysis of economic conditions, production, performance and financial activities. Data is given for the period 1960 to 1975.

750 **The Bank of Ireland, 1783-1946.**
Frederick George Hall. Dublin: Hodges, Figgis, 1949. 523p.

The history and development of a major banking institution, with emphasis on its dominance during the Anglo-Irish ascendancy. Some attention is paid to the architecture of the Bank of Ireland building.

751 **Economic growth in Ireland: the experience since 1947.**
Kieran Kennedy, Brendon Dowling. Dublin: Gill & Macmillan; New York: Barnes & Noble, 1976. 345p.

A useful summary of the Irish economy for the years 1947 to 1972, with data on growth, investments, trade, industry and government policy.

752 **Government and enterprise in Ireland.**
Ivor Kenny. Dublin: Gill & Macmillan, 1984. 149p.

The author charts the negative aspects of private enterprise arising from the growth of government and state power. He is also critical of Irish management, and suggests that major reforms are needed in the organization of both state run bodies and private industry.

753 **Bank of Ireland, 1783-1983: bicentenary essays.**
Edited by F. S. L. Lyons. Dublin: Gill & Macmillan, 1983. 236p.

Various papers separately discuss specific aspects of Irish banking, economic and social history, from the 18th to the late 20th centuries. An authorized company history, this book focuses on the commercial activity and currency transactions of the Bank of Ireland, and on its role as a 'banker's bank.'

754 **The Irish economy since 1922.**
James Francis Meenan. Liverpool, England: Liverpool University Press, 1970. 422p.

A good review is presented of major factors and trends in the Irish economy from 1922 to the 1960s. Detailed tables and data are presented on population, marriage, emigration, labour, production, incomes, prices, economic stability, European integration, trade and tariffs, banking, agriculture, transportation and resources.

755 **Economists and the Irish economy from the eighteenth century to the present day.**
Edited by Antoin Murphy. Blackrock, Ireland (Republic): Irish Academic Press, 1984. 176p.

Several papers trace the influence that events in Ireland have had on the evolution of economic theory, from the 1700s to 1950. Banking, investment, land policies, and the theories of John Stuart Mill all figure in this account.

756 **Economic analysis of an open economy: Ireland.**
Desmond Norton. Dublin: Irish Management Institute, 1981. 414p.

The author examines elements of the Irish economy including supply and demand, public finance, and business policies; he shows its structure to be that of an open system.

757 **The economic history of Ireland from the Union to the famine.**
George O'Brien. Clifden, Ireland (Republic): Augustus Kelly, 1972. 2 vols.

A reprint of a classic 1921 study, covering conditions of the rural population, consolidation of farms, economic distress, government remedies, the great famine, industry, fisheries, manufacturing and public finance. O'Brien has also written *The economic history of Ireland in the eighteenth century* (Philadelphia: Porcupine Press, 1977. Reprint of 1918 edition. 437p.). In the present volume he traces the chief causes of economic disaster leading to the famine. The underlying factors are those traditionally accepted, but the account is lacking some of the detailed statistical analysis of later accounts such as *Why Ireland starved, a quantitative and analytical history of Irish economy, 1800-1850* (q.v.).

758 **The economy of Ireland: policy and performance.**
Edited by John W. O'Hagan. Dublin: Irish Management Institute, 1981. 3rd rev. ed. 300p.

A collection of various writings on the major features of modern Irish economic policies, with information on planning, employment, growth, the cost of living, taxes and other aspects.

759 **Spatial planning in the small economy; a case study of Ireland.**
Helen B. O'Neill. New York: Praeger, 1971. 221p.

The interrelationship between agriculture, urban areas and the regional concentration of industry is explored. Both social change and economic effects are discussed for major Irish cities. Economic models are included. The ways in which a particular region of Ireland is affected by economic change and how it might respond to adequate planning is discussed in a book by C. M. Fanning *Revitalising a local economy: the emerging entrepreneurial response to crisis* (Cork: Cork University Press, 1985).

760 **Ireland.**
Organization for Economic Cooperation and Development, Department of Economic Statistics. Paris: OECD, 1983. 72p. (Economic Survey Series).

A general survey is presented of Ireland's economic well-being, with comments on monetary policies, the fiscal and economic outlook for 1984, persistent macroeconomic imbalances, the growth of the labour force, industrial policy and areas of sustained growth. A chronology of main economic events for 1982-83 is included, with numerous tables comparing ten years of performance.

761 **Planning in Ireland.**
Edited by F. Rogerson, P. Ó hUiginn. Dublin: An Foras Forbartha, 1967. 200p.

This collection of conference papers explores regional planning and economic effects, industrial location, conservation, transportation, resources, and urban areas in both the Republic and Northern Ireland.

762 **Taxation in Ireland.**
New York: Deloitte, Haskins & Sells, 1980. 90p.

A summary of Irish tax law as applied to business corporations. Another short review is Glyn Saunders' *Tolley's taxation in the Republic of Ireland, 1983-1984* (London: Tolley, 1983. 226p.).

763 **Marketing in Ireland.**
US Department of Commerce.   Washington, DC: Government
Printing Office, 1978. 19p. (Overseas Business Report 78-19).
A useful summary of economic conditions in Ireland, potential markets and
business opportunities, government regulations, investments, transportation,
advertising, trade and distribution. This is occasionally reissued with revisions, at
irregular intervals.

764 **Ireland.**
US Department of State.   Washington, DC: Government Printing
Office, 1978. 8p. (Foreign Economic Trends and their Implications
for the United States, no. 78-062).
Major business and economic trends in Ireland are outlined for the benefit of US
commercial interests and firms.

765 **Economic sovereignty and regional policy.**
Edited by John Vaizey.   Dublin: Gill & Macmillan; New York:
Wiley, 1975. 281p.
Conference papers from 1973 discuss regional economic problems existing
between Britain and the Republic of Ireland, showing the strong financial bonds
between the two nations, and Ireland's somewhat dependent position.

766 **Seven seminars: an appraisal of regional planning in Ireland.**
Edited by Michael Viney.   Dublin: An Foras Forbartha, 1969.
112p.
Conference papers sketch 20th-century developments in regional economic
policies throughout Ireland. Remarks are made on growth in the Dublin region,
the need for setting social and economic goals, and the provision of necessary
services.

767 **Interests.**
Thomas K. Whitaker.   Dublin: Institute of Public Administration,
1984. 330p.
Collected essays by a leading figure in Irish banking and government, covering
economic theory, financial crisis, the development of official policies, and some
cultural aspects, such as the use of the Irish language.

Trade

768 External Trade Statistics.
Central Statistics Office. Dublin: Stationery Office, 1968-. annual
An annual publication tabulating exports, imports, commodities, destinations and values. The Central Statistics Office also issues *Trade Statistics of Ireland* (1949-. monthly).

769 Ireland in world commerce.
Charles Hultman. Cork: Mercier, 1969. 160p.
A view of business in Ireland as affected by European, British and world trade patterns. The prospects for Irish trade are assayed in this now dated account.

770 Irish Exporters Handbook.
Dublin: Córas Tráchtála, 1978. 498p.
An occasional publication intended for the Irish businessman, with a review of trade opportunities, regulations, tax advantages, available transportation and exchange systems. The Irish Export Board (Córas Tráchtála) also issues an export directory, listing products, buyers and foreign importers, as well as a periodical, *Export*, providing updated information. A monthly journal, *The Irish Exporter* is published by the Irish Exporters Association and provides current export information.

771 A study of imports.
C. E. V. Leser. Dublin: Economic and Social Research Institute, 1967. 26p. (Its Paper no. 38).
A very brief review of some Irish trade experiences at mid-century. The Institute has issued a number of papers relating to Irish trade.

Industry

772 **Regional studies in Ireland.**
Colin Buchanan and Partners.   Dublin: An Foras Forbartha,
1969. 191p.
A United Nations commissioned study of regional areas in Ireland, their
individual strengths and their potential for industrial development.

773 **Census of Industrial Production in Ireland.**
Central Statistics Office.   Dublin: Stationery Office, 1933-.
decennial.
Basic industrial production figures for the Irish Republic.

774 **The construction industry; sectorial consultative committee report.**
Dublin: An Foras Forbartha, 1984. 132p.
A review of the state of the construction industry in Ireland, with an analysis of its
relationship with government policy. Numerous suggestions are made for
increasing production and performance, with an outlook and forecast to 1989.
Major construction and planning bodies are identified. An Foras Forbartha, the
state body concerned with construction, development and planning, has also
issued *Construction industry statistics, 1984* (Dublin; 1985. 56p.), which provides
information and statistics on the Republic of Ireland's second largest industry.

775 **Managers in Ireland.**
Liam Gorman.   Dublin: Irish Management Institute, 1974. 228p.
Irish managers in major firms are surveyed as to their background, present
positions and training. For a discussion of the decision making process in both
public and private sector management see Laraine Joyce's *Administrators or
managers?* (Dublin: Institute of Public Administration, 1985. 56p.).

776   **Irish industry, how its managed.**
Liam Gorman, (et al.).   Dublin: Irish Management Institute, 1975. 189p.
The performance of various industries in Ireland is examined with regard to finance, employees, products, marketing strategies and other aspects. Statistical tables are included.

777   **A history of Irish steel.**
Sarsfield Hogan.   Dublin: Gill & Macmillan, 1980. 223p.
This volume explores the difficulties involved in staffing the steel industry in Ireland, the failures of the 19th century and the technological advances of the 20th century, labour supply, financial needs, and government support.

778   **IDA Industrial Plan, 1978-82.**
Dublin: Industrial Development Authority, 1979. 77p.
A review of government policies towards the encouragement of economic development, industry and employment. Priorities are set and projections into the short term future are made. The *Annual Reports* of the Authority contain further data on regional efforts, expenditures and development.

779   **Industrialization and regional development in Ireland, 1958-72.**
Kevin C. Kearns.   *American Journal of Economics and Sociology*, vol. 33, no. 3 (July 1974), p. 229-316.
A useful overview of the modernization of Irish industry, as promoted by several government economic programmes. Special emphasis is given to regional concentrations, disbursement and decentralization. Some of the social and economic costs are also noted.

780   **Productivity and industrial growth: the Irish experience.**
Kieran Kennedy.   Oxford: Clarendon Press, 1971. 281p.
A look at Irish manufacturing companies and their productivity, which includes comparisons with other countries. Some performance data is provided for major sectors of Irish industry.

781   **Rural industrialization: the impact of industrialization on two communities in Western Ireland.**
Denis Lucey, Donald Kaldor.   London: Geoffrey Chapman, 1969. 208p.
The effect of new industry upon rural areas in Clare and Sligo is examined. Resulting changes are noted in employment, agricultural organization, management, and the local economy. Detailed data is provided on labourers and managers, showing their changing economic status in rural communities.

782 **A profile of grant-aided industry in Ireland.**
Dermot McAleese.   Dublin: Industrial Development Authority,
1978. 92p.

A review of government supported industry in Ireland (including foreign concerns), with information on trade, location, employment, major products and investments.

783 **Motor makers in Ireland.**
John S. Moore.   Dublin: Blackstaff; Dover, New Hampshire:
Longwood, 1982. 178p.

A general, well illustrated history of the motor car industry in Ireland. For another history of the industry see John O'Donovan's *Wheels and deals* (Dublin: Gill & Macmillan, 1983). O' Donovan presents a history of the motor car in Ireland from the 1890s to the present, the leaders of the industry, and the formation of clubs and trade associations.

784 **Regional policy in Ireland.**
National Economic and Social Council.   Dublin: Stationery Office,
1974. 86p. (Parliamentary Paper no. 4147).

A paper advocating the distribution of new industry through various economic regions. Each region is explored with regard to resources, services and needs.

785 **New dimensions in regional planning.**
Jeremiah Newman.   Dublin: An Foras Forbartha, 1967. 128p.

An important study of Irish regional, industrial and economic planning, the resources available and the needs of each area. The author argues for disbursal of new industry and development in growth centres, but he also notes the necessity of preserving local and cultural values in rural areas.

Agriculture and Forestry

786   **Irish agriculture in a changing world.**
      Edited by I. F. Baillie, S. J. Sheehy.   Edinburgh: Oliver & Boyd,
      1971. 236p.
Several conference papers from 1968 view the position, risks and opportunities of
Irish agriculture and trade in the face of world competition. Demand, sales, and
European regulations are also covered.

787   **Irish forestry policy.**
      Frank J. Convery.   Dublin: National Economic and Social
      Council, 1979. 225p.
The effects of government policy on the forests of Éire are reviewed for recent
years. The forests are considered as a natural resource with an impact on
employment and the economy.

788   **Irish agricultural production: its volume and structure.**
      Raymond Crotty.   Cork: Cork University Press, 1966. 384p.
A statistical and historical review of Irish agriculture from the early 19th century,
with a critique on taxation, land ownership and distribution.

789   **The forests of Ireland, an account of the forests of Ireland from
      early times until the present day.**
      Edited by Harry Morton Fitzpatrick.   Bray, Ireland (Republic):
      Bray Press, 1966. 153p.
Presents a short introduction to Irish trees, covering both their history and
present day environment. This edition was reprinted for the Society of Irish
Foresters, and contains passages on management and education both in Éire and
Northern Ireland. A shorter but more current work is *The forests of Ireland:*

history, distribution and silviculture, by Niall O'Carroll (Dublin: Turoe, 1983. 96p.).

790 **The Department's story.**
Daniel Hoctor. Dublin: Institute of Public Administration, 1971. 304p.

A history of the Republic of Ireland's Department of Agriculture, with a commentary on its leadership, organization and services throughout the 20th century.

791 **Agriculture in Ireland: a census atlas.**
A. A. Horner, J. A. Walsh, J. A. Williams. Dublin: University College Dublin, Department of Geography, 1984. 104p.

A variety of colour and black and white maps plot more than fifty agricultural products and production considerations. 1980 data is used throughout with occasional references to percentages of change since 1970.

792 **The Downshire estates in Ireland, 1801-1845.**
W. A. Maguire. Oxford: Clarendon Press, 1972. 284p.

The organization, economics, production and social history of Ireland's system of great estates is described, based on several 19th-century examples. The estates had a profound influence on agriculture, employment and living conditions.

793 **Irish woods since Tudor times; distribution and exploitation.**
Eileen McCraken. Newton Abbot, England: David & Charles, 1971. 184p. maps.

A summary of Irish forests, including the more plentiful times from the 17th to the 19th centuries. Reasons are given for the sharp decline in the Irish stands, and the problem of modern building techniques and misuse of resources.

794 **A view of Ireland.**
Edited by James Francis Meenan, David Webb. Dublin: Eason & Son, 1957. 254p.

Twelve essays, collected together for the British Association for the Advancement of Science, provide a glimpse of various aspects of Irish rural life.

795 **Meitheal, a study of co-operative labour in rural Ireland.**
Anne O'Dowd. Dublin: Irish Folklore Council, 1981. 181p. bibliog.

A study of cooperative effort and labour in rural communities, which includes a great variety of forms and tasks traditionally shared by those from the surrounding countryside. The volume covers older patterns of work surviving into present times. Cooperative activity is also covered by Patrick Bolger in *The Irish co-operative movement, its history and development* (Dublin: Institute of Public Administration, 1977. 448p.). Bolger charts this widely successful movement that incorporated many agricultural businesses and occupations from the end of the 19th century. Further historical background on this effort towards reform and self-help in agriculture may be found in several biographies of Horace Plunkett, including R. A. Anderson's *With Plunkett in Ireland* (Dublin: Irish Academic Press, 1983), and Margaret Digby's *Horace Plunkett* (Oxford: Blackwell, 1949. 314p.).

796   The quiet revolution: the electrification of rural Ireland.

Michael Shiel.   Dublin: O'Brien Press, 1984. 304p.

A factual, detailed, yet entertaining account of modernization in rural areas following the electrification begun in the 1940s. The book recaptures an era of economic, social and cultural change for agricultural communities where life and work were often difficult.

Transport

General

797 Transport policy in Ireland.
   Sean D. Barrett.   Dublin: Irish Management Institute, 1982. 200p.
This study presents a highly critical review of management policies in CIE (the public transport system in Ireland). Among the targets are bus operations, the fare structure, and public vs. private service.

798 History of aviation in Ireland.
   Liam Byrne.   Dublin: Blackwater, 1979. 150p.
An entertaining, well illustrated history of Irish aviation, covering various early innovations, pioneering attempts, 18th-century balloon ascents, later record holders and transatlantic flights.

799 The canals of the south of Ireland.
   V. T. H. Delany, D. R. Delany.   Newton Abbot, England: David
   & Charles, 1966. 260p.
In the past, Ireland's canals have played an important part in commercial activity. The authors discuss the history, organization and network of the canal system. From the same publisher see also Ruth Delany's, *The Grand Canal of Ireland* (1973, 255p.). Another detailed review of the Irish waterway system is provided by L. Rolt in *Green and silver* (London: Allen & Unwin, 1968. 276p.).

800 **The transport challenge, the opportunities in the 1980's, a report for the Minister for Transport.**
McKinsey International. New York: McKinsey; Dublin: Stationery Office, 1980. [not paginated]. (Parliamentary Paper 9433).
An extensive, technical study of Irish transport and its financial management. Examined are rail and bus operations, roads, freight and urban services. This controversial report recommended a major reorganization of public services, which was not carried out. Numerous charts and statistics are included; transportation data is conveniently arranged.

801 **Coastal passenger steamers and inland navigations in the south of Ireland.**
D. B. McNeill. Belfast: Transport Museum, 1965. 44p.
A very brief, illustrated introduction to the Irish internal transport service and waterways, ships, routes and history. More information is given by the author in volume 2 of *Irish passenger steamship service* (Newton Abbot, England: David & Charles, 1971), which concerns the Irish Republic.

802 **Transport policy.**
National Economic and Social Council. Dublin: Stationery Office, 1980. 161p. (NESC Report no. 48, Parliamentary Paper 8153).
A review of government policy and the organization of the transport sector, covering rail and bus services, the relationship between transport and the economy, aviation, roads, and commercial and urban services. Recommendations for improvements are given.

803 **Travel and transport in Ireland.**
Edited by Kevin Nowlan. Dublin: Gill & Macmillan, 1973. 178p.
Various papers from a 1970 radio lecture series broadly portray the history of all forms of Irish transport from ancient times to modern day aviation.

804 **The B and I line.**
Hazel Smyth. Dublin: Gill & Macmillan, 1984. 250p.
A history of steam packets and later services between England, Wales and Ireland from 1824 to 1982. Company organization, equipment, popular use, and essential services are discussed.

Railways

805 Irish railways since 1916.
Michael Baker. London: Ian Allen, 1972. 224p.

A good review of the rail services in the Irish Republic up to 1970, with data on organization, crews and equipment. The author has also written: *Railways of the Republic of Ireland: a pictorial survey of the G.S.R. and C.I.E., 1925-75* (Truro, England: Barton, 1975. 96p.).

806 Outline of Irish railway history.
Henry Cyril Casserley. Newton Abbot, England: David & Charles, 1974. 303p.

A good introduction to the history of Irish rail transport, especially during the earlier decades when it was a more vital service. A nostalgic look at the railways is provided by the same author in, *Irish railways in the heyday of steam* (Truro, England: Barton, 1979. 96p.).

807 A railway atlas of Ireland.
S. Maxwell Hajducki. Newton Abbot, England: David & Charles, 1974. 70p.

Maps are presented showing the Irish network of passenger, freight and mining railways.

808 Railway history in pictures: Ireland.
W. Alan McCutcheon. New York: Kelley, 1969; Newton Abbot, England: David & Charles, 1971. 2 vols. bibliog.

An illustrated history of Irish railway lines, their equipment and passenger services, from the 1880s.

809 Irish standard gauge railways.
Tom Middlemass. Newton Abbot, England: David & Charles, 1981. 96p.

A short history of the seventeen Irish railway companies, and their gradual decline up to the 1980s. Attention is focused on early lines serving the South and West, during a period of population and economic characteristics which are different to those of today.

810 One hundred and fifty years of Irish railways.
Fergus Mulligan. Belfast: Appletree; Newton Abbot, England: David & Charles, 1983. 176p.

This popular, illustrated history of Irish rail transport from its beginnings to recent times, is enlivened by comments on various oddities of equipment and service, arranged by company. A general rather than technical review is provided.

177

811   **Ireland's first railway.**
   K. A. Murray.   Dublin: Irish Railway Record Society, 1981. 200p.
The establishment of the Dublin and Kingstown line had a profound effect on the
Dublin region after 1834. Both a social and technical history of the times is
presented, with comments on passenger traffic and leading entrepreneurs.

Employment and Manpower

812 **Employment and unemployment policy for Ireland.**
Edited by Denis Coniffee, Kieran Kennedy. Dublin: Economic
and Social Research Institute, 1984. 350p.

An overview of the employment situation in the Republic of Ireland, with an
analysis of the social and economic characteristics of the working population. A
considerable body of supporting statistics is included, with references. The editors
draw recommendations for changes in governmental policy.

813 **The Irish worker.**
J. Deeny. Dublin: Institute of Public Administration, 1971. 97p.

A study of the Irish labour force and its demographic characteristics, occupations,
age, education, and family status. Data are included on agriculture, industrial and
business workers, with accompanying analysis.

814 **The guide to careers and jobs in Ireland.**
Killala, Ireland (Republic); Dublin: Morrigan Book Company,
1983. 96p.

A short guide to finding employment, directed at youth who have graduated, with
information arranged by occupation. Also helpful is the *Student Yearbook and
Career Directory*, (Dublin: Eason, 1982-. annual).

815 **Careers and living.**
Christina Murphy. Dublin: Irish Times, 1981. 171p.

Numerous sugestions are presented on job opportunities for school leavers and
graduates, with comments on job satisfaction and experiences. Originally
published as a fifty part newspaper series, this collection reviews forty-seven
major career areas in Ireland and some 400 specific jobs. Each chapter profiles

one worker as an example of the field. Hints are given on trends in employment, applications and the job interview.

816   **Population and employment projections.**
National Economic and Social Council.   Dublin: Stationery Office, 1975. 84p. (NESC Report, no. 5).

Statistics and projections are provided on employment by occupation and sector for the period 1971 to 1986, and these are related to demographic characteristics.

817   **Strategies for employment.**
Dublin: An Foras Forbatha, 1984. 104p. (Ireland in the Year 2000 Series, no. 5).

The major problem of unemployment is explored both comprehensively and by sector. Areas of the Irish economy with a potential for expansion are identified, with suggestions for their encouragement.

818   **Country labor profiles: Ireland (Eire).**
US Department of Labor, Bureau of International Labor Affairs.
Washington, DC: Government Printing Office, 1980. 80p.

An occasional report for the foreign investor or manufacturer. Information is given on government structure, resources, population, economy, labour force, unemployment, productivity, training, industrial relations, labour standards and working conditions.

819   **Women and employment in Ireland.**
Brendan Walsh, Annette O'Toole.   Dublin: Economic and Social Research Institute, 1973. 154p.

Data from a national survey are provided on the employment and occupational status of women.

Labour Movement and Trade Unions

General

820 **Rise of the Irish trade unions, 1729-1970.**
Andrew Boyd.   Tralee, Irish Republic: Anvil, 1972. 155p.
A short yet comprehensive review of the history of Irish trade unionism. Beginning with early, repressive Parliamentary legislation, the author shows how the development of unions followed that of the nation. An appendix includes a political tract on unions written in 1834.

821 **Leaders and workers.**
Edited by J. W. Boyle.   Cork: Mercier Press, 1978. 95p.
Separate essays discuss nine leading figures from the 18th-century Chartists to the modern day, who have had a major effect on labour organization. James Larkin is included.

822 **Labour in Ireland.**
James Connolly.   Dublin: Irish Transport and General Workers Union, 1944. 346p.
Reprinted many times, this edition includes three essays by Connolly, a major Irish labour leader, on the severe living and working conditions at the turn of the century, on Irish independence, and on the socialist cause. This impassioned account is essential for an historical understanding of modern Irish trade unions but is dated and it is narrow in theory and outlook.

823   **The Irish Transport and General Workers' Union, the formative**
       years.
       C. Desmond Greaves.   Dublin: Gill & Macmillan, 1982. 363p.

An analysis is given of the rapid growth of the Irish Transport and General
Workers' Union (ITGWU) into a major force during the turbulent years from
1909 to 1923, an era of political unrest and great social change. James Connolly,
Jim Larkin and William O'Brien are important figures in this history that charts
early organizational work, involvement in the nationalist cause and later rifts in
leadership.

824   **The rise of the Irish working class, 1880-1914.**
       Dermot Keogh.   Belfast: Appletree, 1982. 248p.

An examination of the Dublin trade union movement which pays particular
attention to the leadership roles of James Connolly and James Larkin. Mentioned
here are the early development of the unions, the state of urban living conditions
at the turn of the century, the famous shut-down in 1913, the conflict between old
and new unions, and the parallel development of socialism and the Irish
nationalist movement.

825   **Trade unions in Ireland, 1894-1960.**
       Charles McCarthy.   Dublin: Institute of Public Administration,
       1978. 671p.

A thorough survey of the turbulent history of Irish trade unionism from the early
organizational attempts of the 19th century, to later maturity as a major political
force. An earlier book by McCarthy reviews the progress of the Irish unions
during the following decade: *The decade of upheaval: Irish trade unions in the
1960s* (Dublin: Institute of Public Administration, 1973. 263p.).

826   **Trade unions and change in Irish society.**
       Edited by Donal Nevin.   Cork: Mercier, 1980. 172p.

Ten essays adapted from a radio series demonstrate major developments in Irish
trade unionism following the Second World War, and the effects that unions have
had on Irish politics and society. Several historians contributed to the volume.

Industrial relations

827   **Elements in a theory of industrial relations.**
       Charles McCarthy.   Dublin: Irish Academic Press, 1984. 144p.

McCarthy, an expert in the field, provides a thorough introduction with an Irish
perspective on the theory and practice of industrial relations.

828 **Personnel and industrial relations directory, 1984-85.**
Edited by Declan McDonagh. Dublin: Institute of Public
Administration, 1984. 3rd ed. 332p.

A useful reference source for the practitioner, this directory provides a list of
more than 750 organizations and services, related media, statistics, some
commentary on current issues, and a survey of recent publications.

829 **The evolution of Irish industrial relations laws and practice.**
B. J. O'Hara. Dublin: Folens, 1981. 146p. bibliog.

This textbook prepared for the Galway Regional Technical College, provides
considerable background on trade unions and the law from the 18th century to
more current Irish and international practice.

830 **Industrial relations in practice.**
Edited by Hugh M. Pollock. Dublin: O'Brien Press, 1981. 160p.
(Issues in Industrial Relations, no. 1).

Eleven contributors from the Irish Republic and Northern Ireland (both
management and labour) discuss the collective bargaining process, personnel
departments, shop stewards, strikes, women employees, low salaries, worker
participation, and the influence of the media.

831 **Reform of industrial relations.**
Edited by Hugh M. Pollock. Dublin: O'Brien Press, 1982. 170p.
(Issues in Industrial Relations, no. 2).

Ten contributors (who represent both trade unions and management) comment
on areas of potential reform, including worker participation, legal requirements,
and quality of work.

Statistics

832 **Census of Ireland, 1851.**
Dublin: Irish Academic Press, 1851. 3 vols. (British Parliamentary Papers Reprint Series).

Official British census papers for 1851 relating to Ireland are reprinted with considerable data on population. They are useful for the study of the rural society, famine conditions and emigration. Irish Academic Press has also reprinted *The Census of Ireland* for 1841 (896p.), which provides a considerable amount of data and commentary on the pre-famine years and on social conditions in the country. The government of the Irish Republic has regularly issued current census data in *Census of Population* (q.v.) since 1926. Irish Microforms of Dublin has also reproduced the *Census of Ireland, 1813-1911* on microfiche.

833 **Irish Statistical Bulletin.**
Central Statistics Office. Dublin: Stationery Office, 1925-.
quarterly.

An important publication providing numerous tables of current data from official sources, with information on demographic and economic trends, social indicators, trade, employment, sales and market performance, population, industry, and similar data.

834 **Statistical Abstract of Ireland.**
Central Statistics Office. Dublin: Stationery Office, 1931-.
irregular.

A major compilation, usually several hundred pages in length, on all aspects of Irish society, economy and resources (including population, demography, industry, agriculture, services and business). Intended to be an annual volume, some years have fallen behind in publication. Briefer information, although with commentary and attractive format, can be found in *Facts about Ireland* (q.v.).

184

835 **Irish economic statistics.**

Frank Kirwan, James McGilvray.   Dublin: Institute of Public Administration, 1983. 236p.

A standard guide and bibliography to the chief sources of published data on the Irish economy. This enlarged edition replaces earlier ones (first published in 1968). Information is limited to the Irish Republic, with heavy reliance on government sources, and includes the topics of population, income, wealth, taxes, trade, prices, manpower, agriculture and regional studies. The accompanying narrative discusses the limitations of the statistics, their applications and uses.

836 **Social statistics in Ireland.**

James McGilvray.   Dublin: Institute of Public Administration, 1977. 204p.

A guide to major social and demographic statistics in Ireland with a commentary on their compilation, use, limitations and gaps. Both official and non-official sources are identified for information on such topics as social services, education, housing, health, income, elections and crime.

837 **Quarterly Economic Commentary.**

Dublin: Economic and Social Research Institute, 1973-. quarterly.

Each issue contains a combination of authoritative articles and tables of current statistics relating to a range of subjects; including the performance of the Irish economy, income and production.

838 **Quarterly Economic Review: Ireland.**

London: Economist Intelligence Unit, quarterly.

Includes current business, marketing and commercial trends and employment data.

839 **Quarterly Review and Forecast.**

Dublin: Coopers & Lybrand Associates, May 1982-. quarterly.

Reviews the major features of the Irish economy, including trade, commerce, construction and agriculture. The data are intended to be timely, and include projections.

840 **Trade Statistics.**

Dublin: Central Statistics Office, 1924-. monthly.

Statistics are presented on exports and imports. The December issue provides an accumulation of statistics for the year. Current news on trade is also provided in the monthly *Trade and Industry in Ireland* (Dublin: Trade Centre).

Environment

General

841 **Man and landscape in Ireland.**
F. H. A. Aalen. London, New York: Academic Press, 1978.
343p. maps. bibliog.
The interplay between man and the Irish environment is clearly noted. Time, technological change, resources and cultural activities are shown to have affected the landscape from the most ancient times to the modern day. In assessing the role of man as a vital force in ecological change, the author draws upon archaeology, folk studies, demography, history and recent planning. There are chapters on the natural habitat of Ireland, prehistoric and ancient cultures, the Middle Ages, contemporary rural landscape, and modern towns.

842 **Promise and performance: Irish environmental policies analysed.**
Edited by John Blackwell, Frank J. Convery. Dublin: University College Dublin, Resource and Environmental Policy Centre, 1983. 434p.
This volume contains thirty-three papers on the Irish environment, conservation and policy by experts in each field. Among the topics covered are water and air pollution, environmental quality, public health, agriculture, forestry, energy, urban systems, law, politics, archaeology, rezoning and interest groups. Numerous maps, tables and graphs are included and suggestions for improvements are made.

843 **Directory of environmental research in Ireland.**
Compiled by M. Conroy. Dublin: National Board for Science and Technology, 1981. 50p.
A list is provided of nearly 250 projects on 286 subjects undertaken by some 27 Irish organizations. The projects relate to pollution, to all aspects of the environment, and to water quality. A *Directory of organizations with environmental interests* by Ann Quinn, with the same publisher (1984. 215p.) forms a companion volume.

844 **Laios: an environmental history.**
John Feehan. Stradbally, County Laois, Ireland (Republic): Bally Kilcavan Press, 1983. 500p.
An extensive study of the changing landscape of County Laois, covering the way it has been affected by development and how it has influenced society there. Few counties of Ireland have been given so deep an environmental analysis, covering land use and landscape, natural resources, buildings and structures. Varied influences are shown from the ancient Gaels, to the Normans, Huguenots, Quakers and English. The book includes supporting illustrations, charts, a bibliography, and placement indexes.

845 **Irish resources and land use.**
Edited by D. A. Gillmor. Dublin: Institute of Public Administration, 1979. 295p. maps. bibliog.
Eleven leading authorities have contributed papers on Irish resources such as agriculture and forestry, fisheries, wildlife, water and the atmosphere, minerals, land and soil, urban space, recreation and transportation. A plea is made for a coordinated and uniform policy towards the exploitation and conservation of Ireland's resources. Two useful earlier works (though lacking current information on the vastly changed fields of Irish agriculture and mining) are *Natural resources of Ireland* by Douglas Bishopp (Dublin: Royal Dublin Society, 1943), and *The industrial resources of Ireland* by Robert Kane (Shannon, Irish Republic: Irish University Press, 1972. Reprint of 1845 volume).

846 **Twenty years of planning.**
Berna Grist. Dublin: An Foras Forbartha, 1983. 60p.
This report evaluates the planning process in Ireland during the years 1963 to 1983, the government structures involved and the effects of environmental, regional, and industrial issues. Criticism is directed at the Local Government (Planning and Development) Act of 1963, its functioning and encumbered operation. The study calls for reform of zoning, development controls, and appeal procedures.

847 **Ireland in the year 2000.**
Dublin: An Foras Forbartha, 1980. 82p.
These proceedings of a colloquy note the prospects for an improved Irish environment. Several papers chart advances and change in the Irish natural habitat and resources, energy, industrial and regional development, urban forms,

and the present state of science, technology and education. Subsequent proceedings on 'Ireland in the year 2000' cover infrastructure, finance and employment (1982), and issues related to a 'national strategy' (1983).

848 **Irish environmental library.**
Dublin: Folens, [n.d.]. 75 pamphlets.

A series of booklets intended for children and young people. Each covers a particular topic relating to Irish culture, environment or history. The majority study nature and the environment, birds, plants, flowers, animals, and geography. Each contains coloured illustrations.

849 **Irish Journal of Environmental Science.**
Dublin: An Foras Forbartha, 1980-. semi-annual.

The journal reports on current environmental research through lengthy articles and brief communications directed at scientists, educators and planners. Papers cover air and water resources, roads, energy, pollution, fish, mammals, and recreational resources.

Town planning

850 **Architectural conservation, an Irish viewpoint.**
Dublin: Architectural Association of Ireland, 1975. 95p.

Nine lectures are presented by leading Irish architects and architectural historians, on building preservation, scale and craftsmanship, conservation areas, the restoration process, and town planning legislation.

851 **The emergence of Irish planning, 1880-1920.**
Edited by Michael J. Bannon. Dublin: Turoe, 1985. 336p.

An illustrated history of Irish planning covering forty years of rapid development, the emergence of regional industrial growth, changing cityscape and new urban problems. This is the first of several volumes, which together review a hundred years of Irish planning.

852 **The development of the Irish town.**
Edited by R. A. Butlin.   London: Croom Helm; Totowa, New Jersey: Rowman & Littlefield, 1977. 144p.

Several scholarly essays study the development of the Irish town within the context of a wider European experience. Numerous examples and contrasts are drawn from both Ireland and Great Britain.

853 **Irish towns and villages.**
L. M. Cullen. Dublin: Eason, 1979. 24p. (Irish Heritage Series, no. 25).

An illustrated pamphlet on the development of Irish townscape and planning from the 15th to the 19th centuries. The growth of more than twenty-five communities is succinctly described with coloured plates and maps.

854 **Urban Ireland: development of towns and cities.**
Curriculum Development Unit. Dublin: O'Brien Press, 1982. 96p.

An illustrated survey of the development, growth and future of Irish towns, written for the secondary school student or general reader. Historic impressions are provided by literary excerpts (from Brendan Behan, Patrick Kavanagh and others), and old prints, maps and photographs are reproduced. Both the ancient roots and modern plights of Irish urban living are given equal discussion.

855 **Dublin: a city in crisis.**
Edited by P. M. Delany. Dublin: Royal Institute of the Architects of Ireland, 1975. 108p. maps.

This report urges immediate steps to be taken in order to preserve the urban fabric of the city. A variety of papers, reflecting the expertise of different authors and groups, address the changing problems, decay, inconsistent building programmes and road networks. While architecture and physical amenities are stressed, the report also considers wider social, economic and community considerations. Numerous maps, charts and examples are given to illustrate the history and potential of the city and surrounding suburban areas.

856 **The town in Ireland.**
Edited by David Harkness, Mary O'Dowd. Belfast: Appletree Press, 1981. 246p. (Historical studies, no. 13).

Ten papers from a 1979 conference provide a glimpse of the development of Irish towns from mediaeval times to the modern day. Particular attention is given to 17th-century plantation towns, 19th-century urban politics, the historical economy of Cork, Dublin city development, and past social conditions in Belfast.

857 **The urban environment; research undertaken by the Planning Division, 1973-1980.**
Irish Government. Planning Division. Dublin: An Foras Forbartha, 1980. 16p.

A handlist prepared by Ireland's leading governmental planning agency of various working papers on the urban environment. This list may be used to chart major trends in Irish research and interest respecting urban areas. Short abstracts of the papers are included.

Environment. Town planning

858 **Streets of Ireland.**
Adrian MacLoughlin. Dublin: Swift Publications, 1981. 299p.
Intended as a city guide, each chapter of this book provides a brief history of twenty-five major communities throughout the Irish Republic. Dublin however is not included.

859 **Urbanization: problems of growth and decay in Dublin.**
National Economic and Social Council. Dublin: Stationery Office, 1982. [not paginated]. (NESC Report, no. 55).
A short study, with current statistics, of social and economic problems, housing, and living conditions in Dublin, at a time of rapid urban expansion, increased population and suburban growth.

860 **Ireland.**
Michael O'Brien. In: *Encyclopedia of urban planning.* Edited by Arnold Whittick. New York: McGraw-Hill, 1974, p. 568-78.
A useful introduction to the history and current practice of town planning in Ireland, with comments on legislation, government administration, and education for the profession.

861 **A sourcebook on planning law in Ireland.**
Philip O'Sullivan, Katharine M. Shepherd. Oxford: Professional Books, 1983. 568p.
This volume for the practitioner provides the text of provisions in major Irish planning legislation between 1963 and 1983. Six chapters discuss planning authorities, development, planning permission, appeals, compensation and enforcement. More than 180 Irish court opinions are cited.

862 **A geography of towns and cities.**
A. J. Parker. Dublin: Educational Company, 1976. 117p.
The relationships between different urban areas, locales, and functions are explored, with a discussion of town planning and metropolitan problems. The traditional evolution of urban centres is emphasized. While the book provides universal formulas, many examples are drawn from Ireland. Primarily for university level, although the many photographs in the book give it a wider appeal.

863 **Regional development and planning in Eire: retrospect and prospect.**
Oxford: Oxford Polytechnic Department of Town Planning, 1977. 122p.
This report presents the results of a study tour by staff and students in a programme on urban and regional planning. Written by various participants, the study presents a range of viewpoints on changing economic conditions in the Irish Republic, the planning process, the evolution of regional policies and the assignment of growth centres to major cities.

864 **Regional planning in the Republic of Ireland: its future development within the European communities.**
Peter Roberts.   Liverpool, England: Liverpool Polytechnic Department of Town and Country Planning, 1975. 79p. bibliog.

The study includes a review of economic and employment conditions in the Irish Republic, population trends, variations in regional policies for local development, and the effects of membership of the European Economic Community (EEC).

865 **The Irish town, an approach to survival.**
Patrick Shaffrey.   Dublin: O'Brien Press, 1975. 192p.

The author provides a forceful argument on the need for local preservation efforts and programmes to enhance existing surroundings. A large number of photographs identify types of city and rural amenities needing preservation. The specific Irish character is shown in buildings, gardens, land and cityscape, and various types of Irish towns are listed, included service, farming, market and commuter centres. The contributions made by good housing, development, parkland, zoning, and architectural details are also shown. An important role is urged for local authorities in encouraging continued growth that is both sensitive to the environment and flexible to local conditions.

866 **Your guide to planning.**
Edited by Patrick Shaffrey.   Dublin: O'Brien Press, 1983. 96p.

A useful guide for the developer, home owner, architect, conservationist, or consultant. Several experts comment on the planning acts, their everyday use and procedure, zoning permission, and the application process. The text of planning legislation is included with a list of appropriate authorities and official bodies. This was compiled in cooperation with An Taisce.

867 **The Dublin region, advisory plan and final report.**
Henry M. Wright.   Dublin: Stationery Office, 1967. 2 vols. maps.

This study prepared for the Ministry of Local Government provides proposals for the orderly planning of growth in the city. Suggestions are made with regard to future population, housing, roads, industry, growth centres and new towns in outlying areas, and the conservation and preservation of important aspects of the existing city. The report is in two parts, the second volume providing more detail and statistics. A number of maps and illustrations are included.

Rural planning

868　Wild Ireland.
Edited by Éamon de Buitléar.　Dublin: Amach Faoin Aer
Publications, 1985. 124p.

These collected papers provide an overview of Irish geology, climate, mountains, flora, fauna, and history, and discuss the prospects for their survival to the year 2034. This zestful, informative, though brief account is suitable for young readers as well as adults. Another view of wildlife and habitat is by Gerrit van Gelderen, *To the waters and the wild* (Dingle, Irish Republic: Brandon, 1985. 128p.). Van Gelderen, an artist and film maker, examines natural life and environment, and argues for the necessity of conservation.

869　The Galway Gaeltacht survey.
Galway, Ireland (Republic): University College Galway Social
Science Research Centre, 1969. 2 vols.

The conditions in the rural, Irish-speaking and often isolated areas in the West of Ireland are discussed, with insights into the economic, social, and linguistic patterns of the region. The social services, governmental organization and administration are criticized. Demographic and economic data are included. A plan for renewal of the region was outlined by the government shortly thereafter in the *Gaeltacht studies* (Dublin: An Foras Forbartha, 1971. 121p.).

870　Irish bogs: a case for planning.
H. van Eck, (et al.).　Nijmegan, The Netherlands: Catholic
University, (1983?). 333p.

A conservation report on the Irish bogs, which were studied for their international significance and applications. The report focuses on the bogs as an important energy source affected by reforestation efforts, turf cutting and local development. The large-scale exploitation and destruction of bogland is plotted in detail.

Environmental protection

871　Areas of scientific interest in Ireland.
Dublin: An Foras Forbartha, 1981. 170p.

An inventory of more than 1,000 sites in Ireland of interest to those doing research in geology, ecology, botany, or zoology. Each location is graded according to its importance and most of these have been identified and discussed by local authorities preparing county reports for the National Heritage Inventory. The existence of many of the listed locations is threatened in spite of their value for scientific research, tourism, education, or recreation. Photographs and a glossary are included.

872 **The state of the environment.**
Edited by David Cabot.   Dublin: An Foras Forbartha, 1985. 206p.
This report, prepared for the Irish Minister for the Environment, provides details on ecological risks and the pressures brought about by social changes, and economic and industrial development. The effects of air, water and noise pollution and waste upon both the urban and rural environment is charted. Each chapter is devoted to one of these problems, with maps, statistics, a list of information needs, and bibliographical notes. For further views on managing the impact of change in rural areas see *Ireland green: social planning and rural development*, by Harry Bohan (Dublin: Veritas, 1979. 128p.).

873 **National survey of Irish rivers.**
L. J. Lennox, P. F. Toner.   Dublin: An Foras Forbartha, 1980. 108p.
Data are presented on water quality and pollution of Irish lakes and rivers. This is the third in a series of monitoring reports on Irish water resources, since 1970-71. A government study on *Water pollution in Ireland* by P. F. Toner has also been issued (Dublin: Stationery Office, 1977. 64p.).

874 **National coastline study.**
Dublin: An Foras Forbartha, 1972-1973. 3 vols.
A technical and planning study of the future development of the coastline, with a strategy for conservation, and a guide to procedures for management.

875 **Today's and tomorrow's wastes: management technologies and environmental quality.**
Edited by J. Ryan.   Dublin: National Board for Science and Technology, 1980. 172p.
Twenty-two papers from a 1979 seminar review various strategies for managing waste in Ireland. Land spreading, sludge processing, incineration, marine dumping, reclamation, and landfill are discussed for municipal, farm, organic and industrial wastes.

876 **Tree projects for schools.**
Edited by Richard Webb.   Dublin: An Foras Forbartha, 1985. 104p.
A handbook intended for primary and secondary school teaching of Irish forest ecology and tree conservation. The depletion of forest resources in the Irish Republic has long been an important conservation problem and major replanting efforts are now underway.

Education

General

877 **Irish education, its history and structure.**
John Coolahan. Dublin: Institute of Public Administration, 1981. 344p.

This competent textbook on Irish education provides a history of the development of a specifically Irish system of education, and its social and economic background. Presentday problems are also considered, including those of comprehensive schools, curriculum development, centralized control, falling standards and teacher training in Ireland. This volume somewhat replaces *Education in Ireland*, by Thomas J. McElligott, published by the Institute in 1966.

878 **Guide to study in Ireland for foreigners.**
Dublin: Morrigan Books, 1983. 48p.

A handy guide to Irish education, the courses available, summer and exchange programmes, and Irish studies. *Guide to schools in Ireland* (1983. 80p.), is also published by Morrigan Books.

879 **Rutland Street.**
Seamus Holland. Oxford: Pergamon Press, 1979. 110p.

A description of a model compensatory education programme centered in Dublin, which is designed for preschool children from socially and economically disadvantaged families.

880 **Investment in education, report of the survey team appointed by the Irish Minister for Education in October 1962.**
Dublin: Stationery Office, 1962. 410p. (Parliamentary paper 8311).
A major review of Irish education by grade level is presented with an analysis of present and future needs, anticipated enrollment and costs. Various reorganization plans are offered. A supplementary volume of statistics and projections was also issued, as Parliamentary paper 8257 (1962. 668p.).

881 **The school survival kit; parents' guide to schooling in Ireland.**
Stan McHugh. Dublin: Wolfhound, [n.d.]. 96p.
A brief introduction to Irish primary and post-primary education, intended for parents of prospective students.

882 **Education in Ireland.**
Edited by Michael W. Murphy. Cork: Mercier, 1970-1973. 3 vols.
Three paperback volumes cover curriculum needs, urban youth, community approaches, use of educational television, teacher preparation, educational history, current research, and the teaching of language, civics and music. The emphasis throughout is on contemporary approaches to instruction.

History

883 **The Irish education experiment: the national system of education in the nineteenth century.**
Donald Harman Akenson. London: Routledge & Kegan Paul, 1970. 430p.
The author traces the beginnings of an Irish system of education, and the 19th-century dimension of politics, social, religious, cultural and economic contentions. The book is based on a number of original sources.

884 **A mirror to Kathleen's face, education in independent Ireland, 1922-1960.**
Donald Harman Akenson. Montreal; London: McGill-Queen's University Press; Dublin: O'Brien, 1976. 240p.
An important review covering the rapid development of an Irish system of education following the attainment of independence. Attention is focused on administrative problems, organization, language training, religious influences and future directions.

885 **Irish education: a history of educational institutions.**
Norman Atkinson. Dublin: Allen Figgis, 1969. 246p. bibliog.
The long history of Irish education is reviewed from ancient Celtic days to modern times. The author discusses the structure of the present system, the role

and influence of the Church, and various pressure groups. Schooling in both the
Republic and Northern Ireland is covered.

886 **Portraits: Belvedere College, 1832-1982.**
Edited by John Bowman, Ronan O'Donoghue. Dublin: Gill &
Macmillan, 1982. 180p.
Collected reminiscences of Irish private schooling are assembled from students
and members of the Belvedere community. A good, historical perspective is
provided of life at the Jesuit school once attended by James Joyce. The pen
portraits range from the factual to the amusing and memorable.

887 **The hedge schools of Ireland.**
Patrick J. Dowling. Cork: Mercier, 1968. 126p.
This account, originally published in 1935, briefly illuminates a period of severe
repression for Irish education between the 17th and 19th centuries. It was a time
during which local schoolmasters surreptitiously provided instruction in Irish
language and culture under great danger, thus insuring the survival of Irish
traditions and ways. Dowling continues this story in his later work, *A history of
Irish education, a study of conflicting loyalties* (Cork: Mercier, 1971. 192p.).

888 **Education in Ireland.**
Sister Anthony Marie Gallagher. Washington, DC: Catholic
University of America Press, 1948. 315p.
A detailed review of the Irish system of education in the 1940s, its historical
antecedents and cultural background. Particular attention is given to the growth
of Irish universities. Numerous statistics are included.

889 **A significant Irish educationalist: the educational writings of P. H.
Pearse.**
Edited by Séamas O'Buachalla. Cork; Dublin: Mercier, 1980.
390p.
The text of the writings of Pearse in the field of education is presented and he is
observed in his role as educational theorist, idealist and headmaster, as well as
rebel. Among the subjects raised in this collection are the philosophy, curriculum
and funding of education, the politics surrounding the creation of a new national
university, bilingual education, and the teaching of foreign languages. Pearse,
patriot, political and literary figure, took an active role in proposing innovations
to reinforce indigenous Irish culture. The book highlights his many proposals,
including dual Irish language training, and education adapted to the rural
Gaeltacht. Pearse's strong attack on English based education in Ireland is
presented in *The murder machine and other essays* (Cork, Irish Republic:
Mercier, 1976. 96p.).

890 **Church, state, and the control of schooling in Ireland, 1900-1944.**
E. Brian Titley. Dublin: Gill & Macmillan, 1983. 224p.
A review of certain aspects of the development of the Irish school system in the
early part of the 20th century. Church domination of the education system during

the years of the Irish Free State is highlighted, along with matters of school finance, the church's insistence on a role in moral education, and the use of schools as a source of religious education. Characteristics of contemporary Irish education have been strongly influenced by a sectarian outlook.

Secondary education

891 **The challenge of change, curriculum development in Irish post primary schools, 1970-84.**
Tony Crooks, Jim McKernan.   Dublin: Institute of Public Administration, 1985. 137p.
Following an extensive survey of school authorities in post-primary education, the authors summarize opinions on the need for constant curriculum review and future change. Included are comments on community school control, science education, and social and environmental studies.

892 **Guide to Dublin schools.**
Dublin: Morrigan Books, 1983. 96p.
A listing of 100 secondary schools throughout the Dublin area, of all types, with descriptive information and costs.

893 **Secondary education in Ireland, 1870-1921.**
T. J. McElligott.   Dublin: Irish Academic Press, 1981. 195p.
Both the accomplishments and the slow, tedious development of a unified school system are traced from their roots in the 19th century, a time when intermediate education was often divided between unregulated Anglican, Catholic, and Presbyterian boarding schools, usually church affiliated. The author traces the growth of Irish education from the days of stringent political control to rigid church dominance in the 20th century. Particular problems confronting secondary education included finances, local control, religious considerations, inadequate teacher training, and poor salaries.

894 **Curriculum and policy in post-primary education in Ireland.**
Donal Mulcahy.   Dublin: Institute of Public Administration, 1981. 256p.
This commissioned study provides a rare, detailed assessment of Irish secondary education with a carefully designed plan for substantial reform. Major changes are recommended, reflecting a shift from traditional, academic courses towards training in business, computing, and technical and vocational fields, in order to deal with increasing unemployment and major population shifts to urban areas.

895 **Post-primary education in Ireland, 1957-1970.**
Eileen Randles. Dublin: Veritas, 1976. 372p.
The growth and development of Irish secondary training in the mid-20th century
is shown against a background of changing economic conditions in Ireland, a new
social outlook, European trends, and domestic political controversy.

Higher education

896 **Report, 1960-1967.**
Commissioner on Higher Education. Dublin: Stationery Office,
1967. 2 vols.
This two part report provides an assessment of higher education in the Irish
Republic, and an attempt to plan for orderly growth. Nearly 1,100 pages are
devoted to a comparison of academic programmes, standards, and the
organization and administration of the colleges. The second volume of the study
provides a review of individual academic and technical colleges, professional
schools, research institutes and medical training programmes. Data on programme concentrations and enrollments are included. Mention is also made of
programmes in Irish studies and languages.

897 **Report on university reorganization.**
Higher Education Authority. Dublin: Stationery Office, 1972.
124p.
A five year review of Irish higher education with suggestions for reorganization.
The Conference of Irish Universities is described and professional education
(medicine, engineering and technology) is emphasized. Special needs in the
Dublin area are noted.

898 **The National University of Ireland and Eamon de Valera.**
Donal McCartney. Dublin: University Press of Ireland, 1984.
56p.
This lecture provides a short history of the relationship between the University of
Ireland, founded in 1908, and de Valera, who was elected Chancellor in 1921. De
Valera served as chancellor for fifty-four of the University's first seventy-five
years, through the turbulent period of Civil War, and the emergence of the
republic. De Valera, once a mathematics scholar, is shown as a political force
defending and encouraging the growth of academic institutions during his
leadership of the government.

899 **Reminiscences of a Maynooth professor.**
Walter McDonald. Cork: Mercier Press, 1967. 299p.
An insider's view of college education is provided in this history of the rather
élitist religious institution during the late 19th and early 20th centuries. This
autobiography provides a good view of society at the time. For the early 19th-

century history of the College see a biography by Ambrose Macaulay of its president, *Dr. Russell of Maynooth* (London: Darton, Longman, 1983).

900　**Trinity College Dublin, 1592-1952, an academic history.**
R. B. McDowell, D. A. Webb.　Cambridge, England; New York: Cambridge University Press, 1982. 580p.

From the foundation of the college as an institution for the privileged, the authors review the history of university teaching in Ireland. Scholarship in Stuart times, the civil war and Commonwealth, political factions and the time of 'Georgian splendour' all influenced the development of the college. The history of academic organization, intellectual life and currents are described, with mention of classical studies, science, and early English law. Special attention is given to the reorganization of higher education in Ireland from the mid-19th to the early 20th centuries. The book includes many colourful descriptions of leading academic figures in times of changing social and political conditions.

901　**Newman's University, idea and reality.**
Fergal McGrath.　London, New York: Longmans, Green, 1951. 537p.

The book reviews an attempt by Newman to establish in Ireland a university programme acceptable to English Catholics. A detailed reflection of the state of university education in Ireland at the end of the 19th century is provided.

902　**Towards a national university; William Delany, S. J. (1835-1924): an era of initiative in Irish education.**
Thomas Morrissey.　Dublin: Wolfhound Press; Atlantic Highlands, New Jersey: Humanities, 1983. 380p.

The career of a leading educator in Ireland is traced from his 19th-century rural college teaching experience to his leadership of the National University, and presidency of the University College Dublin. The volume provides a useful review of higher education in Ireland during the early 20th century.

903　**Maynooth and Victorian Ireland.**
Jeremiah Newman.　Galway, Ireland (Republic): Kenny's, 1984. 250p.

A social and at time amusing history is given of Maynooth, an ecclesiastical college of great influence. The author, a bishop and former president of the school, describes the growing importance of the institution at the time. A companion volume by the same author and publisher is *Maynooth and Georgian Ireland* (1979. 267p.), a somewhat light history of Catholic college education from 1795, with comments on Gaelic traditions, student unrest, educational reforms, learning and culture up to Victorian times.

904 **Gladly learn and gladly teach: a history of Alexandra College and
School, Dublin, 1866-1966.**
Anne V. O'Connor, Susan Parkes.   Dublin: Blackwater Press,
1984. 279p.

A history and nostalgic look is given of the college and its preparatory school
which served as major institutions of Irish higher education for women. Beginning
as a Protestant institution, it helped to train a number of female leaders, writers,
and academics. The somewhat unsteady relationship which it had with Trinity
College and other universities in the early 1900s is reviewed.

905 **Kildare Place.**
Susan Parkes.   Dublin: Church of Ireland College of Education,
1984. 224p.

A history of the training college for the Church of Ireland, between 1811 and
1969. The book broadly discusses Irish education at a time of formidable change.
The creation of a national school system, Church disestablishment, competition
and cooperation under the new government following partition, all affected the
school's mandate.

906 **Trinity College Dublin.**
Fergus Pyle.   Dublin: Eason, 1979. 24p. (Irish Heritage Series).

A short, well illustrated history of Trinity College from its founding in 1592. This
popular booklet emphasizes the architecture of the college.

Learning, Science and Technology

907 **Irish industrial laboratory directory.**
Edited by Miriam Breslin. Dublin: Institute for Industrial
Research and Standards, 1983. 112p.

A directory listing laboratories available for industrial and scientific research, and sources for supplies. Advertisements and a glossary are included. The National Board for Science and Technology has issued a *Directory of state analytical services* by F. M. McSweeney and J. Ryan. Information is given on tests and equipment provided by more than 100 laboratories.

908 **Scientific and technical information in Ireland.**
B. Carroll, N. Wood. Dublin: Stationery Office, 1978. 2 vols.

A study of the availability, use and needs of scientific, technical and medical information in Ireland. Volume one relates to the present use of scientific documentation; volume two is on costs associated with information resources and transfer.

909 **A profit and loss account of science in Ireland.**
Edited by Phyllis Clinch, R. Charles Mollan. Dublin: Royal
Dublin Society, 1983. 151p.

Eleven papers are presented, outlining the success and difficulties of scientific research in Ireland, and prospects for the future.

910 **Science and engineering in Irish higher education.**
John Colgan, Brendan Finucane. Dublin: National Board for
Science and Technology, 1981. 111p.

A descriptive directory of the scientific, research and engineering departments and institutes in Irish colleges and universities. The chief pursuits of each are identified, and personnel are listed.

911 **Ireland, science and technology.**
Compiled by W. Downey, R. Brew.   Dublin: National Board for
Science and Technology, 1979. 108p.
A directory of organizations and official bodies supporting investment, scientific
research and training. Some of the information, however, may require updating.

912 **Sources of scientific and technical information in Ireland.**
Institute for Industrial Research and Standards.   Dublin: Institute
for Industrial Research and Standards, 1983. 84p.
Sources are identified for technical information on various Irish institutes, bodies,
and commercial firms. Personnel handling inquiries are occasionally listed.

913 **George Boole: his life and work.**
Desmond MacHale.   Dun Laoghaire, Ireland (Republic): Boole
Press, 1985. 304p. (Profiles of Genius, no. 2).
A biography of the mathematician famous for the development of Boolean
algebra, and concepts which are adaptable to modern computer programming.
This readable account presents a picture of scientific research in 19th-century
Cork.

914 **The Royal Dublin Society, 1731-1981.**
Edited by James Meenan, Desmond Clarke.   Dublin: Gill &
Macmillan, 1981. 288p.
A comprehensive account by a number of specialists of the history of the society,
and its programmes of research and wide-ranging support for the natural sciences,
the arts, technology and sports. Founded in 1731, the society helped to foster
major Dublin institutions including the National Library, the National Museum,
the College of Art, and the Botanic Gardens. The society has also issued *A
bibliography of the publications of the Royal Dublin Society, 1931-1981* (Dublin:
Royal Dublin Society, 1982. 3rd ed.).

915 **The Royal Irish Academy, a bicentennial history, 1785-1985.**
Edited by T. Ó Raifeartaigh.   Dublin: Royal Irish Academy,
1985. 368p.
The Royal Irish Academy has long served as a leading supporter of academic and
scientific research in Ireland, through its formation of coordinating committees
and grants of financial support. This history includes a wide range of the society's
pursuits. Its library maintains a superior collection of ancient manuscripts, among
other unique resources. The exploratory programmes of the Academy have
concerned antiquities, Irish language and history, literature, biology, marine
science, agricultural research, mathematics, physics, astronomy, geology, chemistry and mapping.

916   **Funding sources for research in Ireland.**
      Sara Whelan.   Dublin: National Board for Science and Techno-
      logy, 1981. 132p.
Aid granting bodies in both Ireland and other countries are described in this short
directory for research funding. The National Board has also published a list of
Fellowships and scholarships available to Irish scientists and technologists by Mary
Gillick (1981).

Literature

General

917 Ireland's literary renaissance.
Ernest Boyd. New York: Barnes & Noble, 1968. 456p. bibliog.
First published in 1916, towards the end of the literary renaissance period, this account reviews the major poetry, fiction, theatre and the great writers of the times. Still useful as a contemporary history.

918 A biographical dictionary of Irish writers
Anne M. Brady, Brian Cleeve. Gigginstown, County Westmeath, Ireland (Republic): Lilliput Press, 1985. 387p.
Short comments, biographical notes and evaluations are given, covering 1,500 years of Irish and Anglo-Irish writing, up to the present day. Some 1,800 entries are included. The dictionary is divided into two parts; the first covers writers in English while the second deals with Gaelic authors.

919 Contemporary Irish writing.
Edited by James D. Brophy, Raymond Porter. Boston, Massachusetts: Twayne (G. K. Hall), 1983. 174p.
The current state of Irish literature and recent Irish writers are discussed in eleven essays, covering Thomas Kinsella, Seamus Heaney, William Trevor, Séan O Riada and others. Included are plot summaries, and chapters on poetry and prose in the Irish language.

920   **The politics of Irish literature from Thomas Davis to W. B. Yeats.**
Malcolm Brown.   Seattle, Washington: University of Washington
Press, 1972. 443p.

Many of the works of popular Irish literature have had strong nationalist,
political, social or revolutionary connotations. Brown reviews the various shifts
and trends among 19th- and early 20th-century writers, and places them in their
historical context.

921   **Escape from the anthill.**
Hubert Butler.   Gigginstown, County Westmeath, Ireland
(Republic): Lilliput Press, 1985. 342p.

A look at Anglo-Irish literature and society from 1745 to 1984. Butler comments
on religion, divergent loyalties and the art of writing in a divided Irish society. He
offers impressions of the leaders of the Irish literary revival and of his later
contemporaries and acquaintances: Sean O'Faolain, Patrick Kavanagh, and other
luminaries. The last part of the book relates to life in Europe between the wars.

922   **Great hatred, little room: the Irish historical novel.**
James Cahalan.   Dublin: Gill & Macmillan; Syracuse, New York:
Syracuse University Press, 1983. 240p.

A study of the Irish historical novel from the 1820s to 1970, spanning romantic
and realist traditions. Political events, social conditions, the famine and
nationalism all figure in some of these 150 novels of the period that have had a
wide appeal for the public. For academic use.

923   **A literary guide to Ireland.**
Susan Cahill, Thomas Cahill.   Dublin: Wolfhound Press, 1979.
333p.

A narrative guide to the literary places of Ireland and to the landscape which has
been made significant by Irish writings. Each part of Ireland is identified with
prominent authors. Although not a travel guide or factbook, this volume is
suitable for relaxed reading or for the traveller with a literary interest. Passages
are quoted from Irish authors, each giving their enthusiastic or special
impressions.

924   **Irish writers series.**
Edited by J. F. Carens.   Lewisburg, Pennsylvania; East Bruns-
wick, New Jersey: Bucknell University Press; London: Associated
University Presses. (Series).

A collection of some forty volumes, each devoted to a single 19th- or 20th-century
Irish author, their literary career, major works, and their background as related
to their writings. Each volume is of approximately 100 pages, and includes a
selective bibliography. Literary criticism is provided, with information on
contemporary attitudes and techniques.

925 **A critical guide to Anglo-Irish literature.**
Edited by Andrew Carpenter, Anne Clune, Terence Brown.
Dublin: University Press of Ireland (Academy Press), 1980. 3 vols.

A collection of papers by some thirty critics and literary scholars. This provides an in-depth view of some aspects of English literature written by the Irish. Volume one covers the Anglo-Irish ascendancy to 1830; volume two the Gaelic renaissance (1831 to 1922); and volume three the modern period.

926 **The writers: a sense of Ireland.**
Edited by Andrew Carpenter, Peter Fallon. Dublin: O'Brien Press, 1980. 224p.

Excerpts are presented from the work of forty-four contemporary writers. Some authors represented have yet to achieve fame, while others have had notable success (Seamus Heaney, Mary Lavin, Sean O'Faolain, Benedict Kiely, and Thomas Kinsella). Prose, poetry and drama are included, and many of the works portray the society and culture of present-day Ireland.

927 **A study of the novels of George Moore.**
Richard Allen Cave. Totowa, New Jersey: Barnes & Noble, 1978. 271p.

Each novel is discussed with regard to its underlying values and outlook on life. A leading biography of Moore is that by Joseph Hone, *The life of George Moore* (Westport, Connecticut: Greenwood, 1973. 515p.). Moore's sensitive, ironic and sometimes bitter outlook is apparent in his autobiography, *Hail and farewell* (Gerrards Cross, England: Colin Smythe, 1976. 774p.). In the present book by Cave, Moore's interest in Irish culture, language and tradition is noted. Varied impressions of Moore are provided in a collection of essays edited by Janet Egelson Dunleavy, *George Moore in perspective* (New York: Barnes & Noble, 1984). That collection provides further biographical information, interpretive commentary and bibliographic notes.

928 **Readings in Anglo-Irish literature.**
Edited by Anne Clune. Dublin: Academy Press, 1979. 550p.

For the general reader or student this sampling provides an extensive survey of Irish literature, through excerpts arranged chronologically. The selections, drawn from 1830 onward, illustrate the development of Irish writing up to the present day.

929 **Literature and the changing world.**
Edited by Peter Connolly. Gerrards Cross, England: Colin Smythe; New York: Barnes & Noble, 1982. 230p. (Literary Studies, no. 9).

A present-day view of Irish literature by an international group of scholars. Comments are offered on Yeats and a changing Ireland, Irish society between 1820 and 1870, the emancipation movements and social ills (such as the landlord system), women writers in Ireland, and the ideal view of the country as seen in poetry. These essays were delivered at the 1979 International Association for the

Study of Anglo-Irish Literature Conference. The papers of the 1982 Conference were issued as the *Irish writer and the city* edited by Maurice Harmon (New York: Barnes & Noble, 1984. 250p.); in 1976 the theme was *Place, personality and the Irish writer* edited by Andrew Carpenter (New York: Barnes & Noble, 1977. 199p.). Each volume has been issued by the same publishers.

930 **Heritage now; Irish literature in the English language.**
Anthony Cronin.   Dingle, Kerry, Ireland (Republic): Brandon, 1982. 180p.

The author views Irish literature written in English as a separate body of literature with its own attributes and identity, which is distinct from a wider English literature *per se*. He identifies major writers, and emphasizes some Irish characteristics of each. Included are James Joyce, Samuel Beckett, W. B. Yeats, Patrick Kavanagh, George Moore, Tom Moore, James Stephens and J. M. Synge. The essays on each writer are short, readable, and contain some biographical information.

931 **The Anglo-Irish novel.**
John Cronin.   Belfast: Appletree; Totowa, New Jersey: Barnes & Noble, 1980. 157p.

In this projected three volume study, volume one covers the Irish novel in the 19th century and the major writers of the period, including Maria Edgeworth, John Banim, William Carleton, Charles Kickham, George Moore and Somerville and Ross. Important novels are discussed in detail and short, selective bibliographies are provided for each writer. Both the gentry and the less polished writers are included. Only one novel by each writer is discussed, so the focus is somewhat narrow.

932 **Celtic revivals: essays in modern Irish literature.**
Seamus Deane.   London: Faber & Faber, 1985. 199p.

Deane presents a collection of essays on major Irish writers and on the relationship between recent Irish history, the public imagination, and the interpretations found in Irish fiction and poetry. In discussing 100 years of literary movements paralleling political change, the author concentrates on the output of the Protestant ascendancy, the play of nationalism in literature, and the accomplishments of major writers such as Yeats, Synge, Montague, Mahon, O'Casey, Pearse, Heaney and Kinsella.

933 **The Oxford illustrated literary guide to Great Britain and Ireland.**
Edited by Dorothy Eagle, Hilary Carnell.   Oxford; New York: Oxford University Press, 1981. 312p.

A guidebook with descriptive information on buildings and places associated with particular authors. Arrangement is by name of location, with the writers indexed. Hundreds of illustrations and maps are included. For popular browsing.

934 **The Irish novelists, 1800-1850.**
Thomas Flanagan. London; Westport, Connecticut: Greenwood
Press, 1976. 362p.
Good portraits are presented of the major Irish novelists just prior to the literary
renaissance period.

935 **A prose and verse anthology of modern Irish writing.**
Edited by Grattan Freyer. Ballina, Ireland (Republic): Irish
Humanities Centre, 1981. 320p.
This anthology serves as an introduction for students to a wide selection of Irish
authors from the mid to late 20th century. Represented are: Brendan Behan,
Clarke, Kavanagh, Montague, Edna O'Brien, O'Connor, O'Flaherty, O'Faolain,
O'Riordain and many others less known. Indeed, the objective of the book is to
bring lesser known authors before an international audience. Poetry, drama and
fiction are included.

936 **An anthology of Irish literature.**
Edited by David Herbert Green. New York: New York University Press, 1971. 2 vols.
A collection of Irish writings from the 7th to 20th centuries. Volume one contains
translations of mediaeval Irish poetry, sagas and narratives, some representing a
much older bardic tradition. The volume concludes with translations of 19th-
century Gaelic writers. Volume two covers Anglo-Irish writers including Swift,
Goldsmith, Moore, Yeats and a fair sampling of the Irish renaissance literature.

937 **Sean O'Faolain: a critical introduction.**
Maurice Harmon. Dublin: Wolfhound, 1984. 2nd rev. ed. 236p.
O'Faolain is noted for his modern day novels, short stories, biographies, and
essays on history, criticism and social commentary. Harmon, in this study
originally published in 1967, reviews his literary efforts, identifying major themes,
social concerns and contentiousness. O'Faolain's novels show Ireland in a period
of change, new mores and lost innocence. *The collected short stories of Sean
O'Faolain* has been published (London: Constable, 1981. 3 vols.).

938 **Dictionary of Irish literature.**
Edited by Robert Hogan, (et al.). Dublin: Gill & Macmillan;
Westport, Connecticut: Greenwood, 1979. 815p.
In this important reference work, entries in alphabetical order cover major
movements in Irish literature and theatre, Irish folklore, some 500 writers, and a
range of publishers. Each entry is well written and most contain a bibliography.
Two introductory essays provide background information on Gaelic literature and
the history of writing in Ireland.

939 **A literary history of Ireland from the earliest times to the present day.**
Douglas Hyde.   London: Benn; New York: St. Martin's, 1980.
654p.

A new edition of a pioneer work first published in 1899. Hyde later became president of the Irish Free State. Covered are Celtic history, the Norman conquest, early poets and writers, and the annals of Irish history up to the 18th century. The language and observations of the book remain interesting but are now somewhat stilted and dated.

940 **Anglo-Irish literature.**
A. Norman Jeffares.   London: Macmillan; Dublin: Gill & Macmillan, 1982. 349p.

A very good overview is presented for those new to the topic of Irish literature in English. Although it includes mediaeval times, the emphasis of is on the 18th to the early 20th centuries. Numerous writers, both major and minor, are mentioned, and accounts of individuals are interwoven into a review of major literary movements, political events and Irish society of the times.

941 **The writings of Brendan Behan.**
Colbert Kearney.   New York, London: St. Martins, 1977. 155p.

A short, scholarly and critical assessment of Behan as author, and the major themes in his work. For further background information see E. H. Mikhail's *Brendan Behan: interviews and recollections* (New York: Barnes & Noble, 1982. 2 vols.). Mikhail captures some of Behan's humour and changing character through an anthology of interviews and shorter writings.

942 **A colder eye: the modern Irish writers.**
Hugh Kenner.   London: Allen Lane; New York: Knopf, 1983.
301p.

An exciting portrayal of an important literary period. This stylish and sometimes amusing account covers Irish writing from Yeats to Beckett, and includes such figures as James Joyce, Sean O'Casey, Oliver St. John Gogarty, Lady Gregory, Patrick Kavanagh, Austin Clarke and Edna O'Brien. Their lives are illuminated with a multiplicity of facts, occurrences, and unusual anecdotes. A full length study of Edna O'Brien, entitled *Edna O'Brien* has been prepared by Grace Eckley (Lewisburg, Pennsylvania: Bucknell University Press, 1974. 88p.). O'Brien is well known for her penetrating novels about Irishwomen in the modern world and their emotional problems. She proves the feminine situation, love, loss and loneliness, humorous incidents, intimate relationships and strengths at moments of great stress. Her novels and screen plays portray the responsibilities and disappointments of life, sometimes in graphic detail. This study contains a critique of her writing, a biography of her 'personal odyssey', and a description of her position as a feminist writer. The characters of her stories are described, and a bibliography and a chronology of her writings to 1972 are included. Among O'Brien's many published works is a collection of twenty-nine stories *A frantic heart: selected stories of Edna O'Brien* (New York: Straus & Giroux, 1985. 480p.).

943 **Lady Gregory: the woman behind the Irish renaissance.**
Mary Lou Kohfeldt. London: Andre Deutsch; New York:
Atheneum, 1985. 366p.

This engrossing, graceful biography of Lady Gregory provides a look into the
circle of writers who contributed to Ireland's literary revival. Lady Gregory's own
position as folklorist, essayist, poet, playwright and supporter of the Abbey
Theatre is well covered. Yeats figures prominently in this account. This is an
interpretive account of her life and motivations, and while it might not be
accepted as definitive, it is one of the most extensive reviews of her life to date.

944 **Studies in Anglo-Irish literature.**
Edited by Heinz Kosok. Bonn: Bouvier Verlag, 1983. 496p.

A wide range of fifty-five essays are presented on the history of Anglo-Irish
literature, by specialists from fifteen countries. The book opens with an essay on
Swift and continues to Behan. The twin directions and tension between the
English and Irish cultures are stressed throughout.

945 **Elizabeth Bowen: an estimation.**
Hermione Lee. New York: Barnes & Noble, 1981. 255p.

A thorough, critical study of Bowen's life and writing of all types. The roots of
modern Anglo-Irish literature, especially fiction, are explored, and the contributions of Bowen as novelist are assayed. A biography, *Elizabeth Bowen* by Victoria
Glendinning has been published (London: Weidenfeld & Nicolson, 1977. 261p.).
Bowen's *Collected stories* have been published (London: Cape, 1980. 784p.).

946 **Oliver St. John Gogarty, the man of many talents.**
J. B. Lyons. Tallaght, Irish Republic: Blackwater Press; Atlantic
Highlands, New Jersey: Humanities, 1981. 348p.

A critical yet sympathetic biography of Gogarty (1878-1957), who combined the
careers of writer, surgeon, senator and humourist. A famous conflict which he
had with Joyce is highlighted.

947 **A short history of Anglo-Irish literature from the earliest times to
the present.**
Roger McHugh, Maurice Harmon. Dublin: Wolfhound; New
York: Barnes & Noble, 1982. 384p. bibliog.

This review, which is useful for students, traces the development of Irish
literature in the English language, and evaluates the achievements of important
prose writers, poets and dramatists. The account is comprehensive, tracing the
literature from its ancient beginnings, through colonial periods, the nationalism of
the 18th and 19th centuries, and revival in the 20th century. A good introduction
to the subject.

948 **The best from *The Bell*.**
Sean McMahon. Dublin: O'Brien, 1978. 187p.

A selection of writings from *The Bell*, one of Ireland's major literary magazines,
for the period 1940 to 1950. Some of the leading Irish authors of the time are
represented.

949   **A book of Irish quotations.**
Edited by Sean McMahon.   Dublin: O'Brien, 1984. 231p.
Memorable phrases are drawn from Irish prose, verse and song, throughout all
periods of Irish writings. Each quote is identified, and the book is indexed by
author. Some quotes have been translated from the Gaelic.

950   **James Stephens: a critical study.**
Augustine Martin.   Totowa, New Jersey: Rowman & Littlefield,
1977. 177p.
An assessment of the writings of Stephens, reviewing their notable success during
the Celtic revival and afterwards. Stephens was noted as a poet, novelist,
playwright, commentator and journalist. A friend of Joyce and other major
writers, his work spans the years 1907 to 1950. Patricia McFate has edited the
Uncollected prose of James Stephens (Dublin: Gill & Macmillan; New York: St.
Martin's, 1983. 2 vols.), containing fifty-nine short stories and other writings.

951   **Anglo-Irish literature.**
Augustine Martin.   Dublin: Department of Foreign Affairs, 1980.
80p. (Aspects of Ireland Series, no. 7).
A brief survey of Irish literature written in English, from the 17th century to 1980.
This is a useful introduction to the literature that produced Swift, Goldsmith,
Sheridan, Shaw, Joyce, Yeats and other major writers. Attractive illustrations are
included.

952   **All the Olympians, a biographical portrait of the Irish literary
renaissance.**
Ulick O'Connor.   New York: Atheneum, 1984. 292p.
These vivid biographical portraits present a feeling of the time of the literary
renaissance, its spark, excitement in national pride, ancient art forms and
contemporary observations. A number of its literary figures are viewed through
the contemporary insights of their fellow writers. Most of the portraits, though
brief, achieve some penetrating observations, with wit and sympathy.

953   **Celtic dawn: a portrait of the Irish literary renaissance.**
Ulick O'Connor.   London: Hamish Hamilton, 1984. 292p.
O'Connor traces the literary renaissance movement from the days of Charles
Stewart Parnell, Douglas Hyde and Michael Davitt. He presents a total picture of
the times, of both major and minor personalities, their commitment to writing,
slow public acceptance, their interest in ancient tradition and the occult, and the
importance of music, theatre and continental trends. This account is well suited to
general readers and students who are unfamiliar with the field. The title of the
book alludes to the title selected by Yeats for his seminal 1893 collection of
essays, *The Celtic twilight*.

Literature. General

954 **Language and society in Anglo-Irish writing.**
Astley Cooper Partridge. Dublin: Gill & Macmillan; New York:
Barnes & Noble, 1984. 394p.

Partridge provides an introduction to the permanent influence of the Irish language, its early literary roots, and its impact on the culture of the country. Although it is not an all-embracing history, the book does discuss ancient Celtic contributions, language, legends and myths in early Irish literature, and later Anglo-Irish writing up to the 20th century. Some emphasis is given to the precise use of certain syntax, to word play and phrases peculiar to the Irish, and the origin of such usage.

955 **Irish literature in English: the romantic period, 1789-1850.**
Patrick Rafroidi. Gerrards Cross, England: Colin Smythe;
Atlantic Highlands, New Jersey: Humanities, 1980. 2 vols.

Volume one of this important study covers the prelude to and development of Romanticism, the major national political movements (Young Ireland, and the insurrection) famine, poetry, literature, ancient traditional roots, folklore, the Irish language (its use, motifs, rhythms), literacy, and connections with French and British literature. Volume two is an extensive bibiliography, with biographical notes. For advanced readership.

956 **Somerville and Ross, a critical appreciation.**
Hilary Robinson. Dublin: Gill & Macmillan; New York: St.
Martin's, 1980. 224p.

A study of the complete works of Edith Somerville and Violet Martin (known as Martin Ross), whose stories have maintained great popularity from the mid-19th century to the present. The two authors placed a sharp focus on the social mores of the Anglo-Irish, particularly those of the country estates, and adopted a humourous though benign brand of satire. Robinson draws on many primary sources for biographical and critical background: letters, personal recollections, journals and notebooks. The novels are viewed as having a style which is separate and distinct from the personality of either author. Another study of the two writers published by Gill & Macmillan is *Somerville and Ross: an illustrated companion* by Lewis Gifford (1983). Gifford provides more biographical background in *Somerville and Ross: the world of the Irish R.M.* (London: Viking, 1985).

957 **Seventy years, 1852-1922, being the autobiography of Lady Gregory.**
Edited with a foreword by Colin Smythe. New York: Macmillan,
1974. 583p.

In the form of a diary, this volume provides a detailed look at youth in the Anglo-Irish landed class, the growth of the Irish literary movement, major writers, anecdotes and incidents. The account serves as a convenient companion to Lady Gregory's *Journals*, volume two of which covers the subsequent years 1925 to 1932. The *Journals* were edited by Daniel J. Murphy (Gerrards Cross, England: Colin Smythe, 1981. 750p.).

958 **Austin Clarke, a study of his writings.**
G. Craig Tapping. Dublin: Academy Press; Dover, New Hampshire: Longwood, 1981. 362p.

A study of the themes found in Clarke's poetry, drama and novels, in which he explored contemporary Irish society with criticism and satire. Both the Gaelic and Anglo-Irish roots of his writings are shown.

959 **A writer's Ireland: landscape in literature.**
William Trevor. New York: Viking, 1984. 192p.

The impressionistic views of Irish writers are combined with photographs, to record the uneasy history and the present nation of Ireland and to predict its future. Extensive quotations are given from the Gaelic poets and from Anglo-Irish writers such as Swift, Goldsmith, Spencer, Yeats, Thackeray, Synge, O'Flaherty, Colum, O'Casey, Shaw, Wilde and many others. This is a book on Ireland as seen through the eyes of its leading literary figures. For recreational reading.

960 **A guide to Anglo-Irish literature.**
Alan Warner. Dublin: Gill & Macmillan; New York: St. Martins, 1981. 295p.

This lively discussion of selected Irish authors provides an overview of the growth and scope of Anglo-Irish literature. Most chapters cover 20th-century authors, some as recent as 1980. Their contributions are shown to have created a sense of Ireland, occasionally with angry observation. Warner provides a balanced view of fantasy imagery, word-play, improvisation, and the ambiguous attitude of many of its writers towards Ireland. A selective guide, the twenty essays which comprise the book provide short, summary studies of particular authors, with brief plot summaries of the more important works and a review of their significance. For the non-specialist.

Prominent writers

Samuel Beckett

961 **Just play: Beckett's theatre.**
Ruby Cohn. Princeton, New Jersey: Princeton University Press, 1980. 313p.

Nearly twenty-five plays of Beckett are analysed with regard to their unique perspective, logic and dramatic technique in this useful summary.

962 **Beckett on file.**
   Compiled by Virginia Cooke. London, New York: Methuen, 1985. 96p.
A checklist of works by Beckett and their performances, with facts about his life briefly outlined.

963 **A student's guide to the plays of Samuel Beckett.**
   Beryl S. Fletcher, John Fletcher. London: Faber & Faber, 1985. 279p.
The book contains a chronology of Beckett's work, a general introduction, and a commentary and notes on individual plays.

964 **Beckett and the voice of species.**
   Eric P. Levy. Dublin: Gill & Macmillan, 1980. 220p.
An exploration of the modern novels of Beckett for a central theme: reality and the meaning of human existence. The evolution of each novel is discussed, and their individual outlook on the world of experience is described.

Oliver Goldsmith

965 **Oliver Goldsmith.**
   Stephen Gwynn. London: Butterworth, 1935. 288p.
A scholarly though readable account of Goldsmith's life, his search for a profession, his travels, career as a writer, and his major works. Critical comments on Goldsmith are included. Goldsmith's most popular works include *She stoops to conquer* (1773) and *The vicar of Wakefield* (1766). His poem, *The deserted village* (1770) provides a long description of hard economic times and repression in an 18th-century village, although the actual setting was drawn from Goldsmith's recollection of rural Ireland, where he was born in 1728.

966 **Goldsmith: the gentle master.**
   Edited by Sean Lucy. Cork: Cork University Press, 1984. 85p. (Thomas Davis Lectures).
The text of a popular radio series honouring the 250th anniversay of Goldsmith's birth. Included is a short biography and reassessment of his position as a major 18th-century writer.

967 **Oliver Goldsmith, a Georgian study.**
   Ricardo Quintana. New York: Macmillan; London: Collier-Macmillan, 1967. 213p.
Outlines Goldsmith's career as a writer, from his earliest attempts, through his service as an essayist for hire, and his achievements in comedy, poetry and drama.

968 **Goldsmith, the critical heritage.**
Edited by G. S. Rousseau.   London; Boston, Massachusetts:
Routledge & Kegan Paul, 1974. 385p. bibliog.

A collection of contemporary reviews and published comments about Goldsmith from his fellow writers and others, including Dr. Johnson, George Eliot and Edmund Burke. An introduction to Goldsmith as an author and a chronology are included. A good, critical commentary of Goldsmith can be found in *The true genius of Oliver Goldsmith*, by Robert Hopkins (1969). Among the best collected editions of Goldsmith's works is that edited by Arthur Friedman (*The collected works*, Oxford: Clarendon Press. 1966. 5 vols.). The Friedman edition includes the text of reviews, poems, and plays, with introductions, notes and indexes.

969 **The life and times of Oliver Goldsmith.**
Oscar Sherwin.   New York: Collier Books, 1962. 2nd ed. 351p.
bibliog.

Directed at the popular audience, this biography stresses Goldsmith's human qualities, including his occasional foolishness and awkwardness, as well as his success. Goldsmith's Irish character is given some attention. The book includes excepts from Goldsmith's writings and summarizes his life, although with insufficient detail.

970 **Oliver Goldsmith.**
Ralph M. Wardle.   Lawrence, Kansas: University of Kansas
Press, 1969. Rev. ed. 330p.

A thorough, scholarly biography, this work provides a modern interpretation of Goldsmith, his character and his work as evaluated by others. This is an authoritative study.

James Joyce

971 **The Joycean way: an illustrated topographical guide to** *Dubliners* **and** *A portrait.*
Bruce Bidwell, Linda Heffer.   Dublin: Wolfhound Press, 1981.
144p.

Through photographs, maps and an interpretative text, the reader is guided through Dublin as it existed in Joyce's day and as it appeared in his novels. Bidwell and Heffer provide a pleasant familiarization with the locale and background of *Dubliners* and *A portrait of the artist as a young man*, and show how the local topography and scene related to the choice of characterization. Both the general reader and the specialist will find this work useful in providing a feeling of place for Joyce's stories.

972 **A companion to Joyce studies.**
Edited by Zack Bowen, James Carens. Westport, Connecticut: Greenwood Press, 1984. 818p.

Sixteen authorities contribute essays which review the published research about Joyce's life, biography, work, novels, correspondence and impact upon modern literature. Each essay includes a timely bibliography of major works. This volume provides a very good introduction to Joycean studies, it will be useful to both scholar and student, and may provide a point of departure for a more detailed exploration of Joyce's novels.

973 **James Joyce and the making of** *Ulysses*.
Frank Budgen. Bloomington, Indiana: Indiana University Press, 1960. 339p.

First published in 1934, this reliable and animated account serves as a lively guide to Joyce's writing and craft. It is based on conversations with Joyce, and recollections by Budgen of their meetings and discussions.

974 **James Joyce.**
Peter Costello. Dublin: Gill & Macmillan, 1980. 160p. (Gill's Irish Lives Series).

A good, basic introduction to Joyce's life, his chronology and particular genius as observed through his novels.

975 **James Joyce's Odyssey: a guide to the Dublin of** *Ulysses*.
Frank Delaney. London: Hodder & Stoughton; New York: Holt, Reinhart & Winston, 1982. 192p.

In an engaging step-by-step retracing of the story, this book follows the progress of *Ulysses* through the Dublin streets in the same circular pattern. Comments by Delaney are offered throughout on the city scene and occurrences. The book is supplied with a generous collection of maps and attractive photographs (both old and recent), and is ideal for recreational reading.

976 **James Joyce: the critical heritage.**
Robert Deming. New York: Barnes & Noble, 1970. 2 vols.

Considerable comment on Joyce's work is drawn from a variety of sources including contemporaneous reviews by notable writers. These are arranged into chapters corresponding to the individual novels. This set allows one to assess how each work of Joyce was reviewed and accepted in his time.

977 **James Joyce letters.**
Edited by Richard Ellman. New York: Viking, 1966. 3 vols.

This collection of Joyce's letters is an expansion of a single volume edition by Stuart Gilbert published by Viking in 1957. In this edition, numerous corrections are made and previously deleted excerpts are restored. A more popular and convenient single volume edition of selected letters was edited by Ellman, *Selected letters of James Joyce* (New York: Viking, 1975. 440p.).

978 **James Joyce.**
Richard Ellman.   New York; Oxford: Oxford University Press,
1982. 2nd rev. ed. 887p.

This definitive life of Joyce has been accepted as one of the major biographies of the 20th century. Ellman, prominent critic and authority on Joyce, writes with sensitivity, poignancy and exceptional detail. The life is chronologically arranged by location (major city) and period. Many excerpts are included from Joyce's correspondence and poems, and the volume also includes various photographs and other documentary sources. This edition is much expanded over that issued twenty-two years earlier. A primary work about Joyce.

979 **Notes for Joyce, an annotation of James Joyce's *Ulysses*.**
Don Gifford, Robert J. Seidman.   New York: Dutton, 1974.
554p.

Interpretative notes are arranged for each line of *Ulysses*, with numbered references keyed to the 1934 and 1961 editions of the book. A useful tool for advanced research. Gifford has also prepared a similar guide to *Dubliners* and *A portrait of the artist as a young man*, in his book *Joyce annotated* (Berkeley, California: University of California Press, 1982. 308p.). Numerous references and explanations are given of passages as they relate to history, events, everyday occurrences and ancient myths.

980 **James Joyce's *Ulysses*, critical essays.**
Edited by Clive Hart, David Hayman.   Berkeley, California; Los
Angeles; London: University of California Press, 1974. 433p.

Each chapter of *Ulysses* is discussed individually by a recognized scholar in separate short essays.

981 **James Joyce's *Ulysses*; a facsimile of the manuscript.**
James Joyce, introduction by Harry Levin.   New York: Octagon,
1984. 3 vols.

The 800 page, handwritten manuscript of Joyce's best known work is reproduced and, for comparison, the text of the first printed edition is included. Also presented is a revised text with 5,000 earlier errors corrected. This has been prepared by a team of leading academics. (Since the original typescript by Joyce is lost, debate will long continue over the exact selection of words). In the present edition a critical introduction discusses Joyce's intended meanings of various passages, phrases and words. An extensive bibliographic preface reviews the evolution of texts and words. For research collections.

982 *Ulysses*: **a critical and synoptic edition.**
James Joyce, prepared by Walter Gabler with Wolfhard Steppe,
Claus Melchior.   New York: Garland, 1984. 3 vols.

A major effort has been made to produce this 'correct' edition, with the text of all extant manuscripts and proofs having been collated by computer. Many thousands of errors in earlier editions had led to erroneous and pointless interpretations. In this edition the left hand pages show variations in the text at different stages of production. The right hand pages contain the corrected passages established by Gabler, though these are still open to some debate. Included in the three volumes are textual notes, an historical collation list, short bibliography and afterword. This grouping of evidence, demonstrating the evolution of Joyce's writing, will be crucial to the research of any Joyce scholar, and will be essential for major collections of modern Irish literature.

983 **Ulysses.**
Hugh Kenner.   London; Boston, Massachusetts: Allen & Unwin, 1980. 182p.

For the advanced reader, this detailed commentary provides significant background and analysis on the language of the novel, its surroundings, hidden meanings, nuances, possibilities, and Dublin setting.

984 **James Joyce.**
A. Walton Litz.   New York: Twayne, 1966. 141p. bibliog. (Twayne's English Author Series, no. 31).

A concise yet competent biography of the author for those who require a short account of Joyce's life in broad outline.

985 **The *Finnegans wake* experience.**
Roland McHugh.   Dublin: Irish Academic Press, 1981. 132p.

A short, often entertaining introduction to *Finnegans wake*, and a search for explanations of words and phrases. McHugh, a leading Joycean scholar, is especially good in his discussion of sounds as a reason for the selection of certain words. McHugh provides a far more detailed page by page exposition of the text in another book, *Annotations to Finnegans wake* (London: Routledge & Kegan Paul, 1980). This is a particularly useful guide for the serious reader to one of Joyce's greatest works.

986 **James Joyce.**
Patrick Parrinder.   London; Cambridge, England: Cambridge University Press, 1984. 300p.

An introduction to the life of Joyce, the Ireland of his youth and the everyday occurrences that were to enter into the elaborate scheme of his novels.

987 **James Joyce: a guide to research.**
Thomas Jackson Rice.   New York: Garland, 1982. 390p. (Reference Library of the Humanitites Series, no. 328).

Some 1,500 entries up to 1981 are listed in this highly selective bibliography of books and essays. Particularly useful are Rice's critical comments and evaluations, which are often laconic, pithy or direct. This list partially supplants *A bibliography of James Joyce studies* by Robert Deming (Boston, Massachusetts: G. K. Hall, 1977. 264p.), and *A bibliography of James Joyce, 1882-1941*, by John Slocum and Herbert Cahoon (New Haven, Connecticut: Yale University Press, 1953. 195p.).

988 **Approaches to *Ulysses*, ten essays.**
Edited by Thomas F. Staley, Bernard Benstock. Pittsburgh,
Pennsylvania: University of Pittsburgh, 1970. 289p.

The essays concentrate on Joyce's fictional technique, his 'allusive' method of writing, his use of motifs, the writing of *Ulysses*, and various characters in the novels.

989 **Allusions in *Ulysses*: an annotated list.**
Weldon Thornton. Chapel Hill, North Carolina: University of
North Carolina Press, 1982. 563p.

A reprint of the 1961 edition, providing a full index and references to allusions in the novel, relating to history, art, music, culture, tales and a multitude of other elements. Useful for advanced research.

990 **A reader's guide to James Joyce.**
William York Tindall. London: Thames & Hudson, 1959. 304p.

Brief notes and comments are offered for each of Joyce's major works. This guide is most useful to those in their initial readings of Joyce.

Sean O'Casey

991 **Sean O'Casey, from times past.**
Brooks Atkinson, edited by Robert Lowery. London: Macmillan;
New York: Barnes & Noble, 1982. 192p.

A collection of theatre reviews, all by Atkinson. This very useful volume treats each work of O'Casey separately, but there is a coherent unity throughout the volume as Atkinson reviewed the majority of plays in their first New York performance. A preface by Eileen O'Casey is included.

992 **The experiments of Sean O'Casey.**
Robert G. Hogan. New York: St. Martin's; Toronto: Macmillan,
1960. 215p.

A detailed and full review of O'Casey's contributions to the modern theatre, his innovations and the new directions he took that reshaped drama.

993 **Sean O'Casey: the man and his plays.**
Jules Koslow. New York: Citadel, 1966. 117p.

This dependable study of O'Casey and his writings has been revised and expanded from an earlier work by Koslow, *The green and the red* (1950).

994 **Sean O'Casey: centenary essays.**
David Krause, Robert Lowery. Gerrards Cross, England: Colin
Smythe, 1980. 257p. (Irish Literary Studies, no. 7).
Several authorities on O'Casey contribute ten essays on the Abbey Theatre, the
art and politics of O'Casey, his friendship with Lady Gregory, his youth and
upbringing, the matter of religion, and his acquaintance with Shaw, Yeats and
Joyce. A chronology of O'Casey's outspoken, productive and sometimes
turbulent life is included. Krause also prepared an early study, *Sean O'Casey: the
man and his work* (1960).

995 **O'Casey Annual.**
Edited by Robert Lowery. Dublin: Gill & Macmillan; London:
Macmillan; Atlantic Highlands, New Jersey: Humanities, 1982-.
annual.
A review is provided of the current literary criticism surrounding O'Casey, the
renowned writer and dramatist. O'Casey has been subject to continuous
reassessment and study and many of the esays here were commissioned from
leading authorities and writers. While giving current views about the author the
essays tend to be specialized, and include observations on O'Casey's use of music,
song, his political views, and his production compared to that of other authors.

996 **Autobiographies.**
Sean O'Casey. London, New York: Macmillan, 1981. 2 vols.
O'Casey's autobiography provides a very detailed sense of a period in Ireland
when intellectual life was dominated by writers. A description is given of his wide
circle of acquaintances, the places he knew, his experiences in Ireland, literary
events, and publishing history between 1880 and 1953. The autobiography was
originally published in six separate volumes between 1939-1954 and each bore a
separate title. Robert Lowery has prepared an index to them, *Sean O'Casey's
autobiographies: an annotated index* (Westport, Connecticut: Greenwood, 1983.
487p.). Ten scholars have contributed chapters reviewing the autobiography in
Essays on Sean O'Casey's autobiographies edited by Robert Lowery (New York:
Barnes & Noble; London: Macmillan, 1981. 249p.). These essays consider
O'Casey's literary style, his politics, Dublin background, the Gaelic League, and
his friendships with G. B. Shaw, Patrick Pearse and others.

997 **A guide to O'Casey's plays: from the plough to the stars.**
John O'Riordan. London: Macmillan; New York: St. Martin's,
1985. 419p.
Each play from four decades of work is given a descriptive chapter with comments
on background, plot, characters, the dramatic craft, staging, production and
acclaim. A useful summation of each dramatic work, but lacking in critical
observation. The prefered edition of the plays is *The complete plays of Sean
O'Casey* (London: Macmillan, 1949-1984. 5 vols.).

998   **Sean O'Casey.**
James Simmons.   London: Macmillan, 1984. 200p. (Macmillan
Modern Dramatists Series).

This biography notes the major public and political events of O'Casey's lifetime,
including his links with the Gaelic League, the Irish Republican Brotherhood, the
1916 rebellion, and his embrace of socialism and eventually communism.
Simmons also portrays O'Casey's very different literary life as a dramatist,
reaching great success with the portrayal of Irish character. Another biography by
Hugh Hunt, *Sean O'Casey* has appeared in the Gill's Irish Lives Series (Dublin:
Gill & Macmillan, 1980. 160p.). Both works provide a short appraisal of
O'Casey's dramatic output, but neither account is definitive.

George Bernard Shaw

999   **Bernard Shaw: his life, work and friends.**
St. John Ervine.   New York: William Morrow, 1956. 628p.

An outspoken account, especially in its criticism of Shaw's later years and
thoughts. A discussion is provided of the plays, their production, and the Irish
theatre.

1000   **Shaw: the critical heritage.**
T. F. Evans.   London; Boston, Massachusetts: Routledge &
Kegan Paul, 1976. 422p.

Contemporary descriptions are given of Shaw's plays and writings as reviewed in
the leading journals of his day. Evans provides additional biographical
information, and background on theatrical production.

1001   **Bernard Shaw: a critical view.**
Nicholas Grene.   London: Macmillan, 1985. 173p.

A balanced evaluation of Shaw and his writings, noting the basic morality of his
plays, his consistent themes and later shortcomings, and providing comparisons
with other authors.

1002   **George Bernard Shaw, man of the century.**
Archibald Henderson.   New York: Appleton, 1956. 769p.

This biography provides a good summary of Shaw's early years, his family, life in
London, and eventual success as novelist, literary critic, Fabian socialist and
dramatist. An early book by Henderson has served as the standard biography on
Shaw: *Bernard Shaw: playboy and prophet* (New York: Appleton, 1932. 872p.).
Stanley Weintraub has compiled *Shaw: an autobiography, 1856-1898, selected
from his writings* (New York: Weybright & Talley, 1969-70. 2 vols.). Weintraub
recreates Shaw's life from an edited selection of Shaw's many letters,
introductions, essays and speeches.

Literature. Prominent writers

1003 **The genius of Shaw.**
Edited by Michael Holroyd. New York: Holt, Rinehart & Winston, 1979. 238p.

A collection of sympathetic essays covering Shaw's life, social ideals, religious philosophy, the plays, and Shaw's role as critic. A number of excellent period photographs are included.

1004 **The universe of G. B. S.**
William Irvine. London, New York: McGraw-Hill, 1949. 439p. bibliog.

Published a year before Shaw's death, this biography provides a valuable review of Shaw's most productive years, and the world in which he wrote. Irvine's appraisal maintains some distance from his subject; it is clear, independent and focused, and serves as a good introduction to Shaw, his surroundings and politics.

1005 **Bernard Shaw: collected letters.**
Edited by Dan H. Laurence. London: Max Reinhardt; New York: Viking, 1965. 3 vols.

A careful selection from Shaw's voluminous outpouring of correspondence, often outspoken, humorous or sharp. Volume one covers 1874 to 1897; volume two 1898 to 1910; and volume three 1911 to 1925. They provide numerous observations on events and personalities of the day with great wit. Volume two provides an extensive review of Shaw's thoughts during his most successful years as a playwright. The last volume, with more than 600 letters, portrays a more serious period of conflict and decline.

1006 **Bernard Shaw.**
John O'Donovan. Dublin: Gill & Macmillan, 1983. 155p. (Gill's Irish Lives Series).

A popular if simplified biography of the playwright, set against the background of Irish theatre and music of the day. O'Donovan emphasizes Shaw's skill as a writer, his advocacy of social reform, and his formidable reputation as a dramatist and music critic.

1007 **Shaw: the style and the man.**
Richard M. Ohmann. Middleton, Connecticut: Wesleyan University Press, 1962. 200p.

A critical study of Shaw's life and plays. His work is evaluated in the light of its place in the modern theatre, several decades after its first performance. Shaw is portrayed as humanist and philosopher.

1008 **Journey to heartbreak, the crucible years of Bernard Shaw, 1914-1918.**
Stanley Weintraub. New York: Weybright & Talley, 1971. 368p.

Part of a trilogy, this volume provides an in-depth review of a productive period in Shaw's writing, which took place during a period of social and political upheaval. Other volumes by Weintraub include *Private Shaw and public Shaw* (1963), dealing with the years 1922 to 1935, and *The last great cause* (1968), on the years 1936 to 1939.

Richard Brinsley Sheridan

1009 Sheridan, the track of a comet.
Madeleine Bingham. New York: St. Martins, 1972. 383p.
Bingham provides a general, pleasant biography that is positive in outlook, although not scholarly. His life is traced through childhood, schooldays, courtship, authorship, and bankruptcy, against the background of English 18th-century literary circles, fashions and political intrigue. The political account overshadows Sheridan's literary accomplishments, and his downfall is vividly portrayed. A short, earlier biography by Lewis Gibbs is *Sheridan* (London: Dent, 1970. Reprint of 1947 edition. 280p.). Gibbs summarizes Sheridan's personal life and popularity with a description of London at that time.

1010 Sheridan.
William Darlington. London: Macmillan, 1933. 144p. (Great Lives Series).
A short, concise and factual review is given of Sheridan's life. Darlington's account is illuminating but is lacking in some details. Sheridan was born in Dublin in 1751, but his rapid rise was centered on the London theatre. His initial success as a playwright of comedies concerning manners is also shown in an earlier biography by L. C. Anderson, *Life of Sheridan* (1890. Reprinted 1974).

1011 Memoirs of the life of the Right Honourable Richard Brinsley Sheridan.
Thomas Moore. New York: Greenwood Press, 1968. Reprint of 1858 edition. 5th ed. 2 vols.
This major biography written in 1827 is more closely contemporary with Sheridan, yet it provides some distance and impartiality in its review of his life. A detailed review is given of Sheridan's life as a playwright, member of the London literary scene, financial backer and partner of the Drury Lane Theatre, orator, and figure in Parliament and government. This account is less thorough in its description of Sheridan's literary accomplishments, but provides more information on his political and social life. The author of the biography was an Irish poet and melodist.

1012 The life and works of Richard Brinsley Richard Brinsley Sheridan.
James Morwood. Edinburgh: Scottish Academic Press, 1986. 208p.
Morwood provides an entertaining account of Sheridan's life for the general reader. The story of the playwright in the London social scene has sparkle and is fascinating. Sheridan's decline through business carelessness and loose living is charted. Another recent biography is by Stanley Ayling, *A portrait of Sheridan* (London: Constable, 1985. 218p.).

1013 **The dramatic works of Richard Brinsley Sheridan.**
Cecil J. L. Price. Oxford: Clarendon Press, 1973. 2 vols.
A critical edition is presented of all the plays of Sheridan, including *The rivals*, *School for scandal*, and *The critic*. Included are the original works, adaptations and improvisations by Sheridan, with additional notes added by Price, and with brief essays on composition and characters. Another standard edition of Sheridan's plays is that edited by Richard Purdy, *Plays and poems*, a 1962 reprint of the 1928 edition in 3 volumes. A discussion of the plays, their structure, composition and production is given by Mark Auburn in *Sheridan's comedies: their contexts and achievements* (Lincoln, Nebraska: University of Nebraska Press, 1977. 221p.).

1014 **Harlequin Sheridan, the man and the legends.**
Raymond Rhodes. Oxford: Blackwell, 1933. 305p.
A substantial biography and study of Sheridan's public and literary life. Rhodes' account provides much detail, but it should be read in conjunction with more recent critical studies. Rhodes also compiled a major edition of Sheridan's writings, *The plays and poems of Richard Brinsley Sheridan* (New York: Macmillan; Oxford: Blackwell, 1928. 3 vols.).

1015 **Sheridan, from new and original material.**
Walter Sichel. Boston, Massachusetts; New York: Houghton Mifflin, 1909. 2 vols.
A very full biography of Sheridan is given, with some stress placed on the 'Irishness' of his character. Some information is drawn from the manuscript diary of the Duchess of Devonshire. In its assessment of the author's life and personality the study emphasizes Sheridan's sensational and at times scandalous behaviour. Sichel provides many insights and facts, but his observations are dated, and are not always accurate.

Jonathan Swift

1016 **Jonathan Swift: a critical anthology.**
Edited by Denis Donoghue. Harmondsworth, England: Penguin, 1971. 454p.
Collected literary criticism, from both Swift's day and from more modern times by a variety of writers. Donoghue has also written *Jonathan Swift: a critical introduction* (1969).

1017 **Swift: the man, his works, and the age.**
Irvin Ehrenpreis. Cambridge, Massachusetts: Harvard University Press, 1962-1984. 3 vols.
A definitive and comprehensive biography of Swift. This detailed and well indexed account is important for an understanding of intellectual thought in 18th-century Ireland. Volume one *Mr. Swift and his contemporaries*, covers family history, Swift's education and early employment. Volume two *Dr. Swift*, includes

his English years, maturity, political writing and move back to Dublin. Volume three *Dean Swift*, reviews his last thirty years, his most productive and important period. Ehrenpreis has also written *The personality of Jonathan Swift* (1958).

1018 **Jonathan Swift: a critical biography.**
John Middleton Murray. London: Jonathan Cape, 1954. 461p.
This convenient biography of Swift provides a useful introduction, covering all the major events in his life, and his most important literary works.

1019 **Jonathan Swift, a hypocrite reversed: a critical biography.**
David Nokes. London, New York: Oxford University Press, 1986. 427p.
A scholarly study of Swift's varied and often contradictory life and outlook. Swift continues to fascinate today's writers with his novel public statements, hilarious satire, amusing utterances, and with his more private and uncertain personal involvements. This book presents a new assessment of Swift, as a patriot noted for his generosity and wit, an occasional opportunist, and a man of changing, sometimes angry moods, irritability and surprise.

1020 **Jonathan Swift.**
Edited by Angus Ross, David Wooley. London: Oxford University Press, 1984. 722p. (Oxford Authors Series).
A collected edition of many of Swift's writings (excluding *Gulliver's travels*.) As a sampler this volume shows the wide range of his literary style and approach to satire. Included are sermons, letters, pamphlets and poems. Each work is given ample notes, with bibliographic references. The standard, most complete edition is *The prose works of Jonathan Swift*, edited by Herbert Davis in a new arrangement of the novels, stories and essays (Oxford: Blackwell, 1939-1968. 14 vols.). Davis's work replaces an earlier set by Temple Scott.

1021 **Jonathan Swift.**
Bernard Tucker. Dublin: Gill & Macmillan, 1983. 143p. (Gill's Irish Lives Series).
Tucker provides a short biography of Swift, including his childhood, education, search for support and return to Dublin. Both his failings and his important contributions as a satirist are noted. A full description is given of *Gulliver's travels*, and its half-hidden critique of society.

1022 **Correspondence of Jonathan Swift.**
Edited by Harold Williams. Oxford: Clarendon Press, 1963-1965. 5 vols.
The most extensive edition of Swift's letters, including many to the leading writers of his time. The correspondence ranges from humorous and satirical, to a concerned tone on social, ethical and personal problems. The final volume contains appendixes with further background on Swift, and a detailed index.

1023 **Swift: the critical heritage.**
Edited by Kathleen Williams. New York: Barnes & Noble, 1970. 347p.
Contemporary accounts, remarks and criticism are reprinted from earlier sources originally appearing between 1704 and 1819. These were written by notable intellects of Swift's time or shortly after, about Swift and his works.

John Millington Synge

1024 **J. M. Synge.**
Eugene Benson. Dublin: Gill & Macmillan; London: Macmillan, 1982. 188p. (Macmillan Modern Dramatists Series).
Benson provides a brief biography of Synge, followed by several essays on his plays and his role as a key figure in the Irish literary renaissance.

1025 **John Millington Synge and the Irish theatre.**
Maurice Bourgeoise. Gerrards Cross, England: Colin Smythe; New York: Arno, 1969. 310p. bibliog.
A study of both the personality of Synge, and his contribution to the Irish theatre, against the background of Irish society and intellectual community at the beginning of the 20th century. Synge is best known for the dramatic portrayal of the Irish poor, the dispossessed, and the fight for survival against the sea, often portrayed in poetic language. Each of his plays is reviewed. This book was first published in 1913 and hence reflects an early stage of Synge criticism. For a more current assessment see Mary C. King's *The drama of J. M. Synge* (Syracuse, New York: Syracuse University Press, 1985. 240p.). King provides a close look at Synge's use of language and its contrast to the action on stage.

1026 **A centenary tribute to John Millington Synge, 1871-1909.**
Edited by S. B. Bushrui. Gerrards Cross, England: Colin Smythe; New York: Barnes & Noble, 1972. 356p.
Individual plays are analysed and various scholars comment on Synge's contributions to world theatre and literature. This book offers a good overall perspective on Synge's continuing influence.

1027 **J. M. Synge, 1871-1909.**
David Greene, Edward Stephens. New York: Macmillan, 1959. 321p.
A full, sensitive biography, in part based on Synge's papers and letters which had then only recently been released. The career of Synge in the theatre, and his contribution to the Abbey Theatre and its performances is explored, although literary criticism is not attempted.

1028   **Synge and Anglo-Irish drama.**
Alan Price.   London: Methuen, 1961. Reprinted, New York:
Russell & Russell, 1972. 236p.
A useful discussion of Synge's work by type: prose, poems, plays and tragedies.
Comments are given on his literary approach, craft, and characters.

1029   **The collected letters of John Millington Synge.**
Edited by Anne Saddlemyer.   Oxford: Clarendon Press, 1983. 2
vols.
The letters of Synge range from the poetic to the sentimental and the deeply
personal. Some reflect the pathos and despair which are found in his plays.
Volume one covers 1871 to 1907; volume two the last years, 1907 to 1909.
Correspondents include Arthur Griffith, Yeats and Lady Gregory. Synge's letters
to Maire O'Neill, his fiancée, reveal a very human side of the playwright. See
Letters to Molly, edited by Anne Saddlemyer (Cambridge, Massachusetts:
Harvard University Press, 1985).

1030   **J. M. Synge and his world.**
Robin Skelton.   London: Thames & Hudson; New York:
Viking, 1971. 144p.
A pleasant photographic essay and biography of Synge, for popular reading.
Included here is the background to his works: the nature of Ireland, local and
rural scenes, the ways of the peasantry, and the Irish theatre. Skelton has also
written *The writings of J. M. Synge* (Indianapolis, Indiana: Bobbs-Merrell, 1971.
190p.), which describes each of the major plays, their structure and performances.

1031   **The collected works of J. M. Synge.**
General editor, Robin Skelton.   Gerrards Cross, England: Colin
Smythe; Washington, DC: Catholic University of America Press,
1982. 4 vols.
A reissue in both hardcover and paperback of the 1962 standard edition of
Synge's work. Volume one contains his poems edited by Skelton; volume two his
prose, edited by Alan Price; and volumes three and four contain the plays, edited
by Anne Saddlemyer. Extensive explanatory notes, corrections, alternative
passages and bibliographic references are included throughout.

1032   **J. M. Synge and the western mind.**
Weldon Thornton.   Gerrards Cross, England: Colin Smythe;
New York: Barnes & Noble, 1979. 170p. (Irish Literary Studies
Series, no. 4).
Thornton scrutinizes the life and background of Synge for influences and future
themes appearing in his work, including family relationships and religious
attitudes. A tension is found in Synge's work between philosophical and moral
beliefs, and everyday reality.

Oscar Wilde

1033   Oscar Wilde: the critical heritage.
Edited by Karl Beckson.   New York: Barnes & Noble, 1970.
434p.
Reviews of Wilde's writings are provided by leading authors and critics between
1881 and 1927. Among the commentators included here are Robert Browning, A.
G. Bierce, Whistler, Shaw and Yeats. An introduction by Beckson covers the
impact of Wilde, his reputation, and the reception of his writings.

1034   Selected letters of Oscar Wilde.
Edited by Rupert Hart-Davis.   London: Oxford University
Press, 1979. 406p.
A selection from Wilde's voluminous correspondence, showing his humour,
varied temperament, brilliant observations and changing circumstances. The
complete *Letters of Oscar Wilde* were also edited by Rupert Hart-Davis (New
York: Harcourt, Brace, World, 1962. 958p.).

1035   The annotated Oscar Wilde.
Edited by H. Montgomery Hyde.   New York: Clarkson Potter;
London: Orbis, 1983. 480p.
A good sampling of Wilde's writings, with selections drawn from his fiction,
poems, plays and letters. Notes, comments and introductory remarks are
provided throughout by Hyde to assist the reader and to establish a continuous
thread. Some 200 illustrations are included.

1036   Oscar Wilde.
Philippe Jullian.   New York: Viking, 1969. 420p.
A biography for popular reading. Wilde's life is covered from his childhood and
upbringing, to his success, the Lord Alfred affair, and subsequent decline. This
vivid account is particularly useful on the later years, and it interprets Wilde's
work in order to discover parallels between it and his own life.

1037   Oscar Wilde: his life and wit.
Hesketh Pearson.   New York, London: Harper, 1946. 345p.
The different stages of Wilde's life are traced: those of critic, writer, wit, talker,
dramatist, and finally exile. Some criticism is given of his plays, but Pearson also
notes how Wilde excelled as a conversationalist in his earlier years.

1038   Oscar Wilde.
Richard Pine.   Dublin: Gill & Macmillan, 1983. 164p. (Gill's
Irish Lives Series).
A biography of the writer who brought controversial change to the literary circles
of 19th-century Ireland. Wilde is shown to have challenged some elements of
society while enjoying a role in it. This well documented study shows the
proponent of art and aesthetics as doomed by his contentious stance and flawed
personality.

1039   **Oscar Wilde.**
Katherine Worth.   London: Macmillan, 1984. 180p.
A review of the plays of Wilde, their innovations of form and content, their production, Wilde's outlook on his society and his motivations as a writer.

William Butler Yeats

1040   **Yeats.**
Douglas Archibald.   Syracuse, New York: Syracuse University Press, 1983. 280p.
This study provides an overview of W. B. Yeats' life. Attention is given to the relationship between William Butler Yeats and his father John Butler Yeats, the influences of friends, particularly Maud Gonne and Lady Gregory, the situation in Anglo and Celtic Ireland prior to 1913, Yeats' pursuit of the occult, public life and his politics up to 1939. This study provides a balanced appreciation of the writer, although it is not an all encompassing biography. Yeats' interaction with both the romantic and modernist literary traditions in Irish literature is briefly summarized.

1041   **William Butler Yeats.**
Anthony Bradley.   New York: Frederick Ungar, 1979. 306p.
An introduction to Yeats as a playwright, with biographical data, and coverage of his mystical impulses, politics and literary movements. The plays are compared, and each is individually analysed, with a review of its plot and possible origin. Emphasis is given to stage production, the growth of the Abbey Theatre and the development of Yeats as a dramatist.

1042   **The identity of Yeats.**
Richard Ellman.   Oxford: Oxford University Press, 1964. Reprinted, London: Faber & Faber, 1983. rev. ed. 342p.
An acclaimed review of Yeats' artistry, this critical assessment presents a balanced interpretation of his life's work. Ellman, in this classic study, charts Yeats' involvements, motivations and output, and evaluates the poems and other writings against the background of his life. Ellman discusses Yeats' style, rhetoric, use of symbols, rituals and iconography.

1043   **Yeats: the man and the masks.**
Richard Ellman.   New York: Norton, 1978. rev. ed. Oxford: Oxford University Press, 1979. 364p.
First published in 1949, this remains a leading assessment of Yeats, based on both published material and on 50,000 pages of manuscripts. More a summary of the author's literary contributions than a full biography, the account includes some family history, an evaluation of Yeats' writing, and many excerpts from his poems.

1044   **Letters to W. B. Yeats.**
Edited by Richard J. Finnerman, George M. Harper, William
Murphy.   New York: Columbia University Press, 1977. 627p.

A selection of 500 letters from 160 correspondents, many of whom were leading
literary figures. The selections are annotated with notes and many contribute to
an understanding of Yeats' interests and concerns, and of the cultural movements
in Ireland at the time. Yeats' own correspondence has been edited by John Kelly
and Eric Domville in *The collected letters of W. B. Yeats, vol. 1: 1865-1895*
(London: Oxford University Press, 1985. 600p.).

1045   **Yeats Annual.**
Edited by Richard Finnerman.   Dublin: Gill & Macmillan;
London: Macmillan; Atlantic Highlands, New Jersey: Humanities
Press, 1982-. annual.

An attractively presented miscellany with varied essays on Yeats, his times,
Victorian society, the new Ireland of the 20th century, the state of literature and
its many movements and directions in Yeats' day. Each volume consists of about
300 pages, and includes book reviews and lists of dissertations completed.

1046   **W. B. Yeats: the poems.**
Edited by Richard J. Finnerman.   Dublin: Gill & Macmillan;
London, New York: Macmillan, 1983. new ed. 747p.

A comprehensive edition of the poems of one of the world's leading writers. The
text, having been restored to its original state, with later emendations by editors
removed, is accurate. Explanatory notes annotate many of the allusions found
throughout. This is the most complete collection of the poems, and the prefered
edition for general use, although earlier Macmillan editions were labelled as
'definitive.' Also useful is *The variorum edition of the poems of W. B. Yeats* edited
by Peter Allt and Russell Alspach (New York: Macmillan, 1957. 882p.). Allt and
Alspach include extensive notes, publishing history and bibliography and provide
alternative versions of the text. It is suited to scholarly use; the Finnerman
volume is recommended for either recreational or academic use.

1047   **The permanence of Yeats: a selected criticism.**
Edited by James Hall, Martin Steinman.   New York: Macmillan,
1950. 414p.

Two dozen prominent English writers of the 20th century present their varied
views on Yeats. Many of the essays have been reprinted from leading journals.

1048   **W. B. Yeats, 1865-1939.**
Joseph Hone.   London: Macmillan, 1967. 504p. bibliog.

A good and convenient (though not definitive) biography of the writer, covering
his schooldays, youth and family, the political events concerning Parnell and their
aftermath, Lady Gregory, Maud Gonne, the Abbey Theatre, Yeats' plays and
controversies, the 1916 rising, his marriage, the Civil War, Yeats' life as a public
figure and his last days.

1049　**A commentary on the collected plays of W. B. Yeats.**
A. Norman Jeffares, A. S. Knowland. Stanford, California:
Stanford University Press, 1975. 313p.
A description of Yeats' plays and their contents, with a chronology of the
playwright's life added. Many explanatory notes on each play are included.

1050　**W. B. Yeats, the critical heritage.**
Edited by A. Norman Jeffares. London: Routledge & Kegan
Paul, 1977. 483p.
A good, broad array of contemporaneous criticism, comments and letters. The
essays and reviews are grouped by Yeats' work which is chronologically arranged.

1051　**Yeats, Sligo and Ireland.**
Edited by A. Norman Jeffares. Gerrards Cross, England: Colin
Smythe; Totowa, New Jersey: Barnes & Noble, 1980. 267p. (Irish
Literary Studies, no. 6).
Various essays are included on Ireland during the Romantic and Victorian
periods, covering the home life of the Yeats family, Yeats' relationship with his
publishers, and some of the characters in his books. Jeffares has also prepared a
fuller biography, *W. B. Yeats: man and poet* (1962).

1052　**A commentary on the collected poems of W. B. Yeats.**
A. Norman Jeffares. London: Macmillan; Stanford, California:
Stanford University Press, 1984. 563p.
A most useful commentary with background notes on each poem, identifying
locations, publications, events, allusions, mythological references, symbolism, and
individuals mentioned in the poems.

1053　**W. B. Yeats.**
Augustine Martin. Dublin: Gill & Macmillan, 1983. 160p.
(Gill's Irish Lives Series).
A short biography of the writer which sets his life against the background of his
family and his times, the emerging literary movements and the newly independent
Ireland.

1054　**The noble drama of W. B. Yeats.**
Liam Miller. Dublin: Dolmen, 1977. 365p.
This very attractive volume reviews the plays of Yeats with an emphasis on the
history of their performances and production. Numerous art nouveau and
programme illustrations are included. While this book provides a pleasant
introduction, it would be useful to follow it with A. S. Knowland's, *W. B. Yeats:
dramatist of vision.* (Gerrards Cross, England: Colin Smythe; Totowa, New
Jersey: Barnes & Noble, 1983. 256p.). Knowland, as a dramatist and producer,
provides a more specialized view of the plays, with suggestions on proper staging,
special dramatic techniques and the use of dance within the plays.

1055 **A guide to the prose fiction of W. B. Yeats.**
William H. O'Donnell. Ann Arbor, Michigan: UMI Research, 1983. 182p. (Studies in Modern Literature Series, no. 12).
A useful guide to the novels and short stories by Yeats. Comments are offered on structure, plot, use of character, major themes and the publication history of each work.

1056 **A readers guide to the plays of W. B. Yeats.**
Richard Taylor. Dublin: Gill & Macmillan, 1984. 197p.
In an introduction Taylor discusses ritual in Yeats' plays, the use of masks and magic and the tragic nature of his drama. Comments are then offered on each play taken in order, the characters of each, their language, style, dramatic rhythms and staging. The prefered edition of the *Collected plays of W. B. Yeats* (q.v.) is that published by Macmillan.

1057 **W. B. Yeats and Irish folklore.**
Mary Helen Thuente. Dublin: Gill & Macmillan; Totowa, New Jersey: Barnes & Noble, 1980. 284p.
Yeats accumulated, preserved and recycled the ancient legends and myths of Ireland from both oral and written traditions. These reappeared in his plays and narrative stories and had a bearing on the style of his writing. This book discusses the folklore that had survived into the 19th century in song, custom and belief, and studies Yeats' use of it. Emphasis is given to Yeats' involvement with Irish myths during the 1880s and 1890s, but actual tales are not described. This scholarly study for advanced research is the only volume to cover the topic.

1058 **Yeats.**
Frank Tuohy. New York: Macmillan, 1976. 232p.
A popular, illustrated account of the writer's life, the Yeats family, 19th and early 20th-century Ireland, Yeats' youth, London years, Maud Gonne, the Irish theatre, Coole Park, politics, the Easter Rising, and Yeats' later life. This attractive volume provides an introduction to Yeats for general readership, and also gives a flavour of the times. A similar volume, with many illustrations, is *W. B. Yeats and his world* by Michael Mac Liammoir and Eavan Boland (New York: Charles Scribner's Sons; London: Thames & Hudson, 1971. 144p.).

1059 **A reader's guide to William Butler Yeats.**
John Unterecker. London: Thames & Hudson; New York: Octagon, 1971. 310p.
This very useful descriptive and explanatory guide to Yeats' literature was first published in 1959. Unterecker has compiled a collection of some of the better essays on Yeats in *Yeats: a collection of critical essays* (1963).

1060 **The autobiography of William Butler Yeats.**
William Butler Yeats. New York: Macmillan, 1953. 344p.
Various recollections of the writer from 1887 to the 1920s, covering Yeats' youth in the post-Parnell period, revolutionary times, the state of literature and of

Ireland, and observations on other writers. These observations, however, were compiled at different dates and lack a continuous theme. The reminiscences do not constitute an autobiography in the formal sense.

1061   **The collected plays of W. B. Yeats.**
William Butler Yeats.   Dublin: Gill & Macmillan; London, New York: Macmillan, 1970. 9th ed. 712p.
This standard, single volume edition of Yeats' plays was first published in 1934. Yeats, founder and director of the Irish National Theatre (later the Abbey Theatre) was largely responsible for the vitality and force of drama during the literary renaissance. The texts of twenty-six plays are included here.

Short stories

1062   **Modern Irish short stories.**
Edited by Ben Forkner, preface by Anthony Burgess.   London: Futura; New York: Viking, 1980. 557p.
This substantial collection presents some of the best short stories in the Anglo-Irish tradition, though omitting the newer works and latest trends.

1063   **44 Irish short stories.**
Edited by Devin A. Garrity.   Old Greenwich, Connecticut: Devin-Adair, 1980. 500p.
An anthology of short stories by numerous Irish writers including Yeats, Shaw, Joyce, O'Faolain, Wilde, Lavin, Lord Dunsany and James Stephens.

1064   **Mary Lavin: quiet rebel, a study of her short stories.**
Angeline A. Kelly.   Dublin: Wolfhound, 1980. 200p.
An introduction to the work of a prominent contemporary Irish writer. The background of Irish middle class society is an important element in the eighty-five stories completed over a forty year period (from 1939 to 1977) that are discussed here. Social attitudes, human relationships, misunderstandings, religious conventions and community norms are some of the major themes of her work. Story plots are summarized and Lavin's approach to writing and the structuring of the stories is discussed. Some of Mary Lavin's work has appeared in *The stories of Mary Lavin* (London: Constable, 1985. 3 vols.). Here, the hardships and anxieties of everyday life are vividly shown.

1065   **The Penguin book of Irish short stories.**
Edited by Benedict Kiely.   Harmondsworth, England: Penguin, 1981. 550p.
A popular selection of thirty-eight short stories ranging from Lady Gregory's retelling of ancient myths, through Victorian and Gothic tales, to more contemporary works showing the concerns of modern society.

1066 **The Irish short story: a critical history.**
Edited by James F. Kilroy. Boston, Massachusetts: G. K. Hall, 1984. 296p.

The evolution of the Irish short story from the 19th century to the present is traced. Several specialists discuss why this form of literature has reached particular heights in Ireland. Historical, cultural and literary influences are covered, and the writings of James Joyce, Sean O'Faolain, Elizabeth Bowen, Frank O'Connor, George Moore, Mary Lavin and others are considered.

1067 **The Bodley Head book of Irish short stories.**
Edited by David Marcus. London: Bodley Head, 1982. 384p.

A collection of thirty short stories with an emphasis on more recent writings.

1068 **The road to bright city.**
Máirtín O Cadhain. Dublin: Poolbeg Press, 1981. 111p.

A collection of short stories in English translation by one of Ireland's best Gaelic writers of the 20th century, who portrayed life and everyday characters as he saw them.

1069 **The Irish short story from George Moore to Frank O'Connor.**
Deborah Averill. Washington, DC: University Press of America, 1982. 328p.

A discussion of the Irish short story tradition represented by George Moore, James Joyce, Seamus O'Kelly and Daniel Corkery, and the masters of the medium: Liam O'Flaherty, Sean O'Faolain, and Frank O'Connor. Bibliographies are included on each, but the typescript body of the text makes reading difficult.

1070 **Short stories.**
Liam O'Flaherty. Portmornock, Dublin: Wolfhound Press, 1981. 2 vols.

Short stories by the popular author of rural life, island existence, the sea and native people. The stories retain a natural strength and Gaelic spirit. O'Flaherty presents a view of the difficulties of a writing career in his autobiography, *Shame the devil* (Dublin: Wolfhound, 1981), and in it tells of life in once turbulent Ireland, which is also portrayed in his well known novel, *The informer*.

1071 **Michael/Frank: studies on Frank O'Connor.**
Edited by Maurice Sheehy. London: Macmillan, 1969. 203p.

O'Connor's stories (about 200 of them) are noted for their portrayal of small town Irish life, comforts and personal relationships, which are pictured with humour, sentiment and warmth. The Sheehy volume provides a good review of O'Connor's writings and their publication. A concise biography is given by James Matthews in *Voices: a life of Frank O'Connor* (New York: Atheneum, 1983. 450p.), that reviews his early life, literary friendships and arguments, and the surroundings of Cork. For a critical assessment of O'Connor's writings, see William Tomory's *Frank O'Connor*. O'Connor's *Collected stories* was published by Knopf (1981.

702p.). A well received, posthumous collection of additional works of O'Connor is *The cornet-player who betrayed Ireland* (Dublin: Poolbeg, 1981. 238p.).

1072   **Selected short stories of Padraic Colum.**
Edited by Sanford Sternlicht.   Syracuse, New York: Syracuse University Press, 1985. 130p.

The thirteen of Colum's stories included here show the wide horizon of Irish life portrayed in his writings, the rural ways and evocative Irish atmosphere. Colum was a significant figure in the Irish literary revival of the early 20th century. An introduction provides a good review of his work as a writer.

Poetry

1073   **Contemporary Irish poetry, an anthology.**
Edited by Anthony Bradley.   Berkeley, California: University of California Press, 1980. 430p.

A useful anthology of forty-three Irish poets spanning more than half a century of endeavour. Included are Clarke, Kavanagh, Kinsella, Montague, Fallon, Heaney and many others. There is a solid introduction summarizing modern trends, descriptive notes on many of the selections, and biographies and photographs of the poets. An excellent introduction to recent writing.

1074   **The art of Seamus Heaney.**
Edited by Tony Curtis.   Bridgend, Wales: Poetry Wales Press, 1982. 152p.

Seven diverse essays probe, often critically, the undercurrents and style of Heaney's poetry. The contributors, writers themselves, discuss his standing as a poet of the 1980s and his potential future directions. A bibliography of criticism on Heaney and excerpts from his works are included.

1075   **New Irish poets.**
Edited by Devin Garrity.   New York: Devin-Adair, 1948. 209p.

This anthology contains representative selections from the work of thirty-seven Irish poets in the first half of the 20th century. This popular volume is illustrated with woodblock prints. Garrity also edited the 1965 edition of the *Mentor book of Irish poetry* (New York: New American Library).

1076   **Modern Anglo-Irish verse, an anthology selected from the works of living Irish poets.**
Padric Gregory.   London: David Nutt, 1914. Reprinted, New York: AMS, 1978. 375p.

This volume still has value because many of the important early writers of the Irish literary renaissance are represented here.

1077   **Irish poetry after Yeats: seven poets.**
Edited by Maurice Harmon.   Dublin: Wolfhound; Boston,
Massachusetts: Little, Brown, 1981. 231p.

A collection of seven major Irish poets: Austin Clarke, Peter Kavanagh, Denis Devlin, Richard Murphy, Thomas Kinsella, John Montague, and Seamus Heaney. Portraits of each and a useful introduction are included.

1078   **1000 years of Irish poetry.**
Edited by Kathleen Hoagland.   Old Greenwich, Connecticut:
Devin-Adair, 1981. 830p.

An excellent source book and reference aid, first published in 1947. The anthology contains hundreds of works spanning the ancient and Gaelic worlds and comparatively recent Anglo-Irish literature.

1079   **Irish poetry after Joyce.**
Dillon Johnston.   Notre Dame, Indiana: Notre Dame Press,
1985. 304p.

In this study of recent figures in Irish poetry the directions taken since 1941 are explored. Among the poets selected Johnston notes a growing 'urban' tradition, and he searches for a unifying 'tone' rather than any central theme. Included in the discussion are Austin Clarke, Peter Kavanagh, Thomas Kinsella, Seamus Heaney, John Montague, Derek Mahon, and others.

1080   **The Penguin book of Irish verse.**
Edited by Brendan Kennelly.   Harmondsworth, England:
Penguin, 1981. 2nd ed. 470p.

A handy collection for recreational reading, this volume contains both early and modern poems, some of which have been translated from the Irish. Although a few later poets are represented, this volume is best up to 1970. A good, concise introduction to the history of Irish poetry is included.

1081   **Irish poets in English.**
Edited by Seán Lucy.   Cork: Mercier, 1973. 224p. (Thomas
Davis Lectures Series).

Essays are included by a number of prominent writers on the development and present state of Anglo-Irish poetry. The contributors themselves have been successful poets and authors.

1082   **Oxford book of Irish verse.**
Edited by Donagh MacDonagh.   London: Oxford University
Press, 1958. 382p.

A selection of Irish poetry, from the 17th to the 20th centuries. (This should not be confused with the *Oxford book of modern verse*, edited by Yeats, published in 1936 and in print ever since, which covers poetry from 1892 to 1935). The present selection of Irish writing is wide and representative of major styles and trends.

1083   **The Faber book of Irish verse.**
Edited by John Montague.   London; Boston, Massachusetts:
Faber & Faber, 1978. 400p.
An excellent, representative selection of Irish poetry, from the periods of ancient
legends and the Book of Invasion in pre-Christian Ireland, early monastic
literature, mediaeval writings of great variety, and the later works of Swift, Egan
O'Rahilly, Goldsmith, Brian Merriman, Thomas Moore and the whole literary
renaissance constellation. Modern Irish writers up to 1951 are also included.
Montague has compiled a 1983 collection, *Book of Irish verse* (New York:
Macmillan) covering poetry from the 6th century to the present.

1084   **Seamus Heaney.**
Blake Morrison.   New York: Methuen, 1982. 95p. (Contemporary Writers Series).
A brief summary of Heaney's poetry to date, with observations on his
autobiographical sources, and his outlook on the political division of modern
Ireland. Heaney's work, resonant, complex, outspoken, direct, yet delicate and
subtle, is well represented in his volume *Station Island* (New York: Farrar, Straus
& Giroux; London: Faber & Faber, 1985. 123p.).

1085   **The poetry of Austin Clarke.**
Gregory Schirmer.   Mountrath, Ireland (Republic): Dolmen
Press; Notre Dame, Indiana: Notre Dame Press, 1983. 167p.
A study of Clarke's impact on recent Irish poetry and the elements in the
character of his writing: introspection, secular outlook, eros, lyricism and ancient
Celtic themes.

1086   **Irish poetry from Moore to Yeats.**
Robert Welch.   Gerrards Cross, England: Colin Smythe; New
York: Barnes & Noble, 1980. 248p. (Irish Literary Studies, no.
5).
Seven major Irish poets of the 19th century are discussed and evaluated: Thomas
Moore, Jeremiah J. Callanan, James Clarence Mangan, Samuel Ferguson, Aubry
Thomas de Vere, William Allingham and William Butler Yeats. Welch notes,
after tracing the biographies and creative work of each, how Yeats established a
completely new direction and art form, breaking from established tradition. For
more advanced academic readers.

Irish (Gaelic) Literature

1087 Medieval Irish lyrics.
Edited by James Carney. London: Oxford University Press;
Dublin: Dolmen; Berkeley, California: University of California
Press, 1967. 103p.
A collection of early Irish poetry in translation, with an introduction on the
structure of Irish verse. Carney has also written *The Bardic poet* (1967), and
Studies in Irish literature and history (1979. 429p.), among other works for the
Dublin Institute of Advanced Studies.

1088 Gaelic literature surveyed
Aodh De Blacam. Dublin: Talbot, 1973. rev. ed. 422p.
A good introduction to the history of the Irish language and literature from
ancient times. First published in 1929, this revised edition includes information on
Irish literature in the 20th century.

1089 Early Irish literature.
Myles Dillon. Chicago: University of Chicago Press, 1966. 192p.
The author reviews the types and structure of Irish literature in the Gaelic
tradition. Included are the cycles of legends, voyages, poetry and sagas. Dillon is
noted for his volumes of *Celtica* published by the Dublin Institute of Advanced
Studies, his book on *Early Irish poetry* (Cork, 1965), and other works on early
Irish society.

1090 The Irish tradition.
Robin Flower. Oxford: Clarendon, 1978. new ed. 182p.
Flower, a major writer, poet and scholar of the Irish language, provides essays on
ancient bardic literature and later poetry.

1091 A golden treasury of Irish poetry.
David Greene, Frank O'Connor. London: Macmillan, 1967.
214p.
A collection of poems from 630 to 1200 AD, with some description and
background. Green has written scholarly works on old Irish, and O'Connor is a
popular, contemporary writer.

1092 The story of early Gaelic literature.
Douglas Hyde. London: Unwin; Dublin: Sealy, Bryers &
Walker; New York: Kennedy, 1895. Reprinted, Folcroft,
Pennsylvania: Folcroft Library Editions, 1973. 174p.
This classic essay studies the early use of writing in Ireland, Gaelic literature,
romances, mythological cycles, annals, and writers. Hyde became president of the
Gaelic League, and later of the Irish Free State.

1093   **A Celtic miscellany: translations from the Celtic literature.**
Edited by Kenneth Jackson.   Harmondsworth, England:
Penguin; Magnolia, Maine: Peter Smith, 1971. 352p.

A good selection of Irish poems, tales and humour, from ancient times to the 19th
century. Jackson also authored *Studies in early Celtic nature poetry* (Cambridge,
England: Cambridge University Press, 1935) which discusses the origin, types and
character of ancient Irish poetry.

1094   **Early Irish verse.**
Edited by Ruth Lehmann.   Austin, Texas: University of Texas
Press, 1982. 132p.

A selection of 101 poems translated from the Irish language, covering the 8th to
the 15th century. Two versions of each are offered: one literal, and one metrical.
The volume is divided into nature poems, devotional and hermit poetry, women's
songs, the sagas and chronicles. An appendix contains the original text of some of
the poems.

1095   **Literature in Irish.**
Proinsias Mac Caba.   Dublin: Department of Foreign Affairs,
1981. 72p. (Aspects of Ireland Series, no. 8).

A pleasant, illustrated introduction for the general reader, providing an overview
of the changing fortunes of the Irish (Gaelic) world of literature, from the 6th
century to the early 1980s. Briefly covered are crisis and evolution in Irish society,
ancient oral traditions, myths and legends, storytelling, the growth of poetry, and
the suppression and subsequent decline of the language.

1096   **The pleasures of Gaelic poetry.**
Edited by Sean Mac Reamoinn.   London: Allen Lane, 1983.
300p.

A collection of essays and poems are presented as an introduction for those who
are unfamiliar with the Irish language. Chapters discuss ancient nature poetry, the
Bardic mind, friendship, old Gaelic traditions, and modern writers in Irish. A
number of recent and current poets write of their own feelings about the Irish
language. The poems and translations included are representative examples.

1097   **Lectures on the manuscript materials of ancient Irish history.**
Eugene O'Curry.   Dublin: Hinch, 1878. Reprinted, New York:
Burt Franklin, 772p.

A very detailed analysis of the early Irish surviving manuscripts, others that have
been lost, the many sources of Irish history, and the content, value, and varied
fortunes of the ancient annals, genealogies and other works. Although
historiography has changed considerably in the century following publication, this
volume remains extremely useful for its gathering of information on the ancient
writings of Ireland.

1098   **An duanaire: an Irish anthology, 1600-1900, poems of the
        dispossessed.**
        Edited by Sean O'Tuama, translated by Thomas Kinsella.
        Mountrath, Ireland (Republic): Dolmen; Philadelphia: University
        of Pennsylvania Press, 1981. 382p.

This handsome volume, which is suitable for both recreational and scholarly use,
presents thirty-one poems written in the native Irish language during a period of
cultural subjugation. The fine examples selected show the quality of writing
during post-Cromwellian times. Translations of the poems are presented side by
side with the original Irish verses. The translations retain rhythms which are
similar to the original. This was a period of change in Irish poetry, with a new
freedom from old formulas.

1099   **Publications of the Irish Text Society.**
        London: Irish Text Society, 1898-.

This series of some fifty volumes, reprints and translates major works in the Irish
language from mediaeval and later periods, including those of history and the
invasions, early literature and poetry, medicine, law and many other primary
texts.

The Arts

General

1100   **Ireland: a cultural encyclopaedia.**
Brian de Breffny.   New York: Facts on File; London: Thames
& Hudson, 1983. 256p.

Six hundred alphabetically arranged short entries cover artists, scholars, writers,
cultural topics, literature, organizations, museums, famous works, architecture,
ruins and artifacts. All the arts are reviewed in succinctly written, short articles,
for all periods, from ancient to modern. An appendix lists facilities open to the
public: museums, art galleries, libraries, houses, castles and gardens. Many
bibliographic references are included.

1101   **The arts in Ireland: a chronology.**
Christopher Fitz-Simon.   Dublin: Gill & Macmillan, 1982. 272p.

This illustrated chronology charts the chief works and events in Irish visual arts
and literature from 7000 BC to 1970 AD. Using parallel charts, the particular
artists and works in painting, sculpture, architecture, drama, music, poetry, and
fiction are identified and plotted alongside social and historical trends both in
Ireland and world-wide.

Visual arts

1102   **A concise history of Irish art.**
Bruce Arnold.   New York: Frederick Praeger, 1968. 213p.
bibliog. (Praeger World of Art Series).

A broad history of the entire range of Irish art, including that of the Celtic era,
Viking invasions, the age of Swift, and the Romantic, landscape, and modern
movements. This convenient, inexpensive volume presents a detailed yet general
introduction to the subject. It provides a well balanced coverage of all periods,
and the illustrations are closely linked with the text.

1103   **Orpen, mirror to an age.**
Bruce Arnold.   London: Jonathan Cape, 1981. 448p.

This biography of the Dublin born portrait and realist painter and teacher also
discusses Ireland's social and cultural circle in the early 20th century. Orpen was
very much a part of that society, and was an acquaintance of Augustus John,
Hugh Lane, and George Moore. This book describe the social setting in which he
worked.

1104   **The painters of Ireland, 1660-1920.**
Anne Crookshank, the Knight of Glin.   London: Barrie &
Jenkins, 1978. 304p.

A thorough history of painting in Ireland, covering local and national themes and
movements, with biographical background on leading artists. The influence of
wider continental styles is charted, with many Irish painters having received their
reputation abroad. The literary, economic and political trends within Ireland are
shown to be reflected in its art. Principal paintings are reproduced.

1105   **Irish art from 1600 to the present day.**
Anne O. Crookshank.   Dublin: Department of Foreign Affairs,
1979. 80p. (Aspects of Ireland Series, no 4).

Major Irish works of art and art movements, primarily from the 16th to the 19th
centuries, are studied in this illustrated essay. Painting, sculpture, stained glass
and applied arts are included.

1106   **Irish sculpture from 1600 to the present day.**
Anne Crookshank.   Dublin: Department of Foreign Affairs,
1984. 72p. (Aspects of Ireland Series).

A capsuled history of more than 300 years of Irish sculpture in stone and wood,
including carved interiors, religious statuary, public monuments, and other forms.

1107 **Harry Clarke: his graphic art.**
Nicola Gordon Bowe. Mountrath, Ireland (Republic): Dolmen, 1983. 112p.
A catalogue and commentary on the life and work of the symbolist artist, illustrator, and stained glass designer. During the 1920s, Clarke successfully encouraged the revival of the Celtic style.

1108 **Irish art and artists, from prehistory to the present.**
Peter Harbison, Homan Potterton, Jeanne Sheehy. London: Thames & Hudson, 1978. 272p.
This illustrated history of Irish art covers ancient archaeological sites, great manuscripts, mediaeval contributions, classical styles, significant architecture, craftsmanship and modern painting.

1109 **Contemporary Irish art.**
Edited by Roderick Knowles. Dublin: Wolfhound, 1983. 232p.
Some 300 photographs provide a sampling of the work of 100 contemporary Irish artists. These are accompanied by comments from the artists themselves and from prominent art critics. This anthology shows the broad range of recent Irish art. Not every style or trend is represented, however, and emphasis is given to environmental art. A final selection provides a directory of 234 artists.

1110 **National Gallery of Ireland: illustrated summary catalogue of paintings.**
Edited by Homan Potterton. Dublin: Gill & Macmillan, 1981. 412p.
An illustrated listing of more than 2,300 paintings in Ireland's leading collection, which are reproduced in black and white. Each is given minor descriptive information in this extensive catalogue.

1111 **The rediscovery of Ireland's past, the Celtic revival, 1830-1930.**
Jeanne Sheehy. London: Thames & Hudson, 1980. 208p.
The Celtic revival movement introduced into arts and crafts of the late 19th and early 20th centuries, the traditional motifs and styles of ancient Ireland. Flowing, curvilinear and interlacing scrollwork, with its inception in mediaeval and even pre-Christian art, was revived in later Irish metalwork, textiles, graphics, glass and book design. The movement, well-illustrated and documented here, is shown to have its parallels in modern literary movements.

1112 **Dictionary of Irish artists.**
William G. Strictland. Dublin: Irish Academic Press, 1984. 1,352p.
A major art reference work, this book lists all significant Irish artists and craftsmen up to the end of the 19th century. Brief biographical information and some illustrations are included, along with a history of art institutions in the Irish Republic. There are useful indexes to artists, pictures, engravings and other works, locations and owners.

1113 **Louis le Brocquy.**
Dorothy Walker. Dublin: Ward River Press, 1981. 168p.
Le Brocquy, Ireland's leading artist of the mid-20th century, has achieved international fame for his infusion of contemporary styles with ancient Celtic themes. His use of the head as a motif in painting, drawing, and tapestry, has achieved international recognition for its many allusions to literature and legend. This book and illustrated catalogue discusses his life and work between 1939 and 1980.

1114 **Masterpieces of the National Gallery of Ireland.**
James White. Dublin: Easons, [n.d.]. 24p. (Irish Heritage Series).
A brief history and description of the contents of the Irish Republic's chief art museum. Many photographs are included of Irish and continental works of art in this popular, pamphlet-sized study.

1115 **Fifty Irish painters.**
Michael Wynne. Dublin: National Gallery of Ireland, 1981. 50p.
A work from each of fifty Irish painters has been selected for illustration and description, and a short biography of each artist is included.

Ancient art

1116 **Irish carved ornament from the Christian period.**
H. S. Crawford. Cork; Dublin: Mercier, 1980. 144p.
A basic, illustrated guide to designs taken from some 300 examples of ancient Irish stone sculptures. The text groups the artwork by theme, motif and style. The illustrations will be of interest to contemporary artists, designers and archaeologists.

1117 **Early Irish art.**
Máire de Paor. Dublin: Department of Foreign Affairs, 1980. 57p. (Aspects of Ireland Series, no. 3).
This very attractive, illustrated booklet provides an introduction to the development of an Irish style of art, from prehistory to the 15th century. It traces indigenous and foreign influences, the development of stone carving, manuscript illumination and metalwork. Máire with Liam de Paor also authored *Early Christian Ireland* (q.v.) which more thoroughly relates Irish art to the cultural background. The present work provides a good, compact summary for the casual reader and includes Megalithic, Bronze, and early Christian art, Roman influences, the Golden Age, the Viking impact, Romanesque and Gothic art.

1118   **Irish art.**
Françoise Henry.   Ithaca, New York: Cornell University Press,
1965. 3 vols.
A major work on art history by a leading authority, showing the gradual
development of a truely native Irish art, from pagan to mediaeval Christian times.
Included are all forms of Irish art of the period: metalwork, sculpture, and
manuscript illumination. Volume one covers the early Christian period to 800
AD; volume two the Viking invasions (800-1020); and volume three Romanesque
art, 1020-1170. The presentation of this detailed review is excellent, and it is
readily understandable. The volumes contain an analysis of motifs and styles,
historical data on sites, diagrams of artistic methods, and numerous black and
white photographs.

1119   **The Book of Kells, reproductions from the manuscript in Trinity
College, Dublin.**
Françoise Henry.   London: Thames & Hudson, 1974. Reprinted,
New York: Knopf, 1977. 228p.
The best scholarly reproduction of the Book of Kells currently available. The
entire text is not here, but copious illustrations are given of all the major pages of
what has been considered Christendom's finest manuscript. Appended are several
studies of the manuscript by Henry who provides a description of the decoration,
ornamentation and construction of the book, and its historical context.
Illustrations include full page reproductions as well as enlargements of detail.
More complete but less attractive editions have appeared previous to this one. A
shorter, less expensive introduction to the *Book of Kells* by G. O. Sims has been
published with eighteen plates of the finer pages (Dublin: Dolmen; Atlantic
Highlands, New Jersey: Humanities Press, 1976. 32p.). Other, short illustrated
introductions are by Peter Brown with a brief essay and forty-eight full colour
plates (London: Thames & Hudson, 1981. 96p.), and Blanche Cirker *The Book of
Kells: selected plates in full color* (New York: Dover, 1982. 32p.).

1120   **Early Christian Irish art.**
Françoise Henry.   Cork: Mercier, 1979. 126p.
A standard, if sparse, introduction to the origins of early Christian art in Ireland,
its growth, flowering (from the 5th to the 9th centuries), and its place in monastic
culture. Henry has contributed some of the most significant and scholarly writings
on early Irish art, over a fifty year period. Pendar Press has announced a three
volume reprinting of her articles in *Studies in early Christian and medieval Irish
art*. Volume one is on enamels and metalwork (1985); volume two will cover
manuscript illumination; and volume three sculpture and architecture. For a
general work providing background on Irish culture and society of the period see
Ludwig Bieler's seminal work, *Ireland, harbinger of the Middle Ages* (London:
Oxford University Press, 1963).

1121   **Irish medieval figure sculpture, 1200-1600.**
John Hunt.   London: Sotheby Publications, 1974. 2 vols.
Hunt, in this massive review of mediaeval stone sculpture in Ireland discusses
major styles, schools and workshops, English and continental influences, the

Norman style in Irish art (1200-1350), an Irish revival period (1350-1450), and the transition from the Gothic to the Elizabethan style (1450-1570). Volume one contains the text; volume two has 340 plates, showing examples drawn from tombs, statuary and armour.

1122 **Celtic craftsmanship in bronze.**
H. E. Kilbridge-Jones. New York: St. Martin's, 1980. 266p.
Examples of ancient Celtic styles of art are shown in surviving bronze artifacts from the 1st to the 7th centuries. Numerous photographs are included.

1123 **Christian art in ancient Ireland, selected objects illustrated and described.**
Adolph Mahr. New York: Hacker Art Books, 1976. 176p. plates.
An extensive survey of ancient art objects in black and white photographs, arranged by type and period. A summary essay is included on the varied styles in Irish art, and detailed notes on particular works of art and ornamentation are provided. For the specialist. This was originally published in two volumes by the Stationery Office in Dublin (1932, 1941).

1124 **Treasures of Irish art, 1500 B.C. to 1500 A.D.**
Edited by G. Frank Mitchell, (et al.). Cork; Dublin: Mercier, 1979. 221p.
Some 3,000 years of ancient art are scanned in this exhibition catalogue, with coverage extending from Bronze Age prehistory to the mediaeval and Gothic period. Five essays highlight particular artifacts and major art treasures from the National Museum of Ireland, the Royal Irish Academy, and Trinity College Dublin. Emphasis is on a description of individual works and a good feature is the colour plates, often showing enlargements of detail, that enhance the text. Vivid impressions are created for a general readership.

1125 **Early Christian, Viking and Romanesque art: motif-pieces from Ireland.**
Uaininn O'Meadhra. Stockholm: Almquist & Wiksell; Atlantic Highlands, New Jersey: Humanities Press, 1979. 199p. (Theses and Papers in North-European Archaeology, no. 7).
A descriptive, illustrated catalogue of trial and practice pieces of ancient Irish art. The objects displayed range from the 5th to 12th centuries and were found in Ireland between 1830 and 1973. They show the formation, development and progress of Celtic interlacing styles. The technical discussion and listing of pieces are among the most extensive available on the topic. For specialized collections in art history.

1126   **The Irish hand: scribes and their manuscripts from the earliest**
       times to the seventeenth century, with an exemplar of Irish scripts.
       Timothy O'Neill.   Mountrath, Ireland (Republic): Dolmen,
       1984. 100p.

An excellent review of the ancient Irish script, through a brief look at major
mediaeval and later works up to the 17th century, which are reproduced here.
The historical importance of each work is briefly discussed. For the general reader
this will serve as a convenient guide to the chief sources of Irish history; for the
calligrapher, it provides an analysis of styles in Irish writing. Both Latin and Irish
language texts are illustrated in a sampling of pages. The twenty-six significant
texts selected represent the development of writing styles over a period of ten
centuries.

1127   **Monasterboice and its monuments.**
       Helen M. Roe.   Dundalk, Ireland (Republic): County Louth
       Archaeology and Historical Society, 1981. 78p.

This illustrated guide book to the great monastic ruin includes notes on
topography, archaeology and the history of its art. The abbey disappears from the
Irish annals after 1100, but its elaborate crosses and figure sculpture remain. This
book updates an earlier guide, *Monasterboice* by R. A. S. Macalister (Dundalk,
Irish Repubic: Dundalgan Press, 1946. 79p.).

1128   **Treasures of Ireland: Irish art, 3000 B.C.-1500 A.D.**
       Edited by Michael Ryan.   Dublin: Royal Irish Academy, 1983.
       203p. bibliog.

The various types of ancient Irish art objects are studied in this collection of
essays. Ninety-one pieces are discussed with excellent coloured illustrations. The
historical background given for each piece provides a basic understanding.
Chapters cover prehistoric art, gold and metalworking, manuscripts, Iron Age art,
early Christian styles, and Viking, Romanesque and Norman influences. A fine
introduction to the topic.

1129   **Irish illuminated manuscripts.**
       G. O. Simms.   Dublin: Eason, 1983. 25p.

A short, illustrated booklet comparing major Irish mediaeval manuscripts, their
production and history.

1130   **Sun and cross: the development from megalithic culture to early**
       Christianity in Ireland.
       Jacob Streit, translated from the German by Hugh Latham.
       Edinburgh: Floris Books, 1984. 223p. bibliog.

This popularly written, personal interpretation of Irish artifacts and early art
styles traces the evolution of the early Irish church. Streit shows the use of
symbolism during megalithic and Celtic periods and suggests the carryover of
certain druidic patterns into later Christian liturgy and rituals. An emphasis is
given to ancient cults and the origin of the sun symbol, spirals and other shapes.
The conclusions drawn on the art motifs are speculative and debatable.

Translated from the German, the book provides an interesting look at the Christian Church in Ireland before St. Patrick.

Design and crafts

1131 Celtic art, the methods of construction.
George Bain. New York: Dover, 1951. 160p.

The most popular introduction to art in the Celtic style, showing its evolution and methods of construction, through numerous step-by-step diagrams. The book contains hundreds of illustrations of examples taken from ancient monuments and manuscripts.

1132 Irish Georgian silver.
Douglas Bennett. London: Cassell, 1972. 369p.

This illustrated study is useful for the identification of Irish silver of the Georgian period, which was a highpoint in Irish craftsmanship. Bennett provides a shorter history of the evolving styles of Irish silver, especially during the 18th and 19th centuries, in *Irish silver* (Dublin: Eason, 1983. 26p.). Lists of silversmiths, hallmarks and other data are presented in his book *Collecting Irish silver* (London: Souvenir Press, [n.d.]).

1133 Irish crochet lace.
Eithne D'Arcy. Mountrath, Ireland (Republic): Dolmen, 1984. 64p.

D'Arcy discusses the beginnings of Irish lace and its motifs, 17th-century needlepoint, and fashions of style into the 19th and 20th centuries. This illustrated account shows, through numerous photographs, fine examples of lace and the various stages of its production.

1134 Belleek: the complete collector's guide and illustrated reference.
Richard Degenhardt. New York: Portfolio Press, 1982. 207p.

An illustrated history of Ireland's best known, exquisite porcelain. Data are presented on specific antique pieces, markings and dimensions. A much shorter history is provided by Michael Archer in *Irish pottery and porcelain* (Dublin: Eason, 1983. 26p.).

1135 Irish art heritage from 2000 B.C.: design legacy from the mid-West.
Hilary Gilmore. Dublin: O'Brien Press, 1983. 96p.

Beginning with the Bronze Age a short review is given of the development of the artforms and styles in which the Irish have excelled. Emphasis is on the applied arts including stone carvings, jewelry, ornament, plaster and iron work, lace, and tools, from 2,000 BC to modern times.

1136 **Waterford: an Irish art.**
Ida Grehan. New York: Portfolio Books, 1982. 256p.
A history of Waterford glass, describing its manufacture, major pieces, and the
master cutters. The changing fortunes of the company are outlined and over 250
photographs show examples of its superior output.

1137 **Celtic ornament.**
Paul Larmour. Dublin: Eason, 1981. 26p. (Irish Heritage Series,
no. 33).
This attractive booklet provides an illustrated introduction to basic Celtic styles in
Irish art, crafts and artifacts. Particular attention is given to the Celtic revival
period and the application of ornament to manuscripts, books, furniture and
religious art.

1138 **Irish lace.**
Ada Longfield. Dublin: Eason, 1979. 26p. (Irish Heritage
Series, no. 21).
An illustrated account of the origin of Irish lace, its manufacture and history,
continental influences, and varied styles and types, including Carickmacross and
Limerick.

1139 **Irish crafts and craftsmen.**
John Manners. Belfast: Appletree, 1982. 120p.
Reviews the traditional crafts and craftsmen of rural Ireland. Included are the
makers of linen and lace, fiddles and pipes, curragh boats, and marble goods
among other products. The commentary is based on interviews with the
craftspeople, as they talk of their work, objectives and society. Photographs of
work activity are included.

1140 **Kilkenny design: twenty-one years of design in Ireland.**
Nick Marchant, Jeremy Addis. Kilkenny, Ireland (Republic):
Kilkenny Design Workshops; London: Lund Humphries, 1984.
212p.
The Kilkenny Design Workshop, founded in 1962, is well known as the national
centre in the Republic of Ireland supporting design innovations applicable to
industry, home use, and interior decoration. Examples are given of some of the
new products and designs developed during the first twenty-one years of the
workshop. A brief discussion is given of its work, organization and funding, and
553 photographs of products are included.

1141 **A handbook of Celtic ornament.**
J. G. Merne. Cork: Mercier, 1977. 104p.
A short textbook on Celtic motifs, methods of construction and application, with
examples drawn from ancient monuments.

1142 **Ireland's traditional crafts.**
      Edited by David Shaw-Smith.   London: Thames & Hudson, 1984. 224p.

In this effective and attractive volume, ten sections discuss traditional methods and production in woodworking, textiles, leather, stone, pottery and metalwork. Step-by-step descriptions are given of forty crafts, including the making of crystal and glass, boats, shoes, walls, lace, musical instruments and bookbinding. Work in progress is clearly shown in 440 photographs, and 14 experts comment on specific crafts and their place in rural society and the economy.

1143 **Weaving: the Irish inheritance.**
      E. Frank Sutton.   Dublin: Gilbert Dalton, 1980. 64p.

An illustrated history of weaving from 700 BC to modern times. Its evolution from utilitarian purposes in ancient times is traced through later periods of linen and cotton industries, to the more modern approach of weaving as an art form.

1144 **Irish glass: Waterford, Cork, Belfast in the age of exuberance.**
      Phelps Warren.   London: Faber; Salem, New Hampshire: Merrimack, 1981. 2nd ed. 256p.

A history of Ireland's preeminent glass industry, covering production and craftsmanship from 1780 to 1830. Examples are shown of cut and moulded glassware, chandeliers and lamps.

1145 **Irish glass.**
      Dudley Westropp, edited by Mary Boydell.   Dublin: Figgis, 1978. rev. ed. 328p.

The standard history of Irish glass from the 16th century to modern times. Shown are the types of glass produced, products and locations, raw materials, the former uses of glassware and the social surroundings. Mary Boydell has also prepared a pamphlet history *Irish glass* (Dublin: Eason, 1983. 26p.). Both accounts are illustrated.

Music and dance

1146 **Irish music and musicians.**
      Charles Acton.   Dublin: Eason, 1976. 24p. (Irish Heritage Series).

This short, illustrated review of traditional music in Irish society covers the instruments used and the players, from the Bronze Age to the 1970s.

1147 **The James Joyce songbook.**
      Edited by Ruth Bauerle.   New York: Garland, 1982. 709p.

A collection of 200 songs either known to have been sung by Joyce or that have been given prominence in his writings. This selection is useful for the interpretation of Joyce's works. Joyce was an accomplished singer, and many popular ballads of his day are included.

1148 Folk music and dances of Ireland.

Breandan Breathnach.   Cork: Mercier, 1980. 160p.

An authoritative review of Irish music and dance, its evolution and present use. An accompanying cassette is available. The Irish Department of Education has supported several Irish language collections of dance music compiled by Breathnach, the third published by An Gúm in Dublin, 1985.

1149 The Christy Moore songbook.

Edited by Frank Connolly.   Dingle, Ireland (Republic):
Brandon, 1984. 142p.

A collection of more than 100 songs on Irish themes by the popular recording artist.

1150 Blood on the harp: Irish rebel history in ballad.

Turlough Faolain.   New York: Whitson, 1983. 553p. bibliog.

The rebel tradition in music is viewed as a form of folk history, shaped by actual events in British-Irish relations, and interpreted by balladeers. The place of great heroes and causes in Irish history is traced from ancient kingships to the political leadership of the 19th century. Numerous songs are included and described against a chronology of historical events. Maps and a lengthy bibliography are provided.

1151 Music in Ireland.

Aloys G. Fleischman.   Cork: Cork University Press; Oxford:
Blackwell, 1952. 371p.

A thorough review of music sources in Ireland. Based on the proceedings of a symposium, information is given on collections and sources for Irish music and instruments in major libraries and institutions.

1152 A history of Irish music.

W. H. Gratton Flood.   Darby, Pennsylvania: Arden Library,
1979. 350p. bibliog.

A history of the music tradition in Ireland, its roots, sources and popular heritage. First published in 1906 this is no longer current. Several appendixes list major music collections, manuscripts and societies of the 18th and 19th centuries.

1153 The Irish bagpipes: their construction and maintenance.

Wilbert Garvin.   Belfast: Blackstaff, 1978. 40p.

A handbook on the construction and care of the Uilleann pipes that produce the distinctive sound of Irish music. Formerly much of this information was unrecorded but passed on orally within families of music craftsmen in Ireland.

The Arts. Music and dance

1154 **Irish minstrelry, or bardic remains of Ireland.**
James Hardiman. Dublin: Irish Academic Press, 1971. 2 vols.
First published in 1831, this is an important basic collection of old airs, ballads
and songs.

1155 **Anglo-Irish music.**
Ita M. Hogan. Cork: Cork University Press; Mystic,
Connecticut: Verry, 1966. 246p. bibliog. pp. 165-235.
A review of the history of music in Ireland's English speaking community
between 1780 and 1830.

1156 **The harp that once–; a chronicle of the life of Thomas Moore.**
Howard Mumford Jones. New York: Russell & Russell, 1970.
365p.
A standard biography (first published in 1937) of Thomas Moore (1779-1852),
Ireland's poet and musician who achieved great popularity. Moore's melodies
have had numerous editions since the 19th century, and several are currently
available, including *Centenary selection from Moore's melodies* edited by David
Hammond (Dublin: Dalton, 1979. 64p.), and *Moore's Irish melodies with
symphonies and accompaniments* (Wilmington, Delaware: Glaziers, 1981).
Moore's diary, memoirs, correspondence and journal have also been published,
but are of more interest in the realm of literary history than music. *The journal of
Thomas Moore* (volumes one and two covering 1818 to 1825) has been edited by
Wilfred Dowden (Cranbury, New Jersey: Associated University Presses, 1985).

1157 **Old Irish folk music and song.**
Patrick Weston Joyce. London, New York: Longmans, Green,
1909. 408p.
A pioneer collection of 842 country tunes collected by Joyce throughout rural
Ireland. His first collection *Ancient music of Ireland*, appeared in 1873.

1158 **The great Irish tenor.**
Gordon T. Ledbetter. New York: Scribners, 1977. 159p.
An illustrated biography of John McCormack, Ireland's greatest tenor.

1159 **Folksongs and ballads popular in Ireland.**
John Loesberg. Cork: Ossian Publications 1982. 3 vols.
A compilation of popular songs, guitar chords and historical background.

1160 **The voice of the people: songs and history of Ireland.**
Michael Mulcahy, Marie Fitzgibbon. Dublin: O'Brien, 1982.
199p. bibliog.
The text is given of 150 Irish ballads, mainly of a political bent, during the period
1796 to 1916. Each chapter contains the ballads of an era, with an introductory
commentary on the social history and major events of the time: the Napoleonic

Wars, the famine, the home rule issue, and the 1916 rebellion. Woodcut illustrations are included.

1161   **The world of Percy French.**
Brendan O'Dowda.   Belfast: Blackstaff, 1981. 192p.

A lively biography of Ireland's gifted entertainer, song writer, and painter. Excerpts are included from French's songs, poems and humorous writings, and some of his watercolours of the Irish landscape are reproduced. French, (1854-1920), achieved international popularity. A volume containing a collection of forty examples of his music is *Percy French and his songs* by James N. Healy (Cork: Mercier, 1978. 172p.).

1162   **Irish street ballads.**
Colm O'Lochlainn.   New York: Citadel Press; London: Pan Books, 1960. 269p.

A collection of vibrant, popular songs of everyday Irish life. O'Lochlainn has compiled several collections of street songs, and pamphlets on Anglo-Irish song writers.

1163   **Irish folk music.**
Francis O'Neill.   Totowa, New Jersey: Roman & Littlefield, 1977. 359p.

This reprint of a 1910 edition presents a compilation of song, dance and instrumental music, with a commentary on the evolution and playing of the pipes. O'Neill was an avid collector of Irish music (and also served as Superintendent of the Chicago Police Force in 1901). In 1906 O'Neill published his great work, *Music in Ireland*. Another of his books (reprinted from a 1922 edition), contains 350 tunes, airs, jigs, marches and reels: *Waifs and strays of Gaelic melody*. (Cork: Mercier, 1980. 186p.).

1164   **Our musical heritage.**
Seán O Riada.   Mountrath, Ireland (Republic): Dolmen, 1982. 84p.

O Riada, trained in the European musical tradition, has had a decisive impact on Irish traditional music of the mid-20th century. This series of radio lectures contains his analysis and discussion of a reawakened interest in Irish traditional music and culture. O Riada's own contribution to a sustained musical revival is recounted in a book by Bernard Harris and Grattan Freyer, *Integrating traditions, the achievement of Sean O Riada* (Ballina, Irish Republic: Irish Humanities Centre; Chester Springs, Pennsylvania: Dufour, 1982).

1165   **Blas meala, a slip from the honey pot.**
Brian O Rourke.   Dublin: Irish Academic Press, 1985. 128p.

A collection of Gaelic folksongs with English translations. Two tapes are also available to accompany the book.

1166 **Irish folk music, song and dance.**
Donal J. O'Sullivan. Cork: Mercier Press, 1974. 56p. (Irish Life and Culture Series).

A basic introduction to the history, rhythms, verses and enjoyment of popular Irish music and dance. This short, illustrated book was compiled for the Cultural Relations Committee of Ireland. O'Sullivan comments on efforts to preserve the old music.

1167 **Songs of the Irish.**
Donal J. O'Sullivan. Cork, Irish Republic: Mercier, 1981. 200p.

A collection of sixty-five popular Irish songs of all types with both the original Irish verse and the English translation. Notes on each are included. O'Sullivan has also written a descriptive introduction, *Irish folk music and song* (Cork, Dublin: Mercier, 1961), which discusses the origin of the music, the dancers, the musicians and their styles.

1168 **Bunting's ancient music of Ireland.**
Edited by Donal O'Sullivan, Mícheál Ó Súilleabháin. Cork: Cork University Press, 1983. 226p. bibliog.

This volume, which originally appeared in 1840, contains the text of 150 pieces with some translations, background information and notes and is an important source for 18th-century Irish music. Additional notes have been added by the present editors. This volume was the third to have been compiled by Edward Bunting. Volumes one and two, (published in Dublin 1796-1809) also provide airs and melodies arranged for piano and harp. They have gradually been reprinted in the *Journal of the Irish Folk Song Society*, vols. 22-27 (1927-39).

1169 **The Petrie collection of the ancient music of Ireland.**
Collected by George Petrie. Farnborough, England: Gregg Press, 1967. 244p.

This collection is reprinted from a University Press edition (Dublin: 1855). Both words and melodies are given for some 300 Irish airs and tunes. Piano arrangements and background material are included. Petrie founded the Society for the Preservation and Publication of the Melodies of Ireland, and as an antiquarian was personally responsible for the collection of rural tunes of various types: those for spinning, ploughing, dancing, the harp and the lullaby. In 1905 Charles Sullivan produced another collection of 1,148 tunes collected by Petrie.

1170 **The Irish harp.**
Joan Rimmer. Cork: Mercier, 1969. 80p. (Irish Life and Culture Series, no. 16).

A review of the historical development of the harp, which has been closely identified as a most characteristic Irish instrument from the 9th century to the present. A book for players is *The Irish harp book, a tutor and companion* by Sheila Cuthbert (Cork: Mercier, 1977).

1171 **The Roche collection of traditional Irish music.**
Frank Roche, introduction by Mícheál Ó Súilleabháin.   Cork:
Ossian Publications, 1984. 234p.
A reprint of a 1927 collection of 566 traditional Irish tunes, dances and marches,
originally published in three volumes. The new introduction to this edition
provides a short biography of Roche.

1172 **Irish folk music studies.**
George D. Zimmermann, (et al.).   Dundrum, Ireland
(Republic): Folk Music Society, [n.d.]. 3 vols.
Several papers are presented on religious and popular song throughout Ireland.
Zimmermann has also compiled *Songs of the Irish rebellion* (Detroit, Michigan:
Gale, 1967. 242p.), a collection of political street ballads and rebels songs from
1780 to 1900.

Theatre

1173 **The Irish dramatic movement.**
Una Ellis-Fermor.   Totowa, New Jersey: Rowman & Littlefield,
1977. 241p.
Reviews the new directions charted by the Irish theatre, and the effect that it had
upon world literature and drama. The author concentrates on the innovations and
contributions of Yeats, Synge, Lady Gregory, Edward Martyn and G. A. Moore.
First published in 1939, this book includes a chronology of the movement.

1174 **The Irish theatre.**
Christopher Fitz-Simon.   London: Thames & Hudson, 1983.
208p.
This short yet comprehensive history is highly recommended as an introduction to
Irish drama. The fortunes of plays, playwrights, productions and actors are traced
from 12-century theatre to the present. The difficulties encountered by Irish
authors over the centuries are noted as are the unique trends developed by them.
Special attention is given to Irish drama during and following the literary
renaissance. Among the playwrights covered are Goldsmith, Congreve, Sheridan,
Wilde, Yeats, Shaw, O'Casey and Beckett. The book is made particularly
attractive by the inclusion of several hundred well chosen illustrations.

1175 **After the Irish renaissance: a critical history of the Irish drama
since *The plough and the stars*.**
Robert Hogan.   London: Macmillan; Minneapolis, Minnesota:
University of Minnesota Press, 1968. 284p.
A history and description of Irish stage productions since 1926. Some 200 plays
and 40 playwrights are mentioned, although this is the period after that of the
titans of Irish theatre.

1176 **The modern Irish drama.**
Robert Hogan, (et al.).   Mountrath, Ireland (Republic):
Dolmen, 1975-1985. 6 vols.

This set provides a history of the Irish theatre from 1899 to 1926, which includes a discussion and commentary, contemporary reviews, selected papers and letters, and lists of casts. Volume one is entitled *The Irish literary theatre*, (1899-1901); volume two *Laying the foundations*, (1902-1904); volume three *The Abbey Theatre: the years of Synge*, (1905-1909); volume four *The rise of the realists*, (1910-1915); volume five *The art of the amateur*, (1916-1920); and volume six *The years of O'Casey*, (1921-1926). This knowledgable account is exceptionally detailed, with references to many minor events. An overall record is presented through the eyes of dramatists, actors, critics and observers. An important set for detailed research.

1177 **Since O'Casey and other essays on Irish drama.**
Robert Hogan.   Gerrards Cross, England; Colin Smythe;
Dublin: Dolmen; Totowa, New Jersey: Barnes & Noble, 1983.
176p. (Irish Literary Studies, vol. 15).

While not a full survey of recent Irish drama, this account nevertheless offers numerous and varied observations on the playwrights and works of the mid-20th century, and some of Hogan's comments are outspokenly critical. A refreshing collection of essays for general readership.

1178 **The Abbey, Ireland's national theatre, 1904-1979.**
Hugh Hunt.   Dublin: Gill & Macmillan; New York: Columbia
University Press, 1979. 306p.

Hunt, a former director of the Abbey and an acquaintance of Yeats, traces the growth of the company from a fledgling amateur group to that of a popular and professional theatre. This illustrated history of what has been described as the oldest state-subsidised theatre in the English speaking world, contains first hand (if opinionated) impressions, along with lists of Abbey productions.

1179 **The story of the Abbey Theatre.**
Peter Kavanagh.   Orono, Maine: National Poetry Foundation
and the University of Maine; Newbridge, Ireland (Republic):
Goldsmith, 1985. 243p.

First published in 1950, this volume covers the first decade of the Abbey Theatre, which was its most important period. Kavanagh studies the triumphs and despair, the great works and the numerous difficulties encountered. The account ends with the death of Yeats. More recent times have been harsh for the Abbey.

1180 **Home before night.**
Hugh Leonard.   Harmondsworth, England: Penguin, 1980. 176p.

The autobiography of a playwright noted for his human, humorous and penetrating look at Irish society, poverty, and personal and family relationships. A collection of three of his plays, *Da, A life, Time was*, has also been published by Penguin.

The Arts. Theatre

1181   **All for Hecuba.**
Mícheál MacLiammoir.   Gerrards Cross, England: Colin Smythe, 1981. 400p.

MacLiammoir provides an anecdotal and impressionistic history of the Gate Theatre in its early years, based on his first hand recollections as a founder. MacLiammoir also authored *Theatre in Ireland* (Dublin: 1950) which provides a short, general introduction to the Irish stage of the Gate and Abbey Theatres.

1182   **The Irish drama.**
Andrew E. Malone.   Gerrards Cross, England: Colin Smythe; New York: Blom, Arno Press, 1965. 352p.

A review of the Irish stage during the creative period from 1896 to 1928. Included are the production notes of some of the plays. A description is also given of the political circumstances surrounding the plays, and the growth of the nationalist cause. First published in 1929.

1183   **A critical history of modern Irish drama, 1891-1980.**
D. E. S. Maxwell.   Cambridge, England: Cambridge University Press, 1984. 300p.

A detailed history and assessment of Irish drama from the start of the Irish Literary Theatre to 1980. Among the major playwrights discussed are Yeats, Synge, O'Casey, Denis Johnston, Samuel Beckett, and Brian Friel. Both the distinctiveness of the Irish theatre, and its continental roots are evaluated.

1184   **Theatre in Ireland.**
Micheál Ó hAdha.   Oxford: Blackwell, 1974. 160p. bibliog.

A general review of the Irish theatre, its history and productions, and period playwrights.

1185   **Aspects of the Irish theatre.**
Edited by Patrick Rafroidi, Raymonde Popot, William Parker. Lille, France: University of Lille; Atlantic Highlands, New Jersey: Humanities Press, 1972. 297p.

A collection of essays on the Irish theatre, its comedies, and the influences of ancient myths, modern politics and contemporary society.

1186   **Ireland's Abbey Theatre: a history, 1899-1951.**
Lennox Robinson.   London: Macmillan; Folcroft, Pennsylvania: Folcroft Library, 1951. 224p.

The authorized history of the Abbey, and its administration, productions and casting. Robinson has also written a general history, *The Irish theatre* (New York: Haskell House, 1982. new ed.), first published in 1939.

1187 **Theatre business.**
Edited by Ann Saddlemyer. Gerrards Cross, England: Colin Smythe, 1982. 330p.

A selection of the correspondence of the first directors of the Abbey Theatre, including that of Lady Gregory, Yeats, and Synge. The first five years of the Abbey are depicted as pioneering, often angry and stormy times in both management and production, with concurrent public scorn and derision. Difficulties were encountered in casting, finance, and even in the nationalist themes of the plays themselves. This book provides the insiders' view of the tribulations and ultimate success of modern Irish drama.

1188 **The Irish drama of Europe from Yeats to Beckett.**
Katharine Worth. London: Athlone; Atlantic Highlands, New Jersey: Humanities, 1978. 276p.

The connection between Irish drama and the continent (especially France) is stressed. Particular attention is focused on production of earlier plays from the time of Yeats, and their potential for future staging in modern surroundings.

Cinema

1189 **The cinema and Ireland, from 1896.**
Liam O'Leary. Dublin: Academy Press, 1979. 224p.

The author reviews some of the early feature film making attempts and documentaries in Ireland, which help to chronicle the living conditions of the early 1900s. He also charts the influence of the Irish in the motion picture industry around the world, and stresses some of the leading figures within Ireland. Dan Ford in a book about his grandfather writes of the great Irish film maker in *The unquiet man: the life of John Ford* (London: William Kimber, 1983). John Ford has achieved lasting fame for his portrayal of Ireland in the films 'The informer,' and 'The quiet man.'

1190 **Rex Ingram, master of the silent cinema.**
Liam O'Leary. New York: Barnes & Noble, 1980. 224p.

Ingram was a leading figure in the early days of Hollywood. This book describes his formative years in Dublin, his important contributions as a film director, his work as a sculptor and artist, and his many acquaintances among writers, statesmen, painters and others. Interesting stills from 27 early films are among the 120 illustrations included.

Architecture

1191 Architectural Heritage.

Dublin: An Foras Forbartha, 1980-.

A series of booklets, each on a specific Irish town, listing and describing buildings of architectural interest. Emphasis is given to the needs of preservation of small, domestic and commercial buildings as well as major landmarks. Each publication is heavily illustrated, showing varied locations, details, facades, and ornamentation. Maps and glossaries are also included. Among the towns covered are Bray, Carlow, Tullomore and Kinsale. Each volume forms part of the National Heritage Inventory, and is by a separate author. Much interest in architectural preservation was generated during the European Architectural Heritage Year (EAHY) in 1975. This resulted in the publication of such studies as the Irish National Committee for EAHY's *Irish architecture, a future for our heritage* (Dublin: An Foras Forbartha, 1975. 6p.), and *Architectural conservation, an Irish viewpoint* (q.v.). The distinctive Irish quality of particular buildings is considered in 'Architectural character of new buildings' in *Planning for amenity and tourism* (vol. 2, part 1 p. 16-19). Brief mention is made of some of the elements that may determine a building's character in the Irish environment: mode of construction, materials, form, colour and siting. Photographs and perspective drawings accompany the text.

1192 Burke's guide to country houses, vol. 1.

Mark Bence-Jones. London: Burke's Peerage, 1978. 288p.

The first in a projected series of volumes on the country houses of the United Kingdom and Ireland. This study is confined to Ireland and presents short paragraphs identifying Irish estates and buildings, and discussing their importance, architectural style, ownership and social history. Some 1,300 illustrations accompany this alphabetical dictionary to country houses, both standing and demolished, prominent and obscure. A glossary is included.

1193 **Georgian Dublin.**
Harold Clarke. Dublin: Eason, 1980. 26p. (Irish Heritage Series).

A short history of Dublin architecture of the Georgian period is given in this booklet, which includes a number of coloured illustrations.

1194 **Ireland observed.**
Maurice Craig, the Knight of Glin. Cork: Mercier Press, 1970. 120p.

An alphabetical guide to prominent buildings, historical and architectural sites. This short reference work is extremely useful for quick identification of major places.

1195 **Irish classic houses of the middle size.**
Maurice Craig. London: Architectural Press, 1976. 200p.

Craig reviews the history of fine architecture in Ireland as represented in town houses, country homes and smaller estates constructed in the last few centuries.

1196 **Architecture in Ireland.**
Maurice Craig. Dublin: Department of Foreign Affairs, 1978. 57p. bibliog.

The history of Irish architecture from the prehistoric era, through early Christian, Romanesque and Gothic periods is summarized. This booklet also reviews the development of castles, later classical traditions, and architecture in the 19th and 20th centuries. A brief essay, this serves as a basic introduction to the varied types of Irish architecture.

1197 **The architecture of Ireland, from the earliest times to 1880.**
Maurice Craig. London: Batsford; Dublin: Eason, 1982. 358p. bibliog.

An excellent, wide-ranging history of the whole of Irish architecture, by a former inspector of ancient monuments in the Irish Republic, and an expert on the topic. Brief coverage is given of early Christian and mediaeval periods, with more emphasis on the later centuries. All kinds of buildings are included: castles, fortifications, towers, churches, estates, cottages, farmhouses, and shops. The character, building technology, and society's use of each type is discussed. Over 250 photographs, drawings and plans are included. For both the general reader and the specialist.

1198 **Ireland's vernacular architecture.**
Kevin Danaher. Cork: Mercier, 1975. 82p.

Irish folk architecture is shown through a sampling of local domestic buildings of different regions, types, forms of construction, design and use. Photographs of each type are included. This brief study was produced for the Cultural Relations Committee of Ireland.

1199   The houses of Ireland.
        Brian de Breffny, Rosemary ffolliott.   London: Thames &
        Hudson; New York: Viking, 1975. 240p.

A general yet thorough history of Irish dwellings, from the 12th century until
1914. Numerous types are included from great castles, palaces and mansions, to
small cottages and farmhouses. The varied forms of homes are related to the
needs of each period of Irish history. Discussed are the ancient Gaelic lifestyle,
early settlements and later town developments, successive Viking, Norman and
English occupations, and the rise of the great estates. Two hundred and seventy-
eight illustrations are included.

1200   **Castles in Ireland.**
        Brian de Breffny.   London: Thames & Hudson, 1977. 208p.

An illustrated history of the Irish castle, its development and various types, and
its towers, fortifications and great halls. Numerous illustrations are included.

1201   **The Georgian Society records of eighteenth century domestic
        architecture and decoration in Dublin.**
        Introduction by Desmond Guinness.   Dublin: Irish Academic
        Press, 1969. 5 vols.

The high points of Georgian architecture in Dublin have achieved international
recognition. This set, with 500 plates, serves as a major reference source in art,
architectural history, and interior design. Volume one covers earlier houses to
1700; volumes two to four relate to dwellings in Dublin in the Georgian style,
many of which still remain; and volume five is on country houses. This is a reprint
of a 1909-1913 edition.

1202   **Irish houses and castles.**
        Desmond Guinness, William Ryan.   London: Thames &
        Hudson; New York: Viking, 1973. 352p.

A good review of the great homes, estates and castles of Ireland, with an
emphasis on the Anglo-Irish aristocracy, their splendid possessions, spectacular
palaces, great interiors, gardens and history. Excellent, colour photographs and
plates are included. The average homes of those with more limited means are not
discussed. For popular reading.

1203   **Georgian Dublin.**
        Desmond Guinness.   London: Batsford, 1979. 235p.

A short guidebook to the important Georgian buildings in Dublin: public,
ecclesiastical and domestic. A brief, general overview is also given on
plasterwork, preservation and infill. The photographs are excellent, and this
volume belongs in every architectural collection with an interest in the period.

1204   **Irish houses: history, architecture, furnishing.**
       Klaus Hartmut-Olbricht, Helga Wegener.   Dublin: Gill &
       Macmillan; Bridgeport, Connecticut: Salem House (Merrimack),
       1984. 274p.

A sampling of impressive 18th and 19th-century buildings is displayed in 260
coloured illustrations. Each building shown is identified with history, and the
location and accessibility of each is given. The buildings chosen represent a
variety of types: great estate homes, city houses, castles and civic places.

1205   **St. Patrick's Cathedral, Dublin.**
       Victor Jackson.   Dublin: Eason, 1982. rev. ed. 26p. (Irish
       Heritage Series, no. 9).

The cathedral, a major structure dating from the 13th and 14th centuries, has had
many important events and personalities associated with it. This pamphlet reviews
the architecture, central importance and long history of Dean Swift's church.

1206   **The Irish castle.**
       D. Newman Johnson.   Dublin: Eason, 1985. 24p. (Irish Heritage
       Series, no. 49).

Introduces the varied forms of the Irish castle, with a brief history of the
development of its architecture. Illustrated with colour photographs.

1207   **Georgian Dublin, Ireland's imperilled architectural heritage.**
       Kevin Corrigan Kearns.   Newton Abbot, England: David &
       Charles, 1983. 244p. bibliog.

The author, after quickly reviewing the development of Dublin's urban patterns
since the 18th century, traces the extent of the remaining Georgian architecture in
the city. He stresses the current threat to historic architecture posed by modern
development. The book documents the loss of great façades, interiors, blocks and
squares, and the processes that inhibit preservation. It also notes successful
preservation and restoration efforts in the decades following 1960.

1208   **Your new home.**
       Patrick J. Kilroy.   Dublin: Ward River Press, 1982. 208p.

A short, handy reference and guide to home ownership and building in Ireland.
Pithy sections offer guidance on buying, renting, selling, construction, mortgages,
taxation, location and contracts. The author suggests future directions of housing
construction, design and availability in Ireland.

1209   **Irish ehurches and monastic buildings.**
       Harold G. Leask.   Dundalk, Ireland (Republic): Dundalgan,
       1955-1960. 3 vols.

An important reference source, this set provides descriptions of church
architecture augmented with numerous plans, photographs and drawings. Volume
one covers early Christian times to the Romanesque; volume two the Gothic
period to 1400 AD; and volume three mediaeval Gothic architecture.

1210   **Irish castles.**
Harold G. Leask.   Dundalk, Ireland (Republic): Dundalgan,
1973. 300p.

Leask, an authority in the field, examines castle architecture in Ireland, the history of its design and uses. Illustrations accompany the text.

1211   **The Irish bungalow book.**
Ted McCarthy.   Cork: Mercier, 1980. 140p.

A useful guide to contemporary domestic building. This book presents seventy plans (many recently developed) for home building. Observations are made on site preparation, financing, planning grants and construction. The illustrations have been produced with care and artistry. A good review is given of the type of mid-20th century house design now preferred in Ireland.

1212   **James Gandon: Vitruvius Hibernicus.**
Edward McParland.   London: Zwemmer; Dublin: Wolfound,
1985. 224p. (Studies in Architecture, vol. XXIV).

The life and work of one of Ireland's greatest architects is described. Gandon did much to reshape Dublin, giving it a distinctive, majestic touch. This is a history of Dublin architecture from the late 18th to mid-19th centuries, a most important phase. Some of the major buildings of Gandon are illustrated by sketches, plans, elevations and photographs, including those of the Four Courts, the Custom House, King's Inn and the present City Hall.

1213   **The buildings of Irish towns, a treasury of everyday architecture.**
Patrick Shaffrey, Maura Shaffrey.   Dublin: O'Brien, 1983. 124p.

Through drawings and text the authors plot the exemplary architecture and scale of courthouse, market, everyday buildings and blocks. They show both the erosion of a once beautiful architectural heritage and some of the positive steps which are being taken for the preservation and renewal of urban amenities. Patrick Shaffrey has also authored *Architecture of Ireland*, also published by O'Brien Press (1979. 192p.), which provides a more general review of architecture.

Folklore, Customs and Festivals

Folklore

1214 **A treasury of Irish folkore.**
Padraic Colum.   New York: Crown Publishers, 1967. 620p.
An extensive collection of stories, ballads, songs and varied excerpts relating to religious and peasant traditions, ancient mythological heroes and historical figures, up to the political and cultural leaders of the 19th century.

1215 **Motif-index of early Irish literature.**
Tom Peete Cross.   Bloomington, Indiana: Indiana University Press, 1952. 537p.
For research collections, this volume provides a numerical classification of particular folk customs, and indexes source references on them. This is intended as an Irish focused supplement to the more universal six volume work by Stith Thompson, *Motif-index of folk literature a classification of narrative elements in folktales. . .* (Bloomington, Indiana: Indiana University Press, 1955-1958. 6 vols.).

1216 **Myths and folk-lore of Ireland.**
Jeremiah Curtin.   New York: Weathervane Books, 1975. 345p.
A collection of twenty tales based on ancient Irish legends, gathered in 1887 and originally published to preserve the old folklore. These tales of the Fenian cycle are suitable for young readers.

1217 **Irish sagas.**
Edited by Myles Dillon. Cork: Mercier, 1985. 4th ed. 175p.
(Thomas Davis Lectures).
Based on a radio lecture series, each of the ancient sagas of Ireland is identified,
described, and placed in its literary and historical context by a leading scholar.
Twelve essays interpret the heroic tales and myths, and the society and customs
represented in them.

1218 **The romance of Cearbhall and Fearbhlaidh.**
Translated and edited by James E. Doan. Atlantic Highlands,
New Jersey: Humanities Press, 1985. 80p.
A translation from ancient manuscripts of one of Ireland's great mediaeval tales,
the love story of an Irish poet and a Scotish princess, which has tragic undertones.

1219 **Early Irish myths and sagas.**
Translated by Jeffrey Gantz. Harmondsworth, England; New
York: Penguin, 1981. 280p. bibliog.
Early Irish stories and myths, some dating from the 8th century, and reflecting the
even earlier traditions of the Iron Age Celts. An introduction briefly describes
existing Irish manuscripts and other extant material, and the Irish method of
storytelling.

1220 **Irish folktales.**
Henry Glassie. New York: Pantheon, 1985. 353p.
A collection of 125 Irish tales drawn from prehistory to the modern era. Some of
these have been previously published and selected from more than forty works,
often by prominent writers. Others have been taped directly by the author and
represent newer contributions. Glassie also discusses the history of folklore
collecting in Ireland.

1221 **To shorten the road, folktales from Ireland's travelling people.**
George Gmelch, Ben Kroup. Dublin: O'Brien, 1978. 189p.
This illustrated volume studies the traveller's (or tinker's) society, through their
stories of fantasy, compiled during the 1930s. An introduction and photographs
provide a current view of their culture. A study of the tinkers as a cultural
subgroup is given by Artelia Court in *Puck of the droms, the lives and literature of
the Irish Tinkers* (Berkeley, California: University of California Press, 1985.
297p.). Court includes a combination of folk-tales, songs and personal interviews.

1222 **The world of the Irish wonder tale.**
Elliott B. Gose. Dingle, Ireland (Republic): Brandon; Toronto;
Buffalo, New York: University of Toronto Press, 1984. 228p.
An introduction to the genre of the Irish tales of fantasy, with comparisons made
beween Celtic, Egyptian and North American myths. Eleven tales are included.
Each is analysed for psychological meaning, universal religious motifs, and
anthropological parallels. The author searches for central themes in this form of

Folklore, Customs and Festivals. Folklore

Irish literature and he finds a consistency of plot, characterization, ancient rites and norms of behaviour, and of the archetypical figure of the hero. Another scholarly analysis combining ancient literature and modern anthropology is Dáibhí Ó hOgain's *The hero in Irish folk history* (Dublin: Gill & Macmillan; New York: St. Martin's Press, 1985).

1223 **The Irish fairy book.**
Alfred Perceval Graves.   New York: Arlington House, 1983. 355p.
A gathering of forty-three tales and legends based on old spoken traditions, transcribed by Yeats, Tennyson and others.

1224 **Cuchulain of Muirthemne.**
Lady Gregory.   Gerrards Cross, England: Colin Smythe, 1970. 272p.
Ireland's classic and heroic tale of ancient warfare and kingship, from a period predating written literature. Lady Gregory's rendering of the story was first published in 1902, and contains a preface by Yeats.

1225 **Visions and beliefs in the west of Ireland.**
Collected by Lady Gregory.   Gerrards Cross, England: Colin Smythe; Toronto: Macmillan, 1970. 365p.
An extensive collection of short folk-tales and observations on rural practices collected first hand by Lady Gregory. This volume, first published in 1920, had an influence upon the Irish literary renaissance. It includes notes and essays by W. B. Yeats.

1226 **The stone of truth and other stories.**
Douglas Hyde.   Dublin: Irish Academic Press; Totowa, New Jersey: Rowman & Littlefield, 1979. 128p.
Sixteen tales of Irish folklore have been selected from a larger edition by Hyde, originally published in 1915. Another volume by Hyde has also been reprinted: *Beside the fire* (Dublin: Irish Academic Press, 1978. 203p.), which contains a Gaelic and English collection of country tales, with an introduction on methods of recording folklore. Hyde was a noted scholar, linguist, and political leader.

1227 **Celtic fairy tales.**
Collected by Joseph Jacobs.   New York: Dover, 1968. 267p.
Originally published in 1892, this is an excellent collection of Irish traditional tales, with wood engravings and drawings. An introduction discusses the process of translation. In 1894 Jacob's *More Celtic fairy tales* was published; it has also been reprinted by Dover. Both volumes are suitable for young readers, but also contain appendixes of scholarly notes and references to original sources, early manuscripts, and comparisons with parallel texts.

1228 **The Tain.**
Translated by Thomas Kinsella. Dublin: Dolmen; London:
Oxford University Press, 1969. 304p.

A translation of the classic Irish heroic epic, based on mediaeval manuscripts. A short introduction reviews the importance of the Táin Bó Cuailnge to Irish traditional history and literature. Drawings by Louis le Brocquy illustrate the text.

1229 **Irish wonders.**
D. R. McAnally Jr. New York: Weathervane, 1977. 218p.

Reprint of an 1888 edition of popular Irish tales and superstitions, arranged by topical themes. Other collections, which have been reprinted include *Myths and legends of the Celtic race* by T. W. Rolleston (London: Constable, 1984. Reprint of a 1911 edition), and *Celtic folklore* by John Rhys (Hounslow, England: Wildwood House, 1985. 2 vols.).

1230 **Celtic mythology.**
Proinsias MacCana. London, New York: Hamlyn, 1973. 136p.

A useful summary of the ancient myths of the Celtic race, with an emphasis on Irish stories of invasions and kingship. Comparisons are made with Gaulic legends and deities. Numerous photographs are included of artifacts, sculpture and architecture.

1231 **Great folktales of old Ireland.**
Compiled by Mary McGarry. New York: Bell, 1972. 112p.

This attractive volume contains seventeen early Irish folk-tales recorded by leading folklorists and authorities, and illustrated with interpretive drawings.

1232 **Saga and myth in ancient Ireland.**
Gerard Murphy. Cork: Cultural Relations Committee of Ireland, Mercier Press, 1971. 75p. (Irish Life and Culture, vol. 10).

A very short evaluation of the chief sources of early Irish myths: the storytelling process and the mythological, heroic, and kingship tales. This history of old Irish literature traces some of the motifs that have been passed on from the pre-Christian period to modern times.

1233 **Irish sagas and folktales.**
Eileen O'Faolain. New York: Avenel, 1982. 245p.

Leading Irish sagas and legends are retold in modern prose, for young adults and older people. Included are the tales of Cuchulainn, the Cattle Raids of Cooley, Finn and the Fianna, and later stories.

1234 **Early Irish history and mythology.**
Thomas F. O'Rahilly. Dublin: Dublin Institute for Advanced Studies, 1976. 568p.

This major work studies the existence of Irish myths prior to the introduction of Christianity in 431. The author searches for evidence from classical sources, linguistic analysis, and historical events. General dates and periods are suggested for each of the successive, invading groups, from which the rich mythology emerged. Early stories are analysed for their historical underpinnings and copious notes are provided on the available data. For advanced researchers and specialists.

1235 **Handbook of Irish folklore.**
Sean Ó Súilleabháin. Detroit, Michigan: Gale, 1970. 699p.

A useful, basic reference guide to a variety of old Irish customs and beliefs. Ó Súilleabháin has compiled a number of collections of Irish tales, stories and beliefs. The present volume, first published in 1942, was considered to be his major contribution. In 1969 his *Folktales of Ireland* appeared (London: Routledge & Kegan Paul, 321p.).

1236 **Celtic myth and legend, poetry and romance.**
Charles Squire. New York: Bell, 1979. 450p.

An interesting introduction to the major themes of Celtic literature and legend in both British and Gaelic traditions. The author discusses customs, religion, conflicts and ancient society, as reflected in the old myths. The work was first published in 1906, and thus does not reflect some of the later historical investigations.

1237 **Ancient legends of Ireland.**
Lady Jane Wilde. Galway, Ireland (Republic): O'Gorman, 1971. 347p.

A collection of folk traditions, superstitions, country ways and beliefs, festivals and legends from the old Irish, largely rural culture, which is now almost extinct. The book is conveniently arranged by topic. This is a reprint of a London 1888 edition.

1238 **Mythologies.**
William Butler Yeats. New York: Macmillan, 1959. 369p.

Traditional stories and legends were collected by Yeats and published in five books, of which the three best known are *The Celtic twilight* (1893), *The secret rose* (1897), and *Stories of Red Hanrahan* (1897). The best stories from each volume are included here. The variorum edition of *The secret rose* has been published by Cornell University Press (Ithaca, New York: 1981. 312p.), and Macmillan (London: 1982. 272p.). *The Celtic twilight* has been republished by Humanities Press and Colin Smythe (1981. 160p.). All were important works in the Irish literary renaissance movement of the 19th and early 20th centuries.

1239 **Fairy and folk tales of Ireland.**
William Butler Yeats. New York: Macmillan; Gerrards Cross, England: Colin Smythe, 1973. Reprinted, London: Pan Books, 1979. 387p.

An important and influential collection of folk beliefs and seventy typical stories collected among the Irish peasants during the 19th century and first published in 1888. The Pan edition includes a useful cross-referencing of the stories to their sources. Yeats' contribution to the preservation of folklore is told in Mary Helen Thuente's, *W. B. Yeats and Irish folklore* (Dublin: Gill & Macmillan, 1980. 286p.).

Customs and festivals

1240 **Researches in the south of Ireland: a source book of Irish folk tradition.**
Thomas Crofton Crocker. Blackrock, Ireland (Republic): Irish Academic Press, 1969. 400p.

A major sourcebook of Irish folk tradition, this pioneering work was written in 1824. Descriptions are given of local beliefs, traditions, farmwork, mining and labour in the countryside of Counties Cork, Limerick and Waterford. This edition has a new introduction by Kevin Danaher. Crocker, an antiquarian famous for his collections of traditional songs and stories, compiled *Legends of Kerry* (reprinted by Anvil Press, Dublin), and *Fairy legends and traditions of the south of Ireland* (Delmar, New York: Scholar's Facsimile, 1983).

1241 **Irish country people.**
Kevin Danaher. Cork: Mercier, 1966. 127p.

A very readable introduction to life in rural Irish society at the beginning of the 20th century, with information on folk ways, culture, living conditions, history, archaeology and traditions.

1242 **The year in Ireland: Irish calendar custom.**
Kevin Danaher. Cork; Dublin: Mercier, 1972. 74p.

Reviews local customs associated with annual events and holidays, many of which are important to rural Irish life. The customs combine ancient traditions and legends, folk medicine and healing, divination, amusements and native sports.

1243 **Gentle places and simple things: Irish customs and belief.**
Kevin Danaher. Dublin; Cork: Mercier, 1976. 125p.

Suitable for recreational reading, this is a popular collection of tales and traditions relating to Irish rural ways and the countryside.

1244 **Irish folkways.**
E. Estyn Evans. London: Routledge & Kegan Paul, 1967. 324p.
bibliog.
A reliable and scholarly, yet entertaining look at customs and everyday life in Irish agricultural society. Twenty topical themes are covered, including homes, furnishings, artifacts, implements, tools, work, modes of transportation, festivals, fairs and superstitions. One hundred useful line drawings supplement the text.

1245 **Gold under the furze: studies in folk traditions.**
Edited by Alan Gailey, Dáithi Ó hOgáin. Dun Laoghaire, Ireland (Republic): Glendale Press, 1983. 256p.
The essays in this volume, which are both scholarly and entertaining, study rural superstitions, architecture, storytelling, traditional crafts, customs and concepts. Some of the twenty essays draw comparisons with life in Scotland and northern Europe.

1246 **The green fool.**
Patrick Kavanagh. Harmondsworth, England: Penguin, 1971. 264p.
This engrossing autobiography provides observations on everyday life and customs in rural Ireland during the early 20th century. Kavanagh, a leading Irish poet, later wrote disparagingly of this book, first published in 1938.

1247 **The festival of Lughnasa: a study of the survival of the Celtic festival of the beginning of the harvest.**
Maire MacNeill. London: Oxford University Press, 1962. 697p.
Dublin: Irish Folklore Council, 1982. 2nd ed. 2 vols.
A major work on rural customs, this volume provides a thorough study of folklore and tradition surrounding the annual harvest festival. The book reviews the record of legends, each recorded location, varied local customs, fairs, and field sports and gatherings, with numerous historical references. It has been heralded as a model study and as an important contribution to ethnological research, tracing the evolution of selected traditions from pre-Christian times to 1950. Its conclusions are based on both ancient accounts and the results of modern questionnaires gathered by the Irish Folklore Commission.

1248 **Irish life and lore.**
Séamus Ó Catháin. Dublin; Cork: Mercier, 1982. 124p.
A look at folk life and everyday customs through 19th and 20th century material largely gathered by the Irish Folklore Commission.

1249 **Life and tradition in rural Ireland.**
Timothy P. O'Neill. London: Dent, 1977. 122p.
The author discusses the traditional ways of life in rural areas that are now disappearing. Included are houses and cottages (with layout), furniture, patterns of work, costume, food, transport, local economy, small industry, and patterns of

play. The author has frequently lectured on folk life and is a former head of the Folklife Division of the National Museum of Ireland.

1250   **Irish popular superstitions.**
   William Wilde.   Dublin: Irish Academic Press, 1972. 140p.

A brief, introductory review of the tales, legends and superstitions of Gaelic Ireland prior to 1850. Folk customs, festivals and medical practices are described, but Wilde's 19th-century outlook lacks discernment or modern interpretation. William Wilde was the husband of the author, Lady Wilde, and father of playwright Oscar Wilde.

Food and Drink

1251　**Irish cooking in colour.**
Vivienne Abbott.　Curragh, Ireland (Republic): Goldsmith Press;
Stirling, Scotland: Johnson & Bacon, 1984. 128p.

A collection of traditional Irish recipes, with comments on the history of Irish cuisine, and coloured illustrations of the best in Irish food. Ingredients native to Ireland are highlighted: fresh fruits, fish, soups and baked goods.

1252　**The Ballymaloe cookbook.**
Myrtle Allen.　Dublin: Gill & Macmillan; London: Methuen,
1981. 176p.

Irish dishes are suggested based on the experience of a County Cork restaurant. Special breads, oyster dishes, steak and stout are some of the native Irish foods covered, but the author, a Parisian restauranteur, also includes more classical and formal dishes.

1253　**The Irish cookbook.**
Carla Blake.　Cork; Dublin: Mercier, 1978. 157p.

Traditional dishes are adjusted to contemporary preferences and tastes and modern methods of preparation, in this practical guide.

1254　**Irish traditional food.**
Theodora Fitzgibbon.　Dublin: Gill & Macmillan; London:
Macmillan; New York: St. Martin's, 1984. 258p.

A very popular guide to Irish country food and servings, presented from an historical perspective. Recipes from the 16th to the 20th centuries are given with a comment on social history and the cuisine of both small farms and large estates, towns and cities. Based on a rich heritage in part from ancient manuscripts and

272

rare documents, Fitzgibbon writes of older practices while offering recipes for sauces, breads, biscuits and beverages. A more recent cookery book by Fitzgibbon is *Your favourite recipes* (Dublin: Gill & Macmillan, 1985).

1255 Cooking Irish style today.
Noreen Kinney.   New York: Irish Book Center, 1977. 128p.
Both original and traditional recipes are included by a regular columnist. Presented are soups, fish, meats (especially chicken), salads and desserts.

1256 An Irish farmhouse cookbook.
Mary Kinsella.   Belfast: Appletree, 1983. 192p.
A collection of 250 Irish recipes which are suitable for preparation in the modern kitchen. The book includes a glossary of terms, and gives measurements for both the American and European reader.

1257 Sean Kinsella's cookbook.
Sean Kinsella.   Dublin: Town House (Eason), 1985. 128p.
A good variety of recommended dishes is included in this volume by one of Ireland's best known chefs.

1258 In praise of poteen.
John McGuffin.   Belfast: Appletree Press, 1978. 120p.
An informative and sometimes humorous history is given of poteen, Ireland's popular albeit illicit form of spirits. The book covers its development, production, and place in rural society and culture.

1259 The Irish cottage cookbook.
Mercedes McLaughlin, Marian McSpiritt.   Dundalk, Ireland (Republic): Careers and Educational Publishers, 1984. 96p.
A convenient, spiral bound collection of seventy recipes from the West of Ireland over a twenty year period. Included are starters, soups, main courses, breads, high teas, and desserts.

1260 Irish whiskey: a history of distilling, the spirit trade and excise controls in Ireland.
Edward B. McGuire.   Dublin: Gill & Macmillan, 1973. 462p.
A scholarly history of the industry. A more popular account of Irish whiskey may be found in Malachy Magee's *One thousand years of Irish whiskey* (q.v.).

1261 Traditional Irish recipes.
John Murphy.   Belfast: Appletree, 1982. 74p.
Some sixty Irish recipes are presented, using local ingredients from rural areas to produce a characteristically Irish flavour. This is a good guide to the country cooking of old, with some unusual combinations, such as Guinness cake, carrigeen moss pudding, pratie oaten, drisheen, and other dishes. Also included

Food and Drink

are soda breads and shell fish. This interesting book, with illustrations and design in a Gaelic style of script, would be a suitable gift.

1262   **Wild and free: cooking from nature.**
Cyril O Ceirin, Kit O Ceirin.   Dublin: O'Brien Press, 1980. 160p.

A hundred recipes are provided, using combinations of twenty-two natural foods, including the blackberry, dandelion, rose, nettle, elder, and crab apple. Suggestions are offered for jams, soups, salads, jellies, and desserts. A calendar shows the seasons for gathering the ingredients, freely available in Ireland.

1263   **Traditional Irish recipes.**
George L. Thomson.   Dublin: O'Brien Press, 1983. 96p.

This interesting compilation includes recipes for various occasions, written in calligraphic script. Each recipe is on a single page and is handlettered in the style of the *Book of Kells* (q.v.). Soups, fish, meat, vegetables, bread, cakes, sweets and drink are included.

1264   **Irish cooking.**
Helen Walsh.   Dublin: Eason, 1985. 26p.

A collection of traditional recipes illustrated with attractive photographs of rural Ireland.

1265   **Guinness.**
Peter Walsh.   Dublin: Eason, 1980. 26p. (Irish Heritage Series).

A brief survey, with colour illustrations, of Ireland's famous brew, the industry, the brewing process, and the now historic buildings. Walsh recounts, with anecdotes, the life of the founders and the social history surrounding them. For popular reading.

Sports and Recreation

1266 100 years of Irish football.
Malcom Brodie.   Belfast: Blackstaff, 1980. 188p.
Published for the Irish Football Association, this illustrated history discusses the leading figures of the sport and some of the major games over the years. Statistics and results are included.

1267 Sport in Ireland.
Noel Carroll.   Dublin: Department of Foreign Affairs, 1979.
105p. (Aspects of Ireland Series, no. 6).
A short, illustrated guide to all the major sports found in Ireland, the games native to the country, the history of their development, the rules, the worldwide participation of Irish sportsmen, and the state of Irish physical education training.

1268 Famous all-Irelands.
Pat Courtney.   Dublin: Canavaun, 1984. 2 vols.
A listing of the results of Irish hurling and football finals, from 1912 to 1980, with a brief commentary based on the reportage of the national newspaper, the *Irish Independent*.

1269 Irish horses.
Monique Dossenbach, Hans Dossenbach.   Dublin: Gill & Macmillan; St. Albans, England: Hart-Davis, 1977. 192p.
The authors provide a good overview of the breeds of horses that have contributed so much to Irish sport and economy, and have focused world attention on the country. The volume contains nearly two hundred illustrations, many in colour. The authors are also noted for their book, *Great stud farms of the world* (1978). An older, related study by Noel Brown is *The horse in Ireland* (London: Pelham Books, 1967).

1270   Fly-fishing for Irish trout.

Niall Fallon.   Kilkenny, Irish Republic: Robert's Books, 1983.
146p.

From years of experience Fallon presents a useful discourse on fly-fishing, with
many suggestions on the major lakes and streams, seasonal conditions, the
various lines, angling tactics, and regulations. A dictionary guidebook to some
800 traditional dressings that may be used is given by E. J. Malone in *Irish trout
and salmon flies* (Gerrards Cross, England: Colin Smythe, 1984. 427p.).

1271   Vincent O'Brien's great horses.

Ivor Herbert, Jacqueline O'Brien.   London: Pelham Books,
1985. 208p.

An account of the times and successes of one of the world's greatest stables, its
staff and sixteen of its famous, prize-winning horses. Interesting background
information is provided on each of the major horses, and on the life of the
trainers. Numerous photographs are included.

1272   The Jimmy Ingle story.

Jimmy Ingle.   Dingle, Ireland (Republic): Brandon, 1984. 96p.

The autobiography of the first Irishman to win a European amateur boxing title
(in 1939). Ingle tells of his early years of poverty in old Dublin, his professional
boxing career and eventual success.

1273   Irish sea cruising guide.

Robert Kemp.   St. Albans, England: Adlard Coles; New York:
Beekmans, 1976. 224p. 27 maps.

A guide to sea-fishing off the Irish coast.

1274   The guide to golf in Ireland.

Edited by Gerry Kennedy.   Dublin: Morrigan, 1984. 88p.

A brief guide to golf in Ireland, some of the leading players and the courses. An
autobiography by a well-known champion, Christy O'Connor, has been
published, *Christy O'Connor, an autobiography as told to John Redmond* by Gill
& Macmillan (Dublin: 1985).

1275   My Olympic years.

Lord Killanin.   London: Secker & Warburg, 1983. 224p.

This autobiography of the Irish President of the International Olympic
Committee, covers the years 1972 to 1980, and reviews the aims and goals of the
committee, and the political crises and dilemmas that surrounded some of its
decisions.

1276   Hunting in Ireland: an historical and geographical analysis.

Colin Lewis.   London: J. A. Allen, 1975. 187p.

The author traces the tradition of the Irish hunt in its two styles, one formal, and
the other reflecting rural ways. Maps, illustrations and much background

information is provided on geographic and locational aspects, terrain, stables, and hounds. An entertaining account, which is also useful as a reference guide.

1277 **The Seven-up Book of Irish Sport.**
Edited by Malachy Logan. Dublin: O'Brien Books, 1982-.
annual.

Presents the results of seventeen major Irish sports including Gaelic football, hurling, rugby, soccer, tennis, boxing, golf and horse-racing. Each volume is illustrated, and contains articles by leading journalists.

1278 **Shrouded in mist.**
Pat Lyne. Presteigne, Powys, Wales: the author, 1985. 247p.

A delightful study of the Connemara pony with historical information, anecdotes and facts on breeding and ownership. The development of the pony from its earliest days to 1963 is traced.

1279 **Falcons and foxhounds.**
Edmund Mahony. Galway, Ireland (Republic): Kenny's, 1985.
127p.

An enjoyable narrative on hunting and field sports in the West of Ireland. With occasional digressions the author comments on Irish horses, hounds and game (fish, fowl and fox).

1280 **Irish gardens.**
Edward Malins, the Knight of Glin. Dublin: Eason & Son,
1977. 24p. (Irish Heritage Series).

This attractive booklet presents an overview of the major styles of Irish gardening throughout history, including great estates and varied conditions of environment. A chiefly pictorial introduction.

1281 **Irish horses.**
H. Meier, Max Reugar. Dublin: Gill & Macmillan, 1977. 192p.

A general introduction to the variety of breeds of Irish horses.

1282 **Postage stamps of Ireland, 1922-82.**
Compiled by Liam Miller. Dublin: Department of Posts and
Telegraphs, 1983. 80p.

The collected output of Irish stamps over a sixty year period are produced in full colour, and accompanied by textual description, with information on designers. The standard philatelic list is the *Hibernian catalogue of the postage stamps of Ireland, 1922-1982* (Dublin: Hibernian Stamp Company, 1983. 108p.). This is regularly reissued with updated information, technical data and prices. A short, illustrated and reliable account is provided by Mairead Reynolds in *A history of the Irish Post Office* (Dublin: MacDonnell Whyte, 1983). This provides fascinating background information on the organization and service of the department.

Sports and Recreation

1283 **A man may fish.**
T. C. Kingsmill Moore. Gerrards Cross, England: Colin Smythe, 1980. 225p.
An enjoyable account of fishing for sea trout in the West of Ireland, the old locations and the people of the area.

1284 **Regency rogue: Dan Donnelly, his life and legends.**
Patrick Myler. Dublin: O'Brien Press, 1976. 168p.
The life of one of Ireland's most famous boxers of the bare-fisted era, who was the inspiration for many ballads, stories and anecdotes.

1285 **The fighting Irish.**
Patrick Myler. Dingle, Ireland (Republic): Brandon; Dover, New Hampshire: Longwood, 1985. 220p.
A history of boxing viewed through the participation of famous Irish and Irish-American contenders.

1286 **Irish gardening and horticulture.**
Edited by E. Charles Nelson, Aidan Brady. Dublin: Royal Horticulture Society of Ireland, 1979. 250p.
An illustrated guide, including some pictures in colour, which is suitable for the home gardener as well as the professional. This provides an excellent reference from a strictly Irish perspective in arrangements, choice of flora, garden design, and indigenous plants. Nelson has also written *An Irish flower garden* (Kilkenny, Irish Republic: Boethius, 1984. 222p.). That volume offers a commentary on the history of 100 chosen plants, and their relationship with particular gardeners, artists, planters and explorers. Drawings and plates accompany the anecdotes.

1287 **Sport in my lifetime.**
Ulick O'Connor. London: Pelham Books, 1984. 141p.
Observations, stories, anecdotes and background material are provided on major sporting figures and events, based on a selection of the author's columns that have regularly appeared in the *Sunday Times* of Dublin.

1288 **The GAA in its time.**
Padraig Puirseal. Dublin: Puirséal, 1983. 2nd ed. 364p.
A good, journalistic and readable history of the Gaelic Athletic Association, the Irish Republic's leading sports group and sponsor. The story of the association is given from 1884 to 1959, through its many vicissitudes of popularity. Championships, the great games and players of Gaelic football and hurling are all stressed, although some attention is also focused on the social and political activities of the GAA, which was conceived as a mainstay of Irish nationalism. An insider's account of the GAA games and the players can be found in *Over the bar: a personal relationship with the GAA*, by Breandán O hEithir (Dublin: Ward River Press, 1984). A well-researched and detailed history of the association is provided by Marcus de Burca in *The G.A.A., a history* (Dublin: Cumann

Lúithchleas Gael, 1981). The National Library in Dublin has issued a short collection of historical documents, photographs and newspaper facsimiles on the GAA, and Michael O'Hehir provides a photographic summary of the organization in *The GAA, 100 years* (Dublin: Gill & Macmillan, 1984).

1289 The Galway hookers.
Richard J. Scott. Dublin: Ward River Press, 1983. 127p.

A history of the working sailboats of Galway and the unique seagoing cruisers that have survived from the last century. Scott explores their origin, builders, sailors, trade and modern racing.

1290 Coins and tokens of Ireland.
Peter Seaby. London: B. A. Seaby, 1970. 167p. (Seaby's Standard Catalogue, part 3).

A collection of short essays, and a descriptive catalogue with values of Irish coins from Norse times through to the 19th century.

1291 Irish fieldsports and angling handbook.
Edited by Albert Titterington. Belfast: Appletree, 1984. 240p.

This volume covers various Irish fieldsports including fishing, hunting and shooting, with a directory of suppliers and services. Maps of locations and illustrations are included.

1292 Fishing in Ireland, the complete guide.
Dick Warner, Kevin Linnane, Peter Brown. Belfast: Appletree, 1980. 200p. maps.

A comprehensive guide to coarse and game fishing and sea angling with a discussion of locations, lists of licence requirements, record catches, and boating services. Some sixty maps of suggested areas are included.

1293 Irish horse-racing, an illustrated history.
John Welcome. Dublin: Gill & Macmillan: London: Macmillan, 1982. 223p.

This volume provides a history of Irish racing from ancient times to 1960, when a transition occured from older Irish flat racing to the more formal setting of park courses (for Derby races). The author enumerates the various champion horses and their contributions world-wide.

1294 The Irish Derby.
Guy St. John Williams, Francis Hyland. London: J. A. Allen, 1980. 432p.

An illustrated account of the Irish Derby from 1866 to 1979.

Museums and
Art Galleries

1295   **A guide to art galleries in Ireland.**
Patricia Butler.   Dublin: Gill & Macmillan, 1978. 32p.

Lists public and commercial art galleries throughout Ireland, with an indication of
subjects covered. The established galleries are also reviewed in Joan Abse's
directory *The art galleries of Britain and Ireland* (Rutherford, New Jersey:
Fairleigh Dickinson University Press, 1976. 248p.).

1296   **The foundation of the National Gallery of Ireland.**
Catherine de Courcy.   Dublin: National Gallery, 1985. 108p.

A look at an important element of Dublin's cultural life is provided in this short,
scholarly review of the history of the gallery during the 19th century. An
illustrated, descriptive listing of some of the major works in the gallery is given in
the booklet by Raymond Keaveney, *The National Gallery of Art: 50 pictures*
(Dublin: National Gallery, 1981. 50p.). For another brief introduction see James
White's *Masterpieces of the National Gallery of Ireland* (q.v.). A detailed listing of
its holdings is contained in the *Illustrated summary catalogue of drawings,
watercolours and miniatures* (Dublin: National Gallery, 1983). A similar catalogue
covering paintings was issued by the Gallery in 1982. For another work on the
National Gallery, see also *National Gallery of Ireland: illustrated summary
catalogue of paintings* (q.v.).

1297   **Museums in Ireland, present and future.**
Irish Museum Association.   Dublin: Irish Museum Association,
1980. 52p.

Papers are reprinted from a 1980 seminar on the present state of Irish museums.
Information is included on museum facilities, treasure trove legislation, staffing,
security, collecting, recording, conservation, display and education. The papers
are very short but illustrate some current concerns.

1298 **Museums and art galleries in Great Britain and Ireland.**
New York: International Publications Service, 1982. 102p.
Major collections and art galleries of both the Irish Republic and Northern Ireland are listed in this guide, although the focus is on Great Britain. For a listing of museum books and educational materials see *A bibliography of museum and art gallery publications and audio visual aids in Great Britain and Ireland*. The 1979-80 edition of the bibliography was edited by Michael Roulstone (Westport, Connecticut: Meckler Publications, 1980. 560p.). The 1978 edition was by Jean Lambert.

1299 **The Natural History Museum.**
C. E. O Riordan. Dublin: Stationery Office, 1983. [not paginated].
A brief guide to the collections of the Natural History Museum in Dublin.

1300 **The Irish museums guide.**
Edited by Sean Popplewell. Dublin: Ward River Press and the Irish Museums Trust, 1983. 208p.
This descriptive guide to 150 museums throughout the Irish Republic and Northern Ireland includes information on opening hours, admission, parking and content.

Libraries

1301 Directory of libraries in Ireland.
Edited by Margaret Barry, Alun Bevan. Dublin: Library
Association of Ireland and the Library Association (Northern
Ireland Branch), 1983. 100p.

A most useful guide listing libraries throughout Ireland, with information on their
location, opening hours, directors, size, subject strengths, equipment and
services. Libraries of all types are included: national, local, government, special,
university and college.

**1302 A history of literacy and libraries in Ireland: the long traced
pedigree.**
Mary Casteleyn. Aldershot, England; Brookfield, Vermont:
Gower, 1984. 255p. bibliog.

Casteleyn traces the history of literacy and education in Ireland from Bardic and
early monastic times through the early days of printing, and thence to the
development of public libraries and university libraries, the great private
collections, and subscription and society libraries. This account emphasizes broad
trends in the development of public institutions, organizations and library
programmes, and is suitable for general readership.

1303 Trinity College Library, Dublin.
Peter Fox. Dublin: Eason, 1982. 26p. (Irish Heritage Series, no.
35).

A brief, illustrated history and guide to one of Ireland's greatest collections, and
its spectacular holdings of ancient manuscripts. The history of the library and the
scope of its collections are described. Coloured photographs show the
development of the library over its 350 year history.

1304   **The National Library of Ireland.**
Noel Kissane.   Dublin: Eason, 1984. 26p. (Irish Heritage Series,
no. 42).
A popular guide to the history and collections of the Irish Republic's chief public
library. A main task of the library is to maintain and document the history of
Ireland's national heritage through its extensive collection of manuscripts, books,
photographs, prints, drawings, maps, genealogical material, newspapers and
microforms. This booklet contains coloured illustrations drawn from the
collections. The April 1977 issue of the *Irish University Review* includes articles
honouring the centenniel of the National Library.

1305   **An Leabharlann, the Irish Library.**
Dublin: Library Association of Ireland and Trinity College, new
series. 1930-. quarterly.
This is the journal of the Library Association of Ireland. Its varied articles are
pertinent to both the Republic and Northern Ireland, and the topics range from
the history of particular collections and libraries to modern computerization and
technology, administration and management. Book reviews are included. Three
volumes appeared between 1905 and 1909. The journal again commenced
publication with volume one in 1930, and a new series with vol. 1 in 1984.

1306   **All graduates and gentlemen: Marsh's Library.**
Muriel McCarthy.   Dublin: O'Brien Press; Totowa, New Jersey:
Rowman & Littlefield, 1980. 239p.
Marsh's Library contains a fascinating and unique collection of volumes published
between the 15th and 18th centuries. The library, founded by Archbishop
Narcissus Marsh in 1638, is located adjacent to St. Patrick's Cathedral in Dublin.
It has been kept intact, with its original arrangement, classification and
furnishings. The story of the library also includes a glimpse of public and
ecclesiastical politics from the 17th to the 19th centuries. This was the first Irish
collection open to the public (in 1708), and Jonathan Swift figured in its history.
Much of this volume is a detailed review of the library's holdings.

1307   **A directory of rare books and special collections in the United
Kingdom and the Republic of Ireland.**
Edited by Moelwyn I. Williams.   Phoenix, Arizona: Oryx Press,
1985. 560p.
Among the collections listed are those of national libraries, universities and
colleges, public libraries, churches, societies, and institutes. Arranged by region,
the collections are briefly described, with information on hours, admission,
services, facilities, and contents.

Libraries

1308   **The life and times of Chester Beatty.**
    A. J. Wilson.   London: Cadogan, 1985. 315p.

The Chester Beatty Library contains a magnificent and invaluable collection of early manuscripts, illustrated books, fine bindings, and Middle Eastern and Asian art. This book covers the life of its founder, Sir Alfred Chester Beatty (1875-1968), a mining engineer. The collection was formed in Dublin in 1953. From time to time the library publishes detailed illustrated catalogues of its holdings. Some of the present volume by Wilson relates to Beatty's earlier years in mining exploration with little relevancy to Ireland.

Publishing and the Book Trade

1309 Censorship: the Irish experience.
Michael Adams.   Dublin: Irish Academic Press, 1968. 266p.
A general history of the exercise of book censorship in the Irish Republic over a forty year period (1929-1968). The volume discusses the origin and operation of the system of censorship, public acceptance and reaction, and some of the major works which have been banned. An earlier period of Irish history is examined in *The freedom of the press in Ireland, 1784-1841*, by Brian Inglis (London: Faber & Faber, 1954. Reprinted, Westport, Connecticut: Greenwood, 1974. 256p.).

1310 Books Ireland, News and Reviews.
Goslingstown, Kilkenny, Ireland (Republic): Books Ireland, 1976-. 10 issues per year.
This, the major publishing journal of Ireland, is especially useful for its general information on the Irish publishing industry and market, news of recent books published, and notices and advertisements of forthcoming books. Most of the journal is devoted to authoritative reviews of new books, usually by leading authors. An index to the journal is issued each year. The illustrations and format make this publication suitable for wide readership. It is a prime source for keeping up to date with new scholarly writing on Ireland, as well as Irish poetry and fiction.

1311 Clé directory of the Irish book trade.
Compiled by Mary Burke, edited by Tony Farmar.   Dublin: CLÉ, 1983. 191p.
A guidebook to the book trade with separate lists of publishers, both general and antiquarian book sellers, libraries, periodicals, the media, publishing services and prizes. For each publisher, data are provided on their address, staff, number of titles and foreign agents. Lists of libraries also indicate size of collections. Other lists cover art councils, editors, indexers and picture sources. Both the Republic and Northern Ireland are covered.

1312 **The Clé manual of book publishing.**
Edited by Tony Farmar, Fiona Biggs.   Dublin: CLÉ, 1981. 350p.
This handbook provides useful information and hints for those starting or managing a publishing firm in Ireland. Some insights into the publishing trade may also be of use to writers, suppliers and those offering services to the industry. The manual includes a directory of publishers and of various other groups and organizations providing technical assistance. Issued in a three-ring binder, the work has chapters on the history of Clé (the Irish Book Publishers Association), editorial matters, contracts and law, design, and book production, distribution and marketing. There are also directories of booksellers and libraries, and a glossary.

1313 **An Irish publisher and his world.**
John M. Feehan.   Cork: Mercier, 1969. 137p.
Feehan reviews the history of Mercier Press and its operations over a twenty year period. He offers insights into the publishing industry in general, and comments on his experiences with individual Irish authors.

1314 **The Irish character in print, 1572-1923.**
E. W. Lynam.   Dublin: Academic Press, 1969. 64p.
This is a study of the development of Irish type and letter forms used in printing as it has progressed from Elizabethan times. Early printed works, political issues and educational and cultural usage are all facets of this history. Examples drawn from early printing illustrate the text.

Mass media

General

1315 **Communications and community in Ireland.**
Edited by Brian Farrell. Dublin; Cork: Mercier, 1984. 133p.
(Thomas Davis Lectures Series).
Several papers present an historical perspective on the mass media in Ireland, the
development of the press (and some of the positions taken later during the Easter
Rising), and the beginnings of Irish broadcasting. Much loss in changing Irish
culture is attributed to television programming and several of the authors deplore
the transformation of Irish character and society. Other issues raised concern
government censorship to control public morality as officially determined, and the
influence of television in the political arena. Reminiscences from the early days of
Irish radio broadcasting can be found in *Written on the wind*, edited by Louis
McRedmond (Dublin: Gill & Macmillan, 1976).

1316 **Media and popular culture.**
Edited by Mark P. Hederman, Richard Kearney. *The Crane
Bag*, vol. 8, no. 2 (1984), 192p.
The twenty-three essays and interviews in this special issue raise and examine
some of the major issues confronting the contemporary Irish mass media.
Observations are offered on popular television, foreign influences on Irish
culture, censorship and broadcasting, government policy and the press,
newspapers, and the performing and visual arts.

Newspapers

1317 The press in Ireland, a survey and guide.
Stephen J. Brown. New York: Lemma Publishing, 1977. 304p.
A somewhat dated description and guide to the leading organs of the Irish press. This is a reprint of a 1937 edition. A comprehensive bibliography of the Irish press is given in *Waterloo directory of Irish newspapers and periodicals, 1800-1900* (Waterloo, Ontario: North Waterloo Academic Press, 1986). Some 4,500 titles are listed, based on the holdings of 50 Irish and British libraries.

1318 Cork Examiner.
Cork: Thomas Crosbie and Company, 1841-. daily.
The newspaper provides regular political coverage, but it is also a convenient source for the interpretation of daily events for those outside Dublin, the larger part of Ireland's population. The outlook of the Dublin newspapers is sometimes noticeably different from that of the rest of the country. The *Cork Examiner* provides a reasonable alternative. Back issues are available on microfilm from Irish Microforms Ltd. of Dublin, and Clearwater Press of New York and Toronto. The reels for the 19th and early 20th century portray vividly the problems confronting rural Ireland, including the effects of the Great Famine, mass emigration, the land struggle, the fight for home rule, the Easter Rising and the War for Independence. *The Cork Examiner* has recently published a collection of 220 historical photographs of old Munster drawn from its archives: *Picture that* (1985).

1319 Freeman's Journal.
Dublin: Irish Microforms; New York and Toronto: Clearwater Press.
This filmed series of the newspaper, from 1763 to 1924, reproduces what was once the major newspaper of Ireland. Its reportage included many of the issues that were taken up by the nationalist cause. Frequent coverage was given to the Great Famine, land struggles, politics, the platforms of O'Connell, home rule, the Easter Rising, the treaty negotiations and the later Civil War. The journal was absorbed by the *Irish Independent* in 1924. For those undertaking historical research, this may be the most important of the 19th-century newspapers.

1320 Arthur Griffith and the advanced-nationalist press in Ireland.
Virginia Glandon. New York, Bern: Peter Lang, 1985. 327p.
Arthur Griffith was an influential journalist who was later involved as a statesman in the emergence of an independent Irish nation. This study examines Griffith's role in publishing while it surveys the issues facing the Irish press in the early 20th century. Griffith's contribution to the nationalist cause, his goals for a united Ireland, and his failure to bring together all factions as head of the provisional government are some of the themes considered in this review of newspaper publishing during the crucial period from 1900 to 1922.

1321 **Inniu.** (Today.)
Dublin: Glun na Buaidhe, weekly.
A weekly Gaelic language journal in newspaper format. Book reviews are included.

1322 **The Irish Independent.**
Dublin: Independent Newspapers 1905-. daily.
This newspaper has had the largest morning circulation in Ireland, and often reflects prevailing public opinion. Originally more conservative, the paper now follows a moderate or middle position in its political and social coverage. Companion papers include the *Evening Herald* (1891-.) and the *Sunday Independent*. Book reviews occasionally appear in the Saturday issues of the *Irish Independent*; cultural news in the *Sunday Independent*. All three papers are available in microfilm from Irish Microforms Ltd. of Dublin, and Clearwater Press of New York and Toronto.

1323 **The Irish Press.**
Dublin: Irish Press, 1931-. daily.
A popular Irish daily with full news coverage and somewhat conservative politics. Companion papers are the *Sunday Press* (1949-.), and the *Evening Press* (1954-.). Presentation of the news tends toward the sensational, and political views are often opposed to that of its competitor, the *Irish Independent* (q.v.). Some book reviews are included in the *Sunday Press*.

1324 **Irish Times.**
Dublin: Irish Times General Services, 1859-. Monday to Saturday.
The *Irish Times* is the most sophisticated of the Irish dailies, with worldwide and national coverage, good book reviews and columns on the arts, literature, business, politics, sports, and auctions. It publishes the best cultural section in Ireland (in the Saturday issue). Highly respected, it attempts a balanced coverage of issues dividing Ireland. It is sometimes disparaged for its élitist positions and pro-establishment outlook. Originally a conservative organ, it is now progressive on many social issues. Back issues are available on microfilm from Irish Microforms (Dublin), or Clearwater Press (New York, Toronto).

1325 **Kavanagh's Weekly, a Journal of Literature and Politics.**
Edited by Patrick Kavanagh. The Curragh, Ireland (Republic): Goldsmith Press, 1981. Reprint. [various pagination].
This weekly paper on Dublin social life and politics had a very short history (it appeared only in 1952), but gained a certain following for the notorious and sardonic wit with which it examined Irish life of the 1950s. Patrick Kavanagh, a well-known Irish writer and poet, passed his frequently disparaging judgements in outlandish style. His life and brief career as a newspaper publisher are told by his brother Peter Kavanagh in *Sacred keeper: a biography of Patrick Kavanagh* (Goldsmith Press, 1982).

1326 **History of Irish periodical literature from the end of the 17th to the middle of the 19th century.**
Richard Madden.   New York: Johnson Reprint, 1867. Reprint. 2 vols.

The long history of Irish newspaper publishing, and that of journals, newsletters and magazines receives an extensive chronicle and commentary in this set. This survey provides a glimpse of public tastes, interests and reading habits among the different classes during periods of great social, political and economic change.

1327 **The Nation.**
Dublin: Irish Microforms.

A reproduction of one of Ireland's most influential newspapers at a time of great upheaval and change, the years 1842 to 1852. As an organ of the Young Ireland movement it included among its publishers Thomas Davis and Charles Gavan Duffy. The newspaper's coverage included the disaster of the Great Famine, and the beginnings of a true Anglo-Irish literature. It was politically alligned with the growth of nationalism and liberalism, and is an essential source of information on political perspectives in 19th-century Ireland.

1328 **The newspaper book, a history of newspapers in Ireland, 1649-1983.**
Hugh Oram.   Dublin: M.O. Books, 1984. 300p.

Three hundred years of Irish newspaper publishing are reviewed in this fact-filled, concentrated history. Covering the period from the time of Cromwell up to the end of 1983, Oram shows the strength of this tradition that continues not only in the national papers but in the many county and regional papers as well. He presents fleeting portraits of a number of leading figures and publishers of the newspaper industry, with many anecdotes. The book includes a chronology and nearly 100 pages of photographs. A more limited though more scholarly history is presented by R. L. Munter in his *History of the Irish newspaper, 1685-1760* (Cambridge, England: Cambridge University Press, 1967. 218p.).

1329 **Sunday Tribune.**
Dublin: Sunday Tribune Company, 1980-. weekly.

A popular newspaper with good coverage of political, social and cultural news conveniently summarized on a weekly basis. Unfortunately, it is poorly distributed outside Ireland, unlike the other major Irish papers.

1330 **Sunday World.**
Dublin: Sunday Newspaper, 1973-. weekly.

Colour tabloid, directed at Ireland's urban population. A similarly popular weekly tabloid in colour is the *Sunday Journal* (Dublin, 1949-.). Both provide coverage of news and society.

Broadcasting

1331 **Irish Broadcasting Review.**
Dublin: Radio Telefis Eireann, 1978-. 3 issues per year.
The varied papers cover the state of broadcasting around the world and in particular countries, the effects of the mass media in Ireland, and the background and experiences of leading figures in Irish broadcasting.

1332 **Issues in Broadcasting.**
Dublin: Radio Telefis Eireann, 1985-. irregular.
A series of brief position papers, studies and reports on issues affecting broadcasting. The first, by Desmond Fisher, is entitled 'A policy for the information age?'; the second by Richard Pine is on 'Leisure and broadcsting'; and the third is by Kevin J. O'Connell, 'Technology and future broadcasting.'

1333 **Television and Irish society.**
Martin McLoone, John McMahon. Dublin: Radio Telefis Eireann/Irish Film Institute, 1985.
Seven essays from a 1983 workshop examine the Irish experience with television over a period of twenty-three years. Particular attention is given to the way that Irish society has been portrayed by certain television productions, programmes and series. A sociological interpretation is sought in the use of stereotypes when depicting the Irish rural world, women, the poor, or the urban classes on television.

General Periodicals

1334 **Counterpoint.**
Dublin: Music Association of Ireland, 1968-. monthly.
Contains articles on musical events and performances in Ireland, and lists concerts and recitals throughout the country.

1335 **Crane Bag.**
Dublin: Crane Bag, 1977-1986. semi-annual.
The journal takes its name from a satchel of alphabetical secrets that once belonged to Manannan, the traditional Irish god of the sea. This is one of the leading intellectual and literary magazines of Ireland, with each issue devoted to a single theme, and including articles by leading Irish and foreign commentators. Recent issues have dealt with the arts and politics, nationalism, mythology, tradition, Anglo-Irish literature, Irish women, Northern Ireland and the All Ireland Forum, minorities in Ireland, language and culture, intellectual life in modern Ireland, and James Joyce. Each issue is intended to explore the many sides of a question. The first ten issues have been reprinted in an anthology: *The Crane Bag, book of Irish studies* (q.v.).

1336 **Film Directions.**
Dublin: Arts Council; Belfast: Arts Council of Northern Ireland, 1977-. quarterly.
Ireland's leading journal on the cinema arts, with articles on film production and reviews of new films.

1337 **Gaelic Sport.**
Dublin: Holyrood Publications, 1958-. monthly.
Ireland's most popular sports magazine, covering major games, results, leading players and teams, and forthcoming events. Illustrations and book reviews are

292

included. Another popular magazine is *Gaelic Games* (Dublin: Sean P. Graham Publications, 1970-. monthly). The official journal of the Gaelic Athletic Association is the *Gaelic World* (Dublin: Tara Publishing, 1979-. monthly.), which includes articles on current football and hurling games, clubs and championships, and the outlook in both the Irish Republic and Northern Ireland. *Gaelic Sport* emphasizes, in general articles, the performance of particular teams and provides biographies of specific players.

1338 Hibernia.
Dublin: Hibernia National Review, 1937-. fortnightly.

A general news publication in tabloid format, with a summary of cultural events, and reviews of recent books, films and plays.

1339 In Dublin.
Dublin: In Dublin, 1976-. fortnightly.

A very convenient guide to major events, cultural activities and entertainment throughout the city. Some feature articles and extensive reviews are included, along with listings of cinema, theatre, restaurants, media and sports.

1340 Inside Ireland.
Dublin: Inside Ireland, 1978-. quarterly.

Current information is provided on Ireland. Included are biographical and directory-type data, a 'who's who' in Ireland, lists of popular places of entertainment, information on how to buy or rent property, on studying abroad, available hotels, and current auctions. This information is directed at the foreign traveller to Ireland. A genealogical consulting service is included with the subscription.

1341 Ireland of the Welcomes.
Dublin: Bord Failte, 1952-. bi-monthly.

An attractive magazine with articles on popular topics of particular interest to the tourist, and with numerous coloured photographs. Some issues have been arranged around a central theme, such as Dublin, the countryside, the sea, folkways, crafts, music, Joyce, architecture, and other broad topics.

1342 Ireland Today.
Dublin: Department of Foreign Affairs, 1949-. fortnightly.

Each brief issue includes topical articles of potential interest to an international audience. Included are foreign affairs, cultural matters, broad economic and social trends, sports, archaeology, and better known writers. Some issues have supplements reprinting important government policy statements or addresses.

1343 Ireland's Own.
Wexford, Ireland (Republic): The People Newspapers, 1902-. weekly.

A short, very popular weekly journal of literature and fiction. Most issues contain an Irish language page, several short stories in English, devotional literature, humour, occasional book reviews, ballads and music, and some illustrations.

1344   **Irish Arts Review.**
Carrick-on-Sur, Ireland (Republic): Irish Arts Review, 1984-.
quarterly.
Designed for an international audience, this attractive, high gloss art magazine provides the art connoisseur with articles on the traditional Irish arts and crafts of all periods, the major movements, great painters, designers, and exhibits. Each issue contains coloured illustrations, advertisements, sale notices, and book reviews.

1345   **Irish Booklore.**
Belfast: Linen Hall Library and Blackstaff Press. New series.
1977-. semi-annual.
For the book collector and bibliophile, each issue contains a variety of bibliographic essays, book reviews and articles on major collections, authors, the history of Irish publishing, and related topics. The journal first appeared in 1971.

1346   **Irish Computer.**
Loughlinstown, Ireland (Republic): Computer Publications of Ireland, 1977-. monthly.
Covers the computer field in Ireland, with articles on new equipment, programmes and applications.

1347   **Irish Field.**
Dublin: Irish Times, 1870-. weekly.
Ireland's major trade and sportsman's publication on horse breeding, training, racing, show-jumping, competitions, and sales. Financial and investment aspects are occasionally included.

1348   **Irish Literary Supplement.**
Selden, New York: Irish Literary Supplement, 1982-. semi-
annual.
Extensive reviews and commentary are provided on recently published Irish books on history, literature, and current affairs. Issued in a newspaper format, this journal is directed at the academic and literary communities. Each issue contains signed reviews by leading scholars, approximately fifty book reviews, notes on works in progress, inquiries, and letters.

1349   **Irish People.**
Dublin: Repsol Publications, 1973-. weekly.
A labour oriented publication on current affairs, political, organizational and industrial activities.

1350 **Irish University Review.**
Dublin: University College Dublin and Wolfhound Press, 1970-.
semi-annual.
Many aspects of Irish culture are included in this journal, with articles appearing on history, mythology, folklore, and literature. Directed at an academic audience, this is published in conjunction with the Irish Association for the Study of Anglo-Irish Literature. Special issues have been devoted to poetry, Samuel Beckett, and James Joyce, and other issues have contained plays, poems, short stories, and book reviews. Beginning in 1972 it has included a bibliographic section on publications by and about Irish authors.

1351 **Irish Woman.**
Dublin: GP Publishing Group, 1959-. monthly.
The official journal of the Irish Countrywoman's Association, with articles on current activities and events of interest to women, handicrafts, and traditional endeavours. A conservative approach is followed, with a woman's perspective.

1352 **Journal of Irish Literature.**
Newark, Delaware: Proscenium Press, 1972-. 3 issues per year.
An academic journal containing articles on Irish literature and drama, interviews with authors, and the text of plays and stories. Some issues focus on particular authors, and book reviews are included.

1353 **Magill Magazine.**
Dublin: Magill 1978(?)-. monthly.
This popular monthly magazine presents outspoken, lively articles on current affairs, politics, business trends, society, religion, cultural affairs, sports, theatre, and travel. The magazine also provides some useful background reports on major news items.

1354 **Motoring Life.**
Dublin: Merit Publications, 1946-. monthly.
A magazine for the motoring public with articles and tips on car care and travel.

1355 **Digest of Irish Affairs.**
Edited by Kathleen O'Brien. Dublin: Academy Press, 1980. 5 vols. plus supplements.
The first five volumes of this set provide coverage of Irish affairs between 1969 and 1978. A comprehensive listing is provided of current Irish news stories and articles with descriptive abstracts or summaries. The citations are arranged by subject, place or individual. It is intended to be used as a reference source in itself, or as an index to Irish periodicals. Book reviews are also noted.

General Periodicals

1356 The Salmon.
Annaghdown, Ireland (Republic): The Salmon, 1981-. quarterly.
Poems, short stories and general literature are presented, with an emphasis on material from the West of Ireland.

1357 Soundpost, Ireland's Music Magazine.
Dublin: Music Assocation of Ireland, 1981-. bimonthly.
For the music and recording public, issues contain news of Irish concerts, reviews of records, interviews with musicians and composers, and general articles on broadcasting and the future of the performing arts.

1358 Studies.
Dublin: Studies, 1912-. quarterly.
A leading academic journal on letters, sociology, philosophy and science. Includes articles on current topics concerning governmental organization and policy, economic and social trends, social problems, literature, the natural sciences, and historical scholarship. Book reviews are included.

1359 An Taisce Journal.
Dublin: An Taisce, 17977-. quarterly.
An environmental magazine serving as the organ of the National Trust of Ireland. Articles regularly appear on the work of the trust, its properties, and on the need for conservation and the preservation of amenities. Taisce refers to a treasure worth preserving, hence An Taisce is the National Trust concerned with historic preservation.

1360 Theatre Ireland.
Belfast: Theatre Ireland, 1982-. 3 times per year.
Issues contain scripts of plays, reviews of productions, and articles on theatre design, the role of drama, and history. Also included are commentaries, interviews, and book reviews. A *Theatre Ireland Yearbook* is also issued.

1361 Woman's Way.
Dublin: J. C. Publications 1963-. weekly.
A popular women's magazine, with general news and commentary, short stories and fiction. Some useful articles are included on household management, and on topics of current concern, such as Irish housing grants.

Professional Journals and Series

1362 Administration.
Dublin: Institute of Public Administration, 1953-. quarterly.
A respected journal of the administrative sciences, with many contributors from positions of leadership. Some articles are thorough and scholarly, and topics include government organization and policy, public administration, the civil service, regional planning, industrial policy, cultural programmes, employment and unemployment, and social welfare legislation. Book reviews are included. Some entire issues are devoted to specialized topics.

1363 Analecta Hibernica.
Dublin: Stationery Office, 1930-. irregular.
Produced for the Irish Manuscripts Commission, each issue presents the edited texts of some historical papers or writings, from ecclesiastical, legal, governmental or private sources. Some emphasis is given to mediaeval documents, for example vol 29 (1980) edited by H. G. Richardson and G. O. Sayles, relates to the 'Administration of Ireland, 1172-1377'. Over the years various publishers have been responsible for the series. These and other publications of the Irish Manuscripts Commission (such as collected correspondence and registers of deeds) are listed in the quarterly *Catalogue of Government Publications* (section 'H'), issued by the Stationery Office.

1364 Anglo-Irish Studies.
Cambridge, England: Cambridge University Press; Atlantic Highlands, New Jersey: Humanities Press, 1975-. annual.
A series of hardbound volumes covering interdisciplinary topics relating to the Anglo-Irish, including literature, history, politics and the social sciences.

Professional Journals and Series

1365 **Architecture in Ireland.**
Dublin: JPS Publications, 1978-. quarterly.
News of the field of architecture, with mention of Irish design, planning and construction in short articles and advertisements.

1366 **Béaloideas.** (Folklore.)
Dublin: Folklore of Ireland Society, 1927-. annual.
This scholarly journal of the Folklore of Ireland Society contains articles on the traditional myths, stories and language of rural Ireland, the tinkers and their dialects, and other elements of Irish society.

1367 **Business and Finance.**
Dublin: Belenos Publications, 1964-. weeky.
A major Irish periodical with news on business, economic trends, regional development, and finance. Included are useful and timely articles, charts and current statistics on economic patterns.

1368 **Conference Times.**
Dublin: Oisin Publications, semi-annual.
Useful for travel agents, planners and the service industry, this publication provides a listing of forthcoming conventions, conferences, exhibitions, exhibits and trade fairs and their locations.

1369 **Economic and Social Review.**
Dublin: Economic and Social Research Institute, 1969-. quarterly.
This scholarly quarterly presents in depth articles on economic policies, changing conditions, the population, marriage, social trends, and related issues in Ireland. A frequently quoted source of current data by economists and sociologists.

1370 **Eire-Ireland.**
St. Paul, Minnesota: Irish American Cultural Institute, 1966-. quarterly.
A scholarly journal of Irish studies, with an emphasis on history, literature and folklore. The articles are thorough and authoritative. Numerous, extensive book reviews are included in each issue.

1371 **Ériu, the Journal of the School of Irish Learning.**
Dublin: Royal Irish Academy, 1904-. annual.
This academic journal studies the use, structure and form of the Irish langue and philology (both old and modern). A discussion of the language as it has been used in some of the ancient Irish legends and texts is included in some issues. This was originally published as the *Journal of the School of Irish Learning* (Dublin). In 1926, the School was incorporated within the Royal Irish Academy, and the Academy continued to publish the journal.

1372   **Etudes Irlandaises.** (Irish Studies.)
Lille, France: Université de Lille. New Series. 1976-. annual.
A leading annual on Irish studies with articles on history, literary criticism, politics and sociology. Some volumes contain more than 400 pages, with the emphasis on modern Irish civilization and sociology. The publication examines issues critically and from an independent viewpoint, removed from the pressures and factions within Ireland. This is the best source for a continental perspective on Irish affairs. The volumes also contain interviews, book reviews, bibliographies, lists of theses, new books, and details of French courses on Irish studies.

1373   **Export.**
Dublin: Córas Tráchtála, 1967-. quarterly.
Current statistics, charts, news and reviews on Irish trade and exports, produced by the Irish Export Board. Irish business and trade patterns are also covered in *The Irish Exporter*, the monthly official journal of the Irish Exporters Association, Dublin (1978-.).

1374   **Irish Banking Review.**
Dublin: Institute of Bankers in Ireland, Irish Banks Standing Committee, 1957-. quarterly.
Short articles comment on news which is of interest to Ireland's banking and financial community. Topics include general economic conditions, industrial growth, national, regional and local development, investment policies and spending patterns. Further financial and economic data, as well as professional articles and book reviews, are provided in the *Journal of the Institute of Bankers in Ireland* (Dublin: Institute of Bankers in Ireland, 1898-. quarterly).

1375   **Irish Builder and Engineer.**
Dublin: Kenlis Publications, 1859-. monthly.
An illustrated leading Irish journal covering architecture, engineering, design and building. Another monthly is *Build* (Dublin: Belenos Publications, 1953-.), which is issued as a supplement to *Business and Finance* (q.v.). *Build* provides information on current developments in the trade. A controlled publication, it includes charts, illustrations, book reviews, statistics, and notices. Solely for the engineering professions is the *Engineers Journal*, the official monthly of the Institution of Engineers of Ireland.

1376   **Irish Business.**
Dublin: Irish Financial Publications, 1975-. monthly.
This widely distributed business monthly includes articles on financial conditions, business prospects and current activity.

1377   **Irish Farmer's Journal.**
Dublin: Irish Farm Centre, 1949-. weekly.
An essential and widely distributed periodical on farm news and conditions, markets, sales and transactions. Other farming journals are the *Irish Farmer's Monthly* (Dun Laoghaire, Irish Republic), and *The Farmer* (Dublin: Baggot Publishing, 1979-. monthly), which serves the agribusiness community.

Professional Journals and Series

1378 **Irish Forestry.**
Dublin: Royal Dublin Society, 1943-. semi-annual.
In this journal of the Society of Irish Foresters, articles range from the technical to the general. Among the topics covered are the economic conditions of the industry, planning, reforestration programmes, end uses, and the history of forests in Ireland. Book reviews, some charts and illustrations are included.

1379 **Irish Geography.**
Dublin: Geographical Society of Ireland, Trinity College, 1944-. annual.
Well researched papers on physical and economic geography, landforms, land use, population and settlement patterns, employment, industrial growth and regional development are included in this important academic journal. There is an extensive book review section, and an annual list of papers recently completed.

1380 **Irish Georgian Society Quarterly Bulletin.**
Celbridge, County Kildare, Ireland (Republic): Irish Georgian Society, 1958-. quarterly.
This journal of art history has an international readership. Articles discuss such aspects as Irish art and architecture of the 18th century, leading artists and craftsmen of the period, landscaping, estate planning, mapping, glassware and other major accomplishments in the arts.

1381 **Irish Historical Studies.**
Dublin: University College Dublin, History Department, 1938-. semi-annual.
A leading academic journal of Irish history, which usually has articles on narrowly defined topics. This is a joint publication of the Irish Historical Society, and the Ulster Society for Historical Studies. Papers of the Irish Conference of Historians have been included. There is a section listing recent writings on Irish history, from both domestic and foreign sources. Book reviews and bibliographies are also included, covering both the Irish Republic and Northern Ireland.

1382 **Irish Journal of Agricultural Economics and Rural Sociology.**
Dublin: An Foras Taluntais, 1967-. semi-annual.
Contains a broad range of articles, covering Irish society and traditions in rural areas, and present economic conditions. Other papers have appeared on farm and home management, marketing, population change, and income levels.

1383 **Irish Journal of Education.**
Dublin: St. Patrick's College, Educational Research Centre, 1967-. semi-annual.
A professional journal with articles on teaching methods and training, courses, problem students, scholastic performance, and new teaching techniques. Many teachers in Ireland also receive the *Turascail*, the official monthly publication of the Irish National Teachers' Organization.

1384   **Irish Journal of Environmental Science.**
Dublin: An Foras Forbatha, 1980-. irregular.
Issued by the National Institute for Physical Planning and Construction Research,
with papers on the general environment, Irish conservation measures, pollution,
energy, roads, development, and wildlife.

1385   **Irish Journal of Psychology.**
Renmore, Galway, Ireland (Republic): Psychological Society of
Ireland, 1971-. annual.
A scientific and academic journal with world-wide distribution, presenting the
results of research and surveys undertaken within Ireland. Book reviews,
bibliographies and tables are included. For those in practice, current information
is provided in the monthly periodical *The Irish Psychologist* (Renmore, Galway,
Irish Republic: 1974-.).

1386   **Irish Law Times.**
Dublin: Smurfit Publications, 1867-. weekly.
The Republic of Ireland's leading legal newspaper and source of information on
current legal developments, new cases and decisions. The publisher has varied
over the years.

1387   **Irish Medical Journal.**
Dublin: Irish Medical Association, 1839-. monthly.
The leading journal for the medical profession, with articles on diseases, health,
medical care and practice in the Republic of Ireland. Book reviews are included.
Current medical and professional news is provided in the weekly tabloid, *Irish
Medical Times* (Dublin: Haymarket Publications, 1967-.). Another professional
publication is the quarterly, *Irish Colleges of Physicians and Surgeons Journal*
(Dublin: 1963-.).

1388   **Irish Naturalists' Journal.**
Belfast: Queen's University, Science Library; Dublin: Irish Field
Clubs, 1925-. quarterly.
This journal has served as the scientific organ of a number of clubs and societies
throughout the Republic and Northern Ireland, including both the Belfast and
Dublin Naturalists' Field Clubs, the Irish Geological Society, the Royal
Zoological Society of Ireland, and the Queen's University Biological Society.
Papers cover a broad range of topics, but biology and geology are emphasized.
Articles have covered fauna, fossils, fish and algae at specific locations. Originally
antiquities and ethnology were also included. Book reviews, bibliographies and
notices of meetings are often given. The journal is a continuation of *The Irish
Naturalist* (Dublin: Eason, 1892-1924).

1389   **The Irish Sword.**
Dublin: Military History Society of Ireland, 1949-. semi-annual.
Articles regularly appear on many aspects of Irish history, of all periods. Book
reviews are included.

Professional Journals and Series

1390 **Irish Journal of Earth Sciences.**
Dublin: Royal Irish Academy, 1984-. semi-annual.
Papers on Irish geology are included, from scientists and geologists throughout both Britain and Ireland.

1391 **Management.**
Dublin: Irish Management Institute, 1953-. monthly.
Articles are presented on business and office management, organization, personnel and training. Some book reviews are included.

1392 **Proceedings of the Royal Irish Academy.**
Dublin: Royal Irish Academy, 1836-. irregular, usually semi-annual.
This prestigious scientific journal contains papers divided into three sections or series: section A covers astronomy, mathematics, and physics; section B biology, chemistry and geology; and section C archaeology, history and linguistics.

1393 **Quarterly Bulletin of the Central Bank.**
Dublin: Economic and Social Research Institute, quarterly.
Information, statistical data and commentary provide a summary of Ireland's economic conditions, trends, balances and national accounts, and factors affecting business and industry. Some timely observations are also provided in the *Quarterly Economic Review* (q.v.), and in the *Quarterly Economic Commentary* (q.v.), which issues a separate section on Ireland.

1394 **Social Studies, Irish Journal of Sociology.**
Maynooth, Ireland (Republic): Christus Rex Society, 1972-. quarterly.
Articles are presented on changing Irish society, social trends, urbanization, rural conditions, and Irish culture generally. The perspective of the journal is from within the framework of religious dogma, presenting a conservative outlook on some, though not all issues of current concern. The journal was published as *Christus Rex* from 1947 to 1971. Many of the papers provide a thorough analysis of an issue, and ethical judgements are explored.

1395 **Studia Hibernica.**
Dublin: Coláiste Phádraig (St. Patrick's College), 1961-. annual.
Research articles are provided on Irish history, folklore, language, place-names, archaeology, and related topics.

1396 **World of Irish Nursing.**
Dublin: Maxwell Publicity, 1972-. monthly.
The news source for the nursing profession, with short articles on health services and care, and nurses training and education. This publication is the official journal of the Irish Nurses Organization and the National Council of Nurses of Ireland.

Encyclopaedias and Directories

1397 **Communications Directory and Yearbook.**
Dublin: Savoy Press, 1973-. annual.
A directory designed for Ireland's mass communications industry and media.

1398 **The Cambridge historical encyclopedia of Great Britain and Ireland.**
Edited by Christopher Haigh. Cambridge, England; New York: Cambridge University Press, 1985. 392p.
This guide presents concise information on many Irish and British events, with emphasis given to English history. The text is arranged in seven chronological chapters covering prehistory (100 BC) to 1975. Some sections are devoted to long thematic topics, and there is also a biographical section on 800 leading figures. The coverage of Irish history is brief and marginal.

1399 **Directory of British associations and associations in Ireland.**
G. P. Henderson, S. P. A. Henderson. Beckenham, Kent, England: C. B. D. Research; Detroit, Michigan: Gale Research, 1986. 5th ed. 506p.
Some 9,000 organizations throughout Ireland, England, Wales and Scotland are listed. Included are virtually all major national associations as well as some local groups which are considered to be of national significance. Each group is identified with its address, chief officers, branches, membership, publications, and a brief description of its goals. The volume includes a subject index. Data for Ireland is abbreviated however.

Encyclopaedias and Directories

1400   **Industrial Register.**
Dublin: Institute for Industrial Research and Standards, 1971-.
occasional.
Various registers provide a listing of products and services related to industry and engineering, and the fields of textiles, chemicals, paper, printing and other businesses. From time to time the institute also issues a handy *Directory of technical information sources*, listing government departments, firms and institutes providing technical data and guides.

1401   **Irish Computer Directory and Diary.**
Loughlinstown, Ireland (Republic): Computer Publications of Ireland, 1978-. annual.
This yearbook contains a directory of Irish computer firms, equipment, and related goods, sales and services, for the Irish market.

1402   **Irish Engineering Directory: Companies, Products and Services.**
Dublin: Institute for Industrial Research and Standards, annual.
The directory lists Irish manufacturers and suppliers of machinery, engineering equipment and components, their addresses, employees, and commercial and technical contacts. Irish Engineering Publications of Dublin has issued a *Directory of Engineers*, which lists Irish engineers, laboratories and technical facilities in higher education and government, and specifications and standards.

1403   **Irish Export Directory.**
Dublin: Coras Trachtala, 1975-. irregular.
An occasional publication for the overseas importer and buyer, providing a listing of Irish goods and services, arranged under the appropriate product or industry. Also of interest to the trader is the directory, *Made in Ireland: the retail buyers guide to Irish consumer products* (Dublin: Institute for Industrial Research and Standards, 1976. 280p.). For the foreign market there is an *Irish Exporter Yearbook and Diary* (Dublin: Tara Publishing, 1979-.).

1404   **Irish Industrial Year Book.**
Dublin: McEvoy Press, 1934-. irregular.
Irish manufacturers are listed alphabetically, and by their location, and the goods and services they provide. Dun & Bradstreet of Dublin has issued a *Guide to Irish manufacturers*, providing an alphabetical list of businesses grouped by industry.

1405   **Encyclopaedia of Ireland.**
Edited by Victor Meally.   Dublin: Allen Figgis; New York, Toronto: McGraw-Hill, 1971. 463p.
Very few encyclopaedias have appeared on Ireland, and the present volume stands alone. Virtually every broad aspect of Irish history and culture is covered here. Geography, literature, politics, entertainment, sports, the arts and other facets of Irish life are included in some 250 articles, many of which are too short. Nearly 600 illustrations enhance the text however, and this volume does present a useful introduction to many topics.

1406   **Thom's Commercial Directory of Ireland.**
Dublin: Thom's Directories, 1844-. annual.

Several series of directories have been issued by Thom since 1844, and antecedents under another name have appeared since 1752. This directory lists major companies and manufacturers, their directors and principal officials, government departments and public institutions, merchants, and trade and professional organizations. The commercial directories are issued annually; a professional directory has also been published. *Thom's Official Dublin Directory* lists streets, residents and traders in Dublin and surrounding areas. The 1973 edition had 984 pages. A 1904 edition, said to have been used by James Joyce in his writing, has been reissued by Irish Microforms of Dublin. Another commercial directory is *Chambers commercial guide to Ireland* (London: Kemp's Group, 1975). In 1923 Thom's issued a collection of 2,500 prominent individuals in *Thom's Irish who's who* (Dublin, 1923. 266p.).

1407   **Who owns whom, United Kingdom and the Republic of Ireland, 1979-80.**
New York: Dun & Bradstreet International, 1979. 2 vols.

A directory to corporations, with volume one listing parent organizations, groups and consortia, and volume two serving as a guide to subsidiaries.

1408   **Who's who, what's what and where in Ireland.**
London: Geoffrey Chapman, 1973. 735p.

A useful and extensive directory listing groups, governmental bodies, educational and public organizations, trade groups and journals. Also included are a glossary of Irish words, a descriptive gazetteer to local places, a list of abbreviations and a subject index. Some 3,000 short biographical notes cover prominent Irish citizens of the time. The directory was compiled by the staffs of Zircon Publishing and *The Irish Times*. The biographical coverage is uneven, and other information is now dated but this remains a useful and convenient compendium.

Bibliographies

General

1409   **Irish Publishing Record.**
Edited by Eithne Bennett.   Belfield, Dublin: University College
Dublin Library, 1967-. annual.
This is the most complete listing of books and other material published in Ireland.
All major and many minor works are included. The bibliographic citations are
authoritative and are carefully prepared. This publication serves as the Irish
national bibliography, and provides a good guide to main entries. Each volume is
divided by subject, and averages approximately 150 pages. Publications from both
Northern Ireland and the Irish Republic are included, and a list of Irish publishers
is included.

1410   **A bibliography of Irish ethnology and folk traditions.**
Kevin Danaher.   Dublin; Cork: Mercier, 1978. 95p.
A useful bibliography bringing together citations to a number of sources, many of
them essential. Citations are divided by subject, and no annotations are given.
Among the topics included are Irish settlements and dwellings, livelihood,
communication, trade, community, way of life, nature, medicine, festivals and
popular beliefs.

1411   **Books on Ireland: a select list.**
Dublin: National Library of Ireland, 1978. 45p.
Several editions of this bibliography have appeared, compiled by C. O'Lochlainn
and others. Intended for the general public it lists several hundred works and
provides annotations for each. Included are directories and yearbooks, descriptions of Ireland, and books on Irish history, society and the economy, the Ulster
question, the Irish abroad, and music, art and culture.

1412 **This arrogant city.**
Henry Boylan. Dublin: A. A. Farmer, 1984. 75p.
A selective bibliography of books about Dublin, of interest to the general reader, the collector, and all those who take pleasure in the city and its history.

1413 **European immigration and ethnicity in the United States and Canada, a historical bibliography.**
Edited by David L. Brye. Santa Barbara, California: ABC-Clio, 1982. 458p.
One hundred citations are given (p. 50-57) of periodicals with papers on the Irish-American experience. Full abstracts are included.

1414 **Catalogue.**
St. Paul, Minnesota: Irish Books and Media, 1982. 145p.
This catalogue lists 1,000 books about Ireland, in print and available in 1982. Good, descriptive comments are provided for each book. Although not all subjects are represented the list does include history (from ancient to modern times), genealogy, folklore, culture, literature and fiction, music, the arts, language, education, travel, children's books, and humour. The annotations are directed at an American audience. All books are available from Irish Books and Media, and the original publishers are not indicated.

1415 **Irish Books in Print.**
Edited by Shane Cleary, (et al.). Wicklow, Ireland (Republic): S. and J. Cleary, 1984. 1,010p.
This major reference and bibliographic sourcebook provides a current listing of literature from or about Ireland. Entries are based on lists submitted by Irish publishing houses, and cover all topics. Further information has been drawn from the computer-generated lists of *British Books in Print* (Whitaker & Sons) for British books about Ireland, and *Books in Print* (Bowker) for US books of Irish interest. Full entries are repeated in separate author, title and classified (broad subject) indexes. Different editions are noted, and there is a supplemental section listing books in the Irish language. A total of more than 8,000 books are cited throughout the volume, and 500 of these are given short annotations in an appendix. In a handy arrangement and with an easy to read format, this lists almost all the books for sale on Ireland, except for some of the more specialized school textbooks.

1416 **British and Irish library resources, a bibliographic guide.**
Robert B. Downs. London; Bronx, New York: Mansell, 1982. 2nd ed. 448p.
This bibliographic guide contains some 6,700 entries listing sources of information about libraries in both Ireland and Great Britain. A wide variety of subjects and collections are indexed. Noted are library catalogues, checklists, calendars of manuscripts, guidebooks, directories, exhibition catalogues, union lists, and journal articles about the collections.

1417   **A guide to Irish bibliographic material: a bibliography of Irish bibliographies and sources of information.**
Compiled by Alan R. Eager.   London: Library Association; Westport, Connecticut: Greenwood, 1980. 2nd. ed. 502p.
This guide presents the most complete listing of Irish bibliographies, whether published as individual works or appearing in another source. Over 9,500 entries are noted, based on the holdings of major library collections in Ireland, England and the United States. Bibliographies in articles, papers, books, catalogues, and numerous primary sources are mentioned, as are many biobibliographies. In addition, this book lists standard, representative works about Ireland that are more general in nature. Entries are arranged under topical headings, and coverage is good for history, Irish geography and topography, localities and biographies. Other topics include philosophy and religion, the social sciences, language and literature, the sciences, professions and the arts. This is an important reference sources for all research collections.

1418   **The Irish language: an annotated bibliography of sociolinguistic publications, 1771-1982.**
John Edwards.   Belfast: Blackstaff; New York: Garland, 1982. 274p.
A bibliography of 800 titles concerning the Irish language, in English. The books and papers are listed alphabetically by author, and deal with education and teaching, cultural aspects of the language, society and history. Works solely in Irish are excluded.

1419   **Environmental bibliographies.**
Dublin: An Foras Forbartha, 1981. 25p.
An Foras Forbartha is the major governmental body and national institute relating to physical planning and construction research. Its library issues numerous bibliographies on the environment, and other narrow, well-defined topics for both urban and rural areas. This pamphlet provides a list of the bibliographies.

1420   **The book of Irish books.**
Tom Kennedy.   Leixlip, Kildare, Ireland (Republic): Albertine Kennedy Publishing, 1982. 3rd ed. 96p.
A listing is given of 1,300 Irish books in stock and available in 1982. Many publishers are represented and books are listed by subject with useful, descriptive annotations. Only books published in Ireland are included, although not all of these are about Ireland.

1421   **A legal bibliography of the British Commonwealth of Nations.**
London: Sweet & Maxwell, 1957. 2nd ed. 7 vols.
Volume four provides a bibliography of Irish law to 1956. Brief entries list treatises on Irish law and especially the English roots, of jurisprudence, practice, rights, obligations, property, landlord and tenant, and other topics.

1422 **A bibliography of published works on Irish foreign relations, 1921-1978.**
Maria Maguire.   Dublin: Royal Irish Academy, 1981. 136p.
Lists material published on Ireland's foreign relations during the period that has seen independence and the establishment of the Irish Free State, the definition and reaffirmation of a neutral position, participation in the United Nations, and changing relationships with the European continent, world powers, and the Third World.

1423 **Irish music in America: a selective bibliography.**
Marsha Maguire.   Washington, DC: Library of Congress Archive of Folk Song, 1981. 10p.
An extensive list of articles, books and dissertations on Irish music in Ireland, the United States and Canada, based on the collections of the Library of Congress.

1424 **The Irish-American experience, a guide to the literature.**
Seamus P. Metress.   Washington, DC: University Press of America, 1981. 220p.
An unannotated bibliography on the Irish-American experience, covering both books and periodicals. Topics covered include anthropology, economics, geography, history, religion, sociology, migration, the labour movement, war, political science, social psychology and regions of settlement. Art and literature are not covered.

1425 **A comprehensive bibliography for the study of American minorities.**
Wayne Charles Miller, (et al.).   New York: New York University Press, 1976. 690p.
An extensive bibliography of the Irish-Americans is presented on p. 381-419, following an essay on the Irish-American experience. Thousands of books and journal articles are listed under headings relating to history, regions, migration, discrimination, economics, politics, education, religion, biography, literature and fiction. Short evaluations are occasionally provided.

1426 **Sources of economic information: Ireland.**
Renuka Page.   Dublin: Institute of Public Administration, 1985. 112p.
A guide is presented to the many sources of economic data on Ireland, especially as found in government publications. Included is a review of the information available from government departments, committees and commissions, research institutes, international bodies, banks, private sources, commercial groups and professional organizations. This volume is particularly useful for economists, business analysts, academics, and those concerned with market research. Among the topics included in the twenty-one chapters are agriculture, tourism, energy, and newspapers. A subject index is also included. For statistical information on Ireland many books, journals and studies are noted in *Irish economic statistics* (q.v.).

1427 **Modern Ireland, a bibliography on politics, planning, research and development.**
Edited by Michael O. Shannon. Westport, Connecticut: Greenwood Press; London: Library Association, 1981. 733p.

This bibliography provides coverage of modern Ireland in its social and physical setting. There are 5,425 entries which cite books, periodicals, reports, studies and research concerning both the Irish Republic and Northern Ireland, primarily during the 19th and 20th centuries. Some of these are annotated. Emphasis is given to history, politics, government, geography and natural history, economic and regional development, employment, sociology, physical planning, social services, programmes and organizations. Part of the volume is divided by local area studies. Excluded are literature, the arts, earlier history, and sports.

1428 **A short bibliography on Irish folk song.**
Hugh Shields. Dundrum, Ireland (Republic): Folk Music Society of Ireland, 1985. 24p.

This bibliography provides a basic list of the chief collections and anthologies of Irish folk-songs, and a listing of works about them.

Government publications

1429 **A select list of reports of inquiries of the Irish Dail and Senate, 1922-72.**
Edited by Percy Ford, G. Ford. Dublin: Irish Academic Press, 1974. 64p.

A list of major Irish reports arising from parliamentary inquiries made since independence and the formation of the Irish Free State. An index to authors of reports and chairpersons of parliamentary committees has been published elsewhere. See Kathleen O'Brien's *Select list of Irish government reports, 1960-72* (Dublin: Central Library and Archives, 1974).

1430 **Government Publications.**
Dublin: Stationery Office, 1923-. quarterly and annual.

The quarterly list provides details of new government publications. Citations to the publications (these are abbreviated) are recorded under the appropriate major departments, with additional sections listing legislative documents (acts, bills, Oireachtas reports, and statutory instruments). A final section is devoted to new general literature in the Irish language. This catalogue is accumulated annually, and is supplemented weekly by offprinted lists and pages from the *Iris Oifigiúil* (The Official Gazette.)

1431 **Official publications of Western Europe. Volume one.**
Edited by Eve Johansson. London: Mansell, 1984. 313p.
Volume one of this two volume bibliography is divided into sections on nine
countries, including Ireland. The set will cover all of Western Europe, and this
volume provides one of the best introductions to Irish official publications.
Comments are given on principal series, method of issue, bibliographic control,
and existing collections. The chapter on Ireland (p. 87-106) by John Goodwillie,
evaluates the official documents of Parliament, the central government departments, state-sponsored bodies, and local authorities. A good description is given
of legislative publications and of the official catalogues of government reports.

1432 **Ireland in the nineteenth century: a breviate of official publications.**
Arthur Maltby, Jean Maltby. New York; Oxford: Pergamon
Press, 1979. 300p. (Guides to Official Publications, no. 4).
A list is presented of some of the government publications of the 19th century
concerning Ireland. All are British, representing the political administration of
the period. Some 600 publications have been selected for inclusion under 12
major categories: government, finance, land ownership, agriculture, poverty and
relief, health, living conditions, transportation and communications, education
and culture, ecclesiastical matters, trade, industry, labour, civil commotions and
other pertinent topics. The chief value of this volume is in the often lengthy
annotations.

1433 **Irish official publications, a guide to Republic of Ireland papers,
with a breviate of reports, 1927-1972.**
Arthur Maltby, Brian McKenna. Oxford; New York: Pergamon
Press, 1980. 388p. (Guides to Official Publications, no. 7).
This volume provides a guide to and description of Irish government publications,
their types, methods of issuance, numbering and other characteristics. The major
part of the volume presents a list of significant government publications, arranged
by subject: government, economics, finance, labour, industry and technology,
agriculture, energy, legal matters, transportation, communications, education,
culture, welfare, health, housing, and town planning. Each category is subdivided
under more specific headings. Some 500 publications are noted and described with
a full summary of their contents, importance or merit. Coverage extends from the
birth of the Irish Free State, and shows the later growth of government
administration and policies. A good subject index is provided, and chairpersons of
important committees are noted. Suggestions are included on acquisitions or a
collecting programme. Some titles of documents are inaccurately given but the
annotations are most useful.

History

1434 **Mediaeval Ireland, 1170-1495: a bibliography of secondary works.**
P. W. A. Asplin. Dublin: Royal Irish Academy, 1971. 139p.
(New History of Ireland, Ancillary Publication no. 1).
A guide to books, periodicals, and bibliographies about mediaeval Ireland, under eighteen main subject headings. Among the topics included are general history, historical geography, military, administrative and ecclesiastical history, social life, economics, literature, the arts, genealogy, and heraldry. Short, descriptive comments are provided on books, serials, collected essays and Festschriften. The author also reviews the more important manuscript collections and repositories.

1435 **Bibliography of Irish history.**
James Carty. Dublin: Stationery Office, 1936-1940. 2 vols.
Based on the collections of the National Library of Ireland, publications are listed on Irish social, political and cultural history leading up to the independence struggle. Volume one covers 1870 to 1911; and volume two 1912 to 1921. Both volumes provide numerous entries showing the extensive amount of books, articles, official reports and other material issued on this crucial period of Irish history. Considerable revision is necessary, however, to account for the even larger amount of material published since this compilation, and for the private papers and archives released since 1940.

1436 **Sources for early modern Irish history, 1534-1641.**
Robert W. Dudley Edwards, Mary O'Dowd. Cambridge, England: Cambridge University Press, 1985. 222p.
In this useful guide to widely dispersed information on the Tudor revival and early Stuart periods, information is given on both primary, extant materials, and on the data that has since been destroyed as in the case of the burning of the Irish archives in the Four Courts. The authors note presently available early writings and original source materials, maps, drawings, important archives, government and administrative documents, and later historiography.

1437 **Annual Bibliography of British and Irish History.**
Edited by G. R. Elton. Brighton, England: Harvester; Atlantic Highlands, New Jersey: Humanities, 1975-. annual.
Published for the Royal Historical Society (London), this annual bibliography lists recent works published on Great Britain, followed by those on Ireland. The section devoted to Ireland is divided by period; both books and articles are listed without annotation. Perusal of these sections will show trends in recent scholarship and current academic interest. Prior to this series, some Irish research had been noted in *Writings on British history*, published by the Royal Historical Society in several volumes. The basic volume of *Writings* covered AD 450-1914, The period 1901-1933 is covered in a 7 volume reprint (London: Cape, 1968-1970). Other volumes of *Writings on British History*, edited by Alexander T.

Milne, have concerned 1934-39; 1937-53, and 1940-45, and are also published by Cape. A shorter, more specific bibliography 'Writings in Irish History', is published each year in the Autumn issue of *Irish Historical Studies* (1938-.).

1438 **Manuscript sources for the history of Irish civilization.**
Edited by Richard J. Hayes. Boston, Massachusetts: G. K. Hall, 1965. 11 vols.

This set provides a union list and index to manuscripts regarding Ireland and the Irish. The manuscripts themselves are located in nearly 700 libraries and archives distributed among 30 nations. Records of them appear on some 300,000 cards, and these are arranged by person, institution, location, subject and date. The manuscripts listed here range from the 5th through to the 20th centuries, and private collections are also noted. A three volume supplement was published in 1979, edited by Alf Mac Lochlainn.

1439 **Sources for the history of Irish civilization: articles in Irish periodicals.**
Richard J. Hayes. Boston, Massachusetts: G. K. Hall, 1970. 9 vols.

A list is provided of articles that have appeared in Irish periodicals between 1800 and 1969. There are some 280,000 citations to articles and reviews in 120 journals. Volumes one to five present a listing by personal name; volumes six to eight contain a subject index; and volume nine consists of a list arranged by place and date of publication.

1440 **Early Christian Ireland: introduction to the sources.**
Kathleen Hughes. Ithaca, New York: Cornell University Press, 1972. 320p. (Sources of History Series).

This study is useful for identifying the major extant sources of Irish history from prehistoric times to 1100. Each type of evidence is evaluated with regard to its importance and reliability. Ancient laws, archaeological finds, historical annals, art, and the various forms of Irish writing are included. This is an important work for graduate research and is written in the style of an essay rather than a bibliography.

1441 **Irish history, a select bibliography.**
Edith M. Johnston. London: Historical Association, 1972. Rev. ed. 76p. (Helps for Students of History Series, no. 73).

A good yet concise bibliography, this serves as a guide to reference and general works grouped by subject, including politics, economics, law, medicine, churches, education, local areas, and geography. Virtually all periods of history are covered: prehistoric Ireland, the Christian, mediaeval and Reformation eras, the famine, Ireland under partition, and the decades from 1922 to 1970. In identifying the major historical works some short comments are occasionally offered.

1442 **The sources for the early history of Ireland: ecclesiastical.**
James Francis Kenny. New York: Columbia University Press,
1929. 807p.
An extensive bibliography with references to a large number of Irish manuscripts
in Britain and on the continent relating to the ancient Church.

1443 **Irish historiography, 1970-1979.**
Edited by J. J. Lee. Cork: Cork University Press, 1984. 238p.
A survey is made of research completed from 1970 to 1979, in this short volume
compiled for the Irish Committee of Historical Sciences. The Committee's own
Bulletin of the Irish Committee of Historical Sciences (1939-.) regularly reports on
new historical studies.

1444 **Catalogue of Irish manuscripts in the British Museum.**
Standish Hayes O'Grady, Robin Flower. London; Oxford:
Trustees of the British Museum, 1926-1953. 3 vols.
Incorporated in the holdings of the British Library (and formerly the British
Museum) is one of the great collections of Irish manuscripts, although they are
located among different holdings, files, and gifts and purchases of rare materials.
This important and scholarly guide to the collection presents the historical context
and a description of the manuscripts and the scribes. Volume three contains
facsimiles. John MacKechnie has compiled a *Catalogue of Gaelic manuscripts in
selected libraries in Great Britain and Ireland* (Boston, Massachusetts: G. K. Hall,
1973. 2 vols.). The Bodleian Library in Oxford maintains Irish manuscripts among
its holdings, and some are listed in its catalogues of slides and filmstrips. In
Dublin the Royal Irish Academy has a collection of Irish manuscripts of
paramount importance. Its *Catalogue of Irish manuscripts* has been published in
28 parts. A *Catalogue of Irish manuscripts in the National Library of Ireland* has
been compiled by Nessa Ni Sheaghdha and issued in 8 fascicles (Dublin: Institute
of Advanced Studies, 1967-1983).

1445 **Sources of Irish local history.**
Thomas P. O'Neill. Dublin: Library Association of Ireland,
1958. 38p.
Several short articles are reprinted, and these offer suggestions for tracing
historical records, maps and documents, and applying them to the study of local
history. Also pertinent to local history are two lists: *A bibliography of British and
Irish municipal history* edited by Geoffrey Martin and Sylvia MacIntyre
(Leicester, England: Leicester University Press, 1972); and Arthur Lee Humphries' *A handbook to county bibliography, being a bibliography of bibliographies
relating to the counties and towns of Great Britain and Ireland* (London: Dawsons,
1917. Reprinted, 1974. 501p.).

Literature

1446   **Bibliography of Irish philology and of printed Irish literature.**
Richard Irvine Best.   New York: Johnson Reprint, 1969. 2 vols.
An important reference source in the study of the Irish language, first published in Dublin in 1913. Many publications in or about the Irish language are listed, including a number of volumes in scholarly series. This list is especially good regarding publications in the 19th century, which was a period that revived interest in native literature, its preservation and analysis. Cited are journals, books, poetry, publications of the Irish Text Society, the Royal Irish Academy, and the Ossianic Society. Best later compiled a *Bibliography of Irish philology and manuscript literature, publications 1913-1914* (Dublin: Dublin Institute of Advanced Studies, 1942. Reprinted, 1969. 254p.).

1447   **Mediaeval Celtic literature: a select bibliography.**
Rachel Bromwich.   Toronto: University of Toronto Press, 1974.
201p.
An annotated list of works published about Celtic and Irish literature of the mediaeval period up to 1450. Most of the works cited have been published since 1940, and include bibliographies, collected editions, catalogues to manuscripts, books in the Irish language, dictionaries and grammars. Also identified are myths, cycles, sagas and poetry of the larger Celtic world. Other useful sources on Celtic literature include Wilfred Bonser's *Anglo-Saxon and Celtic bibliography, 450-1078* (Folcroft, Pennsylvania: Folcroft, 1957. 2 vols.) and the important *Bibliotheca Celtica: a register of publications relating to Wales and the Celtish people and language* (Aberystwyth, Wales: National Library of Wales, 1909-. annual), which is the most extensive listing of current research in the Celtic languages, including Irish.

1448   **A guide to books on Ireland.**
Stephen James Brown.   New York: Lemma, 1977. Reprint.
372p.
Only this volume was issued of a projected series, and that in 1912. It covers prose literature, poetry, music and plays. Some critical studies are listed and comments are provided on entries. The work requires updating. Brown has also compiled *Ireland in fiction: a guide to Irish novels, tales, romances, and folklore* (Dublin: Irish Academic; New York: Burt Franklin, 1969. Reprint of 1916 edition. 382p.). In this second book, descriptive comments are provided on major works of fiction, arranged alphabetically by author.

1449 **Recent research in Anglo-Irish writers.**
Richard J. Finneran. New York: Modern Language Association of America, 1983. 361p.
This list provides information on critical studies and research completed through 1980. The volume supplements Finneran's *Anglo-Irish literature: a review of research* (New York: Modern Language Association, 1976. 596p.). That work contains bibliographic essays on Irish literature, leading 19th-century Anglo-Irish writers and dramatists. Each essay reviews the work of an author, covering their manuscripts, archival holdings, biography, bibliography, and works of criticism. Both the volumes are important for university level research.

1450 **A select bibliography for the study of Anglo-Irish literature and its backgrounds: an Irish studies handbook.**
Maurice Harmon. Dublin: Wolfhound Press, 1977. Reprinted 1980. 187p.
Suggests some works on Anglo-Irish literature and its historical background. Although highly selective, this is a useful guide, which briefly covers the more important reference works, general books on the different periods of the literature, and works on topography, mythology, folklore, language, Gaelic literature, the arts, and archaeology that may provide further information on the roots and direction of the literature. Brief notes are included for some of the entries. Other works by Harmon include *Modern Irish literature, 1800-1967: a readers guide* (Dublin, 1967), which provides a chronological listing of works arranged by subject, and with Roger McHugh, *A short history of Anglo-Irish literature from earliest times to the present day* (q.v.).

1451 **A bibliography of modern Irish and Anglo-Irish literature.**
Frank L. Kershowski, C. W. Spinks, Laird Loomis. San Antonio, Texas: Trinity University Press, 1976. 157p.
A checklist is given of the works of sixty Irish authors with emphasis on the first half of the 20th century.

1452 **Bernard Shaw: a bibliography.**
Dan H. Laurence. Oxford: Clarendon Press, 1983. 1,058p.
An exhaustive listing of Shaw's writings, including his journalism, plays, novels, and essays, and the hundreds of works about him.

1453 **Irish literature, 1800-1875: a guide to information sources.**
Brian McKenna. Detroit, Michigan: Gale, 1978. (World Literature in English, Information Guide no. 13). 388p.
Intended for students, this is a guide to the major sources on the Irish writers who were popular in the 19th century, a period which saw the development of trends culminating in the Irish literary revival.

1454 **J. M. Synge: a bibliography of criticism.**
E. H. Mikhail. Totowa, New Jersey: Rowman & Littlefield, 1975. 214p.

A comprehensive listing of 2,500 citations to criticism about Synge. Another bibliography, edited by Paul M. Levitt, is *J. M. Synge: a bibliography of published criticism* (Dublin: Irish University Press, 1974. 216p.).

1455 **Oscar Wilde: an annotated bibliography of criticism.**
E. H. Mikhail. Totowa, New Jersey: Rowman & Littlefield, 1978. 249p.

Full annotations are provided to some 3,500 citations covering books, journals, reviews, dissertations and other materials relating to Wilde.

1456 **An annotated bibliography of modern Anglo-Irish drama.**
E. H. Mikhail. Troy, New York: Whitson Publishing, 1981. 306p.

Bibliographic coverage is provided on Anglo-Irish drama, with 1,775 publications cited from 1899 to 1977. Although not divided by subject the bibliography has a good subject index. Included are books, periodicals, dissertations, and library collections. The index directs the reader to material on specific Irish theatres, drama companies, and other topics. Primary arrangement is by author, and annotations are very short. This entirely replaces a previous edition from the University of Washington Press.

1457 **Sean O'Casey and his critics: an annotated bibliography, 1916-1982.**
E. H. Mikhail. Metuchen, New Jersey: Scarecrow, 1982. 362p.

A major bibliography on O'Casey listing thousands of works of criticism, editions of O'Casey's work, and reviews, with descriptive annotations. This definitive list can be updated by use of the *O'Casey Annual* (q.v.). Mikhail has grouped the annotations according to reference works, writings about O'Casey, periodicals, reviews of productions, autobiographies, films, dissertations, and recordings.

1458 **A chronological account of nearly four hundred Irish writers.**
Edward O'Reilly. Dublin: Irish Academic Press, 1979. 256p.

First published in 1820 by the Iberno-Celtic Society, this volume provides a list of works by Irish authors from the earliest times up to 1750. While no longer considered an entirely accurate chronology or account, the list does provide many leads and historical information on forgotten works of past centuries.

1459 **A bibliography of the writings of W. B. Yeats.**
Allan Wade. London: Oxford University Press, 1968. 3rd rev.
ed. 514p.

A comprehensive listing of Yeats' works in their various editions. A fourth
edition of the volume was in preparation during 1985.

Index

The index is a single alphabetical sequence of authors (personal and corporate), titles of publications and subjects. Index entries refer both to the main items and to other works mentioned in the notes to each item. Title entries are in italics. Numeration refers to the items as numbered.

320

Annals 194, 272-274, 1092, 1097
  bibliographies 1440
*Annals of the Kingdom of Ireland, by
  the four masters, from the earliest
  period to the year 1616* 195, 273
*Annotated bibliography of modern
  Anglo-Irish drama* 1456
Annotated Oscar Wilde 1035
Annotations to Finnegans wake 985
*Annual Bibliography of British and
  Irish History* 1437
Another life 110
Another life again 110
Anthology of Irish literature 936
Anthropology 109, 497, 1424
Antiquities 63, 75, 83, 198, 215, 234,
  915
  Ossory 96
  Waterford 107
Antiquities of the county of Kerry 108
Antiquities of Ireland 234
Antiquities of the Irish countryside 215
Applied art 1105, 1135
Approaches to Ulysses, ten essays 988
Aran Islands 147, 149, 151, 153,
  155-156
  climate 156
  crafts 156
  folklore 147, 156
  geography 149, 153
  geology 156
  history 149, 151, 153
  in the cinema 147
  in literature 147, 155
  legends 156
  life and customs 149, 151, 153, 155
  photographs 151, 153, 155-156
  settlements 149, 153
  social conditions 153
  trade 156
  travel guides 155
Aran Islands 151, 155
Aran: islands of legend 149
Aran Islands: a personal journey 153
Arbutus trees 169
Archaeology and archaeological sites
  161, 188, 192, 201-216, 245, 260,
  269, 600, 602, 841-842, 1108, 1241
  artifacts 192, 201, 204, 208, 210
  bibliographies 1440, 1450
  Britain 209, 215
  Celtic 198-199, 207, 209, 249, 264

Cork 203
  diocese of Ossory 96
  Dowth 204
  Dublin 211, 281
  early Christian 207, 260
  earthworks 215
  forts 215
  guides 205, 216
  Kerry 93, 203
  Knowth 204, 214
  Limerick 203
  maps 203, 211
  Loch Gur excavations 60
  mediaeval 207, 210
  midlands 104
  Monasterboice 1127
  monuments 206
  Norman 207
  New Grange 202, 204, 213-214
  passage graves 208
  periodicals 1342, 1395
  photographs 209, 212
  round towers 254
  Tipperary 105, 203
  tombs 203-204, 208, 213-215
  Viking Age 201, 207, 281
  Wood Quay 201, 211, 281
Archaeology of Ireland 207, 210
*Archaeology of late Celtic Britain and
  Ireland, c.400-1200 A.D.* 209
Archer, M. 1134
Archibald, D. 1040
*Architectural conservation, an Irish
  viewpoint* 850, 1191
Architectural Heritage 1191
Architecture 75, 865, 1100-1101, 1108,
  1120, 1191-1213, 1245
  Bank of Ireland 750
  Bray 1191
  bungalows 1211
  Carlow 1191
  castles 1196-1197, 1199-1200, 1202,
    1204, 1206, 1210
  Celtic 209
  churches 592, 1197, 1209
  conservation 850, 1191
  cottages 1197, 1199
  country houses 1192, 1195, 1201
  Dublin 116, 122-123, 128, 132, 133,
    1212
  Dublin, Georgian 122, 127, 133,
    1193, 1201, 1203, 1207

Architecture *contd.*
  Dublin, mediaeval 122
  early Christian 1196-1197, 1209
  ecclesiastical 592, 1203
  estates 1195, 1197, 1199, 1202, 1204
  farmhouses 1197, 1199
  forts 1197, 1200
  Gothic 1196, 1209
  history 96, 669, 1196-1197,
     1199-1207, 1209-1210, 1212
  houses 1195, 1199, 1201-1204, 1208,
     1211
  Irish-Canadian 541
  Kerry 93
  Kinsale 1191
  mediaeval 1197, 1209
  monasteries 603, 1209
  palaces 1199, 1202, 1204
  periodicals 1341, 1365, 1375, 1380
  photographs 1197-1198, 1203
  prehistoric period 210
  Romanesque 1196, 1209
  round towers 254
  St. Patrick's cathedral 1205
  shops 1197
  towers 1197, 1200
  town houses 1197, 1204
  towns 1213
  Trinity College Dublin 906
  Tullomore 1191
  vernacular 1198
Architecture in Ireland 1196, 1365
Architecture of Ireland 1213
*Architecture of Ireland, from the
     earliest times to 1880* 1197
Archives 1438
Areas of scientific interest in Ireland 871
Arensburg, C. M. 92, 630
Arklow, Battle of 236
Armagh 62, 68
Armstrong, D. M. 350
Arnold, B. 671, 1102-1103
Around Ireland 76
Art 83, 376, 1101, 1109, 1112, 1117,
     1201, 1335
  ancient 192, 282-283, 1116-1130,
     1135
  applied 1105, 1135
  bibliographies 1411, 1440
  Bronze Age 1117
  Celtic 191, 209, 249, 280, 284, 1102,
     1122, 1130-1131, 1137, 1141

Celtic revival 1107, 1111, 1137
crosses of Kells 283
drawing 1113
early Christian 260, 282, 1116-1118,
     1120, 1123, 1125, 1128, 1130
enamels 1120
Gothic 1117, 1121
graphic 1107, 1111
history 260, 280, 1102, 1104-1106,
     1108, 1116-1130, 1135
landscape movement 1102
manuscript illumination 1117-1120, 1129
megalithic 189, 1117, 1130
modern movement 1102
painting 26, 1101, 1103-1105, 1108,
     1110, 1113-1115, 1161
periodicals 1344, 1380
prehistoric 188-189, 192, 194, 202,
     210, 213, 1128
religious 1137
Romanesque 1117-1118, 1125, 1128
Romantic movement 1102
sculpture 604, 1101, 1105-1106,
     1116, 1118, 1120-1121
stained glass 1105, 1107
stone carving 1117, 1135, 1142
Viking 1118, 1125, 1128
Art galleries 1100, 1295, 1298
  commercial 1295
  directories 1295
  National Gallery 1110, 1114, 1296
  Northern Ireland 1298, 1300
  public 1295
Art galleries of Britain and Ireland 1295
Art of the amateur 1176
Art of Seamus Heaney 1074
*Arthur Frommer's guide to Dublin and
     Ireland* 73
Arthur Griffith 386
*Arthur Griffith and the
     advanced-nationalist press in
     Ireland* 1320
*Arthur Griffith and non-violent Sinn
     Fein* 386
Arthur, P. 443
Artifacts 104, 1100
  prehistoric 192, 201, 204, 208, 210
Artists 501, 1100, 1112, 1115
  biographies 1104, 1112, 1115
  dictionaries 1109, 1112
Arts 4, 8, 13, 22-24, 433, 914, 1111,
     1316, 1324, 1405

322

British Museum
  Irish manuscripts, 593, 1444
British policy and the Irish administration, 1920-22 401
British policy towards Ireland: 1921 to 1941 396
Broadcasting 641, 1315, 1331-1332
  censorship 1316
  leading figures 1331
  radio 1315
  television 1333
Brodie, M. 1266
Brody, H. 95, 134
Broehl, W. G. 506
Bromwich R. 1447
Brophy, J. D. 919
Brothers of the Christian Schools 614
Brown, M. 920
Brown, N. 1269
Brown, P. 1119, 1292
Brown, S. J. 1317, 1448
Brown, T. 376, 925
Brown, T. N. 507
Browne, V. 674
Browning, Robert 1033
Bryant, B. 73
Bryant, S. 698
Brye, D. L. 1413
Brynn, E. 304, 625
Budgen, F. 973
Build 1375
Building
  prehistoric 194
  periodicals 1375
  statistics 1375
Buildings of Irish towns, a treasury of everyday architecture 1213
Buitléar, E. de 49
Bulletin of the Irish Committee of Historical Sciences 1443
Bungalows 1211
Bunting's ancient music of Ireland 1168
Buntús Cainte, a first step in spoken Irish 588
Burgess, A. 1062
Burke 360
Burke, Edmund 356-365, 370, 968
  biographies 358-359, 361-363, 365
Burke, M. 1311
Burke's guide to country houses 1192
Burke's Irish family records 561
Burl, A. 190

Burns, M. 666
Burns, P. 616
Burrell, Augustine 414
Burren, 159
  flora 159
  photographs 159
Burren 159
Bus service 797, 800, 802
Bushrui, S. B. 1026
Business 746, 756, 763-764, 1324, 1393
  EEC policy 730
  law 712-714, 762
  periodicals 1353, 1367, 1373, 1376, 1391
  statistics 834
Business and Finance 1367, 1375
Business law 712
Butler, H. 921
Butler, P. 1295
Butlin, R. A. 852
Byrne, F. J. 408
Byrne, L. 798

C

Cabot, D. 872
Caerwyn Williams, J. E. 577
Cahalan, J. 922
Cahill, K. 508
Cahill, S. 923
Cahill, T. 923
Cahoon, H. 987
Cairnduff, M. 447
Calendar customs 1242
Callanan, J. J. 1086
Cambridge historical encyclopedia of Great Britain and Ireland 1398
Campbell Fraser, A. 349
Canada
  architecture 541
  immigrant farming in 541
  Irish emigration to 521-522, 530, 542, 1413
  Irish in 504, 540-541
  Irish music in 1423
  settlements 541
Canadian Association of Irish Studies 638
Canals 799
Canals of the south of Ireland 799
Canavan, F. 360

Children 130, 147, 150
  child care facilities 646, 661, 663
  social history, 653
Children's books
  bibliographies 1414
Christian art in ancient Ireland, selected objects illustrated and described 1123
Christian Brothers 585, 614
Christianity 194, 197, 274
  early Christian period 207, 210, 260, 282, 1130, 1440, 1442
  history 600
Christus Rex 1394
Christy Moore songbook 1149
Christy O'Connor, an autobiography as told to John Redmond 1274
Chronicles 272, 292, 1094
Chronological account of nearly four hundred Irish writers 1458
Chronologies 19, 29, 91, 233, 243-244, 273, 1150, 1328
  arts 1101
  Beckett, Samuel 963
  Berkeley, major works 348
  Celts 198
  de Valera, Eamon 471
  economic events 1982-83 760
  feast days 601
  Goldsmith, Oliver 968
  Irish-Americans 528
  war of independence 449
  Yeats, William Butler 1049-1050
Chubb, B. 675, 676, 692, 744
Church and state, essays in political philosophy 615
Church and state in modern Ireland, 1923-79 621
Church and state in Tudor Ireland: a history of penal laws against the Irish Catholics, 1534-1603 290, 346, 597
Church and the two nations in medieval Ireland 606
Church history 592, 607, 629
Church in early Irish society 264
Church in medieval Ireland 231
Church now 616
Church of Ireland
  19th century 622, 625
  19th-20th centuries 628, 635
  decline 622, 628

disestablishment 612, 624, 629, 905
  history 628-629
  Kildare Place 905
Church of Ireland: ecclesiastical reform and revolution, 1800-1885 622
Church of Ireland, 1869-1969 628
Church of Ireland in the age of Catholic emancipation 625
Church, state, and the control of schooling in Ireland, 1900-1944 890
Church-state relations 346, 413, 615, 621
  16th century 597
  19th century 320
  and education 890
Churches 62, 1197, 1209
  photographs 1209
  St Patrick's Cathedral 1205, 1306
Churches and abbeys of Ireland 592
Churchill, Winston 115
Cinema 1189-1190
  periodicals 1336
  portrayal of the Aran Islands 147
Cinema and Ireland, from 1896 1189
Cirker, B. 1119
Cities *see* Towns and cities
Civil rights 693-695, 697, 704, 709, 711
Civil service 675, 720, 723, 726-727
Civil war 246, 255, 318, 344, 369, 372, 383-384, 392-393, 400, 410, 420, 429-430, 470, 513, 515, 540, 1048, 1319
  photographs 410
Clan na Gael 507
Clancy, P. 632
Clapham, A. R. 166
Clare 100
  demography 95
  economy 95
  marriage 95
  rural industrialization 781
  rural life 92, 95
  social conditions 95
  travel guides 90
  war of independence 375
Clark, D. 509-510
Clark, R. 712
Clark, S. 305-306
Clarke, Austin 935, 942, 958, 1073, 1077, 1079, 1085
Clarke, D. 615, 914

Guide to Irish bibliographic material: a bibliography of Irish bibliographies and sources of information 1417
Guide to Irish birds 181
Guide to Irish manufacturers 1404
Guide to the national monuments in the Republic of Ireland 206
Guide to political parties in Ireland 686
Guide to the prose fiction of W. B. Yeats 1055
Guide to schools in Ireland 878
Guide to Sean O'Casey's plays: from the plough to the stars 997
Guide to study in Ireland for foreigners 878
Guides
  archaeological sites 205, 216
  cities 858
  education 878, 881, 892
  literary 155, 923, 933
Guillet, E. C. 530
Guinness 1265
Guinness 1265
Guinness, D. 2101-1203
Guilliver's travels 1020-1021
Gur cakes and coal blocks 126
Gwynn, D. 608
Gwynn, D. R. 390, 438, 454
Gwynn, S. 965

H

Hadden, T. 432
Haigh, C. 1398
Hail and farewell 927
Hajducki, S. M. 807
Hall, F. G. 750
Hall, J. 1047
Hallisey, T. 42
Hamlin, A. 264
Hammond, D. 1156
Hand, G. J. 439
Handbook for single women in Ireland 639
Handbook of Celtic ornament 1141
Handbook of the geology of Ireland 42
Handbook of Irish case law 708
Handbook of Irish folklore 1235

Handbook on Irish genealogy 555
Handbook on Irish genealogy: how to trace your ancestors and relatives in Ireland 558
Handbook to county bibliography, being a bibliography of bibliographies relating to the counties and towns of Great Britain and Ireland 1445
Handbooks
  for women 639, 646
Handel, George Frederick 115
Handicapped, the
  social services 662
Handlin, O. 531
Hanly, J. 291
Hanna Sheehy-Skeffington, Irish feminist 640
Hannon, D. 648
Harbison, P. 206-207, 1108
Hardiman, J. 1154
Harkness, D. 856
Harlequin Sheridan, the man and the legends 1014
Harmon, M. 929, 937, 947, 1077, 1450
Harp that once–; a chronicle of the life of Thomas Moore 1156
Harper, G. M. 1044
Harps 1170
Harpstrings and confessions: an anthropological study of politics in rural Ireland 673
Harris, B. 1164
Harry Clarke: his graphic art 1107
Hart, C. 980
Hart-Davis, R. 1034
Hartmut-Olbricht, K. 1204
Harvard encyclopedia of American ethnic groups 551
Has Ireland a population problem? 487
Haughey, Charles J. 679, 691
Haughton, J. P. 28, 57
Hawkins, R. A. 324
Hawthorne trees 169
Hayes, R. J. 1438-1439
Hayes-McCoy, G. A. 235-236
Hayman, D. 980
Hayton, D. 346
Health 842
  bibliographies 1432-1433
  periodicals 1387, 1396

and literature 932
Anglicanism 627
Anglo–Irish 217, 495
Anglo–Irish relations 331, 385, 396,
    401, 405, 414, 737
Anglo–Irish Treaty (1921) 323, 383,
    394, 396, 400, 423, 438-439, 470,
    495, 737
Aran Islands 149, 151, 153, 156
archaeology 96, 254, 260
architecture 96, 1196-1197,
    1199-1207, 1209-1210, 1212
art 260, 280, 1102, 1104-1106, 1108,
    1116-1130, 1135
arts 228, 251, 260, 280
atlases 56
aviation 798
banking 742, 750, 753
bibliographies 231, 244, 1381, 1411,
    1414, 1417, 1425, 1427, 1434-1445
boxing 1285
British policy towards Ireland 219,
    223, 232, 304, 324, 329, 385, 401
canals 799
Catholic Church 320, 594-595, 597,
    607-614, 621, 625
Catholic emancipation 315, 608, 625
Celtic churches 600
Celts 191, 193, 196-199, 209, 219,
    246, 249, 284, 939
censorship 1309
children 653
Christianity 600
church 592, 607
Church of Ireland 622, 628-629
civil war 246, 255, 318, 344, 369,
    372, 383-384, 392-393, 400, 410,
    420, 429-430, 470, 1048, 1319,
    1405
clergy 250, 309, 368, 593, 613
colleges 899
commerce 239
communism 688
constitutional 692
cooperatives 795
Cork 94, 98, 102, 856
cultural 228, 242-243, 245, 251, 253,
    256, 260, 268, 280, 284-285, 310,
    323-324, 346, 485
cultural, of mountain ranges 53
culture, 12th century 279
culture, 16th century 290

culture, 19th century 327, 343
culture, Celtic 196, 200
culture, early Christain 260
culture, prehistoric period 188, 208
culture, Viking Age 281
design 1135
dictionaries 228, 265
documents 98, 220, 223, 226, 233,
    255, 257, 265, 273, 278, 292, 315,
    369, 389, 409, 462, 472, 1363
Dublin 111-112, 116-119, 122, 125,
    132, 398
Dublin, 18th century 127-128, 133
Dublin, 19th century 124, 303
Dublin county 112
Dublin, Viking 201, 281
early Christian period 207, 210, 260,
    282, 1440, 1442
Easter Rising 119, 233, 318, 331,
    334, 367, 369, 375, 379-380, 398,
    406-407, 412, 417, 424-426, 429,
    434, 457, 460, 462, 464, 467,
    469-470, 485, 636, 998, 1048,
    1058, 1160, 1315, 1318-1319
ecclesiastical 96, 271, 276, 291, 309,
    598
economic 98, 132, 228, 239-240, 243,
    245, 268, 276, 295, 300-301, 323,
    332, 413, 745, 754-755, 757
economic, 18th century 321
economic, 18th–20th centuries 753, 755
economic, 19th century 305,
    311-312, 322, 324
education 68, 232, 260, 262, 280,
    346, 404, 413, 877, 882-890, 893,
    898-906
elections 243
Elizabethan 285, 289, 297-298
emigration 311, 347, 525, 551
emigration to Australia 535
emigration to Canada 521-522, 530,
    542, 1318
emigration to United States 316,
    521-522, 524, 530, 542, 545
encyclopaedias 1398
environmental 844
estates 792
European Economic Community –
    EEC 730
famine 220, 246, 306, 308-310, 316,
    332, 347, 405, 481, 524-525, 1160,
    1318-1319, 1327

History contd.
whiskey 651
White Boys 62
wildlife 186
women 277, 636-637, 641
women's suffrage movement 644
World War I 385, 399, 454
World War II 387, 396, 404, 413, 421
Young Ireland 323, 338, 340, 369
York, Viking 281
History and antiquities of the diocese of Ossory 96
History of aviation in Ireland 798
History of the Church of Ireland from the earliest times to the present day 629
History of the city of Dublin 117
History of the county of Dublin, the people, parishes and antiquities from the earliest times to the close of the eighteenth century 112
History of the county of Mayo to the close of the sixteenth century 101
History of Ireland 227, 241
History of Ireland from the earliest period to the English invasion 195
History of Ireland in the eighteenth century 321
History of Irish Catholicism 594
History of Irish education, a study of conflicting loyalties 887
History of Irish flags from earliest times 235
History of Irish music 1152
History of the Irish newspaper, 1685-1760 1328
History of Irish periodical literature from the end of the 17th to the middle of the 19th century 1326
History of the Irish Post Office 1282
History of Irish steel 777
History of literacy and libraries in Ireland: the long traced pedigree 1302
History of medicine in Ireland 665
History of medieval Ireland 276
History of medieval Ireland from 1086-1513 259
History of partition (1912-1925) 438
History of the Presbyterian Church in Ireland 626

History of the Sinn Fein movement and the Irish rebellion of 1916 391
History, topography, and antiquities of the county and city of Waterford, with an account of the present state of the peasantry of that part of the South of Ireland 107
History and topography of Dublin City and County 124
History and topography of Ireland (topographia Hiberniae) 258
Hoagland, K. 1078
Hoctor, D. 790
Hofer, E. 131
Hogan, I. M. 1155
Hogan, R. 918, 938, 1175-1177
Hogan, R. G. 992
Hogan, S. 777
Hogg L. 639
Holiday cruising in Ireland, a guide to inland waterways 87
Holinshed, Raphael 292
Holinshed's Irish chronicle: the historie of Irelande from the first inhabitation thereof, unto the yeare 1509 292
Holland, C. H. 44
Holland, J. 441
Holland, S. 879
Holohan, P. 222
Holroyd, M. 1003
Holt, E. 392
Holy wells 599
Holy wells of Ireland 599
Home before night 1180
Home ownership 1208
Homosexuals 501
Hone, J. 349, 927, 1048
Hood, A. B. E. 263
Hopkins, R. 968
Hopkinson, M. 393
Hoppen, K. T. 317
Horace Plunkett 795
Horgan, P. 707
Horner, A. A. 791
Horse in Ireland 1219
Horse-racing 1271, 1277, 1293-1294
history 1293
Horses 1269, 1271, 1278, 1281, 1293-1294
breeding 1278

356

J

Jackson, J. A. 533
Jackson, K. 1093
Jackson, V. 1205
Jacobs, J. 1227
James I 290
James Connolly 465
James Connolly, a biography 468
James Connolly: selected writings 466
*James Connolly and the United States:
    the road to the 1916 Irish rebellion*
    469
James Gandon: Vitruvius Hibernicus
    1212
James Joyce 974, 978, 984, 986
James Joyce: the critical heritage 976
James Joyce: a guide to research 987
James Joyce letters 977
James Joyce and the making of Ulysses
    973
James Joyce songbook 1147
*James Joyce's Odyssey: a guide to the
    Dublin of Ulysses* 975
James Joyce's Ulysses, critical essays
    980
*James Joyce's Ulysses; a facsimile of
    the manuscript* 981
*James Larkin, Irish labour leader,
    1876-1947* 395
James Stephens: a critical study 950
Janey Mack, me shirt is black 126
Jeffares, A. N. 940, 1049-1052
Jeffrey, D. W. 138
Jennett, S. 100
Jessup, T. E. 352
Jesuit schools 886
Jewelry 1135
Jews 500
    bibliography 500
    demography 500
    documents 500
    history 500
Jews of Ireland 500
Jimmy Ingle story 1272
J. M. Synge 1024
J. M. Synge: a bibliography of criticism
    1454
*J. M. Synge: a bibliography of
    published criticism* 1454
J. M. Synge, 1871-1909 1027
J. M. Synge and his world 1030

J. M. Synge and the western mind 1032
J. M. Synge's guide to the Aran Islands
    155
Johansson, E. 1431
John, Augustus 1103
*John Millington Synge and the Irish
    theatre* 1025
Johnson, D. N. 1206
Johnson, J. E. 534
Johnson, N. 120
Johnson, Dr. Samuel 968
Johnson, P. 240
Johnston, Denis 1183
Johnston, Dillon 1079
Johnston, E. M. 1441
Johnston, G. 350
Johnston, J. 351
Jonathan Swift 1020-1021
Jonathan Swift: a critical anthology
    1016
Jonathan Swift: a critical biography
    1018
Jonathan Swift: a critical introduction
    1016
*Jonathan Swift, a hypocrite reversed: a
    critical biography* 1019
Jones, F. 391
Jones, H. M. 1156
*Journal of the American Irish
    Historical Society* 543
*Journal of the Institute of Bankers in
    Ireland* 1374
Journal of Irish Literature 1352
Journal of the School of Irish Learning
    1371
Journal of Thomas Moore 1156
Journalism 950
Journals 957
*Journey to heartbreak, the crucible
    years of Bernard Shaw, 1914-1918*
    1008
Joyce annotated 979
Joyce, James 115, 121, 129, 930, 942,
    946, 950-951, 971-990, 994, 1063,
    1066, 1069, 1147, 1335, 1341, 1350
    and Belvedere College 886
    and Dublin 121, 971
    bibliographies 972, 987
    biographies 972, 974, 978, 984, 986
    letters 972, 977-978
    photographs 978
Joyce, Joe 679

Kinsella, S. 1257
Kinsella, Thomas 508, 919, 926, 932,
    1073, 1077, 1079, 1098, 1228
Kirby, P. 618
Kirwan, F. 835
Kissane, N. 1304
Knight of Glin (Desmond FitzGerald)
    75, 127, 1194, 1280
Knowland, A. S. 1049, 1054
Knowles, R. 1109
Knowth 204, 214
Knox, H. T. 101
Kohfeldt, M. L. 943
Koslow, J. 993
Kosok, H. 944
Kramnick, I. 359
Krause, D. 994
Kroup, B. 1221

L

Labour 413, 746, 754, 794, 813, 818
    bibliographies 1432-1433
    cooperatives 795
    history 119, 395, 466, 795, 820-826
    Irish-Americans 517
    law 706
    periodicals 1349
Labour conditions 510, 818, 822
Labour disputes 467
Labour force 760, 813, 818
Labour organization 821, 823, 825
Labour Party 685
Labour Party (British) 432
Labour relations 818, 827-831
    collective bargaining 830
    directories 828
    influence of media 830
    law 712, 829
    Northern Ireland 830
    reform 831
    worker participation 830-831
Labour and the Royal 126
Labour history 119, 395, 466, 469,
    820-826
Labour in Ireland 822
Labour in Irish history 466
Labour movement
    women's role 644
Lace making 1133, 1135, 1138-1139,
    1142

    history 1138
    Limerick 1138
    photographs 1133
Ladies' Land League 647
*Lady Gregory: the woman behind the
    Irish renaissance* 943
Laffan, M. 394
Laing, L. 209
Lakes 873
Lalor, B. 122
Lambert, J. 1298
Land law 706
*Land and the national question in
    Ireland, 1858-1882* 302
*Land and people of nineteenth century
    Cork: the rural economy and the
    land question* 98
Land of Ireland 19
Land League 302, 312, 334
Land ownership
    19th century 306, 322, 341
    in 19th-century Cork 98
Land policy 755
Land question 312, 341, 344, 481, 1319
    19th century 302, 306, 308
    in 19th-century Cork 98
*Land question and the Irish economy,
    1870-1903* 341
Land use 844-845, 1379
    in 19th-century Cork 98
*Landlord or tenant? a view of Irish
    history* 312
Landscape 7, 10, 22, 28-29, 31, 39-40,
    43-44, 841, 844, 865
    and literature 923, 971
    in literature 959
    Celtic 215
    influence of geological structure 47
    mountains 53
    photographs 21, 109, 1264
    rural 7, 10, 27, 109
*Landscape of Slieve Bloom: natural
    and human heritage* 157
Lane, Hugh 1103
Language *see also* Dictionaries 9, 22,
    57, 1025, 1056, 1335
    and folktales 573
    and society 569
    Anglo-Irish 567
    bibliographies 1414, 1417, 1446,
    1450
    Breton 566

McCarroll, J. 632
McColgan, J. 401
MacColl, R. 456
McCormack, John 1158
  biography 1158
McCormick, D. 140
McCracken, E. 793
McCracken, J. L. 683
MacCunn, J. 360
MacCurtain, M. 231, 241, 295, 641
McCutcheon, W.A. 808
MacDermont, F. 326
McDonagh, Declan 828
MacDonagh, Donagh 1082
MacDonagh, O. 370, 402
McDonald, W. 899
McDowell, R. B. 226, 327-330, 628,
  900
McElligott, T. J. 877, 893
MacEoin, Sean 418
  biographies 418
McFate, P. 950
McGarrity, Joseph 514
*McGarrity papers: revelations of the
  Irish revolutionary movement in
  Ireland and America, 1900-1940*
  514
McGarry, M. 1231
McGilvray, J. 835-836
Mac Giolla Phadraig, B. 585
McGrath, F. 901
Mac Gréil, M. 499
McGuffin, J. 1258
McGuire, E. G. 1260
MacHale, D. 913
McHugh, Roger 947, 1450
McHugh, Roland 985
McHugh, S. 881
MacIntyre, S. 1445
Mackechnie, J. 570, 1444
McKenna, B. 1433, 1453
McKernan, J. 891
Mackey, H. 459
McKitterick, R. 283
Maclaren, J. 582
McLaughlin, M. 1259
Mac Liammóir, Michael 22, 1058, 1181
Mac Lochlainn, A. 1438
McLoone, J. 502
McLoone, M. 1333
MacLoughlin, A. 125, 858
MacLysaght, E. 296, 403, 559, 560

MacMahon, B. 63, 152
McMahon, B. M. 711
McMahon, D. 737
McMahon, J. 1333
McMahon, S. 25, 948-949
MacManus, F. 404
MacManus, S. 242
McNally, K. 141-142
MacNamara, J. 571
McNeill, D. B. 801
MacNeill, Eoin 196, 265, 267, 408, 426
  biographies 408, 426
McNeill, J. T. 600
MacNeill, Maire 1247
Macneill, Morag 582
MacNiocaill, G. 268
McParland, E. 1212
Macpherson, C. B. 360
Mac Reamoinn, S. 1096
McRedmond, L. 1315
McSpiritt, M. 1259
McSweeney, F. M. 907
McSweeny, B. 733
MacThomais, E. 126
Madden, R. 1326
*Made in Ireland: the retail buyers guide
  to Irish consumer products* 1403
Magee, M. 651, 1260
Magee, P. 714
Magic of the Shannon 78
Magill book of Irish politics 674
Magill Magazine 1353
Magnus, P. 361
Magnusson, M. 312
Maguire, E. J. 545
Maguire, J. F. 540
Maguire, Maria 1422
Maguire, Marsha 1422
Maguire, W. A. 792
Maher, M. 619
Mahon, Derek 932, 1079
Mahoney, T. 362
Mahony, E. 1279
Mahr, A. 1123
Making of Ireland 301
*Making of Ireland and its undoing,
  1200-1600* 232
*Making of 1916: studies in the history
  of the rising* 412
*Making of the Roman Catholic Church
  in Ireland, 1850-1860* 320
Malcolm, E. 651

372

Malins, E. 1280
Mallagh, T. 78
Malone, A.E. 1182
Malone, E. J. 1270
Maltby, A. 1432-1433
Maltby, J. 1432
Malton, J. 127
Mammals 158, 175, 183-184, 849
Man and landscape in Ireland 841
Man from Cape Clear 148
Man may fish 1283
Man of Aran 147
Man of no property 718
Management 752, 775-776, 781, 789, 831
  periodicals 1391
  transport service 797, 800
Management 1391
Managers in Ireland 775
Mandle, W. F. 370
Mangan, J. C. 1086
Manners, J. 1139
Manning, M. 687
Mannion, J. 541
Mansergh, N. 331, 384, 405
Manufacturing industry 757, 780
Manuscript illumination 1117-1120, 1129
Manuscript sources for the history of Irish civilization 1438
Manuscripts 258, 272, 1108, 1126, 1129, 1138, 1219, 1363, 1438, 1442, 1444
  bibliographies 1438, 1444
  Book of Kells 1119
  collections 272, 1303, 1434, 1438, 1444
  ecclesiastical 1442
  Gaelic 570, 1097
  Irish Commission 477
  music 1152
  religious 602
Manx language 566
Mapping 44, 915
  history 55, 58
  19th century 54
Maps and atlases 28-30, 35, 40, 54-59, 71, 79, 86-88, 173-174, 252, 562, 842, 854, 866, 872, 1445
  agriculture 312, 791
  archaeological 203, 211
  Boyne Valley 188

climate 32
Dublin 116, 867, 975
Dublin, historical 125, 971
geological 47, 57
historical 55, 109, 200, 231, 243, 258, 287
islands 140
Kerry 93
linguistic 576
literature 933
Midlands 104
mountains 50
North Bull Island 138
Ordnance Survey 44, 54, 59, 203
railways 807
roads 59
rocks 58
Tipperary 105
Marchant, N. 1140
Marcus, D. 1067
Marine sciences 915
Maritime history 238-239, 245, 288, 801, 804
Markale, J. 197
Marketing 763
  statistics 833, 838
Marketing in Ireland 763
Markets 62
Markievicz, Constance de 377, 429, 636-637
  biographies 637
Marreco, A. 429
Marriage 1-2, 277, 488, 491, 632, 654, 754, 1369
  19th century 305, 489
  County Clare 95
  law 632
  prehistoric period 194, 277
Marriage in Ireland 632
Marriage or divorce: the real issue 632
Marsh, Archbishop Narcissus 1306
Marsh's Library 1306
Martin, A. 950-951, 1053
Martin, F. X. 243-244, 258, 406-408, 426
Martin, G. 1445
Martin, Violet ('Martin Ross') 931, 956
Martyn, E. 1173
Martyrs 283, 596, 601
Marxism 368, 466
Mary Lavin: quiet rebel, a study of her short stories 1064
Mason, T. H. 143

periodicals 1389
Mill, John Stuart 755
Miller, A. P. 363
Miller, K. A. 542
Miller, L. 292, 1054, 1282
Miller, W. C. 1425
Millman, L. 103
Milne, A. T. 1437
Milotte, M. 688
Mineral industry 45
Mineral industry of Ireland 45
Minerals 41, 45, 845
Minerals Yearbook 45
Mining 845
Ministry of Industry and Commerce 12
Ministry of Local Government 866
Minorities 495-503, 1335, 1425
   and government 501
   Anglo-Irish 495
   artists 501
   Catholics, Northern Ireland 501
   education 499
   employment 499
   homosexuals 501
   Jews 500
   mentally ill 501
   mobility 499
   poverty 497, 501
   prejudice and tolerance 499, 501,
     553
   Protestants 496, 501-502
   religion 499, 501
   social class 499
   tinkers 109, 497-498, 501, 503
Mirror to Kathleen's face, education in
   independent Ireland, 1922-1960
   884
Missals 272
Missionaries 256, 262, 280, 596, 600
Mister: a Dublin childhood 130
Mitchell, A. 409
Mitchell, G. F. 29, 1124
Mitchelstown 48
Mobility
   minorities 499
Modern Anglo-Irish verse, an
   anthology selected from the works
   of living Irish poets 1076
Modern Ireland, a bibliography on
   politics, planning, research and
   development 1427
Modern Ireland since 1850 344

Modern Irish drama 1176
Modern Irish literature, 1800-1967: a
   readers guide 1450
Modern Irish short stories 1062
Modernization of Irish society 231, 322
Mokyr, J. 332
Mollan, R. C. 909
Molly Maguires 506
Molly Maguires 506
Moloney, W. 459
Monaghan 97
Monasterboice 1127
Monasterboice 1127
Monasterboice and its monuments 1127
Monasteries 492, 603, 1209
   Monasterboice 1127
   photographs 1209
Monasteries of Ireland, an introduction
   603
Monasticism
   history 260, 264, 281-282, 603, 619
Montague, H. P. 601
Montague John Patrick 932, 935, 1073,
   1077, 1079, 1083
Monuments 83, 206
Moody, T. W. 243-244, 333-334, 442
Mooney, R. 662
Moore, Christy 1149
Moore, D. 245
Moore, G. A. 1173
Moore, George 115, 121, 927, 930-931,
   936, 1066, 1069, 1083, 1086, 1103
   autobiography 927
   bibliography 927
   biography 927
Moore, J. S. 783
Moore, T. 930, 1011, 1083, 1086, 1156
   biography 1156
   diaries 1156
   letters 1156
Moore's Irish melodies with
   symphonies and accompaniments
   1156
More Celtic fairy tales 1227
More Irish families 559
Morgan, D. C. 696
Moriarty, C. 160, 181
Morley, J. 363
Morrison, B. 1084
Morrison, G. 410
Morrissey, J. F. 255
Morrissey, T. 902

Mortality
  statistics 332
Morwood, J. 1012
Mosses 158
Most distressful country 318
Motif-index of early Irish literature
  1215
Motif-index of folk literature: a
  classification of narrative elements
  in folktales 1215
Motor cars
  periodicals 1354
Motor industry 783
Motor makers in Ireland 783
Motoring Life 1354
Mott, G. 20, 592
Mountain year: life on the slopes of
  Slieve Gullion 52
Mountains 50, 52-53, 868
  cultural history 53
  geology 53
  landscape 53
  legends 53
  Loughcrew 189
  maps 50
  photographs 50, 53
  Slieve Bloom 157
  Slieve Gullion 52
Mountains of Ireland 53
Moynihan, M. 472
Muir, R. 215
Muirchu 263
Mulcahy, D. 894
Mulcahy, M. 1160
Mullen, P. 147
Mulligan, F. 810
Munster 100
  19th century 701
  Irish language 576
  photographs 1318
Munster 100
Munter, R. L. 1328
Murder machine and other essays 889
Murphy, A. 755
Murphy, C. 815
Murphy, Dervla 15
Murphy, D. J. 957
Murphy, G. 1232
Murphy, J. 1261
Murphy, J. A. 411, 473
Murphy, M. J. 52
Murphy, M. W. 882

Murphy, Richard 1077
Murphy, W. 1044
Murray, Archbishop 610
Murray, K. A. 811
Murray, J. M. 1018
Murtagh, H. 104
Murtagh, P. 679
Museums 83, 1100, 1297-1298, 1300
  British Museum 1444
  National Museum 914, 1124
  Natural History 1299
Museums and art galleries in Great
  Britain and Ireland 1298
Museums in Ireland, present and future
  1297
Music 10, 23, 953, 1006, 1101,
  1146-1172
  18th century 1168
  Anglo-Irish 1155
  ballads 1147, 1154, 1159-1160, 1162
  bibliographies 1411, 1414, 1423,
    1428, 1448
  Celts 249
  country 1157
  folk 1148, 1157, 1159, 1163,
    1166-1167, 1169, 1172
  folk-songs 1159, 1160, 1162,
    1165-1167, 1214, 1428
  harp 1170
  history 194, 1146, 1152, 1155, 1160
  libraries 1151
  manuscripts 1152
  periodicals 1334, 1341, 1357
  political 1160
  prehistoric period 194
  rebel tradition 1150, 1172
  songs 1147, 1149-1150, 1154,
    1159-1161, 1167
  teaching 882
  traditional 1146, 1164, 1171
  Uillean pipes 1153
Music in Ireland 1151, 1163
Music societies 1152
My fight for Irish freedom 371
My Olympic years 1275
My wallet of photographs: the collected
  photographs of J. M. Synge 155
Mycenae 213
Myers, J. 297
Myler, P. 1284-1285
Mystery of the Casement ship 460
Mythologies 1238

Ireland 370, 382, 388, 401, 421,
426, 439, 470
road atlas 59
society 434, 632
Sunningdale Agreement 435
topography 34-47
travel guides, 73, 79
*Northern Ireland: the background to
the conflict* 434
Northern Ireland question
431-445
bibliographies 1411
religious dimension 443
Northern Ireland, the Orange State 437
*Northern world: history and heritage of
northern Europe, A. D. 400-1100*
284
Norton, D. 756
*Notes for Joyce, an annotation of
James Joyce's Ulysses* 979
Novels 927, 931, 943, 945, 950, 958,
964-965, 971-976, 979-983, 985,
988-990, 1020, 1055, 1070
bibliographies 931, 937, 981-982
historical 922
Nowlan, K. 4, 412-413, 803
Nulty, C. 643
Numismatics 1290
Nursing
periodicals 1396
Nutting, W. 64

O

Oakes, R. 702
O'Baoill, C. 576
O'Beirne, M. 130
O'Brian, R. 483
O'Brien, B. 448
O'Brien, Conor Cruise 6, 249, 335,
356, 484
O'Brien Edna 935, 942
O'Brien, Eoin 669-670
O'Brien, G. 757
O'Brien, J. 1271
O'Brien, J. A. 493
O'Brien, K. 1355, 1429
O'Brien, L. 652
O'Brien, Maire 247
O'Brien, Michael 860
O'Brien, M. H. 543

O'Brien, Smith 313
O'Brien, Vincent 1271
O'Brien, W. 336, 823
O'Broin, A. 25
O Broin, L. 337, 414, 462, 726
O'Buachalla, S. 486, 889
O Cadhain, M. 1068
O'Carroll, J. P. 473
O'Carroll, N. 789
O'Casey Annual, 995
O'Casey Eileen 991
O'Casey, Sean 932, 942, 959, 991-998,
1174, 1176-1177, 1183, 1457
autobiography 996
bibliography 1457
biography 998
politics 994-996
O Catháin, S. 1248
Occult 953
O Cearbhaill, D. 106
O Ceirin, C. 1262
O Ceirin, K. 1262
O'Clery, H. 248
O'Connell, Daniel 313, 317, 475-480,
608, 610, 625, 1319
O'Connell, Daniel
biographies 475, 478-480
O'Connell, J. 36
O'Connell, K. J. 1332
O'Connell, M. R. 477
O'Conner, J. 632
O'Connor, A. V. 904
O'Connor, Christy 1274
autobiography 1274
O'Connor, Frank 463, 935, 1066, 1069,
1071, 1091
biography 1071
O'Connor, U. 415-416, 952-953, 1287
O'Corráin, D. 271, 641
O Crohan, T. 145-146
O Cróinín, D. 586
O Cuiv, B. 572
O'Curry, E. 272, 1097
O Domhnalláin, T. 588
O'Donnell, J. D. 727
O'Donnell, W. H. 1055
O'Donoghue, R. 886
O'Donovan, D. 544
O'Donovan, J. 108, 273, 300, 783,
1006
O'Dowd, A. 795
O'Dowd, L. 632, 634

Tapestry 1113
Tapping, G. C. 958
Tara 213
Tax law 712
Taxation in Ireland 762
Taxation 746, 758, 762, 788
    statistics 835
    laws 760
Taylor, R. 1056
Teach yourself Irish 586
Technical colleges 896
Technology 847, 908, 912, 914
    bibliographies 1433
    directories 911
Television 1316, 1333
    and culture 1315
    and education 882
Television and Irish society 1333
Temperance movement 651
Tennis 1277
Tennyson, Alfred 1223
Tepper, M. 524
*Terrible beauty is born: Irish troubles,
    1912-1922* 416
Thackeray, William Makepeace 68,
    959
*That most distressful nation: the taming
    of the American Irish* 526
Theatre 23-24, 917, 938, 953, 999,
    1006, 1025-1026, 1030, 1058,
    1173-1188
    20th century 1173, 1175-1177,
        1182-1183, 1188
    Abbey Theatre 943, 994, 1027, 1041,
        1048, 1061, 1176, 1178-1179,
        1181, 1186-1187
    and nationalism 1182
    bibliographies 1456
    continental influences 1183, 1188
    Drury Lane 1011
    Gate Theatre 1181
    history 1174, 1176, 1178-1179,
        1181-1184, 1186
    influence of mythology 1185
    influence of politics 1182, 1185
    periodicals 1353, 1360
Theatre business 1187
Theatre in Ireland 1181, 1184
Theatre Ireland 1360
Theatre Ireland Yearbook 1360
*Them and us, Britain, Ireland and the
    Northern question* 436

Theobald Wolf Tone 326
Thernstrom, S. 551
This arrogant city 1412
Thomas, C. 282
Thompson, E. A. 263
Thompson, S. 1215
Thompson, W. I. 425
*Thom's Commercial Directory of
    Ireland* 1406
Thom's Irish who's who 1406
Thom's Official Dublin Directory
    1406
Thomson, G. L. 1263
Thornton, W. 989, 1032
1000 years of Irish poetry 1078
1000 years of Wood Quay 201
Three lives of Gavan Duffy 340
Thuente, M. H. 1057, 1239
Thurneysen, R. 591
Tierney, Mark 241, 343-344
Tierney, Michael 426
Tierney, Myles 729
*Times I've seen: Oliver St. John
    Gogarty, a biography* 415
Tindall, W. Y. 990
Tinkers 109, 497-498, 501, 503, 1366
    culture 497-498, 501, 503, 1221
    folk-tales 1221
    language 498, 1366
    photographs 503, 1221
    poverty 497
    social history 498
    traditions 498
    urban environment, effects on 497
Tinkers and travellers 498
Tipperary 105
    19th century 613
    archaeology 105, 203
    Catholic Church 105, 613
    economy 105
    geography 105
    history 105
    literature 105
    maps 105
    planning 105
    society 105
Tippperary: history and society 105
Tipton, I. C. 354
Titley, E. B, 890
Titterington, A. 1291
*To the golden door, the story of the
    Irish in Ireland and America* 547

Wicklow 65, 109
Wiedel, J. 503
Wild flowers 168, 171
Wild and free: cooking from nature 1262
Wild Ireland 868
Wild, J. 349
Wilde, Oscar 699, 959, 1033-1039, 1063, 1174, 1250, 1455
  bibliographies 1455
  biographies 959, 1036-1038
  letters 1034-1035
Wildlife 175, 868, 1388
  history 186
  survival 182, 186, 845
Wilde, Lady Jane 1237, 1250
Wilde, W. 1250
Wildlife in Britain and Ireland 186
Wilkinson, B. 383
William Butler Yeats 1041
Williams, G. St. John 1294
Williams, H. 1022
Williams, J. A. 791
Williams, J. E. C. 577
Williams, K. 1023
Williams, M. I. 1307
Williams, T. D. 347, 413
Willis, I. 176
Wilson, A. J. 1308
Wilson, D. 284
Wilson, Thomas Woodrow 378
With Plunkett in Ireland 795
Wittke, C. F. 553
Woman in Irish legend, life and literature 638
Woman's Way 1361
Women 4, 466, 636-647, 1335
  and nationalism 647
  arts 642-643
  culture 642
  education 646
  employment 641, 646, 819, 830
  equal rights legislation 646, 693
  handbooks 639, 646, 717
  health 646
  history 636-637, 641, 643-644
  immigrants in 19th century America 516, 540
  immigrants in 19th century Canada 540
  labour movement 646
  legends 638

  literature 638, 643, 929
  periodicals 1351, 1361
  politics 641, 644
  religion 641, 643, 645
  role in the Easter Rising 636
  roles 641, 643
  social welfare 646
  society 4, 466, 636-647
  status 641
  tradition 643
  voting 641
Women and employment in Ireland 819
Women in Irish society, the historical dimension: a study of socialization and role conflict 641
Women's International Year 641
Women's Movement 644-645, 647
Women's rights in Ireland, with a checklist of children's rights 646
Women's studies 641
Wonder tales 1222, 1229
Wood, N. 908
Wood Quay 201, 211, 281
Woodham-Smith, C. 347
Woodwork 1142
Wooley, D. 1020
Work 25, 103
  in 19th century America 516
World of Daniel O'Connell 476
World of Irish Nursing 1396
World of the Irish wonder tale 1222
World of Percy French 1161
World of stone 156
World of stone: life, folklore and legends of the Aran Islands 156
World War I 385, 399, 454
World War II 387, 396, 404, 413, 421
World Wildlife Fund 186
Worth, K. 1039, 1188
Wright, G. N. 133
Wright, H. M. 867
Writer's Ireland: landscape in literature 959
Writers: a sense of Ireland 926
Writings of Brendan Behan 941
Writings on British history 1437
Writings of J. M. Synge 1030
Written on the wind 1315
Wylie, J. C. 716
Wynne, M. 1115
Wynnes, E. 182

Y

Z

Map of the Irish Republic

This map shows the more important towns and other features.

1.	Kerry	10.	Galway	19.	Roscommon
2.	Cork	11.	Offaly	20.	Mayo
3.	Waterford	12.	Laois	21.	Sligo
4.	Wexford	13.	Kildare	22.	Donegal
5.	Carlow	14.	Wicklow	23.	Leitrim
6.	Kilkenny	15.	Dublin	24.	Cavan
7.	Tipperary	16.	Meath	25.	Monaghan
8.	Limerick	17.	Westmeath	26.	Louth
9.	Clare	18.	Longford		

Land over 1000 Feet